Baedeker

Thailand

www.baedeker.com

Verlag Karl Baedeker

SIGHTSEEING HIGHLIGHTS ★ ★

Thailand looks forward to welcoming you! Its perfect tropical beaches and idyllic islands have become a synonym for relaxation and warmth at a time of year when the weather at home makes sun-lovers shiver. But Thailand also has a wealth of interesting cultural attractions. Here we have listed the highlights, so that you know what not to miss.

Krabi
Small statue of Buddha at a temple in the woods

1 Menam Kok
2 Chiang Rai
4 Mae Hong Son
3 Chiang Dao
5 Doi Inthanon National Park
7 Chiang Mai
6 Nan
8 Lamphun
9 Chom Tong
10 Lampang
11 Si Satchanalai
13 Ban Chiang
12 Phu Kradung National Park
15 Sukhothai
14 Wat Phra That Phanom
16 Phitsanulok
17 Kamphaeng Phet
18 Ban Sema
© Baedeker
24 Wat Phra Buddhabat
Wat Prasat Phanom Wan
21
20 Phimai
19 Pa Tham cave paintings
22 Ubon Ratchathani
Singburi
23 Lopburi
25 Khao Yai National Park
26 Ayutthaya
27 Prasat Phanom Rung
28 Khao Phra Viharn
29 Bang Pa In
30 Bridge on the River Kwai
31 Nakhon Pathom
33 Bangkok
32 Ratchaburi
34 Samut Prakan
35 Phetchaburi
36 Trat
37 Ko Chang
38 Ko Samui
39 Chaiya
40 Suratthani
41 Ko Similan
42 Phangnga
43 Nakhon Si Thammarat
44 Phuket
45 Ko Phi Phi
46 Ko Tarutao

Sukhothai
Lotus pond at Wat Phra Si

Sea gypsy village
off the rocky island of Ko Panyi near Phang Nga.

BAEDEKER'S BEST TIPS

Out of all the Baedeker tips in this guide, we have selected the most useful for you. Experience and enjoy Thailand at its most attractive.

🔢 Ayutthaya by boat
From Bangkok you can take a boat trip on the Menam Chao Phraya to Ayutthaya.
► **page 198**

🔢 Bangkok Mass Transit System
The fast trains on an elevated track are a good way to reach many of the sights.
► **page 207**

🔢 Visakha Bucha Festival
On the eve of the festival, pilgrims with burning candles dance around the Marble Temple in Bangkok. ► **page 224**

🔢 In royal style to Bang Pa In
It is now possible to reach Bang Pa In by boat. ► **page 233**

🔢 Treasure hunt
Try your luck as a treasure hunter in the gem mines around Chanthaburi.
► **page 245**

🔢 Leave enough time for Chiang Mai
The city and the fascinating surrounding countryside are definitely worth a trip lasting several days. ► **page 251**

🔢 Night market in Chiang Mai
Every evening a number of streets are transformed into a huge market where typical products of the region, especially those of the hill tribes, are sold from countless stalls. ► **page 243**

🔢 Afternoon visit to Mae Rim
Large numbers of tourist buses head for the elephant camp in the mornings. When they have moved on, you can explore the extensive park on your own in peace.
► **page 263**

🔢 Don't visit without a guide
There could be misunderstandings and unpleasant incidents if you visit the hill tribes without a guide who knows the place and speaks the language.
► **page 269**

🔢 Buffalo race in Chonburi
The celebrations for the great buffalo race, which takes place each October and never fails to draw thousands of visitors to the city, start in the court of Wat Intharam.
► **page 277**

Spirit house
at a crossroads in Chonburi

Chiang Mai
*Said by many to be the most beautiful city
in all Thailand.*

⚠ Sponsor an elephant
In the Elephant Conservation Center in
Lampang you can sponsor an elephant.
► **page 340**

⚠ Blessing of the beloved sons
Mae Hong Son is the place to see the Buat
Luk Khaeo festival, the »blessing of the
beloved sons« at its most colourful.
► **page 354**

⚠ Temple festival
Each November a great temple festival, to
which pilgrims come from all parts of the
country, takes place in Nakhon Pathom.
► **page 362**

⚠ Phansa festival
The dances, markets and boat races on the
Mekong at Wat Phra That in Nakhon
Phanom make this festival in January a top
attraction. ► **page 364**

⚠ Full moon festival
Every year in Nakhon Si Thammarat
thousands of pilgrims dressed in white
stream to Wat Mahathat. ► **page 371**

⚠ Not the place for peace and quiet
If you are looking for a quiet beach
holiday, then in Pattaya the Royal Cliff
Beach Resort and the new Sheraton
Pattaya nearby are the only options likely
to be suitable. ► **page 388**

⚠ Sukhothai by bicycle
The extensive ruins of Sukhothai cannot be
explored thoroughly on foot. Rent a bicycle
at the main entrance in order to get
around the site in comfort. ► **page 467**

⚠ Thailand's loveliest festival ...
... takes place in Sukhothai, when the lake
is transformed into a sea of light.
► **page 469**

The vegetarian festival
*is celebrated in Phuket every September/
October.*

Children at the harbour in Songkhla
▶ page 470

BACKGROUND

PRACTICALITIES

*Monk at the feet of the
32m/105ft statue of Bud-
dha in Wat Inthrawihan
in Bangkok*
► **page 225**

TOURS

*Making shadow puppets in
Nakhon Si Thammarat*
► **page 95**

Price categories

Hotels
Luxury: from £100 / US$200
Mid-range: £55 – 100/US$110 – 200
Budget: under £55 / US$110
for one night in a double room

Restaurants
Expensive: from £15 / US$30
Moderate: £6 – 15/US$12 – 30
Inexpensive: up to £6 / US$12
for a 3-course meal

Pattaya's main »attraction« is its night life.
▶ **page 394**

SIGHTS
FROM A TO Z

The pastry for spring rolls is dried on bamboo trellises.
▶ **page 384**

Girl on Koh Lanta
▶ **page 123**

Background

FACTS ABOUT THE »LAND OF THE
FREE«, THE PEOPLE, THEIR RELIGION,
THE ECONOMY, THE ARTS, THE PAST
AND PRESENT OF A MODERN
COUNTRY WITH A LONG HISTORY

LAND OF SMILES

»By the grace of His Majesty the king, my companions and I had the convenience of two royal steam boats for our journey to the summer residence in Bang Pa In. Navigating the wide Maenam upstream, we stopped at every place that pleased us. When darkness fell, we anchored our steamers in midstream …«. These were the impressions of the German travel writer Ernst von Hesse-Wartegg in his book »Siam – Empire of the White Elephant« in 1899.

Modern travel is far more convenient. Gone are the days when travellers spent their time midstream on a steam boat at night. Air-conditioned hotel rooms are certainly more comfortable. Hesse-Wartegg, whose trip from Europe to Thailand took several months, could not have imagined making the same trip in as little as ten to twelve hours, as modern travellers do.

More than Beaches, Palm Trees and Temples

Thailand, once the kingdom of Siam, has become one of the most popular travel destinations in Asia, not least because of its many unique attractions. Neither the severe economic crisis of the 1990s on the Asian continent nor the devastating tsunami of 26 December 2004, which brought death and destruction to long stretches of Thailand's southern coast, have changed

In Buddha's care
Buddhist temples in all shapes and sizes characterize the »Land of the Free«.

this. With incredible energy. the people in the affected areas have not only repaired the destruction and reopened within an amazingly short time, but have made their tourist paradise in parts even more attractive than before for guests from all over the world. Naturally, the tourists have come back: after a period of stagnation, more guests than ever before visit Thailand.

What is it that casts a spell on visitors? The explanation cannot be only the beaches, where visitors spend carefree days in the shade of palm trees, and the colourful magnificence of temples where monks in bright orange robes sonorously recite Buddhist sutras. An even bigger attraction is the proverbial hospitality of the Thai people, who welcome each guest with a smile. Thais are very proud of their country, and guests who express their interest in Thailand can expect

In the footsteps of Buddha
Theravada Buddhism and its culture, from major festivals down to daily rituals, are a dominant feature of Thailand.

Flowers of Thailand
With around 1,300 native species Thailand is famous for its orchids, although lotus and mallow flowers are also widespread throughout South-East Asia.

Temples
Thailand has more than 30,000 wats built over a span of eleven centuries. They play a multiple role as Buddhist monasteries, temples and community centres.

Buddhism and the banyan tree
It was under a banyan tree that Buddha first achieved enlightenment, and the trees are revered for that reason. They are members of the fig family and can grow to enormous size.

Dream islands
Breathtaking landscapes and paradise beaches have made the islands around Thailand into top destinations for holidaymakers.

Arts and crafts
Hand-painted parasols made of lacquered paper are part of an arts and crafts tradition in northern Thailand that goes back millennia.

an especially cordial greeting. There is much more to Thailand than beaches, palms and temples, and visitors who restrict their vacation to the beach resorts miss the best of the country.

Thailand has a fascinating variety of landscapes, a wealth of historic buildings and many opportunities to make a stay in the kingdom an unforgettable adventure. For those who interested in culture and architecture, magnificent buildings show how cultural influences from India, China and Sri Lanka have left their marks on domestic architecture through the millennia, and how finally a unique Thai style has emerged. For those who prefer a lush tropical environment, there are beaches to enjoy in the south and remote mountains to explore in the north. Active travellers have many opportunities to walk the trails, sail, dive or improve their golf. Others may find time to reflect through Buddhist meditation, learn the art of Thai massage or take a course in Thai cooking. Expect no limits – Thailand has a marvellous vacation in store for every taste and budget.

Buddha Left his Footprints Here

The proverbial hospitality of the Thais is the most welcoming aspect of this »Land of Smiles«. This calm friendliness may have something to do with Buddhism and its open attitude toward enjoying the positive aspects of living. If this life turns out to be lacking, the next one will be better. A creditable life style will help to make the next life better. After all, Buddha himself went through many lives on earth before he reached nirvana, the final state of enlightenment.

This travel guide is meant to encourage a journey of discovery in a fascinating country with an age-old culture, and to inspire curiosity about a land that has never submitted to foreign rule, a fact that remains a powerful source of pride to this day. Of course, this requires travellers to leave the centres of mass tourism behind. But do not worry: travelling today is no longer as laborious as in Ernst von Hesse-Wartegg's time.

Elephants
These majestic animals are trained for work or to be ridden, and also have great spiritual significance.

Facts and Figures

Bustling big cities and tourist centres are just as much a part of Thailand as remote mountain villages and small provincial towns. Thailand is a prosperous modern country, and one of its biggest assets is the friendliness of its citizens.

The Natural Environment

Thailand shares a border with Myanmar in the north-west and west (since 1989 Myanmar has been the official name of the state of Burma).). In the north and north-east, Thailand borders on Laos, in the south-east on Cambodia and in the south on Malaysia. Thailand is about twice as large as the United Kingdom. From north to south Thailand measures 1,620km/1,007mi, from east to west 780km/485mi at its widest point. The narrowest part of Thailand is near Prachuap Khiri Khan, where the Gulf of Thailand and the border to Myanmar (Burma) are only 13km/8mi apart. The Isthmus of Kra on the Malay Peninsula is only 64km/40mi wide. Thailand's coast is 1,875km/1,165mi long on the Gulf of Thailand, 740km/450mi on the Indian Ocean. **National territory**

The capital Bangkok is situated in the lowlands of the Chao Phraya River where the four main regions of the country meet: in the north-west Pak Nya), in the north-east Isan), in the south-east Pak Dai Towan Org) and in the south-west Pak Dai). Bangkok has been the capital of the Kingdom of Thailand since 1782, when General Chakri took power. He later became King Rama I and established the Chakri dynasty. Until then, Thonburi on the opposite bank of the Chao Phraya was considered the capital. In 1970, Thonburi and Bangkok merged and the city experienced explosive growth. Bangkok occupies an area of about 6,500 sq km/2,510 sq mi. **Capital at the intersection between regions**

Topographically Thailand can be divided into five different regions, each with its own unique features and attractions. The climate also plays a big role in forming the many different landscapes. Rainfall is evenly spread throughout the year in the south, and a defined rainy season does not exist. In contrast, seasonal changes characterize the north. The vegetation has adapted to the climate. All year round, southern Thailand up to the Malay Peninsula is lush with evergreen tropical forests and seemingly endless rubber-tree plantations. Northern and central Thailand, however, endures a marked drought period from February to June, which makes this area less attractive, at least at first sight. **Natural regions**

Central Thailand

Central Thailand extends about 270km/168mi north from the ocean. The core of this region is the Maenam basin with the river Maenam Chao Phraya, which runs north-south to the Gulf of Thailand, where the river fans out to form a wide delta (20,000 sq km/7,700 sq mi). The river is regarded as the life blood of the country. Its tributaries **Maenam basin**

← *Children and colourful boats in the harbour of Songkhla*

Natural Environment Thailand

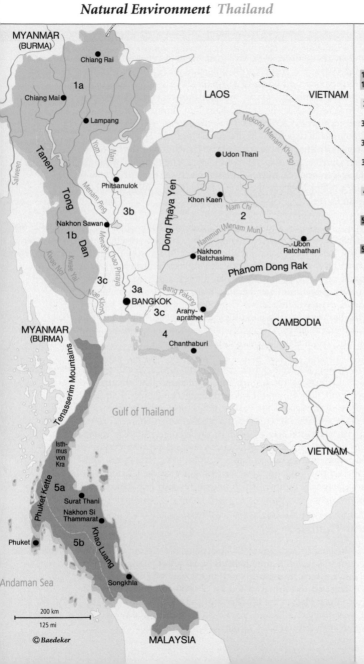

Natural geographic regions

1a	Northern highlands
1b	Western highlands
2	Khorat plateau
3a	Lower Menam basin
3b	Upper Menam basin
3c	Fringes of the Menam basin
4	South-east uplands
5a	Peninsular east coast
5b	Peninsular west coast

are the Ping, Yom and Nan, which merge near Nakhon Sawan. Soon after, the river splits into many arms to form a delta close to the middle of the central basin. In the south, the basin opens to the ocean, while mountains border the other sides. The central mountain range Tanen Tong Dan, which stretches south from the mountains of north Thailand to the Malay Peninsula, forms the western border. Mountains also make up the northern border; the Khorat plateau forms the eastern border area.

The geological formation of the Maenam basin has resulted in two morphologically distinct regions. A hill region with elevations of 500m/1,640ft above sea level forms the transition to the northern mountain range, while an aggradation area (created by sediment deposits) makes up the main basin. In rare places, steep-sided karst cones rise above the plain. The Maenam Chao Phraya carries huge amounts of sediment, which have created the geologically younger central plain and now raise the land in the river delta, thus adding about 5–6m (16–20ft) of land at the mouth of the river every year.

Geology

The wide valley region also features hills and terraced landscapes with fertile alluvial soil. These terraces are intensively used to grow crops, especially rice. Cluster villages of log houses, which are built on piles due to the frequent flooding, are characteristic for this landscape. The Maenam basin lies nearly at sea level (Bangkok is located only 2m/7ft above sea level) and the tides are therefore felt far into the basin. The plain and parts of Bangkok are often flooded during the monsoon rains in October and November. In the long run, the Thai capital may find itself in a precarious situation should the polar ice caps continue to melt and the ocean level rise.

Landscapes

Northern Thailand

To put it simply, northern Thailand can be described as the region north of the 17° line of latitude north. Northern Thailand takes its character from the foothills of the mountain ranges of South-East Asia, which reach to the Malay Peninsula. The highest peak, also the highest mountain in the country, is Doi Inthanon (2,595m/8,514ft). The rivers Nan, Yom, Fing and Wang flow in a southerly direction through the valleys. The large and small basins between the mountain chains are protected from the wind and offer highly favourable conditions for productive agriculture. Precipitation varies greatly in different areas, and many rice fields require additional irrigation. For several decades now, retention ponds and dams have been built to even out the annual water supply.

Mountains and valleys

Two distinct mountain ranges have formed in different geological processes Thailand's core bedrock originated in the Palaeozoic period (about 570–235 million years ago). Limestone and metamorphic sha-

Geology

Mountains in the Doi Phuka National Park

le cover wide areas. Rugged slopes and many caves and caverns characterize the limestone mountains. This older mountain range was pushed up one more time when the Himalayas folded in the Tertiary period. Magma surfaced in the process and solidified to form rounded mountain tops like Doi Inthanon.

Population centres

Population centres have developed in the valleys and the basins between mountains, but most people in the region live in villages rather than towns. The 3,000 settlements of the Akha, Lisu, Yao, Meo and Karen hill tribes, which are scattered through remote, almost impassable terrain, represent an exception to this. Few tribal people have made use of the special government programmes and settled permanently: most have held on to their age-old traditions as migratory farmers, working the land until it is no longer fit for agriculture and then moving on to a new area. Sometimes they use the slash-and-burn method to gain arable land. This turns more areas into karst land.

South-Eastern Thailand

Tropical forest and mountains

The dominant features of south-eastern Thailand are a basin extending in a west-east direction between mountain ranges and a mountain range parallel to the coastline. There is a gradual transition between the two landscapes, with evergreen tropical forests and mountains up to 1,600m/5,250ft high. These granite mountains are part of the ancient Indochinese base rock.

An irregular coastline with deep bays and many islands is also typical for the region. The fishing is good here, as evidenced by the many fishing villages along the coast. Here are the tropical beaches that Thailand travellers dream of, which is why south-east Thailand is the part of the country with the best transport and tourist infrastructure. Beach resorts, among them the famous Pattaya resort, line the coast, and more are under construction farther south.

In this region, mining, too, is economically important. Precious stones are found around Chanthaburi. Rubies and sapphires are mined underground or washed out of the river sand.

North-Eastern Thailand

East of the Maenam river plain rise the characteristic red sandstone and rock-slate formations of the predominantly arid Khorat plateau. On average, the elevation of the plateau is 200m/656ft, its highest point 1,300m/4,265ft. Mountain ranges, the Dong Phaya Yen in the west and the Phanom Dong Rak in the south, distinctly mark the rims of the plateau, which gradually levels off toward the Mekong (Mae Nam Khong) in the east. **Khorat plateau**

Permian (late Palaeozoic) and Mesozoic limestone alternates with red Mesozoic sandstone and rock slate. The limestone is porous, and some of the sandstone has weathered and become the red soil typical for tropical regions. As the soil is ill-suited for agriculture, the area is often called »Thailand's poorhouse«. Part of the natural vegetation still exists. It consists of sparse forests, open savannah and grass steppe. The broad river valleys are completely flooded during the rainy season, which provides conditions suitable for growing rice and jute. **Geology and land use**

The river Mun runs through the Khorat plateau. It is a tributary of the Mekong, the main artery of continental South-East Asia. Dams across the northern Mekong tributaries serve irrigation purposes, and they are the basis for generating hydroelectric power. Overhead lines transport part of the hydroelectric energy as far as the capital Bangkok. Treacherous rapids and the shallow waters all but preclude ships from navigating the river, which separates populations with colliding world-views and political systems. This has often led to military conflicts in the past.

? DID YOU KNOW ...?

■ The Mekong is the tenth-longest river on earth. Over a length of 430km/267mi it forms the border between Thailand and Laos, and drains a catchment area of more than 800,000 sq km/310 sq mi. The Mekong originates at an altitude of about 3,000m/9,843ft in the highlands of Tibet and is 4,500km/2,800mi long. It flows south-east through the province Yun-Nan (in the People's Republic of China) all the way to the South China Sea. More than 1,300 species of fish, birds and reptiles live in and around the Mekong, which is one of the world's richest river habitats.

Western Thailand

Mountainous border to Myanmar

The central South-East Asian mountain range Tanen Tong Dan forms the natural border between western Thailand and the neighbouring Myanmar, formerly Burma. The mountain peaks in this area by far exceed 2,000m/6,600ft. The Khao Sam Roi Yot range (the name means »mountains with 300 peaks«) south of Hua Hin is especially impressive.

Southern Thailand

The elephant's trunk

The outline of Thailand is sometimes compared to the head of an elephant. In this context, southern Thailand would be the trunk. This is the northern part of the long Malay Peninsula, its ridge the continuation of the north-south mountain chains of northern Thailand. The Maenam basin with its western foothills forms the border to the north. In the west, the barely developed, up to 1,500m/4,921ft-high Tenasse mountains are the natural border to Myanmar. The San Kara Khiri mountains in the south separate Malaysia from Thailand. The peninsula is situated between two oceans: the Gulf of Thailand and the South China Sea are part of the western Pacific, while the Andaman Sea in the west is the margin of the Indian Ocean. At the Isthmus of Kra, Thailand is only 64km/40mi wide. A canal across this isthmus would shorten the sea route from coast to coast by 1,300km/800mi. So far, however, the costs of such a canal project have proven prohibitive. Towards the south, the mountain range divides into two parallel north-south chains, the Phuket and the Nakhon Si Thammarat mountains . The highest peak is Khao Luang (1,835m/6,020ft) west of the ancient city of Nakhon Si Thammarat.

Geology

The geology of this terrain is almost the same as in northern Thailand. The foothills of mountain ranges are the most prominent feature. Limestone was deposited on granite base rock, and in some places the granite has surfaced, as often happens in tectonic events and through erosion. These granite surfaces have formed rounded mounds. In contrast, the limestone mountains feature rugged rock towers, which geologists call tropical karst cones. The development of such towers is linked to the hot humid climate. The flat surface is almost always covered with dense vegetation, while most rock walls plunge down so precipitously that the naked rock is visible. However, plants grow wherever the rock surface is rough or creviced. The karst cones often have a smaller diameter at their base, because the rain run-off erodes the stone and protruding stone constantly breaks off.

Coasts and islands

Geological events have also formed the coastlines. The west coast has many bays and islands with sheer limestone cliffs. The attractive wide

The limestone cliffs that rise as islands out of the Andaman Sea are the remains of now-submerged mountain ranges.

beaches on the east coast have recently been developed for tourism. Large fresh-water lakes have been created north of Songkhla through the shifting of beaches. The islands are fascinating, especially those off the shores of Phuket and Phangnga. They rose up when the Malay Peninsula tilted as the result of a tectonic event, lowering the western and raising the eastern part of the peninsula. In the process, entire mountain ranges sank into the Andaman Sea; only their jungle-covered limestone tops have remained as islands above sea level.

Tin mines

Rich tin deposits in southern Thailand were a source of prosperity until the world tin prices and with it the Siamese Tin Syndicate collapsed. Many tin mines, such as the ones on Phuket Island, had to be closed. Little care was taken to fill in the mines, and so they have remained as ugly scars in an otherwise lovely landscape.

Climate

Hot tropical climate Thailand has a tropical climate with summer rains and almost uniformly high temperatures. There are obvious seasonal changes in precipitation due to the monsoon stream over South-East Asia. Three **seasons of differing rainfall** can be defined: the summer monsoon lasts from May to October, the winter monsoon from November to February and the period between monsoons extends from March to the beginning of May. The beginning, end and course of the monsoon may vary. This is particularly true for El Niño years, when there are drastic variations in the barometric pressure above the south Pacific and South-East Asia. With regional variations, there are on average 2,400 to 2,800 sunshine hours per year. The winter climate, in particular, is a holiday-maker's dream.

i Monsoon

- The word monsoon derives from the Arabic word »mausim«, which means »season«, i.e. in this case, seasonal winds suitable for navigation. The south-eastern summer monsoon and the north-eastern winter monsoon occur in the regions around the Indian Ocean. The monsoons of South-East Asia are triggered by the Asian-Australian in-phase climate relationship and ENSO (El Niño-Southern Oscillation). Intense exposure of subtropical Asia to the sun during the northern summer leads to a heat-related depression. In contrast, a high-pressure zone develops at the same time south of the equator over Australia. The opposite happens during the northern winter. The colder temperatures over the Asian continent produce a region of high atmospheric pressure, while a heat-related low-pressure region develops in northern Australia. The resulting difference in pressure across the equator changes polarity in a half-year rhythm. The equalization of atmospheric pressure on a large scale causes the monsoons. The Coriolis force shifts the summer monsoon over Thailand to the south-west, and the winter monsoons toward the north-east.

The **yearly precipitation** range from about 1,000 litres/sq m (about 400 inches) in individual valleys in northern Thailand up to 3,000 litres (about 1,200 inches) in the south-eastern mountains. The local rainfall on exposed south-west slopes may reach more than 5,500 litres (2,565 inches) per year. The entire country receives plentiful south-west rains during the **summer monsoon** from May to October. Summer monsoons usually arrive around 10 May at Thailand's west coast, and two weeks later at the border to Laos and Cambodia. The dry **winter monsoon** brings sunny weather with little precipitation from November to February. However, it picks up moisture over the Gulf of Thailand and releases it over the eastern coast of the Malay Peninsula. This coast is the only region with a winter rainy season.

Sudden embedded rain and thunderstorms (»white squalls«) often sweep through southern Thailand and may cause terrible damage. The **period between monsoons** from March to the beginning of

Climatic regions in Thailand

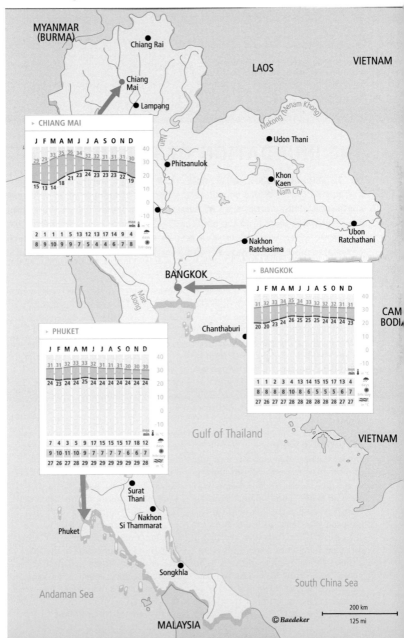

THE INUNDATION OF PARADISE

On 26 December 2004, 00:58 GMT (7:58 locally) the second-strongest earthquake ever recorded convulsed the sea bed at a depth of 25 miles just south-west of the northern tip of Sumatra. It registered 9.3 on the Richter scale (for which there is no top limit) and released such immense energy that the whole globe vibrated for the rest of the day. The resulting tsunami devastated much of the coast of South-East Asia leaving disaster in its wake.

More than 22,000 people died as a result of the tsunami (from the Japanese »tsu« harbour and »nami« wave). Hundred of thousands more suffered injury from breakers as high as 30m/100ft. More than three million lost their homes in the worst-hit coastal regions, north-west Sumatra, the Andaman and Nicobar Islands, Thailand, Sri Lanka and south-east India.

Earthquake Zone

The west coast of Sumatra is a region of particular interest to seismologists. It lies at the junction between two tectonic plates. The Indian-Australian plate is sliding eastwards beneath the Eurasian plate that includes Sumatra at a rate of 10cm/4in a year, creating a so-called subduction zone. This is not a smooth and simple process. The plates frequently jam against one another, dragging down the Eurasian plate that lies on top and twisting it towards the east. The line of the Sunda trench marks the region where the sea bed is crumpling in this way. On 26 December 2004, tensions that had been building for some 200 years reached a point where something had to give. The overlapping region of the plates, an area of some 100,000 sq km/40,000 sq mi, suddenly split. Like a coiled spring, the edge of the Eurasian plate hurtled 13m/45ft westward to its original position – this over a length of 500km/300mi. At the same time the sea bed was raised by two or three metres taking with it a huge column of water that had been above the break. Vast masses of water were set in motion. An asymmetric wave-front composed of massive peaks and deep troughs emanated in all directions at a speed of around 700kmh/450mph. Within the space of the next ten hours, 15 more earthquakes, some almost as ferocious as the first, rattled the sea bed, increasing the cracked region of the ocean floor to a length of 100km/60mi.

An Unstoppable Wave on the Move

Just 15 minutes after the massive rupture, the wave-front broke over the coast of Aceh in northern Sumatra and the Indian-administered Nicobar and Andaman Islands. 30 minutes later the killer wave reached the west coast of Thailand, striking Sri Lanka after two hours and the Maldives after three and a half. The horrific waves were still wreaking havoc some ten hours after the quake, hitting the east coast of Africa before they had finally run their course.

In Thailand the coastal regions of six southerly provinces were hit: Satun, Trang, Krabi, Phang Nga, Ranong and Phuket. The mass of water poured over the exquisite beaches of the offshore islands. Holiday paradises, Khao Lak, Phi Phi Don and Phuket in particular, were laid waste. More than 2500 Thais and as many tourists lost their lives in the flooding.

The destructiveness of the tsunami varied from one bay to another due to the intricacies of the coastline and the differing coastal geography, which had the effect of amplifying or diminishing the approaching mountains of water. Where the coastline projected into the sea, the energy of the waves was spread out, but shallow bays with their sandy beaches tended to focus their power. The construction of hotels at the edge of the water also contributed to the violent consequences of the waves, as did the earlier destruction of pine forests, lagoons, dunes and mangrove fringes that might have provided natural protection from the catastrophe.

Does Every Earthquake Trigger such a Wave?

Not all quakes give rise to a tsunami of this kind. The critical threshold is around 7 on the Richter scale. The speed of propagation of the waves depends on the depth of the sea. In deep ocean basins (5,000m/16,000ft deep on average) they move at speeds of up to 800kmh/500mph, whereas in coastal regions the speed may only be 10kmh/6mph. This is because shallows impede the lateral motion of the oscillating water. This causes the crests to cluster together and reinforce one another with the terrifying effects seen on that fateful day.

Only three weeks after the catastrophe, the governments of Indonesia and Germany decided to build an **early-warning system** for tsunamis in the Indian Ocean. From 2008 it will deliver data from the area most susceptible to seaquakes – the Sunda Arc –, which will be available to all bordering countries for a qick and reliable tsunami warning.

May is characterized by high temperatures and frequent thunderstorms. Although there is usually not much wind in this season, heavy thunderstorms can produce deluges of 50 to 60 litres per sq m (20 to 25 inches) per hour. After the dry winter months, farmers can hardly wait for these first spring rains (»mango rains«). There are up to 22 days of peak rainfall in each of the months of May, September and October. Hardly any rain falls in the northern and eastern mountain valleys from November to March. In this time, some places have less than ten days of rain. Tropical hurricanes are rare. If they occur at all, they only hit southern Thailand.

Temperatures Heat and humidity put a lot of stress on the human body all year round. Especially in the Maenam basin including Bangkok and inland in southern Thailand, people must learn to live in a hothouse climate. In the long term, only the healthy can endure day-time temperatures of 30–35°C (86–95°F) and sometimes up to 40°C/104°F (March and April) and night-time temperatures rarely under 23–25°C (73–77°F). The climate is more pleasant in the mountains, and throughout Thailand in the winter months. In the valleys of the northern and eastern mountains, the climate can be downright cool in January and February when the average daily lows are around 14°C/57°F with extreme temperatures below 5°C/41°F. At 27°C to nearly 30°C (81°F to almost 86°F), the ocean surface temperatures are very high all year round. ▶Practicalities: When to Go.

---

i **Beware the sun!**

■ The perpendicular rays of the tropical sun are extremely intense. Protection is therefore a necessity. A large-rimmed hat will sufficiently protect the entire body around noon, when the sun's rays are almost vertical. Earlier and later times of day are trickier, because the sun is still strong, and strikes at an angle.

Flora and Fauna

Flora

Rainforest and rice fields Thailand's vegetation is characterized by two kinds of biotope. One of them is the tropical rain forest in the northern and southern parts of the country, the other is the Maenam basin with almost endless rice fields and the vast rubber tree plantations on the Malay Peninsula.

Close to half of Thailand is forested. For some time now, this forest has no longer consisted of primary wood that has grown over the centuries. Instead, it is secondary forest. Unrestrained clearances, especially of exotic woods like teak, and a lack of a systematic reforestation have created wide scrubland regions where once there was a jungleland reduced Thailand's forests by about one half. The secindary scrub also makes farming difficult in these regions.

Vegetation *Thailand*

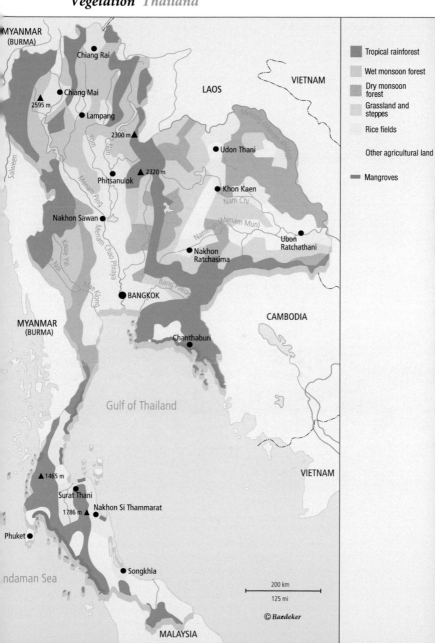

MYANMAR (BURMA)

Chiang Rai

Chiang Mai

▲ 2595 m

Lampang

VIETNAM

LAOS

2300 m ▲

▲ 2320 m

Phitsanulok

Udon Thani

Khon Kaen

Nam Chi

Nakhon Sawan

Ubon Ratchathani

Nakhon Ratchasima

Menam Chao Phraya

Bang Pakon

BANGKOK

CAMBODIA

Chanthaburi

MYANMAR (BURMA)

Salween

Kwae Yai

Mae Klong

Gulf of Thailand

VIETNAM

▲ 1465 m

Surat Thani

1786 m ▲ Nakhon Si Thammarat

Phuket

Andaman Sea

Songkhla

MALAYSIA

	Tropical rainforest
	Wet monsoon forest
	Dry monsoon forest
	Grassland and steppes
	Rice fields
	Other agricultural land
	Mangroves

200 km
125 mi

© *Baedeker*

Depending on climate and altitude, two major types of forests exist **Forest** in Thailand. Most of the woodland in the south and south-east consists of **tropical forest**. The **monsoon forests or tropical dry forests** in the north-east and elsewhere in Thailand are mostly made up of deciduous trees. Decades of deforestation have turned the Khorat plateau into a unique steppe environment. Here, the rivers overflow during the rainy season and form swampy lakes.

The tropical rainforest is **primeval forest** of the kind that most peo- **Rainforest** ple imagine, with an almost impenetrable chaos of many plant species, each at its own level above the ground. On the ground grow shade-loving bushes, ferns and small trees. Dipterocarps occupy the »middle storey« up to a height of 25m/82ft. These are evergreen tropical trees with two-winged fruits, of which more than 400 species exist in Asia alone. Above these trees extend the mighty trunks of yang trees and on the Malay Peninsula takhian trees too. The rainforest is the habitat of an almost indescribable wealth of animal species.

Continuous forests exist today only on the Malay Peninsula, the coastal areas of south-eastern Thailand and in northern Thailand along the border to Myanmar. Experts make dire predictions about the fate of the wildest, most majestic of all forests. Soon, only remnants will remain if deforestation continues at the current pace. This is not only the prediction for Thailand's forests but also for the neighbouring Myanmar and Malaysia. In 1988, the Thai government banned the harvest of tropical woods. However, the effect of this ban is marginal at best, because wood imports from neighbouring countries have increased enormously since then.

> ## *i* Thailand's timber
>
> ■ Since 1988, when the cutting of teak was prohibited, hard bamboo with its lignin and cellulose content has become a substitute for hardwood. Bamboo is used for the construction of buildings, for furniture, household goods and musical instruments. Young bamboo shoots are also a favourite ingredient in Thai and Chinese cooking. Pine, oak and the hardwood yang tree also contribute to the Thai economy. Lianas in the rainforest are the source of a further commercial wood known as rattan, which is mostly used to make furniture. Thailand is one of the largest exporters of rattan in the world.

Until recently, two thirds of Thailand was covered with dense virginal rainforest. Today, it constitutes less than 20% of the country. Unrestrained deforestation of the primary forest without appreciable reforestation efforts, in addition to the traditional slash-and-burn development of arable lands, have led to extensive karst formations. Today, Thailand must import almost half of the wood it needs for construction, while just a few years ago, the domestic forests were still an ample source.

← *Tropical rainforest – as here in the Khao Yai National Park – is an impenetrable tangle of verdant growth.*

Palm trees The various species of palm in Thailand are economically useful. They include **coconut palms**, which grow predominantly in southern Thailand. People eat the coconuts and drink the refreshing coconut milk inside it. The rural population uses the dried outer shell as fuel. Many countries import the oil of the **oil palm** for use as a raw material in, for example, the cosmetics industry.

Coconut harvest on Koh Chang

Mangrove forests are a distinctive feature of southern Thailand. Mangroves demand very little from their habitat and tolerate even salt water. The forest is dry when the tide is out, though the mud remains too deep to walk through the mangroves. At high tide, only the tops of the mangroves stick out of the water. The aerial roots retain a lot of mud, thus contributing to the silting of coastal strips.

A significant cause of the loss of forest acreage is the tradition of preparing land for cultivation by **slash-and-burn deforestation** as a form of migratory cultivation. Through the ages, tribes moved from one settlement to the next by burning the jungle for new fields whenever the old ones were exhausted. The wood ashes served as a natural fertilizer – for a short while. The exhausted idle lands were not reforested. Large savannahs with fast-growing bamboo developed in the deforested areas, because not much of the original forest regenerated itself. Systematic reforestation has only recently started, mainly in the northern parts of the country.

Flowering plants The wealth of flowering plants in Thailand is very impressive. Among the flowers thriving in Thailand are lotus, water lilies, jasmine, hibiscus, lavishly flowering bougainvillea and temple trees (frangipani) with their white, yellow or reddish flowers. The plant with the largest single flower in the world, rafflesia arnoldii, grows in Thailand. The country also provides a habitat for many kinds of orchid. Many hundred different orchid species have been identified, some of them endangered.

Land Animals

A large number of animal species live in Thailand, especially in the sparsely populated western regions and the northern mountains. There are large numbers of primitive primates, jackals, different bear species and big cats. The numbers of tapirs, rhinos and elephants are dwindling, however. To this day, elephants serve as working animals in inaccessible jungle regions.

Tigers, tapirs and more ...

Currently, about 2,000 wild elephants still live in Thailand, most of them along the border to Myanmar in the Tenasserim (Tanintharyi) region. Another 3,000 tame elephants serve as working animals, mainly for the transport of trees through jungle regions; the elephants are also used for riding and in tourist shows. The numbers of working elephants have fallen since the ban on cutting tropical woods in 1988. Elephants have a gestation period of 23 months, and new elephant mothers are then given three years of maternity protection. At birth an elephant weighs around 100kg/220lbs and stands about 75cm/30in tall. A mature elephant weighs in at around four tons. On average, elephants live 80 years, with a maximum age of 100 years. In their prime between 25 and 60 years, elephants work about 8 hours per day. They are rested in the hot months of April and May. At three years of age, young elephants start to train for their future tasks in 'elephant schools'.

Elephants

Tigers are at the top of the list of globally endangered species. They originate on the Indian subcontinent, yet have lost ground in recent decades even there, so that their numbers have dwindled to a fraction of the original population. There are several reasons for this. As predators, they are considered a danger to humans. However, tigers have also been hunted without any consideration for nature or ecology to use some of their body parts as a source of aphrodisiacs. Only a few hundred tigers still live in Thailand. There is still no official protection programme, and it is therefore left to private initiatives to ensure their survival. The best example for such an initiative is Wat Pa Luangta Bua in Kanchanaburi province, where the monks live in harmony with tigers.

Tigers are rare ...

Monkeys usually live in packs and are especially at home in the numerous Thai national parks. However, they also venture into cities (e.g. in Lopburi around Wat Phra Prang Sam Yot). Most monkeys stay clear of humans, but others are adventurous, sometimes even aggressive, and some like to tease unsuspecting visitors. In southern Thailand they are trained to pick coconuts. In some tourist centres, vendors abuse the monkeys by forcing them to pose for pictures with tourists. But in Lobpuri local business appreciate their magnetic effect on tourists and treat them to a full dinner once a year (usually in November) to thank them.

... but monkeys plentiful

A handicap that made her a star: the female elephant Motala is probably the only pachyderm in the world with a false leg.

PEG-LEG MOTALA

Even though an elephant no longer graces the Thai flag, the massive creatures are still among the best-loved animals in the kingdom. Nothing else could explain why an accident to the elephant cow Motala should unleash a worldwide wave of sympathy and help.

The pachyderm trod on a mine in the Cambodian jungle in 1999 and, despite the best efforts of veterinarians, her injuries were so severe that her left front leg had to be amputated. Little attention was paid to this at first, but six years later the 44-year-old elephant, who had been given the name Motala, was to become a centre of attention for animal lovers around the world, and a star of the media.

The doctors in charge of her case had decided to replace the amputated leg with a specially designed prosthetic limb. In view of the enormous cost of such an exercise the vets in Lampang made an appeal to the public. Their pleas did not fall on deaf ears, and a wave of sympathy brought with it a mass of donations for the treatment of the patient. The result was that Motala became the first and almost certainly the only pachyderm in the world with a false leg.

Nevertheless, the situation for elephants in Thailand is not easy, and Motala is certainly not the only one to have faced upheavals to her way of life. Since the prohibition on felling tropical wood, many elephants that had been trained to work with the loggers are unemployed, just like their trainers, the mahouts. Many animals earn money for their owners in elephant shows that take place around the tourist centres, but other mahouts attempt to provide for the elephants, which give them a lifetime of loyalty, by their own efforts. This all too often ends with them begging on the streets of the major cities for food to feed both elephant and mahout – an unworthy existence for so dignified a beast.

This is one of the main reasons why the »Friends of the Asian Elephant« charity was set up in 1993. The trust recognizes the major role that the animals played in Thai history and, in particular, that there were once extensive herds roaming the land. There are now affiliates throughout the world so that, for example, the Brigitte Bardot Foundation set up by the famous actress is now one of the supporters of the group. The FAE has also constructed an elephant hospital in Lampang Province to treat sick and injured elephants.

Cattle, in particular the gigantic gaur, often falsely called the 'Indian bison' (seladang), and also the water buffalo, are common and irreplaceable farm animals.

Cattle

More than 900 bird species live in the rain forest. Many of them exist only in small numbers.

Bird species

The many different tropical butterflies include rare species. In order not to endanger them any further, visitors should resist the urge to buy the prepared butterflies offered in most tourist centres.

Butterflies

The Indian flying fox or kalong (pteropus vampyrus) also deserves mention. It is the largest of all bats with its wing span of up to 1.5m/ 5ft and lives in large colonies. There are many other flying mammals, such as bats and flying dragons (flying lizards). The smallest mammal in the world was discovered in northern Thailand. It is a bat the size of a bumble-bee.

Bats

 Baedeker TIP

Bird watching

Bird watchers will especially like Thailand's national parks. The Bangkok Bird Club organizes regular bird-watching excursions (information: POB 13, Ratchathewi Post Office, Bangkok 10401).

It is best to use effective **mosquito** protection, especially in northern Thailand and on the islands in the south. Mosquitoes are malaria carriers. In these areas it is wise to use the mosquito netting offered in many hotels, to ensure a good night's rest.

In contrast, geckos are completely harmless. They are small lizard-like animals. Attracted by light, they come inside in the evenings making chattering noises. Geckos are welcome house guests because bugs are their preferred food.

Geckos: useful little animals

Giant saurians (crocodiles, monitor lizards) and snakes live everywhere in Thailand. Among the snakes are some venomous species like the cobra and Russell's viper. In general, these poisonous snakes avoid humans, but it is still a good idea to wear closed shoes when wading through rice fields or hiking through the jungle. In Thailand, visitors see crocodiles mostly in captivity in a safe environment on so-called crocodile farms. Nevertheless, some vigilance is indicated when exploring the brackish waters between land and ocean. Saltwater crocodiles (Latin: crocodylus porosus) are especially dangerous. They may attack when they feel threatened.

Reptiles

The Thai people can hardly resist an opportunity for a bet. Cockfights are especially popular in rural areas. The fighting cocks are raised especially for this »sport«. The same is true for the fierce fights between colourful aquarium fish.

Thais like betting on animals

Marine Fauna

Nature conservation The coastal marine environment has suffered considerably from abuse at the hands of the local population and tourists alike. Surprisingly, the tsunami on 26 December 2004 did little damage under water.

Wonderful diving areas are not as numerous as they once were, and untouched waters no longer exist. Diving fans should therefore value the beauty of what still exists under water, and leave it as they find it. Furthermore, it is strictly prohibited to plunder the coral reefs (▶ Baedeker Special p.158).

Corals are marine polyps (cnidarias) with an outer calciferous skeleton. Thus protected, they occur mostly in colonies. Warm water and steady currents along with the strong rays of the sun offer ideal conditions for coral growth. Large coral reefs still exist, especially off the shores of the Andaman Sea. They are so colourful that widely travelled divers compare them to the reefs of the Red Sea. Pieces of coral often break off and wash ashore. It is therefore a good idea to wear protective rubber or plastic beach shoes.

Coral reef in the Andaman Sea

Fish Blowfish (puffer fish) and the bony porcupine (globe) fish, of the genus arothron and tetraodon respectively, are common sights in the diving grounds off the Thai coast. Blowfish can swallow water or air, thus expanding up to five times their original size. They are playful companions of divers. However, blowfish are also an endangered species, as the Japanese like to eat them as an extravagant delicacy (»fugu«). The bile of the blowfish contains a strong poison that is lethal for humans. The preparation of fugu therefore requires expert training and a special permit. It is best to respect the porcupine fish and not tax its good nature. If threatened, its raised spikes can harm a diver. Fish are an important source of protein to complement a rice-based diet. Overfishing, especially in the immediate offshore waters, has unfortunately made fishing the Gulf of Thailand a tedious and unrewarding task (▶ economy). But gamefishing continues to thrive in the Andaman Sea off the west coast of Thailand and around Phuket there there are many opportunities for deep-sea fishing.

From time to time sharks appear off the Thai coasts. While they usually stay far off the coast, it is prudent to be cautious, especially when in the open sea. Those riding water scooters, in particular, should keep this in mind and not venture out too far from the shore.

Beware of sharks

Crustaceans such as lobster or crabs are still plentiful in the south of Thailand off the coastal island shores. The Thais are fond of eating crayfish and mussels.

Lobster, crabs and mussels

Population • Politics • Economy

Population

About 61.6 million people live in Thailand; the population density is 120 inhabitants per sq km/311 per sq mi (according to the most recent census in 1990; the above number of inhabitants has been extrapolated to 2006). The majority (75%) are **Thais**. They include the Siamese, Shan and Lahu populations. There are important minorities: the **Malays** (especially in southern Thailand), the **Chinese**, **Indians** (in the capital and in tourist centres) and people of the **hill tribes** in northern Thailand. Since the Thai government started to emphasize the advantages of birth control in the 1960s, the annual population growth has markedly declined to a rate of currently 0.9%.

Population

Population statistics clearly reflect the generational change in the past decades. Today, 60% of the population are younger than 30 years of age, while only 6% are older than 65. The average life expectancy will increase as medical care improves. In 1960, the life expectancy in Thailand was 50 years for men and 55 years for women. Today, the figures are 67 years for men and 72 years for women.

Demographics

The rural exodus is an ever increasing problem. One out of every seven inhabitants of Bangkok was not born there. More than 6.3 million people, i.e. one Thai in ten, live in an area of only 1,566 sq km/605 sq mi in metropolitan Bangkok. The population count for the entire metropolitan region exceeds 7.5 million. This amounts to a population density of 3,608 inhabitants per sq km (9,552 per sq mi). The number of people living in slums is unknown because the census does not cover these areas. A comparison with conditions in northern Thailand only emphasizes the problem. By size, Chiang Mai is fourth among Thailand's cities, yet only 170,400 people live there. The areas with the lowest population densities are the provinces Tak and Mae Hong Son near the border to Myanmar with 19.9 and 12.6 persons per sq km (52 and 33 per sq mi) respectively.

Rural exodus

The population growth in Thailand has been successfully reined in by government programmes since the 1960s and amounts to just 0.9%.

Bangkok:
a magnet ▶

Metropolitan Bangkok attracts people from less developed parts of the country like a magnet. Every morning hundreds of new city dwellers arrive at the main bus station in Bangkok, where gang-masters are already waiting for them. The new arrivals dream of work and food in the »heavenly capital«. Quite often, their dreams and hopes fade quickly in dark factories where they work under inhumane conditions, earning too little money to make a life for themselves. Young girls and women who are lured into the city with promises of well-paid work instead find themselves captive sex slaves in brothels. The largest group of new Bangkok citizens comes from the poor north-eastern part of Thailand and neighbouring Laos. There is hardly any barrier between Laos and Thailand in terms of the language and alphabet. This and unofficial border crossing have removed almost all barriers to immigration.

Ethnic Groups

Mix of peoples

Thailand's political borders are not ethnic borders. Hill tribes who do not heed government rule live in the remote and undeveloped mountains on both sides of the western border. People of mixed Malay and Thai descent live in southern Thailand. They have close ethnic and cultural ties with the Malay people, and many are Muslims. Remarkably, differences in ethnicity have not kept the Thais from living together peacefully – few exceptions notwithstanding. Conflicts with a few Muslim separatists in southern Thailand do, however, repeatedly occur. Their agenda is political merger with Malaysia.

The Siamese make up the majority (80%) of Thailand's population. The **Shan** at the border to Myanmar as well as the **Lahu** and the **Hmong** (Meo) in northern and north-eastern Thailand are also regarded as Thai peoples. The lineage of the Thais has not been determined with absolute certainty. However, researchers agree that their

Thai
◄ Siamese

origins lie in the Yangtse valley in southern China, where they established their first independent monarchy under the name of Nan Chao around AD 650. The Mongol emperor Kublai Khan conquered Nan Chao in 1253, triggering an extensive migration of tribes. In the course of this migration, the Thai tribes mixed with other southern Chinese tribes on their way to the Mekong delta. In 1257, this mixed population founded the first sovereign kingdom of Siam with Sukhothai as their capital

The **hill tribes** of Tibeto-Burmese or Sino-Laotic descent in northern Thailand have a special position. The Thai government has recognized six different hill tribes and also undertakes efforts to integrate the 58,000 **Hmong** (Meo), the 40,000 **Lahu**, the 30,000 **Yao**, the 24,000 **Akha** and the 18,000 **Lisu**. There are also 246,000 **Karen**, whose settlements reach far into southern Thailand. The hill tribes often build their villages side by side and have unrestrained contacts with

? DID YOU KNOW ...?

■ In 1914, Karl Baedeker's handbook for travellers to India noted that »The Siamese ... are delicate of stature with an olive-bronze skin. They often tattoo their legs and wear their black hair taut like a brush. Their teeth are stained red from chewing betel. Noble women have their teeth enamelled black. Men and women wear similar garb consisting of a brown or white loincloth (panung) with one end brought up between the legs and tucked in at the waist. People also wear jackets, straw hats or head scarves as well as cotton shawls (parkanas). People of means wear gold-embroidered jackets, precious silk sashes, half stockings and buckled shoes ... The religion is Buddhism. The educational system is administered by monks who own countless monasteries but hold on to their habit of going around in the morning with the collecting bowl. The monks wear yellow togas and shave their heads. Once in his lifetime, every free Siamese must spend three months in a monastery. Pilgrimages are a general custom, as is the habit of donating shrines, which are scattered all over the country ...«

each other. Each tribe has a culture of its own, and their lifestyles often appear archaic. They have in common a belief in spirits (animism) and ancestor worship. The people of all hill tribes are admired for their talents in many crafts. They sell their products on the markets of Chiang Mai, Chiang Rai and Mae Hong Son.

Lisu girl

The origin of the Karen is un-known. They are presumed to come from south-western China or south-eastern Tibet. Today, most Karen live in Myanmar. Since the foundation of the state of Burma in 1948, the Karen have resisted the government, which has denied them their own independent Karen state. The so-called God's Army, a militant group of Karen, engages in skirmishes with the Thai army un-der its two juvenile leaders. The Karen who have migrated to Thai-land are, however, among the best-integrated hill tribes. Their villages stretch far south from Mae Hong Son along the border to Myanmar. The assimilated Karen subsist on agriculture exclusively. Opium pro-duction is no longer significant.

The **Akha**, **Lisu** and **Lahu** live in the region north of Chiang Mai up to the »Golden Triangle« and pro-duce opium. Culturally, they be-long to the hill tribes in Myanmar and dress accordingly. Their lang-uage is part of the Tibetan-Bur-mese family. In the early 20th cen-tury, members of the Akha and the Lahu tribes migrated from the southern Chinese province of Yunnan to Thailand via eastern Burma (present day Myanmar) and northern Laos. The Lisu migrated to Thailand from the Salween river valley in China via northern Burma and Kentung. Most members of these three tribes still live in their original homelands; only a few of them migrated to Thailand.

The **Akha** nurture a close connection to their ancestors, believe in spirits in many manifestations and are more strongly attached than the others to ancient traditions, which include asking their ancestors for food and protection from illness and death. The Akha also be-lieve that one day their ancestors will reappear on earth and take possession of their villages. This belief obviously hinders projects of the Thai government to relocate them. The tribal people make a li-ving as farmers, mostly planting rice and vegetables. Here and there some opium fields still exist in villages along the Myanmar border.

A characteristic of the **Lisu** is to strive for primacy. As children they are brought up according to principles of achievement. The large extended families are organized on a strictly patriarchal system, and the strongest clan administers the rule of law in the village. The Lisu make a living by cultivating and selling vegetables.

The languages of the (Meo) and the Yao (also known as the Mien) peoples also belong to the Sino-Tibetan family. Their villages are mostly situated in the provinces of Chiang Rai and Nan. They originated in the central part of southern China, spread from Laos across the Mekong and moved to northern Thailand after a period in refugee camps along the border with Cambodia. They had suffered heavily under the orthodoxy of the communist ruler Pol Pot (1975). Having previously fought on the side of the anti-communist forces, government oppression left them no option but to flee from their tribal homes. Much progress has been made in recent years in settling them in permanent villages. The Yao still retain the language and alphabet of their previous homeland. The Meo primarily make a living from opium cultivation, although alternatives sponsored by the Thai government are increasingly gaining acceptance. In their culture, polygamy is still customary and life is organized along highly patriarchal lines, much as it is among the Lisu. Those two peoples have one more thing in common, in that many of their number lead a nomadic agricultural lifestyle. If, after a few years, the barren, burned-out soil can support no further cultivation, they move on and build new villages elsewhere. **Hmong, Yao**

Little ethnological research has yet been done on the Mabri (»yellow leaves«, since they wear no clothes other than a leaf over their genitals), a tribe of nomadic hunter-gatherers. All attempts at persuading them to settle have so far failed. Around 200 of them live in the mountains around Nan. **Mabri**

In Thailand there are about 2.4 million Muslims (99% Sunni, 1% Shia). They mostly have Arabic-Malayan roots and are mainly concentrated in the south, in particular the four border provinces of Satun, Yala, Pattani and Narathiwat. For years they were considered to be reluctant to integrate and a constant source of unrest. Recently, however, the efforts of the Thai monarchy to incorporate them more into Thai society have met with obvious success. Islam is not merely tolerated in Thailand today; its holy days are now enshrined in law. Bangkok alone has around 100 mosques and there are more than 2,000 in the country as a whole, which along with the existence of 200 Qur'an schools testifies to the importance of Islam in Thailand (►Religion). **Muslims**

Living Conditions

A typical feature of Bangkok and other large cities is uniform tenement housing, built in long, straight streets, largely uninterrupted **In cities**

FAMILY AND SOCIETY

In Asian society there is less focus on the individual and more on the community. The result of this outlook is a constant striving for a compromise that ideally encompasses everyone. It is uncommon for persons to further their own ends at the expense of others, and individuals always keep one eye on the aims of the community.

The reason for this lies in the Confucian tradition that sees people as complete entities ideally living in three-fold harmony: with other people in their sphere, with nature and with the supernatural. In spite of creeping westernization, the Thai people have managed to retain their own cultural and social identity.

The Family as Microcosm

The family is a firmly bonded unit that offers security to all its members as long as the strictly observed relationships in terms of age and status are properly maintained. There are twenty times as many words for interfamilial relationships as those common in Europe. These words reflect the nature of the relationships, whether it be status (senior or junior) or affiliation (mother's side or father's side). These appellations tend to be used more often than a person's actual name.

In a Thai family no-one is alone. Even in a household with multiple rooms, nobody sleeps in a room of their own.

This starts in infancy, when the mother will feed or rock the baby at the slightest sound of discomfort. As soon as it is able to crawl or walk, it is taken everywhere, often with its legs wrapped around the hips of an older sibling who carries it in one arm. This is a position in which the child can sleep, eat and play whenever it wants. Children are not brought up to any specific time plan, e.g. a fixed bedtime. Even very young children are only laid down to sleep when they get tired. Children are seldom scolded, let alone beaten or deprived of attention as a punishment. Their upbringing is achieved by gentler methods. A Thai mother would never say, »if you carry on like that, you're for it« but appeals to the child's sense of shame: »If you carry on like that, everyone will laugh at you.«. Where western parents bring up their children to be independent at the earliest possible juncture, the Asian family seeks to relieve its children of all their troubles, to spare them from conflict and keep them in the bosom of the family for as long as

Women in Thailand: stylised as heroines in legend, in real life they are expected to exhibit virtues such as modesty, shyness and motherliness, and very few emerge as public figures.

possible. This results in a certain collective feeling but can also manifest itself later in life as reluctance to make decisions or enter into conflicts.

Fixed Hierarchies

In Asian society, the respect that younger family members have for their elders is a major factor. The greatest degree of respect is given to grandparents, and the hierarchy extends down via parents and older relatives, also taking in older siblings. Absolute obedience is ingrained into children at an early age. Later on it would be unthinkable to contradict anyone in authority. The consciousness of rank in Thailand is ubiquitous. The word »khun«, for example, is used before a name almost exclusively to people of higher status and only rarely to someone of equal rank.

The Role of Women

Girls are brought up in the same way as boys until the age of about six. It is only then that they start learning the traditional values such as motherliness, shyness, selflessness and modesty.

The role of women in Thai society is heavily influenced by tradition. Western-style emancipation is nonetheless apparent in terms of careers. Although there are few women in leading management positions, they still have access to the same educational and career opportunities as men. Rama V introduced universal access to education, although equality of education for both boys and girls was established only under his successor through a law passed in 1921. Political posts, however, remained closed to women until the 1930s. Elections in Thailand consistently show that women, historically referred to as »the back legs of the elephant«, have to struggle to gain a place in public life.

Foreign Influences

While the rural population has largely kept a traditional Thai identity, western ways and influences from other types of culture are increasingly prominent in the cities, particularly in Bangkok. The cosmopolitan feel and lifestyle of the capital is still not typical of the country as a whole. Most of the populace leads a rather modest life, firmly in the lap of tradition.

apart from some hotels, banks and the offices of multi-national companies. The ground floors often contain shops, workshops or the like, which are mostly shuttered in the evening behind simple roller blinds. The accommodation on the floors above has a strict hierarchy. The first floor houses employees, the second floor is the home of the owners, and the elders of the family live on the top floor. Blocks owned by well-to-do families may well have a roof garden with fencing around it. In the morning these spaces are much used for callisthenics, while in the evening they are frequently the scene of social occasions. As average earners in Thailand can rarely afford a house just for themselves and their family, most such houses are owned by the so-called middle class. They tend to be surrounded by conspicuously high walls, sometimes topped with shards of glass embedded in cement as reassurance for their security-conscious owners. The dramatic fall in the water table in Bangkok has now made it possible to build multi-storey tower blocks, which are increasingly dominating the skyline in the Thai capital. It would once have been impossible to build such towers on the waterlogged ground.

In the country Few remain of the traditional Thai houses that were built throughout the country until about the beginning of the 20th century. Some aspects of traditional building techniques are still employed, e.g. the intersecting, pointed gables, but practical, modern techniques now predominate. The main material for housing is, as it has been for centuries, wood. Traditional houses were built with remarkable craftsmanship and featured no iron components at all, not even nails. Houses were built for stability on teak piles rammed into the ground, and the individual elements were bound together with rattan. The classic Thai house is built on stilts, firstly to prevent the house being flooded during the rainy season and secondly to allow the space beneath to be used for storage, as a workshop or just as a place for the family to congregate. Animals belonging to the family – pigs, dogs or birds – are often kept there. Roofs are usually covered with palm leaves. Even today, particularly in the country, Thais tend to do without glass windows, preferring to protect themselves from the elements with simple wooden shutters that close over the window openings. The layout of the rooms is very simple. There is often just one large room that functions as living room, dining room and bedroom for the whole family. While electric lighting is now standard, running water or even bathtubs are the exception rather than the rule. For a supply of water, large clay butts are used to catch the rain. Some of the middle class can now realize the dream of having their own house. Land, allocated by the community, is cheap. Day labourers and peasants, however, frequently live even now at their place of work in simple straw huts that offer hardly any protection against wind and rain. Government and international efforts are still trying to replace the more than 20,000 homes lost in the tsunami in 2004 and at the same time to increase the standard of rural homes.

Language

Thai, a member of the Sino-Tibetan family of languages, is related to Lao, Shan and various dialects of southern China. It also contains some Sanskrit and Pali vocabulary, which is seldom used nowadays.

Sino-Tibetan languages

Thai, which was formerly called Siamese, is an isolating, monosyllabic language like Chinese, where the pitch of the sounds often distinguishes meanings. Most words are single-syllable and invariant; grammatical functions such as numerals, sex, mode etc. have specific words of their own. Since monosyllabism allows only a limited number of differentiated words, there are seven different pitch inflections, making it a near impossibility for westerners to master the Thai language to perfection. Figures for the number of consonants and vowels are quoted at anything between 50 and 82, many of which are modified in sound according to their positioning within a word. For

Linguistic structures

Life on a Bangkok klong

instance »l« and »r« are pronounced like »n« when they occur at the end of a word, whereas at the beginning of the word they are both pronounced as »l«. In the middle of a word, two »r«s together are transformed into the vowel sound »a« while one »r« becomes silent after an »s«, as seen particularly often in religious and monastic names such as »Sri Ayutthaya«, where the first word is pronounced »Si«.

Written Thai   The Thai alphabet was codified in 1283 by King Ramkhamhaeng. The National Museum in Bangkok displays the royal proclamation, engraved on a stone tablet that documents the very birth of Thai as it is written today. The alphabet includes 44 consonants and 32 vowels, with 14 simple vowels and 18 diphthongs. Words are written one after the other from left to right so that spaces only appear between complete sentences or before proper names. The Buddhist religion, which is dominant all over South-East Asia, contributed to the spread of this alphabet into Myanmar, Laos and Cambodia as well, although a number of modifications were made along the way. The alphabet has undergone very few alterations in the course of the centuries, which explains why any Thai with the ability to read can easily understand, or at least decipher, documents and inscriptions written long ago (for details on the spoken and written language, see ►Practicalities, Language).

State and Government

»Land of the free«   Thailand has never been ruled by foreign powers or peoples throughout its long history. This is the reason why the country adopted its present name of Thailand (or »Prathet Thai« in the local tongue), which literally means »land of the free«. The fact that Thailand has never been colonized, in spite of some tentative attempts (primarily by the British and Portuguese), is attributable in no small part to the successful diplomacy that was conducted, especially during periods of international disorder.

Constitutional monarchy   Subsequent to a coup d'état and the establishment of a new constitution in December 1932, government in Thailand has taken the form of a constitutional monarchy. The people are represented by a parliament of two chambers (Senate and House of Representatives), in which 267 senators (mostly consisting of top officers and officials) are nominated by the king for a period of six years, and 357 are elected by the people for four-year periods by secret ballot. The Thai system of government thus resembles the British model with an upper and a lower house under the aegis of a sovereign.

Local government   Thailand is divided into 73 provinces (changwat), usually named after their capital city. The top tier of local government consists of a provincial governor, who is both a representative of the national go-

Facts and Figures *The Kingdom of Thailand*

Location
► South-East Asia 6° to 20° 30' north 97° 30' to 105° 45' east

Area
► 513,115 sq km/198 sq mi (United Kingdom: 245,000 sq km/94,000 sq mi)

Geography:
► longest river: Chao Phraya River (Maenam Chao Praya) (370km/230mi)
► highest mountain: Doi Inthanon (2,565m/2,805ft) in the north of Thailand
► coastline: 3,219km/2,000mi

Population
► about 65.4 million
► population density: Thailand overall average 121 per sq km/313 per sq mi (United Kingdom: 60 million citizens, 245 per sq km/638 per sq mi); Bangkok: 4,038 inhabitants per sq km/10,458 per sq mi; central region: 138 per sq km/357 per sq mi; northern region: 67 per sq km/174 per sq mi; north-eastern region: 123 per sq km/319 per sq mi; southern region: 114 per sq km/295 per sq mi
► population growth: 0.95% p.a.
► ethnic composition: 80% Thai, 12% of Chinese descent, 4% Malay, 3% Khmer, hill tribes and other minorities

Languages
► predominantly Thai (Siamese), also: Chinese, Malay, English (as the language of business and trade)

Religion
► 94% Buddhist
► 4% Muslim
► 0.6% Christian

State
► constitutional monarchy
► head of state: King Bhumibol Adulyadej (Rama IX)

Economy
► gross domestic product (GDP): about US$ 164 billion (2005)

Thailand

Equator

► GDP per person: about US$ 2,511
► real economic growth: 6.1% (2004)
► business sectors: services 53% industry 37% agriculture 10%
► unemployment rate: 8.8% (2005)

vernment and leader of the local administration. The provinces are made up of 567 districts (amphoe), which are further sub-divided into parishes (tamban). The villages (mu ban) form the lowest level of administration. Finances are the responsibility of the provincial governments, which are funded from Bangkok. The government in Bangkok publishes five-year plans intended to guarantee permanent growth and channel state investment along appropriate lines. Such investment is primarily intended to bring agricultural development to more backward areas of Thailand. King Bhumibol himself has ensured a right of co-determination in this matter.

King The king is the head of state. He has a personal veto on the adoption or rejection of any new law. Thailand also has a special mechanism

The ubiquitous image of King Bhumibol

for introducing laws in the form of a »royal decree«. The king himself may thus declare a law without requiring the consent of parliament. Before the establishment of the new state in 1932, the then kingdom of Siam had been an absolute monarchy, and even today the king's word is sacrosanct. Nevertheless much has changed since the time of Rama I, who ascended the throne in 1782 and was the first of the present Chakri dynasty. The divinity of the monarchy, which until the reign of King Taksin meant that any person touching a member of the royal family would be put to death, has lost credence, as has the belief in the infallibility of the monarch. Nevertheless King Bhumibol (Rama IX) has a tremendous reputation among the people. A referendum in 1987 even awarded him the appellation Bhumibol the Great ► (Baedeker Special p.52).

His word also carries considerable weight in political terms. His intervention after the students' revolt in 1973 persuaded power-hungry military officers to go into exile, and Prime Minister Suchinda resigned after riots in May 1992 when the royal family withdrew all support for him. No criticism of the king is ever uttered, even behind closed doors, and even Thai expatriates maintain respect for the sovereign. Visitors should beware of making any disrespectful utterance about the royal family, let alone an insult.

Role of the army

The army is traditionally the most powerful social group in Thailand. Since 1932 there have been no less than 17 coups. Its political influence is not simply based upon its control of men and arms, but on the fact that officers represent »respected members of society«. Important industrial firms and services, e.g. two of the four TV stations, monopoly control of telephones, airports and the national airline, ports, and until recent times the railways too, all come or have come under control of the officers. Control of the army therefore also means a direct safeguard of economic interests.

In addition, the army being the major consumer of munitions and supplies, the manufacturers of such goods are always willing to make financial contributions to obtain contracts. Corruption has been a key social mechanism in Thailand since time immemorial. In opposition to this excessive power of the military there is an ever-strengthening democratic movement that largely stems from Bangkok-based intellectuals and the middle class, but which also gains surprising support from the royal family (although it is ostensibly almost powerless according to the constitution).

Political parties

Although the political parties of Thailand cover a considerable spectrum, no grouping can claim to represent a defining consensus. Most of them are organizations put together by special interest groups (such as the army or industry) that are mainly concerned with gathering votes for their own candidates. Apart from the Communist Party, the only other party with a recognizable political doctrine is the Palang Dharma, the »Buddhist Party«, led by the former governor of Bangkok, Chamlong Srimuang, who has an admirable reputation for incorruptibility. The Communists are actually officially banned by law, but remain active in the underground, especially among students.

Political consciousness

There is no particular political consciousness in Thailand that transcends all class differences. Voters favour whichever candidate promises to relieve their most pressing needs most quickly. It is also commonplace for votes to be bought and sold, especially in the country where pronounced respect for authority and an almost feudalistic traditional order remain. The intellectual class has a quite different outlook; here democracy has its deepest roots.

Foreign policy

Thailand's foreign policy has generally been closely tied to that of the United States, which has provided large amounts of aid for improvements to the infrastructure of the north-east. This is one principal reason why Thailand agreed to allow US troops to be stationed in the country during the Vietnam war. A more vigorous policy of in-

The image of the monarch is ubiquitous: outsized paintings alongside busy motorways or miniatures in souvenir shops. The love of the Thais for their king and queen is common to all strata of Thai society.

THE ROYAL FAMILY

Pictures of the king are displayed even in the tiniest huts: King Bhumibol is everywhere in Thailand. The current monarch is seen as a symbol of unity in a country with a volatile parliament and a military that has launched 17 coups d'état since 1932.

King Bhumibol was born on 5 December 1927 in Cambridge (USA) and now bears the title Rama IX, as the ninth ruler of the Chakri dynasty that has controlled Thailand since 1782. The current monarch was the third and last child of Prince Mahidol of Songkhla, a son of Rama V (Chulalongkorn). When the king's father died early, his mother resettled the family in Switzerland, where the children were to receive an international, yet essentially middle-class education in a democratic milieu.

After the abdication of his uncle and the mysterious death of his brother, Bhumibol Adulyadej found himself declared king. He remained in Switzerland to complete his education but finally returned to Thailand to take up his official responsibilities in 1951, having already been crowned in Bangkok on 5 May 1950. During the decades of his reign, the king has earned such love and respect from the populace that he has been dubbed »Father of the People«. Visits to all parts of the country have been one of the most important aspects of his

royal duties. He personally oversees many development projects, and his devotion to duty has earned him the rare title of »Bhumibol the Great«, an honorific bestowed by the people themselves a few months before his 60th birthday in May 1987. The 50th jubilee of his coronation in May 2000 was commemorated with magnificent celebrations. King Bhumibol is not only ubiquitous in Thailand, he is now the longest-reigning monarch on earth at the present time and has ruled for longer than any other king in Thailand's history.

Queen Sirikit

The present queen **Sirikit Somdech Phraborom Raijninath** is no less popular than her husband. She was born on 12 August 1932 and is also descended from the famous King Chulalongkorn, as a great granddaughter on her father's side. She got to know her distant cousin Bhumibol when she was just 15 and studying in France. The young Bhumibol exhibited a passion for fast cars, which ended in an accident from

which he suffered serious eye injuries. His recovery in hospital in Lausanne was accelerated, however, and his wishes came true when a beautiful and attentive visitor arrived at his bedside: the future Queen Sirikit, definitely a sight for sore eyes. They became engaged and were able to share their final year of study before their return to Bangkok. Along with all members of the royal family, the queen has been active in charitable work and activities for social causes. She is not only the president of the Thai Red Cross but also works on behalf of disadvantaged women and children and promotes traditional skills (such as hand weaving).

The Children of the Sovereign

Among the four children born to Bhumibol and Sirikit, princesses **Chulabhorn** (born 1957) and **Sirindhorn** (1955) stand out. They have supported their mother in the accomplishment of her social and charitable aims. The reverence in which they are held among the populace has even led to the abandonment of the 700-year-old tradition decreeing that the throne may only be occupied by the most senior male heir. This means it is theoretically possible that the successor to the present king might not necessarily be **Crown Prince Vajiaralongkorn**, who is the eldest son, born

in 1952, but that the crown might yet be offered to his younger sister Sirindhorn. An elder sister, **Ubo Ratana**, has already relinquished all claims to the royal succession, having left the country to get married. While Prince Vajiaralongkorn studied in Australia at the famous Duntroon Military Academy, his sister Sirindhorn, a doctor of archaeology, undertook duties of state and joined in efforts for social and cultural advancement to an extent that has earned her the award of the title, »Maha Chakri«, which in terms of protocol elevates her to the same level as the prince. The youngest princess, Chulabhorn, studied agriculture and forestry in Chiang Mai and Bangkok.

Princess Mother

The mother of the present king (1900–1995) remained a regular traveller throughout the land until the last years of her life. She was particularly concerned with the development of medical care in remote areas and with the advancement of the hill tribes of the north. The »Princess Mother« was a Thai commoner who met her husband-to-be, the doctor Prince Mahidol, while working as a young nurse in Boston USA. She was dubbed »the royal mother from the sky« (Mae Fah Luang) by the hill peoples.

dependence in the late 1970s, however, led to America being requested to give up its bases. Since that time Thailand has been consistently more independent in its foreign policy.

Membership of international groupings

Thailand has been a member of the United Nations and its special organizations since 1946. It was involved in the Colombo plan of 1950 that had the aim of »raising living standards in all member countries« according to a model exemplified by the Marshall plan. It was also a founder member of the Association of South East Asian Nations (ASEAN), which published its constitution in Bangkok in 1967.

Education and science

Teaching of general knowledge and basic reading and arithmetical skills was almost exclusively the domain of monks in the temples until the 19th century. It was not until the reign of King Mongkut (Rama IV, 1851–1868) that a school system was developed with the aim of teaching the entire population. Even then, English was one of the compulsory subjects. However, it was not until 1917 that compulsory education was enshrined in law. The Thai schooling system begins for children of pre-school age at institutions resembling nursery schools. Children then have six years of primary teaching (which is free, although the obligatory school uniform and some books still need to be paid for). Out in the country, teaching sometimes still takes place in Buddhist monasteries. A secondary system formulated along British lines builds upon this primary system, with three years of secondary education in so-called high schools followed by an optional three years equating to sixth-form education. There are a total of 32 universities and technical colleges in Thailand. Among the 20 institutions of higher education in Bangkok itself, the largest is the internationally renowned Chulalongkorn University, founded by Rama VI in 1917. Training colleges are spread throughout the country and play a major role in the Thai education system. In particular they teach modern farming techniques to villagers. As late as 1970, 17% of 35- to 40-year-olds could neither read nor write. By the mid 1990s this figure had been reduced to 6%.

Higher education, training colleges ▶

Illiteracy ▶

Economy

One of the »Four Tigers«

A serious economic crisis emanated from Thailand in February 1997 and affected the entire Asian continent, leading to economic uncertainty throughout the world. It came at the end of a veritably intoxicating economic boom that had benefited South-East Asia for a number of years. Around the beginning of the 1980s, Thailand had started catching up with Asian emerging economies, the so-called »Four Tigers« of Hong Kong, Singapore, South Korea and Taiwan. These countries had become a major factor in the world economy. The calamity arose primarily as a result of a construction boom in Thailand that had been financed mainly by foreign credit. As the supply of new high-rise offices in Bangkok increasingly exceeded demand, much of this foreign credit could not be repaid. Even reputable financial institutions such as the Bank of Thailand found themselves in difficulties and the Thai baht fell victim to currency speculators from all over the world. This resulted in an unexpected collapse in exports, a run on the currency and dramatic falls in share prices. The traditional high level of corruption also played a role in this collapse of the Thai economy, from which the country is only now beginning to recover. The crisis also refuted one of the hard-and-fast rules of national economics. According to all the books, the devaluation of the baht should have led to a rise in exports, but in this case banks simply did not have the funds to provide new credit for the purchase of raw materials overseas, for example. The economic catastrophe was not totally unexpected. Critics had warned the government in Bangkok about the developments, but their cautions fell on deaf ears. Their long-held fear was that the country had beco-

◄ The role of corruption

◄ Fatal interdependencies

A merchant people: mobile traders on the ferry to Ko Samet

me too dependent on the capital and goodwill of foreign investors. The World Bank was called in to help, but it made the release of funds conditional on structural reforms to the economy. Compelled to act as instructed, a considerable loss of face for Thailand, the government, then under the leadership of Prime Minister Chavalit, merged several insolvent banks. These moves, however, were not enough to prevent the resignation of Chavalit and his cabinet some months later. Yet even his successor had difficulties dissolving the political and economic structures and hierarchies that had become

► *Traditional trade deficit* entrenched over the preceding decades. The economic crisis was not the first time Thailand had run a trade deficit. Its foreign debt is around 17 billion US dollars. The countries of the European Union are highly regarded in Thailand and as a bloc constitute the country's third-largest trading partner. Thailand now has many export goods (gems, textiles, rice, fruit and vegetables, fish) that are of interest to western countries. By the

i   Wages in Thailand

- The average wage in the Bangkok region is about 5,700 baht per month (€120 or £80). Unskilled workers take home about 3,200 baht (approx. €67 or £45).

year 2000 the crisis had already bottomed out and exports rose by 9%, of which cars, clothes and electronic goods made up the largest proportions.

Mining and energy   Thailand possesses rich mineral deposits including tin, zinc and fluorites. The south is part of the south-east Asian tin belt that extends into Malaysia. As the world's fourth largest producer of tin, Thailand also suffered from a worldwide trading crisis (caused by the collapse of the International Tin Cartel) over the past few years that has led

► *No nuclear power stations* to a drastic fall in the price of the metal. Thailand has no nuclear power stations. Instead, natural gas, oil and the lignite that is customarily strip-mined in the north furnish practically all of the country's energy supplies. About 7.6 million tons of lignite coal are mined every year. Abundant supplies of natural gas will also play a key role in supplying energy to Thailand in the future. Extensive gas fields in the Gulf of Thailand are to be exploited intensively. Utilization and export of natural gas should bring in billions of dollars in earnings and benefit Thailand's balance of payments for years to come. Considerable deposits of oil were also discovered in the Gulf of Thailand during the 1980s, which has led to a major reduction in oil imports. Domestic energy sources now cover a third of the country's energy needs. This also includes a number of large dams that have been constructed in the north and east of Thailand.

Agriculture, forestry and fishing   **Rice** remains the central crop in Thailand's traditional agricultural regions (it is sometimes called the »rice bowl of South-East Asia«). Two harvests in a year are often possible. However, only the so-called »white rice«, which takes longer to grow and is more labour-intensive to cultivate, is suitable for export. The »sticky rice« that is mainly grown in the north and »Na Muang rice« from central Thailand are both grown almost exclusively for domestic consumption. Only about 60% of existing rice paddies are actually cultivated at present. Increasing industrialization, particularly in the Maenam basin and around Bangkok, have contributed to this decline. **Coconut palms** are also used intensively. The wood is suitable for building houses and the nuts contain delicious coconut milk. The fruit can of course be eaten, or dried to make copra, which can itself be processed to extract coconut oil. The shells are burned as fuel in country districts. Over 70% of northern Thailand (30% of the land area of the entire country) is thickly forested. Half the cover is made up of dipterocarp trees; of

Rice harvest in northern Thailand

which the yang trees (or wood-oil trees) are put to particularly great use. The rest is mixed woodland with valuable teak that can be economically exploited. The tropical rain forest has been badly damaged by slash-and-burn clearance, shifting cultivation and excessive felling. Vegetable cultivation has more than doubled since the 1960s, and production of fruit has increased by even more. Thailand and the Philippines are the world's leading producers of pineapples. With the exception of rice, the most important export crops are cassava, sugar cane and maize. Raw rubber production is also increasing in importance. Thailand is one of the world's major exporters of tuna fish. Even though catches have somewhat stagnated since the 1970s, the tonnage of the fishing fleet increased six-fold between 1976 and 1988. In 2000 Thai fishermen landed close on two million tons of fish. The catch is processed and canned in modern plants, mostly for export. In the area around Bangkok alone, about 30 fish factories make products for export.

◄ Cultivation of fruit and vegetables

◄ Fishing

Industrialization is becoming increasingly important. This brings its own problems. In spite of a consistently expanding economy, a major chasm between metropolitan and rural districts remains one of Thailand's most intractable difficulties. Thousands of rural inhabitants flood into Bangkok, especially in years when the harvest is poor, to seek their fortune in the capital. Programmes established by the government to compensate earnings in such years have gained acceptance, but they need time to take effect. Bangkok is the epicentre of both industry and commerce in Thailand. All foreign firms

Industry

with a presence in the country set up their headquarters in the built up area around the kingdom's main city. For domestic companies, too, there are no major alternatives to Bangkok with its comprehensive transport links. The city centre is dominated by office blocks occupied by multi-national corporations and service companies. The government is nevertheless seeking to boost the attractiveness to industry of regions other than Bangkok itself, but this will first require improvements to the infrastructure.

i **Sex tourism**

■ A significant proportion of the almost 10 million annual visitors to Thailand are in search of sexual experiences. Their »needs« are often met by women or young girls and boys who have been abducted by (or occasionally sold by parents to) sex traffickers brothel owners and pimps from all the major cities of Thailand. What is particularly horrifying is the increase in prostitution involving children and young teenagers. According to the international aid organization »Médecins Sans Frontières« more than 200,000 children and teenagers have been forced into prostitution. In Pattaya alone there are said to be some 20,000 prostitutes, of whom half are boys and girls between the ages of 10 and 14. Now, after many years of procrastination, the Thai government is taking action against child prostitution. Dubious premises are being investigated, and sex tourists who are caught are severely punished and afterwards deported from the country.

The Thai textile industry can now match the quality of even the most renowned textile manufacturing countries. The **silk industry** has long been of central importance and Thailand is one of the world's main suppliers of silk. Cotton and other fabrics are also imported from abroad and processed within the country.

It is not generally known that the kingdom of Thailand is the second-biggest **manufacturer of jewellery** in the world after Italy. Rubies and sapphires are mined mainly in the south-east of the country, while diamonds and other gems are sent to Thailand from producing countries throughout the world for finishing.

Alongside traditional areas of the economy such as agriculture or fisheries, **tourism** has become a major source of earnings for the country over the last three decades. Throughout this period the number of visitors has increased year on year. In 2004 around 11.65 million people came to Thailand. The largest proportion of visitors from countries outside Asia, are from Europe, especially Germany. Even the tsunami that struck on 26 December 2004 reversed the upward trend only for a very short time. In 2005 there was a further rise in visitor numbers of the order of 3%.

Employment policy
In 2004 unofficial figures estimated that the total workforce in Thailand numbered some 34.1 million people. One specific characteristic of South-East Asia is the relatively high number of children in work. In 1997 1.1 million young people between 11 and 15 were earning a wage, around 16% of the age group. Low wages and competitive tax levels mean that companies have good reason to expect further expansion of the economy.

Religion

More than 95% of the population in Thailand is officially Buddhist (about 58 million). Hinayana Buddhism, literally »the way of the lesser vehicle«, is the main branch of the religion in the country. The second-largest group, about 12% of Thais,, follow Mahayana Buddhism (»the way of the greater vehicle«). Buddha himself is not worshipped as a God but honoured as the founder of the religion. Buddhism has been declared the state religion in Thailand, but other religious groups are protected by law: i.e. Hindus (approx. 65,000 people, mainly of Indian origin), Muslims (4%, mainly Malays in the southern provinces) and Christians (0.6%). Only 0.4% of the population claim to have no religion.

Buddhism – state religion

Buddhism

The name Buddha comes from Sanskrit and has a meaning akin to »The Enlightened One«. Buddha was born with the name **Siddharta Gautama** around 563 BC. He was the son of a rich landowner in what is now Nepal at the foot of the Himalayas. Although his life was initially sheltered amidst the luxury of his parents' estate, he is said to have escaped his confines on three occasions, during which he learned of the plight of humanity from the sight of an old man, a sick man and a dead man. The moment that changed his life, on a fourth such excursion when he was 29 years old, was a meeting with a hermit who encouraged him to abandon the life he had led and become a wandering ascetic seeking the meaning of human life. The story as told emphasizes how earnest this decision was, since on the very day of his departure a son was born to his wife. After seven years of wandering, during which he sought to find a middle way between self-indulgence and self-mortification by intense meditation, he found himself sitting under a pipal tree next to the Nerajara river in India. His meditation took him deep within himself, he passed through four separate planes of consciousness and finally found enlightenment. His first sermon in the Indian town of Benares elucidated the Four Noble Truths: »There is suffering«, »How suffering is caused«, »There can be an end to suffering« and »The way to the end of suffering«. In only three months after this sermon he had already gathered 60 disciples. He instructed them to »bring the joyous word to all who can hear. No two of you should go the same way«. He himself spent 45 years travelling through India preaching his message of the **»Dharma wheel«** (dharmachakrapravartana). He survived murder attempts by his cousin Devadatta, for example by taming an elephant that had been set on him by the strength of his own merciful love. Although Buddhist texts claim that Buddha entered into a state of **nirvana** in 543 BC aged 80, historical analysis sets the date of his death around 480 or 470 BC. Nevertheless the

The history and teaching of Buddha

Buddhist calendar still uses 543 BC as its origin. Visitors often meet with dates that differ from the Christian calendar by that number. For instance the year 2006 in the western calendar translates to 2549 in countries where Buddhism is the state religion.

Roots of Buddhism The roots of Buddhism emerged from Hinduism. From there came the concept of karma, the immutable law of the cosmos. Karma implies that all good deeds and bad deeds have consequences that are atoned for in the course of regular reincarnations, in the sense that good deeds are rewarded in the form of a better existence in the next life. The cycle is unavoidable. Buddhist traditions relate that Buddha himself had to experience more than 500 lives in various bodily forms. Nevertheless it is possible for people to influence their progress through the cycle by dedicating their own lives to the basic beliefs propounded by Buddha. Those who are closest to nirvana are the monks who spend their whole lives studying the teachings of Buddha. This is why monks are so highly respected in Thailand.

> ### ? DID YOU KNOW …?
>
> ■ The legend about the form of the Indian dagoba and thus of the chedis that decorate all Thai temples relates it to some of the last words of Buddha, who was asked by his disciples how he should be remembered. He answered, »Build little hills of sand like a mound of rice, for that is what everyone needs.«

Mahayana and Hinayana Buddhism The differences between Mahayana and Hinayana Buddhism are to be found in the possibility of breaking the cycle of birth, death and reincarnation. Whereas Hinayana Buddhism assumes that this has to be achieved by all believers individually with no support, the Mahayana Buddhism that emerged in the first and second centuries AD recognizes the concept of **bodhisattvas**. This refers to people who have already attained a state of enlightenment, but who still remain (unrecognized as such) on earth to guide others along the »Noble Eight-fold Path« to self-recognition so that they can find the true way to nirvana. Buddha himself is considered to have been such a bodhisattva, having been through the cycle of birth, death and rebirth 500 times before reaching nirvana.

Modern beliefs The first Buddhist monks entered the Thai region of Nakhon Pathom, having been sent by the Indian ruler Ashoka in the 3rd century BC. The beliefs that are still taught today developed in this region. The teachings of the enlightened Buddha became mixed with **elements of Hinduism**, including for example the Hindu vision of the world. One of the many depictions of this world view is attributed to King Loei Thai (1299–1347). It conceives of a world existing in an infinite space that splits into a world of senses, a world of pure form

Buddhist monks at prayer →

and a world of the unexplainable. The world of senses includes both cold hells and hot hells, while the world above them contains the earth in the form of a disc with the mountain of Meru at its centre and populated by people, animals and spirits. The highest world is the world of the gods, who spend millennia in a state of meditation and have abandoned any kind of tangible form. Beyond the three worlds lies nirvana, which is beyond any human description or imagining. Whereas Buddha's own teachings do not mention gods, beliefs have developed over the course of the centuries that involve worshipping the gods of related religions (like Hinduism). Thus, certain aspects of Hindu mythology have been adopted, such as the trinity of **Brahma** (creator of the universe), **Shiva** (the god with the third eye that exposes all evil) and **Vishnu** (the benefactor, protector and saviour). They also appear in the Buddhist religion in a variety of incarnations: Vishnu, for example, as Rama, the hero of the Ramayana epic.

Animism Another central feature of religious life in Thailand is the belief in good and bad spirits, an element of animism. Buddha himself specifically stated that, as long as no harm is done to the teachings or to another creature, the pantheon of gods, though subordinate to the great teacher, do not lose their power to allay the cares of daily life, as long as people are able to retain their favour. An individual is composed of three components, the material body or »kai«, an individual soul »winyan« and a free soul »khwan«. If the »khwan« can be bound to the body, health, prosperity and success in work are assured. After illness or death, the »khwan« departs from the body, but sometimes it roams restlessly to haunt the living. Every funeral involves an elaborate ritual to prevent such spirits of the dead, or their »khwan«, from returning to earth. The hill tribes of the north have specific rites of their own, since for them spirits play an even more crucial role. There are bad spirits and, of course, there are also good spirits such as the earth spirit »phi ruan« and the household spirits »phra phum«. Good spirits are adopted into families as soon as they are identified, whereas the bad spirits find a home in **spirit houses**, »saan phra phum«, where they are appeased with daily offerings. Evil spirits are thought to be the souls of dead people who have been denied reincarnation and thus the next stage of their journey to nirvana. »Phra phum« means »protective spirit« and represents real comfort in the everyday lives of the people, since the spirit lives among them – not under the same roof or in the shadow of their house, but right next door. The spirit lives in its own beautifully constructed building that resembles a palace or a temple and is set on a post at eye level. It is surrounded by a terrace or gallery on which the offerings are left. »Phra phum« is usually depicted in person, too, in the form of a wood or clay figurine leaning against the back wall of the house with a fly-swat in one hand and a large book in the other. From there the figure is able to keep an eye on all goings-on through the open front entrance to the house. All important family events are entered in his book. He punishes any disrespect with nightmares or, in serious instances, with robbery, burglary or fire.

The Thais bring rice, tea, orchids and other offerings in order to request intercession, particularly by the good spirits. Under special circumstances, e.g. in the event of illness, a birth in the family, indebtedness or if there is hope of winning a prize in a lottery, the entourage of servants and companions around the house of »phra phum« is supplemented by horses and elephants, slaves and dancing girls, all daintily made out of cardboard or wood. Such spirit houses also stand at dangerous sections of road where accidents occur. Although most of these spirit rites are incomprehensible to foreigners, it is nevertheless worth taking a look at the Erawan shrine on Rama I Road in Bangkok, which is visited by hundreds of Thais every day (it is actually an ordinary spirit house but is especially revered) or Lak Muang opposite the great palace complex in Bangkok.

Daily offerings are made to spirits

Religious Festivals and Customs

There are estimated to be 200,000 monks in Thailand. For more than half of them this is a lifelong decision. Old monks are particularly respected, since it is assumed that their ascetic lifestyle will, by their

Monks

time of life, have brought them close to a state of redemption. Monks are not allowed to accept alms from women, although this is not based on any instruction from Buddha himself. Words have since been put into the founder's mouth that minimize the role women play in the world. Despite knowing this, monks still avoid taking food or money from a woman. The monasteries, though, are also home to Mae Ji, female attendants who are not subject to the same rules as the monks themselves. For example, they are permitted to handle money and are often responsible for running the household inside a monastery.

Life in a monastery Practically every male Buddhist in Thailand spends at least one period of his life in a monastery, often while he is still young. In the summer holidays, for example, numerous temples are set up for boys, some as young as six. A period in the temple is intended to give young Buddhists access to the teachings of the Enlightened One. The day that an individual enters the monastery is celebrated by his entire family as well as friends and relatives from distant places. The ceremony involves his head being shaven as a sign of modesty, after which he receives his saffron-dyed monk's robe. During the subsequent weeks, his day will include several hours studying holy scripture, as written in the sutras. Young monks are also initiated into the art of meditation, which is not always easy at a young age. Just like their adult role models, young monks are expected to venture out early in the mornings to gather alms. These mostly consist of rice, vegetables and a small amount of meat, given to monks by believers, or occasionally they may consist of offerings such as lotus blossoms or orchids, which they will be bidden to lay before the Buddha figure in the temple. Monks do not normally offer any thanks for these gifts. On the contrary, if a monk accepts an offering, the giver will usually thank the receiver with a respectful »wai« gesture with the hands pressed together in front of the face. It is hoped that this will be a contribution to the redemption of the soul.

Funerals For a funeral, close relatives gather for seven days around the coffin in the house of the deceased, dressed in black or white mourning wear, to listen to recitations of the sutras by monks seated in rows on raised pedestals. On the day of the cremation (the intervening period of time is generally longer for people of higher social standing, perhaps even as long as a year), the coffin is brought to the temple complex, where all the funeral guests will be given small straw stars that they will throw as a symbolic gesture onto a bonfire of stacked wood topped with an elaborate paper pagoda, before the most honoured guest sets the fire ablaze. The actual location for the cremation is selected only by the closest intimates of the deceased.

Hindu gods in everyday life Whereas high Brahman ceremonials are celebrated at major family feasts, harvest blessing, and the night before the initiation of monks, everyday prayers for hope and so-lace are made to stone or marble Hindu idols. Usually quite modest offerings suffice, such as a few smoky candles, a garland of flowers (pyan malai), a small bowl of rice or other foodstuffs and, of course, simple humble obeisance. Special reverence is offered to »Tao Maha Prom« (on the corner of the Four Seasons hotel in Bangkok), or

»Erawan«, the three-headed elephant (in front of the art academy next to the national theatre) and »Phra Mae Torani« (in a shrine on the klong behind Bangkok's Royal Hotel), all of which are very po-pular. A stream of water flows from the plaited tresses of the goddess (Mae Torani means Mother Earth) and is believed to bestow bles-sings. It is especially venerated during the Loy Krathong festival in November, perhaps Thailand's most beautiful festival.

»Pyan malai« garlands, artistically plaited from fragrant jasmine blooms, orchids or roses, are offered for sale to drivers at practically every set of traffic lights in the evenings. They are put over the necks of successful examination candidates or receivers of honourable titles to bring them luck, as well as being draped over statues of the Bud-dha or laid at the feet of the animist god »phra phum«.

Garlands of flowers

Temples

Although sacred architecture usually bears the unmistakeable hall-mark of the dynasty of its time, almost all temple complexes in Thai-land also reveal the influence of foreign cultures. Indian and Sri Lan-kan elements arrived in Thailand with missionaries or merchants. For centuries the (Mon) Khmer defined the architecture of temples along the trade routes, but their buildings in the north-west have been more or less left to decay. In the north, magnificent Burmese and Lao buildings are the paradigm to this day. In the 19th century European styles and materials also began to make their mark (one splendid example of this is the Wat Benchama-bo-bitr temple in Bangkok). In terms of temple construction, as with many other cul-tural achievements, the Thais adopted elements from their neigh-bours but proved to be masters at perfecting and refining those ele-ments. Many temple sites also demonstrate a variety of styles, since they have seen additions in several eras.

Varied influences

Free-standing temples in the form of towers developed in India du-ring the time of Gupta (AD 310–500) and supplanted the previous cave or cliff temples. These towers initially consisted of a cubic block built on a square terrace. Above the main room inside the block, the

Hindu temples

cella, rises a pyramid-shaped tower, mostly stepped, that can be accessed only from one side. Steps lead up to the terrace on all four sides, whereas the cella is entered from one side only. The oldest remaining example of such Indian tower temples are the temple to Shiva in Geogarh (5th century with a tower about 13m/43ft high), the tiled temple of Bhitargaon near Khanpur (5th century) and the Buddhist Mahabodhi temple (built around 562 with a 51m/167ft tower) in Bodhgaya, where Buddha attained enlightenment (the temple viharn of Wat Chet Yot in Chiang Mai is a smaller copy of the same temple). Not long afterwards, a meeting hall known as a mondop (mondhop or mandapa) came to be added to the cella, then an »antarala« (cloister) between the cella and mondop. The cella also received richly decorated gateways (gopura). This established the basic shape of a Hindu temple. Various aspects of this style are mirrored in the Thai »wats«.

Khmer temples   Along roads that no longer exist in their full length but which may once have crossed Thailand from north to south, many Khmer holy sites can still be found in various states of preservation. It has been established that the Khmer built temples along their trade routes so that that travellers could fulfil their religious obligations. In the 1st and 2nd centuries BC the Khmer had the mightiest empire in South-East Asia. Their sphere of influence stretched from the domain they themselves controlled, in modern-day Cambodia, deep into Thailand and Burma. Architects in Thailand adopted many of the characteristics of Khmer temples, such as the prasat. Although they were more artistically decorative, they retained their original form. Khmer architecture developed from the Baphuon style, which revered »holy mountain« (Meru) was and was therefore heavily influenced by the Hindu original. The Khmer were generally true to the original in the layout of their temples.

Prasat ▶   The central shrine of the rectangular Khmer temples is the prasat, usually a tall building surrounded by pillars arranged in a floor plan resembling a Greek cross. Outside this, all four sides were ringed by prangs (▶p.71). Above the crossing where the four roofs with multiple steps intersected was a tower decorated with countless bas-reliefs of people and animals. If the building was used for religious ceremonies or as a place of memorial, the tower is itself a prang. If, however, it was used by the king as an audience chamber or if king's body was laid out there before his funeral, the tower normally ended in a spire. Khmer shrines were enclosed by an inner wall while a larger, and usually higher wall would form the perimeter of the temple complex as a whole. Moats around the temple symbolized the oceans of the world; inside were fonts studded with many gems from which the priests would distribute holy water. The Khmer temples display outstanding craftsmanship. The carvings of animals, people and plants around the doors and windows show their creators to have been masters of their art. Many Khmer temples still exist, especially

One of the most beautiful temples in Thailand is Wat Phra That Luang in Lampang.

in the north-east of Thailand. Particularly fine examples can be seen in Phimai and near Prakhon Chai (Wat Prasat Phanom Rung).

The Thai wat
◀ Temples

The word »wat« is often translated as »monastery«. This is not inaccurate. Like monasteries of the Middles Ages in Europe, a Thai wat is a place of refuge or retreat. They also take on the roles of schools, hospitals and orphanages. The wat is very often the place in a village for celebrating events and festivals. The name wat applies to the full extent of the monastery grounds, including the sacred precinct and the monks' dwellings, where there are seldom any ceremonial buildings. The two parts are usually separated by a wall (the »kamphaeng kheo« or jewelled wall). The monks' apartments (khana), the main sermon hall (viharn), the courtyard and chapels that surround it, the temple itself, the refectories and service buildings are all components of the complete temple complex. Depending on the size of the complex, there may also be a library, where sutras (holy words of Buddha) are kept, as well as one or more cloisters in which the monks may meditate. Typical buildings within a wat include the »bot«, the »viharn«, the »sala«, the »ho trai« and the »kambarien« (see below).

The temple compound may also contain one or more viharns, named after the statue of Buddha that is always inside them. The most prominent building on the site is likely to be the chedi or the prang that towers over the whole complex. These are typical of wats in Thailand. The wat may also have a belltower (»ho rakang«) with a drum or a gong suspended at its base. It is common to see statues in the form of »jaks« (temple guards of Chinese origin), »kinnari« (bird women), »garudas« (the steeds of Vishnu) and others, mostly from Hindu mythology.

Bodhi trees ► Bodhi trees are particularly revered. They often grow in temple compounds and may be decorated with yellow or saffron ribbons. It was under such a tree that Buddha first attained his state of enlightenment.

Bot The most sacred building in a temple complex is called the bot, or ubosoth, which only monks may enter. It is used for celebrating the ordination of a monk. Eight boundary stones or »sema« mark the perimeter of the sacred precinct and set it apart from the surrounding unconsecrated ground. They commonly have pointed spires and are decorated with bas-reliefs, often showing scenes from the life of Buddha. To protect them from the weather and from magical forces, they are frequently topped with a tabernacle shaped in the form of a chedi. The bot itself is a long rectangular building with windows along the sides. The entrance is always on the eastern side. Larger bots have three entrances, the central one being much smaller than the other two. There may also be a cloister, often with statues of Buddha. The portals and window shutters are often decorated with elaborate gilded carvings or mother-of-pearl inlay work. It is characteristic for the thick walls and columns to taper towards the top.

Entrances ► The entrances of temples in northern Thailand, which usually emulate the Burmese style, are particularly magnificent in their decoration. Balustrades have the shape of horned vipers, their heads and bodies speckled with dozens of tiny glass mosaic tiles. The stacked and slightly curving roofs of temple buildings are often covered with colourful glazed tiles arranged in a specific pattern and end in stylized snakes that wind symbolically towards the heavens. Little bells hang from the roof overhangs and jingle in the breeze. The sound is made by tiny sheets of metal shaped to resemble to the heart-shaped leaves of the sacred Bodhi tree.

Interiors ► The interiors of larger buildings are divided into three aisles, whereas smaller buildings have a single aisle. On the western side opposite the entrance sits the most revered of the Buddha statues, often surrounded by many other figures, garlands of flowers, offerings and a trough of sand into which believers place joss sticks. Apart from the proportions of the room and the branching structure of roof joists (often with a magnificently decorated wooden coffered ceiling

The famous Wat Phra Kaeo in Bangkok: →
a single temple the size of a whole suburb

suspended between them), the main contribution to the atmosphere derives from the harmonious colour schemes, in which red, gold, blue and black are the popular shades. Paintings on the wall mostly depict scenes from the life of Buddha or from his previous lives (jataka).

Viharn
The viharn is similar to the bot and serves as the meeting place for lay people. It too has one or more statues of Buddha and is enhanced by innumerable artistic details. Temple complexes may contain either one large viharn or several smaller ones.

Chedis and stupas
The Indian stupa and its Thai equivalent, the chedi, developed from the mounds that once covered the graves of holy monks. The first stupas are said to have been erected by the Indian king Ashoka (273–231 BC), for example the four at Pattan (Nepal).
The stupa in Anuradhapura on Sri Lanka is also one of the oldest. On the island they are known as »dagobas«. Stupas and chedis are not like churches that people enter to worship a god. They are cult buildings without access which house relics of Buddha and may be regarded as among the most striking monuments of Buddhism itself. In Laos stupas bear the name »that«, while in Burma, Nepal, Java and Bali they are called »pagodas«. The basic shape consists of a hemispherical or bell-shaped body built of baked clay and then plastered or stuccoed. Above that is a rectangular section, then a multi-layered upper part, a symbol of holiness. The largest chedi of an especially holy temple will be topped by a gilded or even a solid gold steeple. To show respect for Buddha, a stupa or chedi should be circled in a clockwise direction. For this purpose there is a terrace surrounded by stone balustrade (upon which no woman may walk). The balustrade is punctuated by four large gates, one on each side. The building itself is richly decorated with sculptures.

In Thailand stupas developed from the form of their Indian forerunners in two ways: to chedis and prangs. They are essential components of any wat and they clearly demonstrate the development from the original form of the stupa. Whereas a traditional stupa has a squat, almost stumpy base, the Thais made the chedi bell-shaped and crowned it with a spire (often with rings making up the middle section) that initially imitated the shape of a lotus flower but gradually

Development of the Chedi

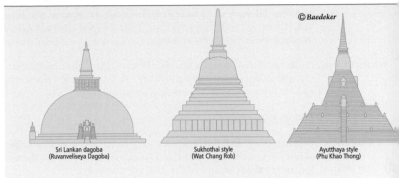

© Baedeker

Sri Lankan dagoba
(Ruvanveliseya Dagoba)

Sukhothai style
(Wat Chang Rob)

Ayutthaya style
(Phu Khao Thong)

became ever narrower. The spire lends the stupa an elegance that is typical of Thailand. A chedi often houses relics of Buddha (to which there is no access), although they may also contain the mortal remains of kings or the holiest of monks.

Prangs were developed by the Khmer, who influenced Thailand for a great many years. They too emerged from the Indian dagobas. Unlike a chedi, the prang has no spire, but is topped by a dome. The silhouette is slender above the base and tapers only slightly inwards toward the top. Some prangs, however, particularly those from the 16th century, seem quite squat. Inside there are relics in a chamber with a roofed porch accessed by a stairway. Prangs are usually highly decorated and adorned with sculptures. The most impressive prang in Thailand is at Wat Arun in Bangkok.

A **sala** is a small, open hall with a roof supported on pillars. They are located at various positions in a temple compound and normally function as places for visitors to rest.

The **ho trai** is the library where holy writings and cult objects are kept. It usually has a tall cubic base structure (to protect the writings from insects and damp), partly surrounded by a pillared walkway. The roof is pyramid-shaped and stepped, its surface often richly decorated with plaster ornament (as for example at Wat Phra Kaeo in Bangkok). In northern Thailand there are still some well-preserved ho trais built of teak. Depending on its importance, a temple may have one or two ho trais.

The **kambarien** is one of the most important yet least ornamented buildings in a wat. Here monks recite their sutras every day from noon till 1pm. Inside there is often a richly decorated teak pulpit from which the monk speaks.

Wat mahathat

Very important temple complexes also have an additional (wat) phra mahathat (»temple of most holy relics«). All the seats of the kings had at least one wat phra mahathat, with a Buddha relic (a hair, a bone, a tooth) in its chedi or prang.

Residential area

In the residential area of a temple, the monks lead their quiet, reserved and often strictly regimented life. Visitors should respect this and not disturb the monks with loud behaviour.

Other Religions

Constitutional freedom of religion

Religions other than Buddhism are allowed to be practised, as stipulated in the constitution of 1978. This is a further demonstration of the cosmopolitan outlook of the Thai government.

Islam

The history of Sunni Muslims in Thailand probably goes back to the 13th century, as Islam spread from the Malay peninsula and found many converts in southern Siam. Even though most of the Thai population elected to remain Buddhist, some small Muslim principalities did form. Around 1786 the Thais started to annex these regions and demand tribute. This was done with little care as regards cultural and religious traditions. Officials from Bangkok showed considerable lack of tact, and many were unable to speak the local Yawi dialect. The dialect was then forbidden and schools taught exclusively in Thai. This led to resistance and underground guerrillas fighting against the hated Buddhist system and the Thai royal family. Acts of violence by the natives led to equally violent responses from the rulers. In the 1950s and 1960s there was considerable activity from separatist groups. It was not until the Thai government showed a change of heart that peace returned to the region. The royal family has worked hard to encourage integration of the Muslim minority, permitting lessons in and use of the Yawi dialect. Women have once again been allowed to wear the traditional Islamic head scarf, the chador, in public. The king decreed the building of a summer residence for himself close to Narathiwat and financed the establishment of a university in Pattani. King Bhumibol also paid for a translation of the Qur'an into Thai from his own pocket. The privy council includes a respected representative of the Muslim community to deal with Muslim issues among the Thai community. Muslim state officials are allowed a half-holiday on Fridays for the »djum'a« (gathering for Friday prayer) and a four-month paid holiday at one point in their lives in order to make the pilgrimage to Mecca.

Hinduism

In Thailand there are more than 50,000 Hindus. In Hindu schools, apart from the obligatory Thai curriculum, Hindi, Sanskrit and English are all taught. Hindus in Thailand live mostly in the cities. The Brahman Hindus have great respect and often officiate at public functions of the royal household.

In the 16th and 17th centuries Jesuits from Spain, Portugal and France brought **Christianity** to South-East Asia. Nowadays the approximately 220,000 Christians in Thailand are highly regarded as a result of their charitable work there. Responsibility for orphanages, old people's homes, hospitals and schools for the deaf and dumb has been given by the state to church institutions, as is common in Asia. Thailand has about 100 Christian churches, half of which are Catholic and half Protestant. Many of the churches were built in a European style, for example the Notre Dame cathedral built by French Christians in Chanthaburi, which is the largest Christian church in Thailand.

Moslem children in southern Thailand

History

The Thais remain proud to this day of the fact that their country has never been occupied by foreign powers. The kings pursued a clever policy that tolerated the presence of foreigners but allowed them no more influence than desired.

Potters and the First Buddhists

About 4000 BC	Bronze tools and ceramics from Ban Chiang
AD 250 approx.	Buddhism arrives in Thailand.
AD 800–1000	The Khmer extend their influence into Thailand

Origin of the Thais

The origin of the Thai people was a matter of debate for many years. Nowadays it is believed that they were driven from their original lands during the fearsome conquests of the Mongol Kublai Khan. Kublai Khan, grandson of the notorious Genghis Khan, attacked the southern Chinese kingdom of Nan Chao in about 1253 – before he had actually been acclaimed as ruler of all Mongolia. The kingdom is thought to have been established in around AD 650. Theory has it that the migration of peoples triggered by the invasion brought some fugitives into Thailand.

Sensational finds in Ban Chiang

In 1967, a startling find not far from the village of Ban Chiang provided proof that the Thai people, with their southern Chinese heritage, were not the first to settle the lands of modern Thailand. At Ban Chiang archaeologists uncovered a host of finds leading to the conclusion that the region was already inhabited 4,000 years before Christ. That implies that while central Europe remained in the Neolithic era, there was already a flourishing population around Ban Chiang. The greatest sensation was the discovery of bronze tools at the site. These have been dated to around 2000 BC, the time when the first bronze implements were being manufactured in Mesopotamia. It had been thought that the latter were the first examples of bronze made by any people in the world.

The arrival of Buddhism

About 300 years after Buddha, the Enlightened One, passed into nirvana, King Ashoka of India despatched monks to all points of the compass to spread the teachings of Siddharta Gautama. Some of the missionaries came to the region around what is now Nakhon Pathom, where the inhabitants proved a receptive audience for their words.

The Khmer era begins

The Khmer, one of the most powerful peoples of South-East Asia, extended their influence between AD 800 and 1100. The temple city of Angkor Wat (in modern Cambodia) became the centre of their empire, but they built a great many shrines along their trade routes. These were apparently to serve the spiritual needs of their merchants, who travelled as far as China. However, some small areas in the north-east were settled by immigrants from Burma and Cambodia.

← *Capture of a white elephant in Siam*
  (French colour print from 1911)

These people have the best claim to be regarded as the original inhabitants of Thailand. At its height the Khmer empire included the entire northern half of Thailand.

The First Siamese Kingdom

1253	Establishment of the kingdom of Siam
1279	King Ramkhamhaeng ascends the throne.
1350	Ayutthaya becomes the capital.

Ramkhamhaeng – the mighty ruler The sovereign kingdom of Siam was first declared in 1253. The first powerful ruler was **King Ramkhamhaeng**, who ascended the throne in 1279 and made Sukhothai the capital of his kingdom. His major legacy is the introduction of the Thai alphabet that is still used today. The alphabet draws on the Indian Devanagari script. The king became legendary for his »declaration of government«, which he had engraved in stone and includes a surprising number of democratic elements. The stone tablet is now kept in the Bangkok National Museum. Other Thai principalities also emerged in the regions around Chiang Rai and Chiang Saen that adjoined Ramkhamhaeng's kingdom.

Chiang Mai becomes capital **King Mengrai** is another monarch who played a major role in Siamese history. After conquering the kingdom of Haripunchai in northern Thailand, he founded a new town alongside the Maenam Ping river and named it Chiang Mai (»new town«). Chiang Mai became the capital of the Lan Na kingdom (»kingdom of the 100,000 rice paddies«) as successor to Lamphun, which had been subject to frequent flooding.

The Rise and Fall of Ayutthaya

1350	King U Thong founds Ayutthaya.
1512	The first Europeans arrive.
1569	Ayutthaya is briefly occupied but spared destruction.

Ayutthaya, the new capital The heyday of the Sukhothai kingdom ended shortly after the death of Ramkhamhaeng. Disagreements among his successors meant that the kingdom was split into several principalities. Sukhothai's influence was gradually superseded by the might of the new capital Ayutthaya, whose kings were constantly able to widen their sphere of influence, until eventually even Sukhothai itself was subsumed and its king, **Liu Thai**, reduced to the status of governor. The foundations for this development were laid by **King Rama Thibodi I** (also known as U Thong) in 1350. Before the city fell in 1767 Thailand had become the most powerful state in South-East Asia.

The first Europeans to visit the kingdom of Ayutthaya were **Portuguese**. In 1512 they sailed from Malacca (in modern-day Malaysia) up the Maenam Chao Phraya at the behest of Viceroy Alfonso d'Albuquerque, having conquered Malacca the previous year, to be told that the land was in fact in possession of the »King of Sayam in Ayuthia«. They offered to supply artillery and gunpowder for a campaign against the Burmese and thus met with a sympathetic hearing from **King Rama Thibodi II**. In response he granted them the right to reside and trade in Ayutthaya and gave them permission to pursue their Christian religion.

The first Europeans arrive

In 1556 the Burmese conquered Chiang Mai, which remained under their control until the 18th century. They even managed to occupy Ayutthaya in 1569 after a number of unsuccessful previous attacks. Nevertheless they chose not to destroy the city. 28 years later **King Naresuen** managed to escape from Burmese imprisonment, having won in man-to-man combat. His forces managed to reconquer Ayutthaya. In the years that followed, the city experienced unprecedented prosperity. More than a million people lived within its walls and visitors from Europe described it as »the most beautiful city ever seen« or »teeming with gold and diamonds«. What was later to become Bangkok was a modest village in a grove of olive trees and attracted little attention at first. However, as European traders came to recognize its strategic and economically advantageous position, they started establishing their first trading posts there on the shores of the Maenam Chao Phraya.

The heyday of Ayutthaya

King Narai ascended the throne in 1656 and soon recognized that the Europeans who had been treated so hospitably were not simply there to trade, but also had military objectives. In 1664 Narai was forced to sign a highly unfavourable trade agreement when Dutch warships took up offensive positions outside Bangkok. However the king took note of the French missionaries who had arrived in 1656 and saw them in this situation as a »sign from heaven«. The monarch sent a royal fleet to **King Louis XIV**, but the ships vanished under mysterious circumstances near Mauritius. A second Siamese delegation, which made its way to Versailles in 1684, was respectfully received. A year later, Louis XIV of France sent a diplomatic mission to Siam led by Chevalier de Chaumont. This was accompanied by a rather large contingent of Jesuits seeking to convert the Thais to Christianity. The French delegation left Siam a year later, its ships laden with valuable Chinese porcelain and other parting gifts. The next envoys, Cébéret and de la Loubère arrived in Siam with 1,400 sol-

Reign of King Narai

diers. King Narai and his Greek advisor, Constantine Phaulkon, received these aristocrats with considerable mistrust. A group of nobles led by the commander of the royal regiment of elephants, **Phra Petraja**, took advantage of a serious illness that befell Narai to accuse Phaulkon of treason and beheaded him at Lopburi. Petraja took the throne himself in 1688 and expelled all »farangs« (foreigners) from the kingdom. From then on, Siam remained closed to westerners for 130 years.

The Burmese threat Border conflicts with Burma forced the Siamese to be ever alert. The only period of peace was during the reign of **King Boromakot** (1732–1758). Ayutthaya was further expanded, and art and culture reached their zenith.

The conquest of Ayutthaya After a siege of 15 months Burmese forces under King Hsinbyushin (1763–1776) conquered and destroyed the capital at Ayutthaya, murdering Siam's King Ekatat. Only a few of the population of over a million survived, including 500 soldiers under the command of an officer called Taksin, who managed to flee to Thonburi near Bangkok. Before the end of the year Taksin had gathered a powerful army that he led on Chiang Mai, where his victory drove the Burmese out of the country. In 1768 the same **Phya Taksin** was declared king. He made **Thonburi** his capital. Nevertheless, there was never time for him to adorn the city as he was too involved with military campaigns against domestic rebels and with expanding his kingdom as far as Laos and Cambodia.

The Chakri Dynasty

1782	Accession of King Rama I
1830 approx.	The first university is founded at Wat Pho in Bangkok.
1851	Rama IV becomes the great reformer.

Bangkok the capital King Taksin, who was treated with great mistrust by the people as an inevitable consequence of his own megalomania, was eventually indicted and condemned to die, sewn into a silk sack and beaten to death. After the execution, the crown was offered to his friend and army commander Chao Phya Mahakasatsuck who took the throne at the age of 45 as **Rama I** (Phra Phuttayodfa Chulalok). He thus became the first monarch from the Chakri dynasty, which rules Thailand to this day. Rama I moved the royal residence from Thonburi across the Maenam Chao Phraya to Bangkok on the opposite bank, and is regarded today as the founder of the city. When he died in 1809, revered by his people, his son Phuttaloetla Nabhalai became his successor and is now known as **Rama II**. In 1818 he re-established official ties with Europe after an interval of 130 years. The Portuguese, Carlos Manuel Silveira, was granted authority to build vessels and initiate trade. The same privilege, though, was denied four years later to the Briton John Crawford.

During the reign of Rama III (1824–1851), a monarch who was especially keen to encourage art and science, the first university in Thailand was opened at Wat Pho in Bangkok, attendance being free of charge. In political terms, one key factor for the kingdom of Siam was the involvement of Britain in South-East Asia. For **Rama III**, the British conquest of Burma was a stroke of luck that relieved him of the need to defend his western borders constantly. The king displayed his recognition of this fact and signed up to an alliance and trade agreement. In a far-sighted move, however, the British were not granted any privileges beyond trading rights. The same applied to the American merchants and missionaries who were despatched by President Jackson in 1833.

The reign of Rama III

When Rama III died aged 63, his son **Rama IV** (also known as Mongkut), who had lived as a wandering monk since he was 20, ascended the throne. He encouraged the educational and medicinal efforts of the Christians but did not himself convert. He also reorganized the police and army along European lines. The king passed more than 500 new laws during his reign, including a law guaranteeing equality of treatment for all, with no discrimination on the basis of rank or position in society, relieving conditions for slaves and permitting freedom of religion. When King **Rama V** (Chulalongkorn) took power in 1868, the kingdom of Siam opened up even further to the West. His predecessor had already made an alliance and trade treaty with the British governor of Hong Kong, but some clever diplomacy now ensured that both Britain and France would leave Siam unmolested as a buffer state between their own colonies in Asia.

Opening up to the West

In 1869, the country's first paved road was opened for traffic in Bangkok. It was significantly named Charoen Krung (»may the capital prosper«) and was 8km/5mi long. To make construction possible, some of Bangkok's famous klongs (canals) had to be filled in for the first time. Only a year after Charoen Krung opened, the first street map of Bangkok appeared, issued by Dr. Bradley's Mission Press in Singapore. It indicated the presence of four Christian churches and more than 80 Buddhist temples. The transport infrastructure also extended into the country. In 1882, the first railway line was opened for passengers, a 70km/44mi route from Bangkok to Ayutthaya. In the capital itself, 1883 saw the opening of a 10km/6mi-long, single-track, electrically powered tramway. In 1910, in the reign of the westward-leaning **King Rama VI**, German engineers built another line leading south from Bangkok to Surat Thani.

Building transport systems

One name is not In 1920 all Thai citizens were obliged to adopt surnames. Before that,
enough people were commonly known by only one name. Even today, people
are still officially addressed by their first name. Lists of names, such
as telephone books etc., are also sorted alphabetically by first name.
It is also common to use nicknames among relatives and friends.

From Monarchy to Democracy

1932	King Rama VII abdicates.
1932	The first constitution of the kingdom of Siam
1939	Siam is officially renamed the Kingdom of Thailand.

Ultimatum for Prince Paripatra, who was deputizing for **Rama VII** while the king
the king was on holiday, was arrested on 24 June 1932. An ultimatum was delivered to the king at his summer palace Klai Klangwan in Hua Hin.
He subsequently announced his abdication in a memorable speech.
A regency council for the callow **King Rama VIII**, then attending
school at Lausanne in Switzerland, took over responsibility for government. Meanwhile, democratic forces gained the upper hand. On
27 July 1932 a constitution was agreed based on the concept of creating a constitutional monarchy. It came into force in December
1932, when Phaya Monapahorn Nitithada became the first prime minister of the country. However, he was unable to prevent the 1932
reformers from splitting into civil and military camps, a schism that
still plays a key role in Thai politics to the present day.

Siam becomes For nearly 350 years, the country now called Thailand had been
Thailand known to the world as the Kingdom of Siam, the name given to it in
1592 by the Englishman Sir James Lancaster. In June 1939 Siam was
officially renamed the Kingdom of Thailand, or **Prathet Thai** in the
Thai language, which approximately equates to »Land of the Free«,
in recognition of the fact that Thailand had never been colonized or
occupied by foreign powers. This remained the case throughout the
Second World War. The Japanese did march into Bangkok in 1941,
where they appropriately made the Oriental Hotel their headquarters. However, this occupation did not extend beyond the capital and
a few neighbouring provinces such as Kanchanaburi, where nevertheless hundreds of prisoners of war were forced into working on
the construction of the notorious »Bridge on the River Kwai«.

The king is On 9 June 1946 the Thai public was shocked by a mystifying and tra-
dead ... gic incident. King Rama VIII, at the age of just 21and only weeks after ascending the throne, was found dead in his bedroom on the
morning of 9 June. The cause of death was established to be a guns-
hot, but the circumstances of the tragedy have never been resolved.

The sudden death of the sovereign brought his younger brother **Bhumibol Adulyadej** to the fore. Whereas he would normally have had no expectation of succeeding to the throne, he suddenly found himself confronted with all the responsibilities of kingship. In order to cope with this, he changed the subjects he was studying, turning his back on the natural sciences that he came to call his »hobby« and instead spending three years in Switzerland attending lectures at the department of politics and law. On 28 April 1950 he married **Queen Sirikit**, the daughter of the Thai ambassador to France. They were crowned together on 5 May 1950 in Bangkok (► Baedeker Special p.52). The new king rapidly gained respect and approval among the people. He played a major part in the signing of the SEATO treaty (South East Asia Treaty Organization) by Thailand, Australia, Britain, France, New Zealand, Pakistan, the Philippines and the USA at a conference in Manila in 1954. In 1956 Bangkok was selected as the headquarters of SEATO.

... long live the king!

King Bhumibol was nevertheless unable to prevent repeated military coups for power in the land. In 1957 General Sarit Thanarat brought down the incumbent prime minister Phibul and held power, ruling with an iron hand until he died in 1963. The desire of the Thai people for freedom could only be suppressed by brutal means. On 28 October 1958 he declared martial law, so that certain crimes, primarily communist activities, were prosecuted by court martial.

The army seeks power

Editors of glossy magazines all over Europe were thrilled when the Thai royal couple followed their state visit to the USA in 1960 with a tour of 15 European countries.

Visit to Europe

Three years later there was a significant power shift in Thailand as Field Marshall **Thanom Kittikachorn** became Sarit's successor. He started work on a new constitution that would be based on the 1932 version and would contain democratic elements, but would also grant considerable rights to the army, which had always had played a major role behind the scenes of Thai politics. Nevertheless, this did not affect the holding of Thailand's first-ever free elections in 1969.

Thanom Kittikachorn takes power

The aid that had been provided by the USA since the 1950s, which had amongst its aims the improvement of infrastructure in the north-east, proved to be militarily advantageous to the Americans in the course of the war in Indochina that developed into the Vietnam war from 1954. The Thai government approved the establishment of American bases on its territory, from which the US Air Force was able to launch air raids on Vietnam. American troops remained in the country until the mid-1980s, when the base at Sattahip was finally given up.
It was not until 2004 that the last refugees who lost their homes (in Laos) due to the Vietnam War were premanently resettled in the USA.

Vietnam war

Founding of ASEAN

ASEAN (Association of South East Asian Nations) was established in 1967 with the aim of raising the living standards of its citizens. Its members include Thailand, Indonesia, Malaysia, the Philippines and Singapore.

Declaration of martial law

Once again the army claimed power: the National Executive Council (NEC) adopted prime minister Thanom Kittikachorn as its leader on 17 November 1971, suspended parliament and the constitution and declared martial law. Even though the royal family is not accorded any effective political powers, King Bhumibol was required to announce an interim constitution in December 1972. Instead of the NEC, a government was formed that included 28 cabinet members with Thanom as prime minister. The 299 members of the law-making body, the National Assembly, were to be named by the king. Two thirds of them were high-ranking officers and only a third were government officials or civilians. The actual sovereignty in the land was, however, in the hands of Thanom, his son-in-law Narong and police chief Prapass.

The People against the Army

From 1973	Students protest against politicians.
1979	New elections change nothing.
26.12.2004	A major tsunami claims over 5,000 lives in Thailand.

Student unrest

In October 1973, peaceful demonstrations in Bangkok turned to violent confrontation between students and the army. The trouble began at the famous Thammasat University. The demonstrations were broken up with gunfire and it was left to the king to put a stop to the hunting down of demonstrators. Many students escaped through the canals to the royal residence of Chitralada where they were given sanctuary. As Kittikachorn, Narong and Prapass fled into exile, the king named an interim government under Professor Sanya Dhammasak. On 7 October 1974 he declared a new democratic constitution that set in stone the right to general elections. The brothers Seni and Kukrit Pramoj, both over 70 years old but explicit anti-militarist democrats, became successive leaders of the government.

However, peace lasted for little more than a year. When Thanom Kittikachorn returned from exile dressed as a monk, the news spread like wildfire among students. There were renewed protests against him on the Thammasat campus in Bangkok, but the army stopped the demonstrations in bloody fashion, reassumed power under General Kriangsak and abolished the new constitution, declaring a national emergency. A gradual return to democracy was promised but the civilian government put in place by the general lasted only 13 months. New elections called in 1979 resulted in no change to the situation. The general remained in power but the democrats suffered severe losses. Nevertheless, in 1980 a novel event in the history of Thai democracy took place. After a successful motion of no confidence in General Kriangsak, he was replaced by the defence minister General Prem Tinsulanonda.

Bangkok's bicentennial

Great pomp and ceremony marked two hundred years of Bangkok's existence and simultaneously of the Chakri royal dynasty. **Rattanakosin** (jewelled city), the original name of Bangkok and a name that is still frequently used for the old city, was the scene of innumerable processions and festivals. The celebrations provided a reason for the newly renovated royal barges to be brought out for the first time in many years to take part in a procession along the Maenam Chao Phraya. Rama I, the founder of Bangkok, was posthumously awarded the title of »Rama the Great«.

Conflict with Cambodia

The north-east border was the scene of serious conflict with Cambodia in 1984. Thai soldiers attempted to repel a Vietnamese unit who believed that Khmer Rouge rebels were present on Thai soil. Shortly afterwards, large areas near the Cambodian border were placed under martial law. The conflicts ended only with a cease-fire agreement in 1987.

Floods

Serious floods in southern Thailand caused hundreds of deaths in 1988. One major contributory factor to the dreadful consequences was logging in the region's forests. This caused King Bhumibol to finnind mi nutralled felling and order replanting measures. However, this could not prevent a rise in imports of tropical wood from neighbouring countries..

Another military putsch

A putsch by a group of generals under the leadership of Suchinda Kraprayoon in February 1991 succeeded in bringing down the government of prime minister Chatichai Choonhavan that had ruled since 1988. General Sunthorn Kongsompong formed a »National Peacekeeping Council« that accepted 59-year-old diplomat Anand Panyarachun as the new head of government. The new government instituted a campaign against sex tourism and the spread of Aids. A more decisive line was to be taken against prostitution involving children and young people.

The return of Choonhavan

The Chart Thai party named the deposed prime minister Choonhavan as its leading candidate for the elections of 1992. In September 1991 there was a successful end to negotiations between the four sides (including the notorious Khmer Rouge) in the Cambodian civil war that had raged for 20 years and taken 2 million victims. A peace treaty intended to enable the country to return to democracy was signed in Paris on 23 October. Prince Sihanouk, who had lived in exile in France since he was deposed in 1970, was to play a major role in the work of integration.

Fruits of successful government Anand's government called new elections. One of its final acts was to pass a law on environmental protection that would be one of the strictest in South-East Asia.

Khao Phra Viharn accessible again Peace negotiations with Cambodia had one result in 1992 that was of special importance to Buddhists. The cave temple of **Wat Khao Phra Viharn**, located precisely on the border between Thailand and Cambodia, had been granted by the international court to Cambodia in 1976. Now it once more became accessible from Thailand, a religious symbol of peace between two former enemies.

General Suchinda becomes prime minister In March 1992 there were new elections, but no party was able to gain a workable majority. The new head of government was General Suchinda Kraprayoon, the same man who had pulled the strings in the February 1991 putsch. However, he himself was not actually a member of the parliament. In 1992 three of the politicians who had been mired in corruption at the time of the Chatichai Choonhavan government, which Kraprayoon himself had toppled, were appointed to the cabinet. This led to mass demonstrations, particularly in Bangkok, Chiang Mai, Khon Kaen and Hat Yai. With events threatening to get out of the government's control, a state of emergency was declared in Bangkok and four neighbouring provinces on 18 May. The same day saw significant confrontations with soldiers shooting into the crowd near the royal palace and around the Democracy Monument. There were hundreds of injuries and many dead. More than 2,000 demonstrators were arrested. The royal family, however, put pressure on Suchinda and on 24 May he resigned.

Military government ends A few days after Suchinda's resignation, the parliament amended the constitution so that the head of government was required to be an elected official. King Bhumibol nevertheless named Anand Panyarachun prime minister once more, since the man was accorded such great trust. Anand called new elections and at the end of July 1992 sacked the leading military officers, who had been responsible for the use of violence in May.

Chatichai's comeback fails In the elections of 1992, Anand was not a candidate and the surprise winner was the democratic party of lawyer Chuan Leek Pai.

Economic crisis The Thai economy had become used to almost astronomical growth over a lengthy period of time, but in 1992 it suffered a serious blow. Within days share prices had plummeted and the Thai baht was under serious pressure on the international exchanges. The International Monetary Fund approved new credit to the country only on condition that the ailing banking system underwent wide-ranging reforms. The Thai government had to accept a devaluation of the baht amounting to one third of its value. This temporarily calmed the situation but still cost many citizens a large part of their savings.

The telecom billionaire **Thaksin Shinawatra** and his »Thai Rak Thai« (»Thais love Thais«) party were the clear winners of elections in 2001. However, there were once again serious allegations of vote-buying and fraud during counting.

Billionaire in government

On Boxing Day 2004 a severe undersea earthquake off the coast of Sumatra triggered a massive **tsunami** that reached as far as the west coast of Thailand. The coastal districts of Phuket and Khao Lak were the worst hit. Official estimates put the number of dead at more than 5,300 and there were also countless injuries. Whole villages were destroyed, as well as many hotels and tourist facilities. On the island of Ko Phi Phi practically all of the main town was wiped out. More than 800 died in this one place alone.

Disaster of the century – the tsunami

Elections on 2 April 2006 once again triggered a national crisis when the opposition claimed manipulation. King Bhumibol instructed the constitutional court to find a way out of the mess. The court declared the election to be illegal and ordered a new one. Prime Minister Thaksin, accused of abuse of power, tendered his resignation.

National crisis

Arts and Culture

Temples and chedis in all corners of Thailand, on close inspection, are like a picture book that relates the history of the land and its rulers. Traditional dance, theatre and music have fused together into a narrative dramatic art that is unique in the world.

Art History

Thai culture was influenced by neighbouring countries. To this day Thailand has continued to absorb the cultures of other peoples and, strictly speaking, it has not created any entirely new style, but only refined what was already in existence. Nevertheless this refinement has been undertaken with considerable artistic talent. Indian influences (such as the Ramakien epic) are undeniable, as are those of Malaysia (e.g. shadow puppetry). A certain artistic independence nevertheless began to emerge towards the end of the 13th century, as King Ramkhamhaeng founded the first state that approximately corresponded to the area of modern Thailand, and did much to encourage art and culture. The best example of this is the evolution of the somewhat stumpy and awkward-looking Indian and Sri Lankan **dagoba** into the elegant, almost playful Thai **chedi**. Later, as Ayutthaya became the cultural centre of all South-East Asia in the 16th and 17th centuries, influences spread in the opposite direction, from Thailand itself.

Early influences

Not until the 1970s did the Thais develop a cultural consciousness and an accompanying interest in the emergence of their culture. Before that time, conservationists at Bangkok's National Museum were more concerned with preserving great monuments of religious importance, such as temples and statues of Buddha. Much that has been critical to the development of Thailand therefore still remain unknown.

Historical research

It is impossible to say what kind of culture existed in the Thais' supposed place of origin in southern China. What is certain is that, in their new country, they adopted a culture that was distinctly dominated by Indian influences and modified it relatively freely according to their own religious ideas. They took over symbolism not solely from one religion, but combined Buddhism with various Brahman and Hindu elements. The oldest known remains of art and buildings were not built by the Siamese, who came into the land from southern China some centuries later, but by the Khmer, the Burmese and the Laos.

Emergence of Thai art

Artistic Styles

The culture extant at the time of the Dvaravati or Mon kingdom (from the late 6th century till the 11th/12th century) is most recognizable on the central plain of Thailand and in the north. The few remaining buildings bear witness to a Thai cultural identity that was just beginning to develop. One particularly splendid example of a

Dvaravati style or Mon style

← *Outstanding art: the murals of Wat Phumin in Nan*

chedi from the Dvaravati era is at **Wat Kukut** in Lamphun. Even in these early remains, the Buddhist influence is clear. Paintings of the wheel of life, referring to the first sermon given by Buddha after his enlightenment in Benares, have survived. Buddha sculptures, certainly those of the early Dvaravati periods, also draw on Indian forerunners.

Srivijaya style The modern tradition of Thai art can be traced back to the Dvaravati style, yet at the time there was something of an artistic duality. The Dvaravati style is wholly devoted to the teachings of Buddha, whereas the Srivijaya style (7th to late 13th century) that emerged from the eponymous kingdom on the Indonesian archipelago was initially devoted to Hinduism. Vishnu, the god with the many arms, appears here, far from his Indian origins, as well as the linga, the phallic symbol that represent the god Shiva. Influences from Java can also be seen, for example in the Buddha statues of Songkhla. Towards the end of the Srivijaya period, some forms adopted from the Khmer style were also added, many of which survive. Examples can be seen in the National Museum in Bangkok.

Khmer style Contemporary to the two styles already mentioned, the Khmer style (also called the Angkor Wat style ; 7th–13th centuries) was also developing. Remaining examples clearly testify to its influence on the culture of the Dvaravati/Srivijaya kingdom. The outstanding buildings here are in the so-called Angkor style of the late 9th century. The style is named after the city of Angkor, home to the mighty temple complex of **Angkor Wat**, the most impressive building of its era. In the Khmer kingdom, which extended from modern day Cambodia deep into what is now Thailand, Hindu cults were practised alongside Mahayana Buddhism. In cultural terms, Lopburi, the cultural centre of the Mon kingdom, was also highly influential. Its Buddha images have angular faces with fierce features. Few buildings have survived from this era. The most beautiful and complete are in the temple complexes of Phimai or Prakhon Chai. One very typical feature of the Angkor Wat style that became more influential through the Khmer is the Buddha wearing a crown and sitting on the coiled body of a Naga snake, whose seven heads form a shade over him. This depiction also goes back to a legend. 42 days after his enlightenment, Buddha was said to have sat beneath a tree where he was protected from a ferocious rainstorm that lasted many days by the snake king Muchalinda (Naga) stretching out his heads. Apart from religious scenes and scenes from history, images from the everyday life of the Thai people were also being depicted by this time.

Chiang Mai style The chief centres of this style (11th century to mid-16th century) were the towns of Chiang Mai, Chiang Saen and Lamphun. It was a style that typified the Lanna kingdom to which all the three towns belonged. There are no longer any examples of the Chiang Saen architectural style, since all of its buildings were destroyed. The Buddha statues of the time had fierce, almost arrogant features, chunky bodies and barrel chests. They are largely seated on two rows of lotus leaves with their stamens. Many of the images of Buddha were carved from semi-precious stones such as rock crystal. One of the key works of art of the Chiang Mai era is the famous jade Buddha that is now kept at **Wat Phra Kaeo** in Bangkok.

The **U Thong style** (1220–1350) is typified by sitting or standing Buddhas, mostly made of bronze and making the Bh mispar a Mudr (gesture of touching the earth). The artists also adorned their figures with a narrow headband and a long sash over the shoulders.

One of Thailand's most splendid statues of Buddha is in Wat Traimitr in Bangkok.

As the town of **Sukhothai** rose to become the capital of the new kingdom (1279), the Khmer style that had dominated until then seemed to have fallen out favour. Nevertheless Khmer temples were not demolished. Instead their exteriors were refurbished to reflect the new artistic fashions of the Sukhothai style (late 13th to early 15th century). One aspect seen for the first time during the Sukhothai era was the form of the **walking Buddha**. One of the finest examples of this way of depicting the Enlightened One was at **Wat Si Iriyabot** in Kamphaeng Phet, of which little now remains. The Sukhothai style is often said to be the most beautiful style of Thai architecture. It was associated with nine kings, of whom the third, the artistically minded Ramkhamhaeng (reigned 1279–1299), made the most lasting impression. There are examples of the Sukhothai style not only in Sukhothai itself, but all over Thailand. One particularly fine example is the Buddha statue in the northern viharn of the **Phra Pathom**

chedi in Nakhon Pathom. The Buddha statue at **Wat Traimitr** in Bangkok is especially valuable since it is cast from pure gold.

Ayutthaya style   The second major culture to develop in Thailand emerged during the kingdom of Ayutthaya (1350–1767), where a search for new shapes resulted in a unique flowering of artistic creativity. Whereas sculpture, in particular, was initially clearly influenced by earlier styles, in architecture idiosyncratic forms emerged with elegant outlines, towering proportions and vivid decoration. The distinctive features of this era of cultural awakening include elongated, graceful forms in sculpture. An individual cultural identity is also demonstrated by some of the statues of the originator of the religion, Buddha himself. Their sheer immensity shows the importance of the kingdom and how its rulers sought to make their own mark. The most important achievements of this culture were incinerated when the Burmese occupied Ayutthaya in 1767. All that was left was a vast field of ruins that permits no more than a faint glimpse of the magnificence of the famous city. There were said to be 400 temples in this city alone, which many visitors described as the most beautiful they had ever seen.

Thonburi style   After the destruction of Ayutthaya, new styles developed haltingly under King Taksin in Thonburi. The period mostly reflects earlier epochs. Only in the sphere of painting were new energies released. The architecture (exemplified by the Khmer prang of Wat Arun in Bangkok) displayed few innovations.

Bangkok style   The new capital of Bangkok spawned some splendid buildings, which increasingly betrayed the influence of the West. The rulers of the Chakri dynasty sponsored much of the building in the city they had made their home. Their legacy is not, however, distinguished by an expressive effervescence of spirit. The Bangkok style (1780–1930; also called Rattanakosin style) exhibited little that was new, but is characterized more by its refinement of forms based on existing styles, as can be seen in the rich decoration and vivid ornamentation of many temples in the city. Some of these buildings are threatened with collapse since many temples are built of wood. In order to demonstrate historical continuity, famous statues from all parts of the country have been collected and re-erected in Bangkok.

Art in the present day   Since the 1930s Thailand has been attempting to adapt to modern western ways. This applies less to the building of temples, where traditional forms are favoured, despite the use of modern materials (such as the Italian marble of Wat Benchama-bo-bitr in Bangkok). Increasingly, the original Thai art of remote provinces is being rediscovered, and efforts are being made to open up archaeological finds and sites to young artists as well as to tourists. In general, a return to traditional Thai styles can be seen.

Portrayal of Buddha and Gods

Unlike the present day, the early era of Buddhism did not produce portraits of Buddha. At this time, the symbols of the religion were lotus blossom, the Bodhi tree, the wheel of life, the sacred footprint and stupas. The earliest known images of Buddha date from the 1st century AD and emerged from the kingdom of Kubhana in northern India in the reign of the art-loving King Kanishka. They were made simultaneously in the towns of Mathura and Ghandara, which were main centres of Indian art at the time. In the latter, a style developed that probably was a major influence on Persian artists. As Persia was then part of Alexander the Great's Greek empire, it has become known as the Greco-Buddhist style.

Early images of Buddha

These early pictures show the Buddha Shakyami either seated or standing. A fixed canon of proportions, attributes and gestures appears to have emerged already, illustrating a desire to capture a »true likeness« that would be valid for all time. The proportions of the body derive from speculation on cosmic numerical relationships: there are 32 main characteristics to Buddha's body, and another 80 would

Attributes of Buddha

Buddha Statues *Styles*

© Baedeker

Mon style

Khmer style, 13th century
Buddha depicted as a healer

Lan Na style, late 15th century

Sukhothai style

Thai style 12th-13th century
Suphanburi/Sankhaburi

Ayutthaya style

Protective hand gesture

later be added. They include, for example, the ushnisha, the symbol of omniscience that grows out of his head; the curl (urna) between the eyebrows, often shown as a birthmark or as a jewel radiating multi-coloured light; and the wavy or curly hair, a halo around his head or his whole body, a symbol for energy. The body is androgynous and the palms or the soles of the feet sometimes display the wheel of life. Buddha mostly wears a simple monk's garb with the right shoulder exposed. The oval face is peaceful and fulfilled, frequently with a happy smile. The extended earlobes testify to Buddha's noble origins, since only the rich could afford the heavy jewellery that caused them to lengthen. There have been hardly any changes since these early images of Buddha came into existence. To this day Buddhist artists avoid free representation of the image, preferring to adhere to the inherited canon. In a traditional ceremony life is breathed into new figures of Buddha, so that the spirit of Buddha himself can enter into them. Nine items of great symbolic importance are also incorporated into the body. If a statue is broken, it loses all value as its power escapes. This also applies to a headless statue, which explains why the Burmese decapitated hundreds of them during their sack of Ayutthaya in 1767.

Postures of Buddha

The Buddhist religion acknowledges four possible depictions of its first Enlightened One: standing, sitting, walking or reclining. There are five postures each for seated or standing images, as well as five precisely defined hand gestures, all of which have a symbolic meaning. Depictions of a reclining Buddha represent the moment when he entered nirvana or perhaps the moment of his death. Many variants of the traditional postures derive from the body language of Indian (and Thai) dance. The laughing Buddha (Budei) is technically not an image of Buddha but of the Maitreya, a future Buddha.

The classic sitting postures have legs crossed in such a way that the soles of the feet are not visible; legs crossed with the soles of the feet visible (the diamond, lotus or meditation position); alternatively a posture with one leg lifted beneath the body while the other extends straight down (relaxed sitting position); or the sitting position common in Europe, with both legs dangling (typical of the »future Buddha« or »Maitreya«. It is not uncommon for the sitting Buddha to be seated on the body of a Naga snake, one of the demi-gods of Indian mythology who lives in a legendarily beautiful underworld. Muchalinda, king of the Naga, protected Buddha during his meditation from a heavy rainstorm by spreading his many heads over the monk. **Sitting postures**

Bodhisattvas are transcendent beings that appear exclusively in Mahayana Buddhism. They are more slender than most Buddha depictions and are also androgynous. They wear a crown and jewellery on the neck, chest, arms and legs. The torso is unclothed apart from a sash or shawl around the shoulders. The posture is more casual than normal Buddha figures and they often have multiple arms and heads, which are clearly meant to indicate supernatural spiritual and physical capabilities. One form, for example, is an eleven-headed Bodhisattva with a thousand arms that surround the body like spokes of a wheel. **Bodhisattvas**

Of the Brahman deities, Brahma, Shiva, Vishnu, Indra, Ganesha and the goddess Lakshmi are most frequently depicted, usually in a distinctively Thai variant. Brahma, the all-knowing, all-seeing creator of the universe, is shown with four crowned heads aligned to the four directions of the compass and four hands holding a rod, a jar with water from the Ganges and a string of prayer beads. Shiva is seen with a snake over one shoulder or with his steed, the bull Nandi, dancing to symbolize the cycle of change. Alternatively, his linga (phallus) may be worshipped in the form of a stone column many metres tall. He is often depicted with his wife Parvati. Vishnu, the guardian of life, is depicted along with his steed the bird-king Garuda (who has the head, wings and beak of an eagle but the body of a man) or sitting on the snake of the world or with his wife Lakshmi, who herself often sits on a lotus blossom. **Brahman deities**

Other pictures derived from Indian Brahmanism show Indra, the invincible, who conquers all enemies and restores the balance of nature with his mace (vajra) and the three-headed elephant Erawan, as well as the elephant-headed god Ganesha with his four hands holding a lotus blossom, a shell, a discus and a club, who despite his lower ranking among the gods is still seen as a bringer of good fortune and a remover of obstacles.

Theatre

Lakon Thai theatre encompasses a combination of dance, mime, music and singing. The Thai word for it is »lakon«. There are four forms of lakon, of which the most important is probably lakon nai (indoor theatre, commonly called »kon« in slang). Originally it was performed exclusively within the walls of royal palaces by the ladies of the palace, but now forms an essential cornerstone in the repertoire of the Bangkok national theatre. Actors undergo hard training as dancers and musicians. Students are selected as a result of tough examinations between the ages of 11 and 14. All masculine roles of high-ranking characters (e.g. kings and princes) are portrayed by young female dancers, while demons and animals (principally apes) are given to the male alumni of the college with their acrobatic training.

Ramakien The subject matter for this classical dramatic dance consists of episodes from the Ramakien saga, a Thai version of the Ramayana epic, of which copies exist from as early as the third century BC. The language of the dance is made up of 68 gestures – primarily movements of the hands and head. Emotions are not clearly expressed but hinted at. The story tells of a battle between gods and demons, a kind of tale of chivalry told in 24,000 quatrains.

Shadow theatre The second popular category in Thai theatre is the shadow play (nang yai). The beautiful artistry of the nang yai forms, cut from a water buffalo hide measuring about a metre in length, was used for both ceremonial as well as entertainment purposes until the end of the absolute monarchy. When a royal cremation took place at Sanaam Luang, the field in front of the palace complex in Bangkok, shadow stencils would be erected in front of the fire on bamboo stilts more than 20m/65ft high to project a dramatic series of episodes from the Ramakien. Nowadays this kind of theatre has been more or less completed superseded by cinema.

Shadow puppets By contrast, shadow puppet theatre (nan) has continued to thrive – particularly in southern Thailand. Although the puppets are cut with equal artistry from tanned buffalo leather, they are just 20–50cm (8–20in) tall and are moved in front of a backlit linen screen. The participants (mostly members of a single family) include a narrator, a musician and two puppeteers. They often move as many as 100 figures across the stage as the plot demands. The Indonesian-Malaysian origin of the puppet show is undeniable, but there is a distinctively Thai twist in that the figures are exclusively black-and-white and the plays are entirely devoted to a few epic tales. Even in Bangkok, plays such as these are often seen at local festivals or in temple gardens.

Making shadow figures in Nakhon Si Thammarat →

Likay

»Likay« is possibly the most popular kind of theatrical performance in Thailand. It is a mixture of operetta, cabaret and even circus performance, with colourful backgrounds and lights contributing to the magic. For those unfamiliar with the language and local politics, the plays are all but incomprehensible, which makes them less attractive to western eyes. Nevertheless, the huge audiences of people of all ages and from all walks of life are a fascinating of these events.

Puppet shows

The fourth theatrical form in Thailand is the puppet show, but the only way visitors are likely to get to see one is to make the acquaintance of Thais or have contact with cultural institutes. Mostly they are presented by private citizens as part of a celebration. The shows are not advertised and are not really meant to be seen by strangers.

Ensembles and instruments

A traditional orchestra (»phi phat«) seems to accompany everything that is ceremonial or otherwise of importance: temple or court ceremonies, classical dramatic dance or even the popular likay or shadow plays (nang yai) and Thai boxing. The ensemble consists of between five and a maximum of fifteen musicians. Most players have some sort of percussion instrument. Melodies are played on xylophones with wooden bars or metallophones (with metal bars) or even on hemispherical gong drums. The rhythm instruments include cymbals, gongs and drums. There are also wind instruments, such as a four-reed oboe and a bamboo flute, and string instruments such as a tubular violin, zither and lute.

Dance

Traditional dance

Traditional dance in Thailand is based on techniques handed down for centuries. As in the theatre, very young girls from all over the country must pass tough examinations before they are taken on for an artistic education in Bangkok that involves several years of study. Future dancers are also taught locally in the villages by older inhabitants, so that the skills continue to be handed down directly. There are plenty of opportunities for dancers to exhibit their skills, from celebrating the sowing season to thanksgiving for the rice harvest. Among the hill tribes, many dances have a spiritual significance. Luckily, there is still enough awareness of tradition in Thailand for the dances to have largely retained their original form, even when they are being performed for tourists.

Bamboo stick dance

The bamboo stick dance is perhaps the most classical dance of all and is famed the world over, since it is often performed by touring Thai dance groups. Eight male dancers line up in pairs, each pair gripping two bamboo sticks which they beat together in time to the music. The pairs stand in the middle of the floor and dance in alter-

Girls start learning dance at a very early age.

nation between the sticks, when they are held apart, or to the side when they are thrust together.

Dance of the long nails

The famous fingernail dance originated in northern Thailand. Originally it was danced almost exclusively at major festivals. Nowadays it is a staple of events that are put on specifically for their photogenic quality, e.g. in the Rose Garden of Nakhon Pathom or at Old Chiang Mai in Chiang Mai. Over their own nails the dancing girls wear long pointed nail extensions that are either made of gold-covered cardboard or silver. As with all Thai dances, every movement of the hands or the fingers has its own special meaning, although few foreign spectators will be able to follow this. The candle dance has the same symbolic meaning as the dance of the long nails, except that the dancers have burning candles on their fingers instead of extended nails.

◄ Candle dance

Magic fowl dance

The magic fowl dance is one of Thailand's oldest dances. It is mostly danced in the north of the country. It is based on an ancient game featuring a conflict between two northern Thai cities and is concerned with love, death and mourning.

Dances of the hill tribes The hill tribes of northern Thailand also have a dance tradition that is centuries old. However, they place less emphasis on ancient stories and epics than on animistic or mystical themes. In one dance that conjures the spirits of the elders, the ghosts of ancestors are invited to possess the bodies of the dancers. It is danced by those hill tribes where ancestor worship is practised. When the dancers give a high-pitched scream, it is an unmistakeable signal to the spectators that the ghost has taken possession for the brief duration of the dance, in order to share in the enjoyment of the movement. Once the dance has ended, the spirit will have had its fun and leave the dancer's body again.

Traditional Sports

Kite flying From the middle of February the Sanaam Luang field in front of the royal palace in Bangkok is given over to trials for the annual Kaeng Wau kite-flying contests for a cup instituted by the king himself. The contest is combined with a chess tournament and culminates in a final in the second half of April, where a huge audience gathers on the stands, enthusiastically following the action while eating and drinking and laying bets. The kite battles take the form of an aerial »battle of the sexes«. The kites are artistic masterpieces, as tall as a man with a span of over one metre. There are also strict rules regarding the construction and the fighting procedure. For example, the frame of the kites must be made from carefully peeled, three-year-old bamboo.

In **takraw** (pronounced »daggro«) players can use any part of their body other than their hands either to propel a cane ball about 12cm/5in in diameter into a net through a hoop suspended 2.75m/9ft above the ground or, in another version of the game, to play the ball into the opponents' field of play across a net 2.5m/8ft high (a little like volleyball with no hands – the game is often called kick volleyball). »Net« takraw has now been adopted into the annual ASEAN Games, in which all the countries of South-East Asia compete. In Thailand itself, though, »circle takraw« is actually more popular. It features six to eight players and may or may not have a target hoop above the middle of the ring. In this form of the game the players stand equidistant from one another around the edge of a ring and compete by making the most artistic contortions to play the ball. The longer the ball stays aloft, the more convoluted the movements, the higher the jumps to head the ball and the more varied the leaps and body parts used to keep it up, the more points are scored. The most vaunted move is a kick where the hands are held so that the arms form a hoop and the ball is kicked through them while the player is on or off the ground. It can even be played with the arms behind the back. If the ball touches a player's hand or arm or if it touches the ground, it is considered a »dead ball«. A game lasts 40 minutes with no breaks. The minimum rally must have nine different moves including somersault moves or rolling the ball over different parts of the body. Anyone who can keep this up for ten or twelve minutes could perform in a circus in Europe, and in Thailand would be considered rea-

! *Baedeker* TIP

Takraw tournaments

Net takraw can be viewed every week in Bangkok from February to May outside the City Hall (next to Wat Suthat). At the same time the circle takraw season culminates in an annual super-tournament on the Sanaam Luang field, where the winning team is presented with the Royal Gold Cup by a member of the royal house. Takraw games can also be seen all over Thailand at any other time of year, especially in the late afternoon.

sonably good. Before 1900 the game was played with a ball made of feathers or strips of bamboo. In the reign of King Naresuan (around 1579), a version of the game featured elephants playing with a ball containing a condemned criminal, so that the miscreant suffered execution by being trampled to death.

Sword fighting

»Kraboo krabong«, is the Thai version of fencing. It derives from duels between elephant riders (often members of the royal family) and is many centuries old. Even though modern rifles have replaced swords on the battlefield, the skill has been maintained into the present century, with King Chulalongkorn decreeing that all princes should be taught the art. The king himself performed many »sword dances« on the back of elephants, not to duel but to honour Buddha. Nowadays, the swords are blunted but injuries are still common.

Thai boxing

According to legend King Naresuan freed himself from Burmese captivity in 1560 by defeating the finest wrestlers in Burma. Nowadays Muay Thai, Thai boxing, has developed into the national sport. It was originally a form of self-defence that was even taught to monks in the monasteries. It bears little resemblance to western boxing. Boxers use their hands and feet, shins and elbows to hit any part of the opponent's body that is exposed. The stomach and kidneys are favoured places to attack. Thai boxing is extremely popular. When major fights take place on Saturday nights at the national boxing stadium in Bangkok, the entire nation is encamped in front of the television. Tickets are nearly always sold out long in advance. Muay Thai is one of the martial arts forms that together developed into kickboxing.

Famous People

A German who wrote the Thai national anthem, an former US secret agent who became the director of a smart hotel and a producer of silk, an Irishman who gave orphaned children the chance of a future and Siamese kings who left a lasting impression on their subjects: all these are people who found happiness in the country and gave back something in return.

Father Ray Brennan (1933–2003)

Founder of orphanages

»Lord, it's hard to be humble when you're Irish« said a sign on the door of his office. This is typical of the character of the Irish Redemptorist priest. The are an order of missionaries founded in 1732. Father Brennan was sent to South-East Asia and, after a period spent in the refugee camps along the border with Cambodia, arrived in Pattaya in the early 1970s. One morning a baby was abandoned at his door. It was the first of many. Within a few months he had a dozen children to deal with. He soon became known all over Pattaya, not least because he would take his collection box during the evenings and go to all the restaurants and bars to collect donations for »his« children. It was not long, though, before such excursions became unnecessary. Hotels put on benefits at Christmas or New Year for the Pattaya orphanage and collection boxes were to be found all over the city. Donors and sponsors came from all over the world. There was no end to the good deeds of the priest, who was always careful to limit influence from the state. He founded the first private schools in Thailand for blind and deaf children and gave them the chance of an education. He also took in street children who would spend the nights begging in Pattaya's bars. When Father Ray Brennan died of heart failure in 2003, he left behind a down-to-earth charity that was unique in all Thailand. The story of his life has been published in a book entitled *In the Name of the Boss Upstairs*. The Father Ray Trust (www.fr-ray.org) manages the assets of the charity and arranges for donations and adoptions. Visitors are always welcome.

Father Ray and his orphans

Peter Feit (1883–1968)

Musicologist

Peter Feit was the son of a Thai mother and a German immigrant from Trier on the river Moselle. At a very young age he gained a job as a music teacher and composer at the Siamese court. Feit was the first to annotate the Thai music that had previously been handed down from memory, and thus managed to preserve valuable cultural heritage. King Chulalongkorn commissioned him to write what in 1932 became the national anthem of Thailand.

← *Rama V pictured on a state visit to Germany with Chancellor Bismarck*

Anna Harriett Leonowens (1831–1915)

Teacher at the court of Rama IV Anna Harriett Leonowens was born in Wales in 1831 and became one of the most controversial western figures in the history of Thailand. There are still debates to this day about the real role of the woman who published her memoirs of King Rama IV in a book entitled *The King and I*. Anna was the daughter of an army captain who applied at the age of 28, when she was already the mother of a young son, for a job as governess at the court of Rama IV. The king was keen to provide his children with an upbringing along western lines. However, it remains unproven whether the governess to the king's 58 children was really as close to the monarch as described in the book and whether he really did consult her regularly for advice. The last phase of her life is, however, undisputed. In 1876 she travelled to Halifax in Canada and founded the Nova Scotia School of Art and Design. She died in Montreal in 1915.

The most recent filming of Anna Leonowens' memoirs was released as »Anna and the King« in 1999 with Jodie Foster in the title role.

Leonowens' story has been used as the subject matter for several other works. In 1944, Margaret Landon wrote her novel *Anna and the King of Siam* based on Leonowens' memoirs, and the story was made into a film by John Cromwell just two years later. In 1951, Richard Rodgers and Oscar Hammerstein wrote their musical *The King and I*, which was also made into a film in 1956. In 1999, another film was made by director Andy Tennant from a script by Steve Meerson with Jody Foster and Chow Yun Fat in the leading roles.

Alma Link (1898–1989)

Alma Link trained as a nurse in Russia, Germany and England and after working in London, Manila, Bangkok and Baghdad, married the Bangkok-based German industrialist Herbert Link in 1939. In Bangkok Alma discovered her life's work as she founded a branch of Cheshire Homes in Thailand. Leonard Cheshire was a British airforce officer who had witnessed the attacks on Hiroshima. His visits to hospitals had made it clear to him that terminally ill people without the requisite support from relatives needed to be provided with »homes« where they could experience a family atmosphere. Alma Link made it possible to open the first Cheshire home as early as 1965. She was the first, and currently the only western woman to be granted the royal appellation of »khunying« (roughly similar to a dame or a knight).

Benefactress

Constantine Phaulkon (1647–1688)

The Greek adventurer Constantine Phaulkon was one of the most interesting of the foreign figures who influenced the Thai state and people. He was born in Argostoli on the Greek island of Cephalonia in 1647. Early on he joined a British ship, but when he made acquaintance with the brothers Samuel and George White, who were seeking adventure in the hope of making huge profits from the trade with Asia, he joined their enterprise. They initially worked for the East India Company, which had a monopoly of English trade with Asia, but after a few years could afford to work for themselves. Phaulkon went to Ayutthaya in 1670 in the service of the brothers and was introduced to the royal court, not least because of his remarkable skill in the native language. Phaulkon ended up as royal translator and eventually rose to be a counsellor of King Narai. He reached the height of his influence when Narai elevated him to first minister. In his attempts to persuade the king that the only way to counteract Dutch pressure for power and influence in Siam was to encourage the French, he pursued a rather risky policy that unnerved many nobles and government officials. Nevertheless, Phaulkon succeeded in allowing a garrison of French troops to be stationed at the mouth of the Maenam Chao Phraya, although there was a contingent of Jesuit priests in their midst, who Phaulkon hoped would be able

Royal adviser

Eng and Chang Bunker were the conjoined pair for whom the name »Siamese twins« was coined.

DOUBLE LIFE

The twins Eng and Chang Bunker (1811–1874) were discovered by the British merchant Robert Hunter when they were eighteen. Ever since then, surviving pairs of monozygotic twins conjoined at the head or hips have been popularly known as Siamese twins.

The original »**Siamese twins**«, the first such conjoined pair known to western medicine, were born in 1811 in Mae Klong in the province of Samut Songkhram, about 60km/35mi from Bangkok. They were two of the ten children born to a fishermen of Chinese extraction and his Thai wife. They were joined together from the buttocks to the shoulder. In those days, of course, there was no question of an operation to separate them. They led an existence out of the public eye until the merchant Robert Hunter heard about the unusual pair and mentioned their existence to the missionary Captain Coffin. Coffin persuaded the boys' mother to allow him to take them to Europe and introduce them to an astonished medical profession there. Thereafter they were to settle in America as free citizens of the United States.

What was felt to be most remarkable was the fact that the brothers, who took the name Bunker in their new homeland, had so successfully adapted to the condition of enforced togetherness in spite of their quite different characters (in fact there were differences of opinion that sometimes led to public arguments).

As time went on they proved to be excellent chess players and they even learned to swim. The money that they had earned from public appearances they invested in a plot of land in North Carolina in 1839, where they built a house. Amazingly enough, both of them later married, Eng took Sarah Yates as his wife and Chang was wedded to her sister Adelaide. 21 children were born of this unusual union that involved the brothers staying three days with one wife then three days with the other, and so on. It was not unusual, considering the times and their place of residence, that the families kept slaves. But the Civil War (1861-65) broke their fortunes, as that of many others, and they were forced to make several more personal appearance tours to support their large family. Eng and Chang lived to the age of 63 before Chang died of a bronchial infection. His brother, despite being unaffected by the illness, died of shock a couple of hours later.

to convert the king to Christianity. This proved too much for the royal courtiers. Under the leadership of one Phra Petraja, they took advantage of a serious illness to the king to arrest Phaulkon, forcing him to give up his fortune and then executing him. When Narai died, Petraja himself took the throne and expelled all foreigners from the country. The kingdom was to remain closed to westerners for the next 130 years.

Rama IV (Mongkut; 1804–1868)

King of Thailand

Rama IV, also known as Mongkut, ascended the Siamese throne at the age of 46. He had been a monk since he was 20 and had led a wandering monastic existence that took him all over Siam. He had also been the abbot of Wat Bovornives in Bangkok. Unlike his predecessors, who had been brought up in the palace surrounded solely by courtiers, he was well aware of the tribulations and needs of people from all walks of life. In terms of religion, the king has gone down in history as the monarch who rejuvenated Buddhism in Thailand. He had the Pali sources translated, emphasized the original message of the belief and founded the strict monastic order Dhammayut Nikaya, members of which are easily identifiable since their robes are of a darker colour. His most memorable achievement, however, is that his speedy responses successfully averted the colonial threat to Thailand. Rama IV had studied not only the science but also the languages of the west. The princes and princesses of the realm were brought up by a British governess. The king was also privately interested in astronomy, a hobby that indirectly caused his death. In 1886, he predicted a total eclipse of the sun but, having entered a swamp to observe it, he caught malaria and died.

Rama V (Chulalongkorn; 1853–1910)

King of Thailand

King Rama V, also known as Chulalongkorn, was brought up by his British governess Anna Harriet Leonowens and became king at the age of 16. He was very open to western practices: one of his first acts as monarch was to declare all his subjects to be »Thai« (= free). In 1905 he prohibited all forms of slavery, though he was also aware of the problems this would bring: »From one day to the next the slaves will be forced to contend for their own food and a roof over their heads. They will never have learned how to fend for themselves.« In order to mitigate the impact of these foreseeable difficulties, at least to some extent, he ordered that any personal service must be payable. Rama V was particularly concerned with the economic development of his country. He went abroad to learn modern management techniques, instituting railway construction, telegraphy and a post office upon his return. He sent young Thais to study in Europe and the USA, and brought hundreds of engineers and scientists in the opposite direction. His political strategies guaranteed independence, peace and freedom for his country. »By way of diplomacy« he allowed British and French dominion over large swathes of land that had been conquered by his predecessors in the preceding 650 years (Laos, Cambodia and four provinces of what is now Malaysia). Even though these countries added up to an area larger than England, he sacrificed no soldiers for their defence. The result, however, was that Britain and France viewed the kingdom of Siam as a buffer state between their own Asian colonies and, as such, they left it unmolested.

Chin Sophonpanich (1910–1987)

The headquarters of the Bangkok Bank Ltd is 32 storeys high and the tallest building in Bangkok. It was opened in 1982 by the bank's founder Chin Sophonpanich on the occasion of his 72nd birthday. More than 4,000 guests from all over the world were there to honour him. He was born the son of Thai-Chinese parents in Bangkok and was sent by his father to spend some years studying in Canton. Money ran out when he was 17 years old and he returned to his home town, where he carried sacks of rice and cooked noodles in the city's Chinatown. The first milestone in his subsequent career was four years later, when he became manager of a small building supplier, selling wood for building and tools as well as tinned foods. During the Second World War he exported rice to Indonesia, ran sawmills and finally, in 1944, founded the Bangkok Bank. Chin became one of the richest industrialists in South-East Asia and had shares in more than 140 companies, covering a full spectrum of prosperous concerns. His bank still finances around 40% of all exports from Thailand and controls perhaps a third of the inland banking business.

Banker and industrialist

Sunthorn Phu (1786–1855)

It is believed that the Thai poet Sunthorn Phu was born in Thonburi. His mother left his father early in his life to become a wet nurse at the royal court in Bangkok. The young Phu grew up at the palace, learned to read and write and also picked up a grounding in the art of poetry. Sunthorn Phu had a distinct preference for easy living and came to »commute« between the Bangkok court and the monastic life. He was an especially frequent visitor to a monastery on the island of Klaeng near Rayong, where his father had once been abbot. Whereas Rama II sponsored Sunthorn Phu and commissioned him to rework the Ramakien epic and other literary works, he fell out of favour with Rama III. For the next 18 years he led a nomadic life, reciting and writing poems to order, as well as being an alchemist and a monk. It was in this period that his most beautiful Nirat works were created. It was only when Rama IV ascended the throne that Sunthorn Phu was restored to a position of honour and was even given the appellation »Sunthorn, the enlightened one«.

Poet

James (Jim) Thompson (1906–1974?)

Architect and bon vivant

US architect James (Jim) Thompson arrived in Bangkok after the Second World War as a member of the American secret service, the OSS, although he left that organization very soon afterwards. He chose to make Bangkok his permanent home and, after a brief interlude as director of the Oriental Hotel, then already a celebrated institution, he discovered the traditional silk weaving of the Thai people. That Thai silk is nowadays renowned the world over is largely owing to Thompson. He developed modern production methods while simultaneously encouraging the return of traditional techniques. Himself a highly talented designer in terms of textiles and colours, he was instrumental in building up a silk industry that remains essential to the Thai economy today. The English writer Somerset Maugham was a regular guest of Thompson's and wrote the following in his guest book after being invited to visit his factories and dine at his home: »You not only have beautiful things, but what is rare you have arranged them with faultless taste.« Jim Thompson travelled extensively to all corners of Thailand and wherever he went, he brought art treasures back with him to Bangkok, rescuing many from decay and destruction. The buildings created in the traditional Thai fashion which he had dismantled at their original location, then brought to the capital and re-erected, are the most beautiful legacy of his collector's passion. The foresight of this is apparent to this day, for there are few places in Thailand where wooden buildings are to be found in such good repair. At the peak of his collecting frenzy, he suddenly vanished at the age of 61. To this day the circumstances of his disappearance are not known. He had been taking a short holiday on the Cameron Islands in western Malaysia, when all trace of him was lost on Easter Sunday 1967. An intensive search failed to find him. He was finally declared officially dead seven years later in 1974. His collection remains in the possession of a charity that works on behalf of social causes.

Prateen Ungsongtham (born 1951)

Schoolteacher

»Certainly the youngest recipient of this Far Eastern version of the Nobel prize, and probably the least educated in academic terms,« said Ramon Magsaysay of 27-year-old Prateen Ungsongtham, when she was awarded the prize in Tokyo in 1978 as a result of her campaign for the education of slum inhabitants and their children. She herself had been born in what was then the world's third biggest slum around the harbour of Klong Toey. Nevertheless, she learned to read and write and by the age of 16 she had begun to give lessons to the children of her own neighbourhood. Only when this »illegal school« was threatened with eviction from the premises where Prateen had set it up did the city council finally respond and act to keep the school going (1974). The young teacher used the 10,000 US dollars from the highly regarded prize to set up a trust. Since that time she has enjoyed the utmost trust and assistance from the authorities in Bangkok who, along with many private donors, have provided support for Prateen to achieve her objectives. She now teaches almost 2,000 children and employs more than a dozen conventionally trained teachers. The trust is called the »Duang Prateep Foundation« (»Flame of Hope«). With its fees of 1 baht per day the school has become a model for all the developing countries of South-East Asia. Nowadays the curriculum also offers adult education, family planning and vocational education, as well as training in health and hygiene. Donations from home and abroad assist the foundation in offering scholarships and monastic training, sport and leisure programs as well as financing schemes to combat crime among youths and the unemployed.

Pierra Vejabul (1900–1964)

Pierra Vejabul was to become the first female doctor in Thailand, but to achieve that aim she was forced to leave her home. She emigrated to Paris, where she financed her schooling and a university degree by working as a cleaner. Having qualified, she spent a period working in the Charité hospital in Berlin before returning to Bangkok in the early 1930s. There she was given responsibility for a department treating women and girls with sexually transmitted diseases. At the time, such patients, even girls under 14, were tattooed by the health authorities. This was the first thing the forceful Pierra Vejabul dispensed with. Later she started to adopt children abandoned by her patients, for which her family disowned her. The name by which she is known means »kind and patient doctor« and was awarded to her along with the honoured title of »khunying« by the royal family. Khunying Vejabul ran an orphanage for around 3,000 children until the day she died in 1964. Many of her charges have gone on to highly regarded careers and become important people. She also ran a clinic and oversaw a re-education centre on the outskirts of Bangkok, taking in pregnant prostitutes or those seeking to undergo rehabilitation and giving them a chance of an education and a career.

Doctor

Practicalities

WHAT SHOULD YOU PACK
WHEN GOING TO THAILAND?
HOW DO YOU FIND A HOTEL?
HOW SHOULD VISITORS TO THAILAND BEHAVE SO
AS NOT TO »LOSE FACE«? READ THE ANSWERS
HERE – IDEALLY BEFORE YOUR JOURNEY BEGINS.

Accommodation

For many years Thailand's hotels have had an excellent reputation. The accommodation available ranges from luxury hotels to the most basic places to sleep in guest house and bungalow villages. Travellers who leave the areas of well-developed tourist infrastructure can expect a lower level of comfort and facilities. To compensate the prices are much lower than in popular tourist places.

Royal Orchid Holiday Thai Airways International offers a »Royal Orchid Holiday« programme, with reduced room rates as part of a package including stopovers or the planning of the complete trip (can be booked only before starting the trip; www.royalorchidholidays.co.uk).

Prices Hotel rooms are of course more expensive in Bangkok and the tourist resorts, but here too there is a range of options. A night in the legendary Oriental Hotel in Bangkok costs upwards of £700/US$1400, a stay in a basic guest house no more than £7/US$14. A room in a low-cost hotel outside the main tourist resorts costs between £10 and £30 (US$20 to 60). In the off-season (March to October) even high-class hotels are sometimes willing to bargain over the price of a room. **Reservations ▶** It is necessary to book well in advance for the high season (November to the end of February), but at other times there is usually enough capacity in the desired category of accommodation.

Finding a room The Thai Hotel Association has a counter in the arrivals hall of Bangkok airport, which not only finds a room but also organizes transfer to the hotel. There are similar accommodation desks at all the other airports in the country. They open when a plane lands or is expected.

Accommodation for Young People

Basic but reliable In addition to budget accommodation in many small hotels and hundreds of guest houses, there are also youth hostels of acceptable standard in the larger towns. They are open to travellers of all ages. The standard is basic, and rooms are shared with other guests. But most hostels and guest houses also have private rooms at a slightly higher rate. Beware of thieves (who are most likely to be other tourists)! Avoid accommodation in suspicious-looking areas, which may be the haunt of drug dealers and under observation by the narcotics squad of the police, who often carry out searches. Nevertheless, Thailand has had lots of experience with budget travellers and knows how to accomodate them.

The lobby of the legendary, exclusive Oriental Hotel in Bangkok, →
which opened in 1876 as the first grand hotel in Thailand

Camping

Insignificant In Thailand camp sites specially equipped for the purpose do not exist, but wild camping is permitted. Ask the owner of the land for permission first. Camping in national parks and nature reserves is not allowed without permission from the park rangers. In some nature reserves the rangers hire out tents and other equipment, sell food and drinks and allow sanitary facilities to be used for a small fee.

Arrival • Planning the Journey

How to Get There

By air ... Most visitors to Thailand arrive by air, of course. The journey of roughly 10,000km/6,000mi from Europe takes about ten hours without stopovers. From the west coast of the USA the journey time is 15 hours or more, from Australia (Sydney) about nine hours. The international airports in Thailand, apart from Bangkok, are in Chiang Mai und Phuket.

... to Bangkok **Suvarnabhumi International Airport**, which opened in 2006 and is one of the world's most modern airports, is about 25km/15mi east of Bangkok. More than 50 airlines fly there. From Europe Thai Airways and several major carriers such as British Airways, Air France, Lufthansa and KLM fly direct to Bangkok, but it is also worth considering a charter flight. From North America there is also a good choice of connections.

An excellent road network, including five highways, links the airport to the Thai capital; nevertheless, allow at least 45 minutes for the journey into the city. There is also a fast rail connection from the centre of Bangkok to the airport.

Ticket prices vary greatly according to the time of year. The round trip from Europe can cost anything between €400 and €800, more for flights without a stopover. It is worth searching by internet for the best offers and asking around, particularly at travel agents specialized

Bangkok Airport at a Glance

- **Official name:** Suvarnabhumi International Airport
- **Architects:** Murphy/Jahn (Chicago / USA)
- **Start of work:** 19 January 2002
- **Cost:** about 4 billion US$
- **Area:** about 3,232ha/7,985 acres
- **Runways:** two (4,000 / 3,700 m; later four)
- **Traffic:** up to 76 take-offs and landings per hour
- **Passengers:** 50 million / year (later 100 million)
- **Baggage:** 9,600 pieces per hour
- **Freight traffic:** 3 million t / year (later up to 6.4 million t)
- **And:** at 132m/433ft, the control tower of the new Bangkok airport is the tallest of its kind in the world.

in Asian trips. From London, for example, 20 airlines or more offer flights to Thailand, though only British Airways, Thai Air and Qantas fly non-stop.

Domestic flights in Thailand: see ►Transport

Travellers coming by car from Singapore or Malaysia use one of the three entry points in the south of Thailand, in the provinces of **Songkhla**, **Yala** and **Narathiwat** (Sungai Kolok). Entering the country by car is permitted only at these three points (daily until 6pm). The »Asian Highway« from the Bosporus to Singapore has been interrupted since Myanmar (Burma) closed its border to motor vehicles.

By car

There are trains daily from Singapore and Malaysia. The fares are low, the journey is comfortable and the trains keep to the schedule reliably. The journey time from Singapore to Bangkok is one and a half to two days. To travel first class or to use a sleeper car, it is advisable to book in advance. See ►Transport, Rail.

By train

The luxurious Eastern & Oriental Express connects Singapore and Thailand; the three-day journey is wonderful but not cheap (information and bookings: www.orient-expresstrains.com).

◄ Eastern & Oriental Express

Cruise ships stop infrequently at the river port of Bangkok (usually between pier 9 and pier 12); they also stop off Pattaya, Sattahip and Phuket, so that passengers can go ashore in smaller boats.

By ship

● AIRLINE ADDRESSES

IN AUSTRALIA
► **Thai Airways International**
75-77 Pitt Street
Sydney 2001
NSW 2000
Tel. 02 98 44 09 99
Fax 02 98 44 09 36
www.thaiairways.com.au

IN UNITED KINGDOM
► **Thai Airways International**
41 Albemarle Street
London W1S 4BF
Tel. 020 74 91 79 53
Fax 020 74 09 14 63

IN USA
► **Thai Airways International**
Lincoln Building

60 East 42nd Street
New York NY 10165
Tel. 212 9 49 84 24
Fax 212 2 86 00 82

► **Thai Airways International**
222 North Sepulveda Blvd
suite 100
El Segundo CA 90245
Tel. 1 800 4 26 52 04
Fax 1 310 322 87 28

IN THAILAND
► **Thai Airways International**
Bangkok Head Office
89 Vibhavadi Rangsit Road
Chatuchak
Tel. 02 / 5 45 36 90 92
Fax 5 45 38 32

Immigration Regulations

Travel documents A passport and permission to enter Thailand are required. For a stay of up to 30 days, a visa is stamped in the passport at the airport or the border crossing. Visas for a longer stay must be applied for at a Thai consulate (▶ Information, Embassies) before the journey. Passports must be valid for six months beyond the date of departure. Children must either have their own passport or be included in the passports of their parents. The children's identity cards used in some European countries are not accepted!

Types of visa In addition to the 30-day visitor's visa, it is also possible to obtain a tourist visa for 60 or a non-immigrant visa for 90 days. If you know that you may want to extend your stay in Thailand, it is best to apply for the two-month visa from the very beginning, as an extension of the 30-day visa costs a considerable amount of time and money. A recently introduced annual visa for persons over the age of 55 entitles the bearer to enter the country more than once, but is issued only before departure from the traveller's country of origin. In addition, the holders of this type of visa may not stay in Thailand for more than three months at one time and must provide proof of their financial means.

! **Baedeker TIP**

Visa information

The latest information about passports and visas is posted on the website of the Thai Ministry of Foreign Affairs: www.mfa.go.th/web/12.php.

Visas for neighbouring countries Visas for visits to **Myanmar** (Burma), **Laos** and **Vietnam** are available only from these countries' consulates in Bangkok, not at the border. The processing of a visa application may take several days. **Malaysia** issues an entry visa valid for 90 days at the border post or the airport. If you plan to leave Thailand, for example to make a trip to Hong Kong or Burma, and to return to the country, apply for a multiple-entry visa, which is valid for entry up to three times.

Visa applications Visa application forms for Thailand are available from travel agents. Two forms, two passport photos, the passport and, in the case of a package holiday, confirmation of booking from the tour company, should be included, as well as a stamped addressed envelope if the application is made by post. As visa fees must be paid in cash, it is advisable to send applications as a registered letter.

Visa extension A visa extension must be applied for from the **Immigration Department** (tel. 1900 222 323; 9 baht / min. to make an appointment) before the original expiry date. The fee for extending the visa is high. Visitors who overstay the time specified in their visa are liable to a fine of 500 baht per day, with a maximum fine of 20,000 baht.

Everyone leaving the country who has spent 90 days or more per year in Thailand needs to present a tax clearance certificate, which gives exemption from taxes in Thailand. The certificate must also be presented by travellers who have a Thai work permit or have been in the country for more than 14 days on a business trip.

Tax clearance certificate

If you **lose your passport**, the embassy has to obtain replacement entry documents from the Immigration Department. To get a replacement passport, certification of the loss, obtainable from the Thai police, is necessary.

When renting a car in Thailand, it is usually sufficient to present a national driving licence; however, it is advisable also to have an inter-

Driving licence

 ## ADDRESSES FOR VISAS

TAX CLEARANCE CERTIFICATE

▶ **Tax Clearance Sub-Division**
Central Operating Division
1 Chakrapongse Road, Bangkok

▶ **Revenue Department**
Rajdamnoen Road, Bangkok
Tel. 02 / 2 81 57 77

IMMIGRATION DEPARTMENTS

▶ **Opening times for all offices:**
Mon–Fri 8.30am–noon, 1–4.30pm

▶ **Bangkok**
507 Soi Suan Phlu
Sathorn Tai Road
Tel. 02 / 28 73 10 11
Fax 2 87 13 10, 2 87 15 16
www.immigration.go.th

▶ **Chiang Mai**
71 Airport Road
(at the airport)
Tel. 0 53 / 27 75 10

▶ **Kanchanaburi**
100/22 Mae Klong Road
Tel. 0 34 / 51 33 25

▶ **Ko Samui**
Near the post office in Nathon
Tel. 0 77 / 42 10 69

▶ **Krabi**
Uttarakit Road, Krabi Town
Tel. 0 75 / 61 10 97

▶ **Pattaya**
Beach Road, Soi 8
Tel. 0 38 / 42 94 09

▶ **Surat Thani**
Don Nok Road (City Hall)
Tel. 0 77 / 27 32 17

▶ **Phuket**
South Phuket Road
Phuket City
Tel. 0 76 / 21 21 08

THAI DRIVING LICENCE

▶ **The Department of Land Transport**
1032 Phahonyothin Road
opposite Chatuchak Park
Bangkok 10900
Tel. 02 / 2 72 31 00

! *Baedeker* TIP

Passport photos and copies

It is advisable to take extra passport photos when travelling to Thailand. They are needed for entering the neighbouring countries. It is also recommended to make a photocopy of travel documents (including the page with the Thai visa) and keep them in a separate place from the originals. This makes it much easier to obtain replacements in case of loss.

national driving licence. If you lose your driving licence in Thailand, it may be worthwhile trying to get a Thai driving licence from the Department of Land Transport by showing police certification of the loss.

There is normally no point in trying to take dogs or cats to Thailand, as they are placed in quarantine for three months on entry.

Customs Regulations

Entering Thailand

Items for personal use such as clothing and toiletries are not subject to customs duty. Visitors over the age of 18 may also import 200 cigarettes or 250g of tobacco or 50 cigars, 1 litre of wine or spirits, a still camera and a video or film camera. Medicines for personal use can also be imported, but in order to avoid misunderstandings, it is best to bring them in the original packaging. It is forbidden to import drugs and pornographic literature. Hunting weapons and ammunition require authorization from the Police Department. Harpoons for underwater hunting may not be imported.

Return to EU countries

Thailand is shopping heaven, but it pays to remember that on return to a country of the European Union, goods to the value of more than €175/£120 are subject to customs duties and value added tax. All personal items that travellers take to Thailand with them are exempt from duty, but it is advisable to take purchase receipts for high-value items bought in your home country, in order to avoid problems when you return home. Persons 18 years of age or older have the following duty-free allowance: 200 cigarettes or 100 cigarillos or 250g of tobacco; 0.25 litres of eau de toilette or 50g of perfume; 1 litre of spirits over 22% by volume or 2 litres of sparkling or fortified wine, and 2 litres of wine. Import of foodstuffs is not allowed, as a measure to prevent infectious disease.

Currency regulations

There is no limit on the amount of foreign currency that can be imported. Thai currency up to a limit of 50,000 baht per person may be imported or exported without a licence.

Washington Convention

The Washington Convention on International Trade in Endangered Species prohibits trade in and therefore the import of exotic animals, whether living or dead. No parts of endangered animals may be brought back from Thailand. You may be subject to checks at the airport on returning, and heavy fines can be expected for those who

break the regulations. Be careful not to buy animals or animal products which may be from endangered species; this includes certain types of shell, corals, birds and reptiles, including bags and shoes of crocodile leather.

Travel Insurance

It is highly advisable to take out health insurance for the trip. Insurance packages that include baggage, accident and liability insurance as well as cover for medical treatment are available.

Health insurance

Beaches

With a coastline 1,875km/1,165mi long on the Gulf of Siam and 740km/460mi long on the Indian Ocean, it comes as no surprise that Thailand has a great number of extremely attractive beaches. Many of them, of course, are popular with the Thais themselves, who like to cool off in the sea at weekends and in the summer holidays (May–July). The beaches that can be reached from Bangkok in two or three hours by car tend to be overcrowded at these times, and the quality of the bathing water sometimes deteriorates, especially in places which are also destinations for foreign tourists.

Superabundance of perfect beaches

There are clean and lovely beaches in **Phuket**, **Hua Hin**, **Koh Samui**, **Koh Lanta** and **Khao Lak**, as well as on the islands off the east coast (**Koh Chang**, **Koh Samet**). The main beach of Pattaya is not to be recommended, but here too there are clean beaches with clear water and fine-grained sand just a few miles outside the town and on the outlying islands.

Underwater currents are a danger even for strong swimmers. They cannot be seen from the land and occur particularly in the monsoon season. The areas mainly affected are the beaches on Phuket, where

Red flag: danger!!!

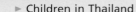

Thailand is famous for its pristine tropical beaches.

it is important to pay attention to the warning signs. Beaches in Thailand do not normally have a lifeguard service. Red flags on the beach mean that swimming is prohibited!

Jet skis are for hire on many beaches. Do not venture too far out to sea on them: sharks have been known to attack!

Thailand is not a country for nudists: **nakedness in public is not acceptable** to Thai moral values. Topless sunbathing is possible on some beaches, but is tolerated rather than expressly allowed.

Children in Thailand

Children are welcome everywhere and often find a holiday in Thailand a great experience. This does not necessarily mean spending the days on one of the wonderful beaches. There are a great many alternatives to this, such as a visit to an elephant camp, where it is possible to touch and ride the animals. For older children a trip to the tiger temple in Kanchanaburi province could be the highlight of the holiday.

BANGKOK

► Dreamworld
Km 7, Rangsit-Nakhon Nayok
Mon–Fri 10am–6pm, Sat and Sun to 7pm.
Large fun park based on Disneyland.

► Siam Park
99 Sukhapiban 2 Road
Bungkum, Bangkok
Mon–Sun 10am–6pm.
An attractive combination of fun park and water park for swimming.

► Rose Garden
Phet Kasem Road
32km/20mi from Bangkok
Mon–Sun 8am–6pm; daily cultural performance at 3pm. Elephant riding and cultural attractions on a large area.

► Safari World
99 Ramindra 1, Min Buri
Mon–Sun 9am–5pm
Zoo with wild animals in open enclosures and a sea aquarium with a lot of colourful fish.

AROUND BANGKOK

► **Ancient City**
(►Sights from A to Z, Samut Prakan) Thailand in miniature – all the sights in one place

► **Kanchanaburi**
Tiger temple (in Wat Pa Luangta Bua; ►Sights from A to Z, Kanchanaburi). Have you always wanted to stroke a living tiger? It takes a little courage, but you can do it here.

PATTAYA

► **Pattaya Elephant Village**
on the road to Siam Country Club, about 5km/3mi from Pattaya
Mon–Sun 9am–6pm; elephant show 2.30–4.30pm, elephant rides

► **Pattaya Park**
345 Jomtien Beach
Mon–Sun 9am–6pm
For everyone who loves water – fun for all ages

► **Ripley's »Believe It or Not«**
in the Royal Garden Plaza

Mon–Sun 10am–midnight
A collection of curiosities from all around the world

► **Go-Karts**
Thepprasit Road (Jomtien Beach)
Mon–Sun 10am–6pm. Training for would-be Formula One drivers

PHUKET

► **Phuket Aquarium**
Phanwe Cap (about 10km/6mi outside Phuket Town)
Mon–Sun 8.30am–4pm. An enormous sea-water aquarium full of marine life

► **Phuket Kart Race Track**
Above Patong Beach on the road to Phuket Town
Mon–Sun 10am–5pm
The counterpart to the go-kart track in Pattaya

► **Phuket Zoo**
At Chalong Beach
Mon–Sun 9am–6pm
A variety of shows with elephants, monkeys and crocodiles

Drugs

In Thailand as in the whole of South-East Asia, the authorities have   **Just don't!**
changed their attitude in recent years to those who deal in, possess and consume drugs – including so-called soft drugs. Pressure from Europe and the USA, among other influences, has led the Thai police to take an extremely tough line on such offences. Do not be tempted by offers from the locals, who may be police informants. And never »do a favour« for someone by taking a package »for a friend back home«, as you may unknowingly become a courier for drugs and end up in court. The possession of comparatively small quantities of drugs can be punished by long prison terms, and even by a sentence of death. Prisons in Thailand are not like those in western countries! Persons accused of drug offences can expect only the most basic help from the diplomatic representations of their home country.

Electricity

The power supply in all parts of Thailand is 220-volt AC, 50 to 60 Hertz. Two-pin sockets are the norm. Adapters are widely available from shops and at hotel reception desks.

Emergency

Tourist police The **Tourist Assistance Center** (TAC) is a department of the Tourism Authority of Thailand (TAT) that provides information in English. The tourist police, many of whom patrol on motorbikes, speak English.

Few normal policemen speak good English, so communication can be a problem, but it is important to call them in case of difficulties, so that they can record details of any incident.

▶ EMERGENCY NUMBERS

▶ **Ambulance**
There is no telephone number used nationwide. In case of accident, call the nearest police station.

▶ **Tourist Police**
Tel. 11 55

▶ **Police**
Tel. 191

▶ **Fire service**
Tel. 199

▶ **Tourist Assistance Center**
HQ in Bangkok
Tel. 02 / 2 81 50 51 or
Tel. 02 / 2 82 81 29
Daily 8am–midnight

Etiquette and Customs in Thailand

Worth knowing Even in an age of increasing western influence, Thai society still has its firmly established rules of behaviour. A description of the Thai national character would begin with politeness, tolerance and a deeply rooted love of life. Hospitality plays an important role, especially towards foreigners. However, visitors to the kingdom of Thailand should take note of a few rules of conduct in order to avoid unintentionally arousing disapproval.

Curiosity, in the best sense of the word, is a natural characteristic of adults as well as children. It is a matter of genuine personal interest, even of decency, to ask questions about a visitor's age, partner, number of children, profession etc. Women are often asked if they are alone (»kon di o«) by Thai men trying to work out their chances. To counter this question, answer »mai chai« (not true) or »bai pop sami« (I'm about to meet my husband). The simplest response, however, is to say »mai khau jai« (I don't understand). But never forget to smile: the firmer the negative answer, the friendlier the smile. It is considered impolite to express irritation, anger and outrage by speaking loudly.

Smiles are important

Girl on Koh Lanta

Physical contact – especially between the sexes – is avoided by the Thai way of greeting, the wai, which involves putting the palms of the hands together, as in prayer, and holding them in front of the face. As a sign of particular respect (for example towards a monk), the hands are also raised to the level of the forehead or higher. Strangers and persons of the same age and status hold their fingertips at the level of the chin or nose. A friendly smile is part of the greeting.

Wai

In buses and boats people do not offer their seat to the elderly, mothers with small children and pregnant women. This privilege is sometimes according to monks, who also have a right to the back seats in buses. Europeans who offer their seat will be thanked for the gesture, but with a hint of amusement in the smile.

Monks can sit

It is difficult for visitors from the west to get used to their conversation being ignored, for example during a meal. Even when all the Thais in the group can understand English, they pay attention only to subjects that interest them. Interruptions in Thai to a personal conversation are absolutely normal, even when the foreign visitor is the host.

Conversation

If you invite a Thai couple for a meal, the man is likely to bring one, two or even three friends instead of his wife, who sends her apologies. An invitation to a Thai's family home is a mark of special hospitality to a visitor from the west. Thais usually invite several guests in order to get an interesting circle of people together. Dress codes exist only for official occasions, but guests should still be dressed in a seemly manner – not in shorts and t-shirt, and on no account in black, which is the colour of death.

Invitations

Nine spirits Nine different spirits live on a property and in the house. Take care not to offend one of them, the spirit of the threshold, directly on arrival. If the door has a threshold, do not tread on it but step over it.

It goes without saying that guests take off their shoes before entering the house. Guests are expected to bring a small present: flowers for a lady, toys for children. Never give baby clothes to a pregnant woman, as this brings bad luck!

Physical expressions of affection between man and woman in the presence of others (including the couple's own children) are frowned upon. Nowadays holding hands is tolerated for young couples. On the other hand, it is absolutely normal for two women or two men to link fingers on the street or even to embrace each other warmly.

Besides the subject of physical contact, there are **deep-seated taboos** about the head and the feet. Thais regard the head as the seat of their human dignity and do not like to be touched there. Even a well-intentioned stroking of a child's head can have the opposite effect to the one desired. Thais also avoid passing any object over the shoulder, as it is easy to touch a person's head unintentionally while doing so. Try never to look down on the head of another person in Thailand, especially not the head of an older or higher-ranking person. Visitors from western countries, who are generally taller than the

Cultural sensitivity is called for when visiting temples.

locals, will not always be able to avoid this, but the important thing is to try, for example by bending forward, or sitting when the other person is standing. Nobody watches a procession or a parade from the window of an upper storey or a balcony. If the king is present, it is sacrilege to do so, as no-one may stand higher than the king. The feet are the opposite of the head: they are unworthy, insulting and dirty. It is an affront to point your feet at a Thai. To cross your legs when seated, a posture normal in the west, is also inadvisable except perhaps if they are concealed under the table, as the soles of your feet might be pointing at the person opposite.

In an international city like Bangkok, in contrast to the provinces, some unseemly behaviour is forgiven or judged mildly. This, however, applies to matters of etiquette and not to sacrilege, which is defined in law and punished by heavy fines, in serious cases even by imprisonment. Sacrilege is »an action against an object or a place of religious veneration or against a religious community in such a manner as to denigrate the religion concerned« (§ 206 of the criminal code). This includes touching a statue of Buddha without authorization, pointing a foot at it or climbing on it. Thais do not like to see images of Buddha used as the backdrop for holiday photos. Humorous photos posed in front of pictures of the royal family also cause offence.

Sacrilege

The law protects not only Buddhism, the religion of the majority of the population, but also all other religions. It is forbidden to disturb prayers in Buddhist or Hindu temples, in churches or mosques. When visiting religious sites such as the palace precinct in Bangkok, wear decent clothing, i.e. never bare-chested, in shorts or a short skirt. Shoes must be removed before entering the inner bot (temple) in Wat Phra Kaeo. Buddhist monks may not touch a woman or take objects directly from a woman. If a woman wants to give something to a monk, a man must touch it first.

Visiting religious sites

Some time ago the Thai government took up the fight against smoking. Cigarette companies are now forced to print photos with a strong deterrent effect on each pack. Restaurant proprietors are obliged to ban smoking in air-conditioned rooms.

Smoking

Festivals, Holidays and Events

 WHAT • WHEN • WHERE?

PUBLIC HOLIDAYS

► **1 January**
New Year

► **6 April**
Chakri Day. This holiday is in memory of Rama I and all other kings of the reigning Chakri dynasty; the people have access to the eight statues of the kings in Wat Phra Kaeo in Bangkok on this day only. The foundation of Bangkok in 1782 is also commemorated.

► **13–15 April**
Songkhram festival. The Thais celebrate their traditional New Year festival, when the sun comes into the sign of Capricorn before the rice is sown. Offerings are made to monks, and fish and birds are released from captivity. Statues of Buddha are given a symbolic »bath« by sprinkling them liberally with water. Carnival-style processions are held all over the country. From the second day of the festival until it ends, there are »water fights« in the streets between girls and boys. Rice powder and even coal dust are often mixed into the water.

► **1 May**
The day of labour, with mass meetings of trade unions. Offerings are given to monks. There are performance of music and theatre in Lumphini Park in Bangkok especially the popular »krabi« (comedies).

► **5 May**
Coronation day. National holiday to celebrate the anniversary of the coronation (1959) of the ruling royal couple, King Bhumibol and Queen Sirikit.

► **12 August**
Queen's Birthday. A day of merry celebration, especially in Bangkok. Queen Sirikit takes part in religious ceremonies and distributes offerings to monks in Chitralada Palace.

► **23 October**
Chulalongkorn Day in honour of the popular king Chulalongkorn (Rama V), the grandfather of the present ruler, who died in 1910. In Bangkok cadets march past the equestrian statue of King Chulalongkorn on the square in front of parliament.

► **5 December**
King's Birthday. The birthday of King Bhumibol (Rama IX, born 1927) is celebrated with great pomp. A few days after this event, the traditional yacht regatta for the King's Cup, which Bhumibol sponsored, takes place off Phuket.

► **8 December**
Prachuap Khiri Khan: a light-and-sound show and a big fair commemorate the victory over the Japanese invaders

► **10 December**
Constitution Day. In memory of the first democratic constitution, passed in 1932. Monks receive offerings.

FESTIVALS AND EVENTS: JANUARY

► **Bangkok**
In Lumphini Park and elsewhere: Red Cross Festival. Bazaars with cooked food stalls, exhibitions, entertainment. The ambassadors accredited to Thailand traditionally take part. The proceeds go to charity.

► **Chaiyaphum and Surin:**
Elephant festivals with colourful processions and markets

LATE JANUARY/ EARLY FEBRUARY

► **Nationwide**
Makha Bucha, one of the most important Buddhist festivals, is held at full moon to commemorate a sermon preached by Buddha

and attended by 1,250 disciples. In the evening, by the light of the moon, processions of the faithful circle the temples.

► Saraburi
Around Wat Phra Buddhabat: folk music, Thai dancing and theatre and a large fair

FEBRUARY

► Nakhon Phanom
Temple festival at That Phanom (folk music and dancing, boat race on the Mekong)

► Chiang Mai
1st weekend in February: flower festival, parade with wonderfully decorated floats. Exhibitions with an unrivalled variety of orchids, workshops about flowers, botanical guided walks.

LATE FEBRUARY/ EARLY MARCH

► Nationwide
Chinese New Year with an array of noisy events, especially in China-town in Bangkok. Chinese businesses are closed at least on this day, if not for the whole week.

LATE FEBRUARY TO MID-APRIL

► Nationwide
Kite-flying season (at its best at Sanaam Luang in Bangkok)

MARCH

► Mae Hong Son
Buat Luk Khaew festival (dedication of sons)

APRIL

► Pattaya
Pattaya Festival (originally Songkhran Festival) with water activities, car and motor cycle racing and a big fair

MAY

► Bangkok
Ploughing ceremony. According to Brahman rites, grains of rice are blessed and given to farmers, who come from all parts of the country to Bangkok, to bring luck. High-

Kite-flying season on Saanan Luang in Bangkok

ranking persons dressed in white and gold parade past the king and his bodyguard on Sanaam Luang in Bangkok with a plough, the symbol of a good harvest.

▶ **Nationwide**
At full moon in May: Visakha Puja (public holiday in all Thailand), the most sacred Buddhist festival (the day of Buddha's birth, enlightenment and death), is celebrated with candlelight processions and temple festivities.

▶ **Yasothon**
Mid-May: Boon Bang Fai rocket festival. Home-made rockets are fired into the sky to bring rain. Whether it then rains or not, this is the occasion for a big fair.

JUNE

▶ **Chiang Rai**
Lychee festival. The best lychees come from this region, and the harvest is marked with a great festival.

▶ **Loei**
Phi Ta Khon, a festival to commemorate the return of Prince Vessandorn, the last incarnation of Buddha, to the town. A procession of greeting, in which the spirits (phi) also took part. In memory of this event, young men disguise themselves as spirits, carry a statue of Buddha and tease the onlookers.

JULY

▶ **Nationwide**
At full moon: Asanrha Puja. In memory of Buddha's first sermon to his five disciples. All over Thailand there are temple festivals and processions at night beneath the full moon.

▶ **Nationwide**
Khao Phansa. Start of the Buddhist time of fasting. The celebration is particularly enjoyable in Ubon Ratchathani: enormous, beautifully carved wax candles are carried in procession.

AUGUST

▶ **Surat Thani**
Rambutan festival

SEPTEMBER

▶ **Hua Hin**
Elephant polo (▶Sports and Outdoors)

▶ **Nakhon Pathom**
Harvest festival with a parade of fruit and flowers, cookery demonstrations and lots of entertainment

▶ **Kamphaeng Phet**
Khluai Khai (banana festival). The best bananas in Thailand come from this area. The end of the harvest is the occasion for a great celebration.

▶ **Phuket**
Vegetarian festival (late September/early October): Thais of Chinese descent eat vegetarian food for a week. Many restaurants take account of this. Processions and occult performances (people in a trance walk over hot coals, for example).

OCTOBER

▶ **Chonburi**
Water buffalo race

▶ **Sakhon Nakhon**
Festival of wax locks at the end of the Buddhist period of retreat for

the rainy season. Miniature temples of beeswax are carried in procession and boat races are held.

► **Thot Kathin**
End of the three-month-long Buddhist fasting period. The rural population celebrates the end of the rainy season and completes the main rice harvest. Monks are given new robes and the king visits Wat Arun in Bangkok. On this day he now uses the royal barques, which have now been restored, in magnificent parades on Menam Chao Phraya once again. The colourful boat races in Phra Fa Daeng (opposite Paknam) and Phitsanulok are an interesting spectacle.

NOVEMBER

► **Nationwide**
Loy Kratong, one of the most enjoyable festivals in Thailand. It originated as a festival of light in honour of Mae Kongka, the goddess of the waterways; according to legend a princess once sent her lover little boats with burning candles at evening on the Menam Chao Phraya. At full moon the lights of countless thousands of little boats of banana and lotus leaves, which carry candles, joss sticks and sometimes coins, float on the rivers and canals. The most romantic celebrations take place in Sukhothai (with fireworks and folk dances) and Chiang Mai. In Bang Sai (near Ayutthaya) the national longboat championships are held on the Menam Chao Phraya.

► **Surin**
Elephant round-up, a big festival lasting several days

► **Nakhon Pathom**
Pilgrimage to the world's most sacred Buddhist sanctuary. Great temple festival with a fair.

► **Bangkok**
Golden Mount Fair. On 22 November hosts of pilgrims walk up to Wat Sakhet to revere relics of Buddha.

LATE NOVEMBER / EARLY DECEMBER

► **Mae Sarieng**
Sunflower festival

► **Kanchanaburi**
River Kwai Bridge week

► **Khon Kaen**
Silk festival with the Phuk Sieo ritual

DECEMBER

► **Chiang Mai**
Food festival. Many restaurants in Chiang Mai offer Thai specialities and cookery courses. Musicians and artists stage a lively programme of events around Cherng Doi Market in Canal Road.

Every November: Loy Kratong light festival

Food and Drink

National hobby   It has been said of the Thais that while half of them are thinking about food, the other half are actually eating. This is undoubtedly true: why else should there be roadside food vendors everywhere, even in the smallest village, that find customers for snacks almost round the clock? Fixed mealtimes, as in the west, are common only among families of higher social classes. Most people often go to the cooked food vendors and eat five or six times a day, though only small quantities. Breakfast in the European or American style is uncommon; the usual way to start the day is a bowl of rice or vegetable soup. Thais do not eat with a knife and fork, as these utensils are seen as symbols of aggression, and chopsticks too are used only by Thais of Chinese origin. Instead the food is cut up into spoon-sized pieces, and is served is this way in restaurants. The rule is that a piece of meat and a small amount of rice together form a mouthful.

Varied influences   Thai food is varied and closely related to that of other countries of South-East Asia. Indian, Chinese and Sri Lankan dishes have gained a typically Thai character through the use of different spices. The openness of the Thais is also evident in their adoption of western recipes: in the centres of tourism many restaurants provide international food.

! *Baedeker* TIP

Tips and tricks: Thai cooking

Cookery courses at the famous Oriental Hotel and Peninsula Hotel in Bangkok teach the finer points of Thai cuisine. Many other hotels, too, offer cookery courses, including instruction in how to cut fruit into different shapes. Just ask at reception.

The principle of classic Thai cooking is to use main ingredients that are simple but fresh. Everyday dishes use fish, vegetables and rice; beef or pork are normally eaten only on feast days. Until a few years ago, fish was a special treat in the north of the country, but the farming of tilapia in the irrigation canals of the rice paddies has made it affordable there too. Dried fish, a speciality of south Thailand, is eaten as a delicacy in all parts of the country.

Spices   Thai food can in general be described as medium spicy. It gets its own particular flavour from the combination of many different spices (such as curry, coconut milk, onions, chilli, ginger, coriander, basil, mint, lemon grass, shrimp paste and garlic) and the use of sweet, sweet-and-sour or hot sauces. Salt is hardly used at all; fish sauce (nam pla) is provided instead. Soups and main courses are usually served with a selection of spices for individual seasoning. Beware: the small pickled red and green peppers (nam prick) are very hot! The larger ones are milder.

Floating cooked food stall in Damnoen Saduak near Bangkok

Most soups are made as creamed soups. They taste wonderful and are very nutritious. There are vegetable soups as well as soups made from poultry, meat and fish, which are often served with noodles. **»Tom yam gung«**, vegetables and shrimps in a strong broth, is one famous soup; **»tom ka gai« soup** (chicken with coconut milk) is also delicious. Soups are generally very spicy; if this is not to your taste, say »mai sai prick« (»not spicy, please«) when ordering.

There are many typical Thai dishes. All are prepared with generous amounts of garlic and onions, and most served garnished with different types of salad. Pork (»mu«), beef (»wua«), chicken (»gai«) and fish (»pla«) of every imaginable variety are a prominent feature of menus. Steaks, too, are popular. To go with the meat or fish, rice (»kau«), noodles (»bami«) or potatoes (»man farang«) are served. To order fried rice with pork, for example, just say »kau phad mu«; for beef, just say »kau phad wua«.

Meat is usually fried, grilled or deep fried. The classic meat dishes include beef with rice noodles, fried beef with basil leaves, soya sprouts or bamboo shoots (»sen mi nua yang«), and chicken curry with coconut and rice (»kaeng kau khiao wan kai«).

Fish and shellfish (lobster, langoustines, crabs) are cheap, always fresh and expertly cooked: sweet-and-sour fish curry (»kaeng som«), for example, or poached fish with hot tomato sauce (»pla nueng yaeo

Lychee   *Durian*   *Jackfruit*

FROM PINEAPPLE TO RAMBUTAN

When it comes to fruit, Thailand is a luxuriant garden of Eden, with tropical delights unknown to many people in western countries. Restaurants often have fresh fruit on the menu, depending on the time of year. When buying fruit on the market, do not forget to wash it thoroughly.

Bananas (kluey), of which there are 15 different sorts, can be bought all year round. Those on sale on the street in the evening have mostly been dipped in sweet coconut milk and grilled. The smaller the banana, the better it tastes.

Coconut (ma prao onn) milk is a healthy, refreshing drink; the white inner part of the coconut is removed with a long pointed spoon.

The somewhat floury flesh of the durian, which is often called »stink-fruit« on account of its pungent smell, is prized as a delicacy by the Thais (April to June). Many hotels ask their guests not to bring durian onto the premises.

Farang fruit (guava) is usually eaten with sugar and a pinch of salt. It is called »farang«, meaning »foreign«, as it seems like an outsider amongst the fruits of the country (September to January).

Grapefruit (som o thong dee), usually the especially luscious pink variety, is available throughout the year. Thais eat it with a pinch of salt and chili.

The sweet aromatic jackfruit (ka nun), a round fruit weighing several kilograms, is cut into slices and served on ice-cream (August to September).

Langsat (langsard) is a delicious, light-brown berry with a thin but tough skin that has to be cut off with a knife. Be careful: the sweet flesh of the fruit conceals an extremely bitter stone (June to September).

Round, green limes, the Thai equivalent of the lemon, are available all year round. Yellow lemons have to be imported and are expensive.

Longan (lamyai) is a fruit from the northern provinces that only stays fresh for a few days. In Bangkok it is sold at fairly high prices, as it has to be transported over a long distance (July to September).

Lychees (hong huay, gimjeng, ohia), which used to be a luxury tinned product imported from China, are now grown in Thailand, especially in the north. The three different names refer to three different price categories, which correspond to their vulnerability to pests. There is little difference between the taste of the

Longan   *Langsat*   *Mangosteen*

varieties. They are fresh and ripe (with a red shell) from May to August.

Next to pineapple, mango (ma muang) is undoubtedly the most popular fruit with tourists. It is sweet, juicy and aromatic only when fully ripe (yellow skin, does not keep long). It is cut apart in the middle and the flesh removed with a spoon or sucked out. Mangosteen (mang khud), which is available from June to November, is purple on the outside. The flesh is white and has a sweet taste similar to lychees.

Oranges (som) have a thin green skin in Thailand and are sold all year round. They taste particularly sweet when they have turned yellow.

Papaya (malakhor), often served halved with »menau« (lemon) as part of a hotel breakfast, is the cheapest fruit in Thailand and can be bought on markets at all times of the year. Beware: large quantities of papaya have a guaranteed laxative effect.

Pineapple (sapparot) is available fresh from April to July. There are no less than eleven varieties. It is low in calories and high in vitamin C. Some types are normally eaten in a part-fermented state, and can have an undesired laxative effect.

Rambutan (ngor) is called »hairy fruit« by Americans because of its curly hairs, which are green, or red when the fruit is fully ripe. Cut open the skin with a knife and eat the juicy flesh but not the stones (May to October).

Rose-apples (chompu) are pear-shaped with rust-coloured, waxy skin and porous white flesh inside, both of which are edible. As the fruit is slightly sour, it is normally eaten with sugar and a pinch of salt (January to March).

The Thai art of carving fruit and vegetables is linked to an ancient legend: a poem by King Rama II tells of a queen, whose rival won the king's favour. She was banned from the palace, but returned as a kitchen maid and caught the attention of her son by carving events from her former life on pieces of vegetable for the soup. The son recognized his mother, asked the king to pardon her and was able to gain permission for her return to court. Today hotel kitchens employ specialists who are true masters of the art of sculpture in fruit and vegetables.

makhua tet«). Many restaurants display their seafood in refrigerated glass cases. Giant prawns are a much-loved speciality on the coast in the south of the country. They are grilled on charcoal and served with a variety of side dishes.

! *Baedeker* TIP

Learn to cook Thai-style

Thai food is one of the world's best cuisines. Here are addresses where you can learn how to do it for yourself.
Chiang Mai Thai Cookery School
Tel. 0 53 20 63 88
www.thaicookeryschool.com
Oriental Hotel Cooking School, Bangkok
Tel. 0 26 59 90 00

Beans, cabbage, Chinese greens, turnips, aubergines and mushrooms are usually only cooked for a short time, often in a wok, and therefore keep most of their vitamins. Fat is hardly used; many ingredients are steamed.

The Thais like extremely **sweet, garishly coloured desserts** (»khong wan«). Little, dry raisin cakes are also popular. Desserts made with rice are called »khanom«. The Thais have also learned how to make ice-cream in the American style, and produce delicious ice-cream coupes imaginatively served (in a hollowed-out pineapple, for example).

Drinks

Tea with everything
Good restaurants provide cold weak tea (»chaa«) free of charge with the meal. Hot tea (»chaa rom«) has to be ordered separately. Coffee comes either with milk and sugar (very sweet) or as »o'liang«: black, cold and usually with ice. Italian espresso-style coffee has also taken hold in Thailand. Fresh milk (»nom«) is available in plastic bags, usually from Danish producers. Insist on »mai waan«, or you will be given sweetened milk. When ordering fruit juice, it is best to ask specifically for fresh (»sod«) juice, as fruit drinks in Thailand are normally very sweet and brightly coloured. »Soda« is generally understood as a term for mineral water.

! *Baedeker* TIP

A sea of ice!

Drinks are often served with a mass of unwanted ice cubes. For most people, it is better to learn the phrase »no ice, please« (»mai sai nam-khaeng«) than »with ice, please« (»kor sai namkhaeng«).

Alcoholic drinks
Thai beer such as Singha, Amarit and the German-style Kloster comes in small bottles (»koad lek«) and large bottles (»koad yai«). It is fairly expensive, as hops cannot be grown in Thailand and have to be imported. Imported European beer is available in places frequented by tourists.
»Maekong« is a typical Thai drink; it is a spirit made from rice containing 28 per cent alcohol, and is drunk with cola, soda water or a lemon (»menau«).

Remarkably, vines have successfully been cultivated in Thailand in recent years, by taking European vines as a basis to develop plants suitable for a tropical climate. The country now produces about 1.5 million litres of wine per year. The wine-growing areas are the cooler regions of the north. The best-known producer is called Chateau de Loei. Wine imported from France, Italy, the USA and Australia is relatively expensive and is often not stored properly.

Thai wine?

Health

The Thai health system has two main pillars: on the one hand there are modern, well-equipped western-style hospitals (especially in Bangkok and the tourist areas), on the other hand (in rural areas) a large number of small clinics. In Bangkok the doctors are particularly well trained. Many have studied or completed specialist training in Europe or the USA and speak English.

Good medical attention

Hotels and the local representatives of tour companies can find doctors, who will go to the hotel in urgent cases. In rural areas it is sometimes difficult to find a doctor. The first place to turn to is the local police station, which will know where the nearest doctor or hospital can be found. A number of embassies in Bangkok (►Information) keep lists of doctors.

Finding a doctor

Thailand does not have a sophisticated emergency service. There are no rescue helicopters. In case of accidents, it may take some time for the emergency service to arrive, as the distance to the nearest town can be considerable. You can usually rely on the willingness of the Thais to help.

Emergency and rescue services

Visitors must pay for the costs of treatment and medicine. Most hospitals accept credit cards as well as cash. In emergencies, ask the embassy of your country for a loan. You are strongly recommended to take out a travel health insurance policy that will also cover the costs of transport back home.

Payment

Serum against snake bites can be obtained in Bangkok from the Pasteur Saovapha Institute (Saladaeng Road), at weekends and on holidays from the Chulalongkorn Hospital (Saladaeng Road). If you are bitten by a snake in a country area, go to the nearest police station straight away and inform the locals. There is no central emergency phone number for this eventuality.

Snake bites

The shops marked »ram kai jaa« in Thai or often in English as »pharmacy« have a large selection of commonly used medicines. The

Pharmacies

prices are often only a fraction of those charged in western countries for the same product. To avoid making the wrong purchase, take with you the packaging of medicine that you need, if possible. Doctors give a prescription for a medicine only in exceptional cases. Instead the patient is given a plastic bag with the medicine needed for the next few days. The opening times of pharmacies are Mon–Sat 9am–7pm, often 8pm. Many are closed on Sundays.

Hospitals In Thailand every provincial capital has a public hospital and often private clinics, too, with doctors who studied in Europe or the USA. There are also hospitals run by church organizations and charities. Ask at the hotel reception where the nearest hospital is to be found.

Plague of mosquitoes In the evenings it is advisable to be well protected against mosquitoes. Long trousers and long-sleeved shirts are useful as well as an anti-mosquito preparation..

Information

 USEFUL ADDRESSES

IN AUSTRALIA

► **Tourism Authority of Thailand (TAT)**
Level 2, 75 Pitt Street
Sydney, NSW 2000
Tel. 02 92 47 75 49
info@thailand.net.au
The TAT has an excellent range of informative brochures.

IN BRITAIN

► **Tourism Authority of Thailand (TAT)**
3rd Floor, Brook House
98-99 Jermyn Street
London SW1Y 6EE
Tel. 020 79 25 25 11
tatuk@tat.or.th

IN USA

► **Tourism Authority of Thailand (TAT)**
61 Broadway, Suite 2810
New York NY 10006
Tel. 212 432 04 33
tatny@tat.or.th

► **Tourism Authority of Thailand (TAT)**
1st Floor
611 North Larchmont Blvd
LA, CA 90004
Tel. 323 461 98 14
tatla@tat.or.th

IN THAILAND

► **Tourism Authority of Thailand (TAT)**
1600 New Phetchaburi Road
Makkasan,
Ratchathewi
Bangkok 10400
Tel. 02 / 2 50 55 00
Fax 2 50 55 11
www.tourismthailand.org;
Open daily 8.30am–4.30pm

► **TAT Airport and by Phone**
Bangkok International Airport
Arrival hall, Terminal 1
Tel. 02 / 5 04 27 01-2
Arrival hall, Terminal 2
Tel. 02 / 5 04 27 03, 25 35 26 69
Open daily 8am–midnight.
TAT Call Centre (English and
other languages): tel. 02 / 16 72;
8am–8pm

► **Local TAT offices**
All large towns have a tourist
office, which can supply detailed
information and maps about the
sights in the surrounding area.
They can also help by booking
accommodation, tours and travel
tickets. Please refer to the entries
about individual places in the
main section of this book for local
addresses.

**THAI EMBASSIES AND
CONSULATES**

► **Australia**
Thai Consulate
Level 8, 131 Macquarie Street
Sydney, NSW 2000
Tel. 02 92 41 25 42
http://thaisydney.idx.com.au

► **Canada**
Thai Consulate
1040 Burrard Street
Vancouver BC V6Z 2R9
Tel. 6 04 687 11 43
www.thaicongenvancouver.org

► **UK**
Thai Embassy, 29-30 Queensgate
London SW7 5JB
Tel. 020 75 89 01 73
http://thailand.embassyhome
page.com

► **USA**
Thai Embassy

351 East 52nd Street
New York, NY 10022
Tel. 212 754 17 70
http://thaiconsulnewyork.com

**EMBASSIES AND
CONSULATES IN THAILAND**

► **Australian Embassy**
37 Th Sathon Tai, Bangkok
Tel. 0 22 87 26 80
www.austembassy.or.th

► **Canadian Embassy**
15th Floor, Abdulrahim Bldg
990 Th Pra Ram IV
Bangkok
Tel. 0 26 36 05 40
http://geo.international.gc.ca/asia/
bangkok/

► **UK Embassy**
1031 Th Withayu, Bangkok
Tel. 0 23 05 83 33
www.britishemb.or.th

► **United States
Embassy**
120-22 Th Withayu, Bangkok
Tel. 0 53 25 26 29
http://bangkok.usembassy.gov/

INTERNET

► **www.tourismthailand.org**
The official English-language
homepage of the Tourism Authority of Thailand has a lot of
valuable information, including
suggestions on where to go.

► **www.sawasdee.com**
Well-presented site in English with
a great deal of useful information
about Thailand

► **www.asia-discovery.com/
thailand.htm**
Information about hotels, tours,
trekking and sports

Language

Basics The most important expression, a phrase that most tourists hear soon after arriving in the country, is »mai pen rai«, which means »it doesn't matter!« and is a good description of the Thai mentality. With this phrase, to which Thais mostly add »ka(p)«, »please«, small mistakes in conduct are considered as pardoned. The »farang« (a word for foreigner which is probably a corruption of »français«, as the French were the first Europeans seen in Thailand) encounter a second linguistic peculiarity when greetings are exchanged. Thais say »sawadee«, accompanied by »wai«, the respectful Buddhist greeting, and add the word »kap« if they are men, »kaa« in the case of women. »Sawadee« is the expression used from morning to evening: no distinction in the form of greeting is made according to the time of day.

Transliteration There are considerable variations in the western way of writing Thai words and names, according to whether the transliteration follows the letters or the sounds. This produces a confusing variety of spellings for persons and places, streets and buildings. In this guide the attempt has been made to render Thai names in a consistent manner, but it was also necessary to take account of the way names are written locally.

For example: (Wat Phra) **Khaeo** (temple name) is also written Kheo or Keo; **Ko** (island) can also appear as Kho, **Prasad** (temple building) as Prasat and **Ratchadamnoen** (street name) as Rajadamnoen or Rachadamnern.

Pronunciation To start with the most important point: r is usually spoken as l, e.g. »rai« always »lai«. Ph, th, kh are aspirated p, t, k; p, t, k sound like b, d, g of they are not aspirated. W is a soft sound, as wh in what.

Pitfalls Many pitfalls await those who try to learn the Thai language. Two examples give an idea of the problem. The word »mai«, depending on the tone in which it is spoken, can mean »widow«, »silk«, »wood«, »burn« or »new«. And if someone says he has »eaten enough« (»por« in Thai) and emphasizes the o, it means that he has eaten his own father.

Basics Visitors are recommended at least to learn the greeting »sawadee« and to express regret with a quick »mai pen rai kaa(p)«. If you manage this, you can be sure of a beaming smile from your Thai counterpart.

Forms of address Differences in status are expressed in forms of address. Here are some general rules: the word »khun« precedes words addressed to a stranger; among people who know each other, the first name suffices. »Khun nai« or »Khun nuh« are used by a person of lower rank addressing higher-ranked person.

At the end of a sentence, »kaa« is spoken by women, »kaap« by men as an expression of politeness.

By speaking English it is almost always possible to get along in Thailand.

English spoken here

Literature

Handley, Paul M.,, *The King Never Smiles: A Biography of Thailand's Bhumibol Adulyadej*, Yale 2006. A substantial work that illuminates not just the personality of the king but the recent development of Thailand.

Phongpaichit P. and Baker C., *Thailand's Boom and Bust*, 1998. The background to the economic growth of Thailand from the 1980s and the subsequent crash.

Phra Peter Pannapadipo., *Phra Farang: An English Monk in Thailand*, Arrow Books, 2005. Insights into Thai society and Buddhism.

Stevenson, William., *The Revolutionary King*, Constable and Robinson 2001. The life of the popular monarch Bumibol (Rama IX).

Wyatt, D. K., *Thailand: A Short History*, Yale 2004. Update of a standard work to include the rapid social and economic development of the last 20 years.

Cooper, R., Cooper, N., *Culture Shock Thailand*, Marshall Cavendish 2006. How the Thais think and feel, and how to avoid putting your foot in it.

Hand, Elizabeth, *Anna and the King*, Harper Collins 2000. The novel taken from the film re-make, adaptation of the screenplay by Steve Meerson und Peter Krikes.

Kepner, S (ed.), *The Lioness in Bloom*, University of California Press 1996. Eleven short stories and excerpts from five novels illuminate the situation of women in Thai society.

Landon, Margaret, *Anna and the King of Siam*, Amereon 1999. The original novel that inspired the films.

Moore, Christopher G.,, *A Bewitching Smile*, White Lotus Books 1992. The Canadian expatriate Moore has written a series of thrillers set in the underworld and go-go bars of Thailand.

Somtow, S.P., *Jasmine Nights,* St Martin's Press 1995. The best-selling Thai author, who also writes science fiction, goes back to his roots near Bangkok in the 1960s in this semi-autobiographical novel.

Sudham, Pira, *Monsoon Country,* Breakwater Books 1990. The author, who grew up in the north-east of the country, writes in this and other fictional works about rural Thailand.

Pettifor, Steven, *Flavours: Thai Contemporary Art,* Thavibu Gallery 2004. A survey of the contemporary art scene in Thailand.

Warren, William, *Thai Garden Style,* Periplus Editions 2003. A sumptuous coffee-table book for lovers of Asian gardens.

Warren, William, *Thai Style,* Times Editions 2002. A classic work on Thai architecture and interior design, illustrated with superb photos by Luca Tettoni.

Bhumichitr, V., *A Taste of Thailand,* Pavilion 2005. Authentic recipes and background on the country that created them.

Massage

Traditional Thai massage has nothing to do with prostitution. The masseurs use methods that are taught and applied all over the world

for medicinal purposes. In Wat Pho, one of the oldest temples in Bangkok, there is a school devoted to the classical method of massage, a combination of »western« massage and foot zone massage (reflexology). The skilled fingers of the well-trained masseurs and masseuses produce a feeling of relaxation and well-being.

Everywhere in Thailand there are steam baths, with strict separation of the sexes, where massage is also offered. Genuine masseurs, usually of the same sex as the customer, will come to a hotel for a small additional fee; the reception desk can organize this service. In Wat Pho in Bangkok (to the right of the main entrance) experienced masseurs are available at low prices. In

Massage school in Chiang Mai

Chiang Mai classical massage is on offer at Wat Suan Dok and in various other places, where it is also taught in courses.

Prostitution, which goes on more or less openly, is known as »massage for tourists« and is found particularly in the bars and »massage parlours« of Bangkok, Phuket and Pattaya.

Media

Newspapers and magazines in English are available in all centres of tourism, sometimes only one day after printing, but they are expensive. For a Thai view of the world, read the dailies *Bangkok Post and Nation.*

Newspapers, magazines

All large towns have their own radio station, and broadcasts from Bangkok can be picked up almost everywhere in the country. Some channels broadcast news in English. Local stations in Pattaya and on Phuket transmit a programme of light music and world news in English. Reception of BBC World Service, Voice of America and Radio Australia is generally good.

Radio

Four stations, one of them a propaganda channel for the army, and a range of satellite channels, especially sports channels, can be picked up in all parts of Thailand. Some programmes are in English. Many hotels also have English-language channels.

Television

Money

The unit of currency in Thailand is the baht (THB), subdivided into 100 satang (colloquially known as dang).

Currency

The smallest coin in circulation, the salung (25 satang) is now rarely seen. There are also coins to the value of 50 satang (2 salung), 1 baht, 5 baht and 10 baht. Banknotes are in the following denominations: 20 (green), 50 (blue), 100 (red), 500 (purple) and 1000 baht (grey-brown). The value appears not only in the Thai alphabet but also in Arabic numerals.

Coins and banknotes

The exchange rate for banks is fixed by the government and published in the business section of daily newspapers. The rates offered by a money changer may well be better than the official rates from a bank. Change money at hotels only in emergencies, as their exchange rate is less favourable as a rule.

Exchange rates

► EXCHANGE RATES

1 baht (THB) = 0.03 US$
1 US$ = 32 baht
1 baht = 0.015 £ (GBP)
1 £ = 64 baht
1 baht = 0.02 €
1 € = 43 baht

Bank and credit cards Cash can be obtained at practically all banks in every part of the country using **bank cards** from cash machines (ATMs).

The usual **credit cards** are accepted by most hotels, restaurants and shops, travel agents and airlines. Mastercard and Visa are the most commonly accepted cards, followed by Amex. Local car hire companies tend not to accept credit cards; if you want to pay by this means, hire from an international company. After making payment by credit card, compare the original and the copy to ensure that both bear the same amount; tear up any carbon paper that was used for the copy. It is of course possible to withdraw cash from ATMs by credit card with the PIN number, but the charges for doing so are high.

! *Baedeker* TIP

Lost your credit card?

Phone these numbers in Bangkok if you have lost your credit card:
Amex tel. 0 22 73 50 50
Mastercard tel. 001 800 11 887 06 63
Visa tel. 001 800 441 34 85.

Banks Thailand is well supplied with branches of banks. They offer all the usual financial services, as well as international money transfer by telegraph. Some banks have mobile branches, especially in the main tourist centres, where cash and traveller's cheques can be converted to local currency.

Opening times ► Banks: Mon–Fri 8.30am–3pm, Sat 8.30am–noon. Money changers: Mon–Sat 9am–8pm, Sun usually closed.
Sometimes the money changers shut up shop, as they have run out of baht.

National Parks

Thailand has 63 national parks in all regions of the country, many of which have only recently been established. The most attractive are described in »Sights from A to Z«.

The main purpose of the national parks is to preserve the typical regional flora and fauna, and they are also of course areas for recreation. They are under the control of the **Forestry Department**, which employs rangers to care for them. For a small fee the national park offices sell basic maps, on which paths for walkers are marked.

Administration

Signs in the parks provide information about what is and is not allowed. Camping, for example, is permitted only in specific places (information from rangers). There is a general prohibition on picking flowers, felling trees, hunting and fishing. Offences are punishable with heavy fines. Fires may be lit only in places equipped with a hearth.

Code in national parks

▶ THE BEST NATIONAL PARKS

▶ **Ang Thong**
(▶Surat Thani)

▶ **Ao Phangna**
(▶Phangna)

▶ **Doi Luang**
(▶Phetchaburi)

▶ **Doi Inthanon**
(▶Vhom Thong)

View of Dai Inthanon National Park near Chong Tong

National Parks *in Thailand*

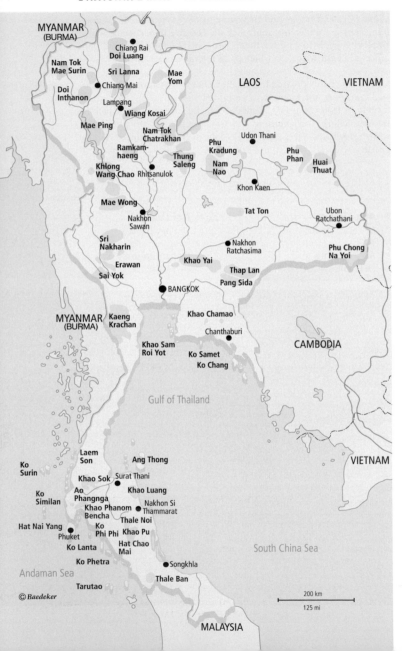

MYANMAR
(BURMA)

Chiang Rai
Doi Luang

Nam Tok
Mae Surin
Sri Lanna
Mae
Yom

Doi
Inthanon
Chiang Mai
LAOS
VIETNAM

Lampang

Wiang Kosai

Mae Ping
Nam Tok
Chatrakhan

Udon Thani

Ramkam-
haeng
Thung
Saleng
Phu
Kradung
Phu
Phan
Huai
Thuat

Khlong
Wang Chao
Rhitsanulok
Nam
Nao

Khon Kaen

Mae Wong
Tat Ton
Ubon
Ratchathani

Nakhon
Sawan

Sri
Nakharin
Nakhon
Ratchasima
Phu Chong
Na Yoi

Erawan
Khao Yai

Sai Yok
Thap Lan
Pang Sida

BANGKOK

MYANMAR
(BURMA)
Kaeng
Krachan
Khao Chamao

Chanthaburi
CAMBODIA

Khao Sam
Roi Yot
Ko Samet
Ko Chang

Gulf of Thailand

VIETNAM

Laem
Son
Ang Thong

Ko
Surin
Khao Sok
Surat Thani

Ko
Similan
Ao
Phangnga
Khao Luang

Khao Phanom
Bencha
Nakhon Si
Thammarat

Thale Noi

Hat Nai Yang
Ko
Phi Phi
Khao Pu
South China Sea

Phuket

Ko Lanta
Hat Chao
Mai

Ko Phetra
Songkhla

Andaman Sea
Thale Ban

© Baedeker
Tarutao

200 km
125 mi

MALAYSIA

► **Doi Pui**
(►Chiang Mai)

► **Erawan**
(►Kanchanaburi; Khao Salop)

► **Hat Nai Yang**
(►Phuket)

► **Kaeng Krachan**
(►Phetchaburi)

► **Khao Chamao**
(►Ko Samet)

► **Khao Khiew**
(►Chonburi)

► **Khao Luang**
(►Nakhon Si Thammarat)

► **Khao Phanom Benche**
(►Krabi)

► **Khao Sam Roi Yot**
(►Hua Hin)

► **Khao Sok**
(►Phangnga)

► **Khao Yai, Ko Chang**
(►Trat)

► **Ko Phi Phi**
(►Ko Phi Phi)

► **Ko Samet**
(►Ko Samet)

► **Ko Similan**
(►Phuket)

► **Ko Tarutao, Lan Sang**
(►Tak)

► **Phu Kai**
(►Saraburi)

► **Phu Kradung, Phu Phan**
(►Nakhon Phanom)

► **Thale Noi**
(►Phattalung)

► **Thung Saleng**
(►Phitsanulok)

► **Wang Takrai**
(►Prachinburi)

Personal Safety

In Thailand the rate of crimes, theft and assault is not higher than elsewhere in the world, and the kingdom is one of the safest countries for travellers in South-East Asia. Theft often results from carelessness on the part of the victim. Bear in mind that tourists often carry more cash with them than the annual income of a hotel employee. It is a question of tact and discretion not to flaunt wealth. Valuable should be deposited in the hotel safe. Do not carry more money with you than you expect to need.

Precautions

Most hotels provide deposit boxes or room safes without charge. Larger valuables such as camera cases should be left at the reception, as the hotel is not liable for items stolen from rooms. Hand in the room keys at the reception desk when you leave the hotel.

Safes

Beware of pickpockets! Skilled pickpockets are at work, especially in the centres of tourism. Keep your valuables in a money belt or concealed under your shirt or blouse.

Scams The danger of excessive charges and scams is higher is areas of »classic« Thai nightlife. Do not fall for touts who want to take you to dubious establishments.

Post • Communications

Stamps The Thai postal service is fast and reliable. Letters to Europe or North America take about six days by air mail (par avion). If they are not marked as air mail, they go by sea and overland, which can take as long as three months. Letter boxes are red. In Bangkok there are letter boxes for post sent to addresses within the city. Hotel reception desks have post boxes and sell stamps. All towns and airports and some villages have post offices, all of which take poste restante deliveries.

Postal charges Air mail letters cost 28 baht, postcards 12 baht. Registered letters cost more, but it is advisable to pay the supplement for important letters.

Parcels Parcels sent abroad have to be wrapped and sealed in the presence of a customs officer, who can be found at the »customs window« of the post office, where the packaging material can also be purchased. Parcels can have a maximum weight of 20kg/44lb. Customs duties do not normally have to be paid for presents and personal items.

 TELEPHONE CODES

TO THAILAND

The country code for Thailand is 66, preceded by the prefix for international calls (e.g. 00) and followed by the local area code without the zero.

WITHIN THAILAND

Always dial the area code, even when making a call within a city. The codes 01, 06, 08 and 09 are mobile codes. See »Sights from A to Z« for the area codes of destinations in Thailand.

FROM THAILAND

► **To Australia**
Tel. 00 61

► **To Canada**
Tel. 00 1

► **To Ireland**
Tel. 00 353

► **To United Kingdom**
Tel. 00 44

► **To USA**
Tel. 00 1

There are public telephones, usually card phones, in all Thai towns.   Telephone
Larger towns have public telephones that accept payment by credit
card. Phone cards in various denominations are available from post
offices and from the Seven-Eleven
shops that stay open almost all
hours.

Internet cafés are to be found in
all sizeable towns. They compete to
offer the lowest prices. Almost all
hotels have an internet connection
for their guests.

All operators of **mobile phone net-
works** in Thailand are linked to the
roaming network, which means
that mobile phones from western countries can be used directly
upon arrival in Thailand. But beware: costs vary greatly. It is advisable to check the current tariffs before leaving for Thailand and make a
comparison with the prices at your destination: if you want to use
your mobile phone there, it may be best to buy a prepaid card in
Thailand and remove the SIM card from your home country. Prepaid cards are sold at Seven-Eleven shops.

> **? DID YOU KNOW …?**
>
> ■ … that the costs of mobile phone calls that
> you receive when in Thailand are charged to
> you from the border of your home country?
> This applies even if you have switched off the
> mobile phone in Thailand but have activated
> your mailbox at home. In this case the call not
> taken in Thailand is sent back and can be
> charged double.

Prices • Discounts

Prices in Thailand are still very low for visitors from Europe and   Prices
North America. This is due to exchange rates and the difference in
standard of living. Public transport and services in regions off the
main tourist track, in particular, cost only a fraction of the price paid
in western countries. There is therefore no reason to be outraged if,
as is often the case, higher prices are demanded from »rich« foreigners than from the locals for goods on markets and for services in
hotels, fun parks etc. Even government institutions such as the national parks take advantage of the »two-tariff system«, which is perfectly
legal. Neither is a visit to a temple necessarily free of charge for tourists: the larger temples have fixed admission charges, and in the
small ones a donation is expected.

The Thais are commercially-minded people; fixed prices apply only   Bargaining
in modern department stores and supermarkets. Elsewhere bargaining is part of the fun of shopping.Get to know the prices, in order
not to lose face or annoy the shopkeeper by making a ridiculously
low offer. It is important to conduct even tough and lengthy negotiations with a friendly smile at all times.

HOW MUCH DOES IT COST

Basic accommodation
from £8/US$16

Simple dish
from £1.20/ US$2.40

Bottle of Thai beer
from £0.45/ US$0.90

Sleeper car Bangkok – Chiang Mai
£9/US$0.17

1 litre of petrol
from £0.30/ US$0.60

Cup of coffee
£0.35/US$0.70

Rail pass — Rail travel in Thailand is enjoyable and cheap. The Thai national rail network offers a rail pass that is valid for 20 days of travel around the kingdom. Information and booking at Hualampong railway station in Bangkok (▶Transport, Rail).

Discover Thailand — Discover Thailand is an offer by **Thai Airways**, which permits the holder to take three domestic flights within three months for a price of currently US$169. Further flights can be booked for US$69 each.

Road Traffic

Roads — Thailand has a good road network. However, only the national routes that lead from Bangkok to all parts of the country and are officially known as highways meet western standards. With the exception of some rural and mountain routes, the roads are passable even in the rainy season (June to September).

Road signs — As signposts are in both Thai and English, it is not difficult to find the way, although the spelling of place names can vary. The road signs correspond the standard international system, with a few exceptions that are easy to understand.

Speed limit — In built-up areas the speed limit is 60kmh/37mph, on country roads and highways usually 100kmh/62mph. However, few drivers observe these limits, and most drive as fast as the traffic conditions allow. There are speed checks, especially on highways and other fast roads. One thing to note: multi-lane one-way streets in Bangkok often have a bus lane on which buses can drive against the flow of one-way traffic. Do not fail to look in both directions when crossing a one-way street.

It is extremely inadvisable to tackle the confusion of Bangkok's traffic in a hired car. Even experienced drivers have problems in chaotic conditions that bear no comparison to what they are used to at home. Reduce stress and avoid accidents by taking a bus or taxi.

Outside Bangkok road traffic is much lighter, but here too drivers must take great care. It is not unusual to encounter animals, playing children and street traders on the roads – and even people asleep at the side of the road. Drive with caution: do not follow the example of the Thais. Long-distance buses are a hazard to drivers all over the country. At night they race each other along the highways and often cause serious accidents. At night large numbers of trucks travelling between the capital city and the provinces without adequate lighting or even with no lights at all are a further danger.

A trip in a three-wheeled tuk-tuk costs only half as much as by taxi.

There are said to be 16,000 taxis in Bangkok alone, not including the services of private cars driven as a second job. Taxis also play an important role in country areas. Many have air-conditioning that functions tolerably well and run on environmentally friendly liquid petroleum gas. Make sure that the taxi driver has liability insurance; this is shown by a sticker on the windscreen with the current year (note the Buddhist calendar: 2008 + 543 = 2551, for example). Taxis can be ordered from the hotel reception desk. Taxis with an officially calibrated taximeter are a recent innovation in Bangkok and other large towns. They can be recognized by the sign »taxi meter« on the roof, and are licensed and adequately insured. The price for the first 2 kilometres is 35 baht, the third kilometre costs 5 baht, the 4th to 6th cost 4.50 baht, and from the 7th kilometre the price is km 3.50 baht per km. Every minute spent motionless in a traffic jam costs 1.50 baht extra. **Taxis**

The classic means of transport in Thailand is a tuk-tuk, a three-wheeled vehicle powered by a noisy two-stroke engine. The price is negotiated before the start of the journey. If the driver demands too much, wave the next tuk-tuk over. For short distances a tuk-tuk trip is a real experience, but during daytime in Bangkok it is best to take a taxi. **Tuk-tuk**

Limousine
service

Large hotels have their own limousine service, which is available for general use. Limousine taxis are expensive but well maintained, air-conditioned and insured. The price is not open to bargaining except on long trips.

Shopping

Souvenirs

Crafts

The varied ethnic roots of the Thai people are evident in their crafts, even though much of what is sold on markets and in souvenir stores is not typical for particular sections of the population. Visitors should not buy products made from ivory (should they still be found), or the framed butterfly pictures that are often offered for sale, as they are one of the principal reasons why certain types of butterfly are threatened with extinction in Asia.

Woven fabrics from Nan province

The many different types of wood carving are mostly produced in the poorer regions of Thailand and are the work of families, who have often been carvers for generations. In place of teak, which may no longer be felled in Thailand, other types of wood are increasingly used. The difference is hardly noticeable. Earthenware jugs, vases and plates, as well as porcelain, are made in central Thailand. Good-quality leather goods are also produced. *Wood carving*

The north of the country is known for its pewter products and fabrics woven from the famous Thai silk. Painting and embroidery on silk are also done to a high standard. Many furniture producers around Chiang Mai make beautifully carved chairs, tables and cupboards, and can organize transport by ship to Europe and America. The parasols made of rice paper and painted with country scenes can be made into lampshades with a little care. The people of the hill tribes are skilled at making dolls and marionettes, which look like antiques thanks to an artificial process of ageing. When buying brass cutlery take care that the products have been carefully finished after the casting process. The women of the hill peoples make beautiful woven fabrics, mostly from cotton, and silver jewellery. *Products from the north*

Shadow puppets, cut from hard buffalo leather and painted, are typical of the south. Attractive table sets and coasters are made from the same material. *Shadow puppets*

Thailand is the land of bespoke tailors, even though the monopoly of this business seems to be in the hands of Indian Sikhs. Any item of clothing can be precisely made at a low price. It takes at least three days to make a suit, including two fitting sessions, which are definitely recommended. Excellent but expensive tailors for men and women work in many hotels, especially the large ones. The innumerable tailors' shops in the tourist resorts are at least as good. The names of the good tailors are passed round by word of mouth. *Tailors*

Samples in the shop windows provide an impression of the quality of the final products. If you have difficulties in deciding what to order, ask for a fashion magazine, as catalogues from western countries are often available. After ordering and taking measurements it is usual to ask for a deposit, which should not be more than 20% of the price.

Thailand is famous for the quality of its **silk**, which is extremely pleasant to wear. It can be recommended for men's shirts as well as for evening wear for ladies. Chinese silk is more expensive but wrinkles

? DID YOU KNOW ...?

■ ... that clothing bearing international brand-names is protected by law? Be aware of this should you get into a shopping frenzy on the markets in Thailand; otherwise, when you arrive home, attentive customs officials at the airport will be happy to inform you about the law. Home-comers have been known to have the entire contents of a suitcase confiscated for this reason.

less than Thai silk. Every good tailor has a wide range of fabrics which meet western standards in terms of quality and design.

A man's suit made of wool (jacket, waistcoat, trousers) costs about £50–100 or US$100–200 including the material, a shirt of pure silk about £15 or US$30. Ladies' clothing is more expensive, but special wishes are taken into account.

◄ Prices

Thailand is one of the world's largest exporters of textiles. The range of clothes on offer, especially in the main centres of tourism, is simply overwhelming. It includes textiles that are made in Thailand but would never be worn in a subtropical climate, such as anoraks for cold winter weather. Be careful when buying, as the information on the labels is not always accurate. Expensive cotton is sometimes mixed with artificial fibres. Statements such as »100% cotton« should therefore be viewed with suspicion.

Other fabrics

Antiques

The export of antiques is strictly controlled by the Thai government, which aims to prevent a sell-out of its cultural artefacts. The export of antique items which could be of historical interest for the country is prohibited. This applies to statues of Buddha or parts of them, whether they are originals or reproductions. The problem is that production and sale are allowed in Thailand, but export is permitted only in exceptional cases.

Export only with a permit

The export of other antiques is equally subject to state control. It takes about two weeks to process an application, as the ministry of trade has to give its consent and the export duties have to be set.

Do not on any account try to take antiques out of Thailand without a permit. Random checks are regularly carried out at the airports, and the fines for breaking the law are high. If in doubt, consult the Tourism Authority of Thailand (► Information). Reputable antique dealers know the export regulations and usually take steps to observe the formalities. If you buy genuine antiques in a neighbouring country and import them to Thailand, you must be able to present a certificate of origin.

Be careful: border controls

It is sensible to take a sceptical attitude to the authenticity of antiques. Few originals are found in the hands of dealers, who are subject to state control.

Authenticity

A certificate of authenticity can be obtained on payment of a fee from the **Fine Arts Department** (Bangkok, Na Phratat Road, by the National Museum, tel. 02 / 2 81 67 66 or 6 28 50 32; branches at the National Museum Chiang Mai, tel. 0 53 / 22 13 08 and in the National Museum Songkhla, tel. 0 74 / 31 17 28).

← *Weekend market in Bangkok*

Precious Stones

Paradise for gems

Thailand, especially the south-east, is naturally rich in precious stones, and the Thais have a reputation for being skilled goldsmiths. After Italy, Thailand is the world's second-largest producer of jewellery. The **Asian Institute of Gemmological Science** in Bangkok is an internationally recognized place of training for gem-cutters, goldsmiths and jewellery dealers from all over the world.

Purchase tips

In view of the enormous range of products on offer, it is tempting to buy precious stones in Thailand, but those without expert knowledge should confine themselves to reputable specialist stores. If you buy wonderful-looking gems from a hawker on the beach and later find that they are not genuine, you have only yourself to blame. Reputable dealers give detailed information before the sale is made and provide a certificate of authenticity. A piece of jewellery must be stamped with its content of precious metal, and if it contains gems, the carat weight must also be shown. The price is normally agreed by bargaining.

Precious stones

The stones produced in Thailand are principally sapphires in a variety of colours, deep red rubies, emeralds and a transparent green type of beryl. Diamonds occur less often. The mining of gems can be seen in, for example, **Chanthaburi** on the east coast, where jewellery and uncut stones are of course cheaper than in the tourist centres.

Jade

The main market for jade, long a popular material for jewellery, is in Hong Kong, but Chiang Mai is also a centre of jade working. Two different substances are known as jade: **nephrite** is normally dark green (like the famous jade Buddha in Wat Phra Khaeo in Bangkok), but can also be pale or medium-dark green. **Yellow jade** is a yellowish or brown type of nephrite, which takes its colour from being deposited for a long period in yellow Chinese loess. Most of the jade on the market in Thailand comes from Myanmar and is a different mineral known as jadeite. Its spectrum of colours ranges from greenish white to green, brown, red, orange, yellow, purple and black. Speckled stones, too, can often be found.

Precious metals

Pure gold is 24-carat gold; 18 carats means 18 parts of gold and six parts of other metals such as copper or silver. Silver should have at least 90% purity. Be aware that the purity of gold stated in Thailand does not always correspond to the carat weight by international standards. Always ask explicitly for the »international weight«! Gold is cheaper in Thailand than in, for example, Europe.

Markets: lively and colourful

The markets that are held every day in all parts of the country are perhaps the best places to experience the typical life of the Thais. They usually take place in the centre of towns and villages, and are

Thai markets are normally held early in the morning.

not just places to supply the population with all types of products, but also centres of communication and social life. Thai markets are a confusing jumble, with all types of goods mixed up together. Fish is sold next to toys, living animals are on offer next to plastic flowers and household goods. This is what makes the markets in Thailand so interesting, even though western visitors sometimes find the smells hard to take. Markets begin very early in the morning, usually about 6am. The traders often arrive the previous evening and spend the night at the site of the market, so that they can catch the very first customers. Most markets close again at about 10am. The Thai word for market is talaad – if you combine this word with the question »ti nai?« (where?), every Thai will gladly show you the way to the nearest market.

Sports and Outdoors

Centres for meditation are not only for the local Buddhists. Tourists **Meditation** are welcome too. It goes without saying that they are then expected to show a real interest in the teaching of Buddha. Information about places for meditation and a list of monasteries that are open to foreigners is available in Bangkok from the **World Fellowship of Buddhists**. This organization regularly organizes evenings of meditation and talks by Buddhist monks.

Information: World Fellowship of Buddhists, 616 Benjasiri Park, Soi Medhinivet, Sukhumvit 24, Bangkok 10110, tel. 02 / 661 12 84-87, fax. 02 / 661 05 55, Opening times: Mon–Fri 8am–noon.

Several meditation centres have an international reputation, including **Wat Mahathat** in Bangkok (monks speak English), **Wat Umong** and **Wat Ram Poeng** in Chiang Mai, and **Wat Suan Mok** near Surat Thani. In Surat Thani courses in meditation are held monthly in English; early booking is advisable.

Spectator Sports

Thai boxing (Muay Thai), the most popular spectator sport in Thai- **Thai boxing** land, is practised all over the country. According to legend the art of Thai boxing goes back to King Naresuen, who succeeding in gaining

! *Baedeker* TIP

See Thai boxing

Tickets for the big fights are usually sold out long in advance, but with a little luck it is sometimes possible to get hold of one. Thai boxing contests are held in Bangkok in Ratchadamnoen Stadium (Ratchadamnoen Nok Road) every Monday and Wednesday at 6pm, Thursday at 5pm and 9pm and Sunday at 4pm and 8pm. There are also fights in Lumphini Stadium (Rama IV Road) on Tuesdays and Fridays at 6pm and on Saturdays at 5pm. Visitors to Phuket can watch boxing on Tuesdays and Fridays at 8pm in Phuket Boxing Stadium.

his freedom from imprisonment at the hands of the Burmese in 1560 by defeating the best fighters. Thai boxing as it is taught today thus derives from a form of self-defence and was even taught in monasteries by the monks.

Muay Thai bears little similarity to the western form of boxing: the boxers use not only their fists, but kick their feet at all exposed parts of the opponent's body. The stomach and kidneys are favourite targets. Scratching, strangling, biting and spitting are prohibited.

Boxing fights often empty the streets. When the big fights from the National Box Stadium in Bangkok are broadcast live, the whole country is glued to the television. Tickets for these fights are greatly sought-after.

The show fights staged in tourists resorts are often quite serious contests. The events become ridiculous, however, when small boys wearing boxing gloves larger than their heads take the ring.

Takraw At takraw the players use all parts of the body except their hands to propel a woven rattan ball about 12cm/5in in diameter through the air; either through a 2.75m/9ft-high hoop into the opponents' net or – the more usual version – over a high net into the opponents' half of the field. The game lasts 40 minutes without a break. The ball is dead if it touches a player's hand or arm, or lands on the ground. Takraw is a game of great skill that is popular all over Thailand (▶ Nature, Culture, History; Traditional Sports).

Elephant polo Elephant polo has a long history and was already enjoyed by Indian kings. The elephant polo tournament in Hua Hin, which takes place every September in the beach resort Hua Hin, has become a favourite event of high society. Teams from Thailand and other countries compete one week long for a trophy donated by King Bhumibol.

Sports and Outdoor Activities

Trips in a hot-air balloon are becoming more and more popular. **Hot-air balloons**
They are on offer in all larger towns, particularly in places where
tourists are to be found. A balloon trip in the north of Thailand is
especially enjoyable.

In recent years Thailand has become a mecca for golfers. There are **Golf**
26 international-standard golf courses in the Bangkok area alone,
formerly including what was probably the world's strangest golf
course, situated between the two runways of the old Don Muang airport. Offices of the Tourism Authority of Thailand (► Information)
send on request a 90-page brochure that describes all the golf courses
in the country. For details of golf holidays in Thailand, see www.asia-
tours.net/golf/thailand.

Almost every large hotel in Thailand has tennis courts, often floodlit. **Tennis**
The equipment can be hired or bought locally.

Many operators, especially in northern Thailand, organize guided **Trekking**
trekking tours through the wonderful mountain scenery of the region. Many last several days and include a section of the journey on
the back of an elephant. Information is supplied by the local TAT office, e.g. in Chiang Mai and Chiang Rai.

Water Sports

At the beach resorts on the coasts of the Gulf of Siam, conditions are **Every concei-**
ideal for every conceivable type of water sport: surfing, sailing, snor- **vable activity**
kelling, diving, parasailing, motorboat trips and of course swimming
– and all of this at year-round water temperatures that Europeans
dream of.
Equipment is available for hire at low prices. It pays to be careful
when hiring so-called water scooters (jet skis). They are very powerful and require a certain amount of skill from the driver. Serious accidents occur repeatedly, usually as a result of inexperience in hand-
ling the machine or irresponsible
behaviour. Sometimes the machines are in poor condition, and
users are held responsible for damage that they did not cause. Follow the instructions given by the
hire company and use the machines only in the areas permitted.

The Gulf of Siam and the coasts of
the Andaman Sea are ideal for **sailing**. Island-hopping is a popular

! **Baedeker TIP**

Chartering a Boat

To charter a boat, an international sailing licence
must be presented. An alternative is to charter a
boat with a complete crew or at least an
experienced skipper who knows the waters. See
the information provided by TAT offices or local
operators.

Slow-growing treasures:
corals in the Andaman Sea

PARADISE FOR DIVERS

A coastline fully 1,600 miles long, a myriad small and tiny islands fringed with beaches of snow-white coral sand, and tourist facilities of a standard that is easily high enough to please even spoiled visitors: all excellent reasons to go diving in Thailand.

It is true that the underwater world is not intact as it once was. It is also true that the enigmatic climatic phenomenon known as El Niño, a sudden warm-water current that appeared on many of the world's coasts in 1998, has caused lasting damage to the coral reefs of Thailand, too – in contrast to the tsunami, which did astonishingly little harm to the reefs even though it hit the Thai coast with enormous force. Despite all damage, the underwater world that remains is truly impressive in places such as the diving waters of Ang Thong Marine National Park, about 40km/25mi north-west of Ko Samui. Around 40 islands belong to this protected area, which was created in time to prevent the marine environment from deteriorating. To put the problem in simple terms: certain types of coral grow no more than two or three millimetres per year, which means that a single kick from a careless diver suffices to destroy a beautiful, centuries-old work of nature. The Thais themselves bear considerable responsibility for the destruction, for example through the formerly widespread practice of fishing with dynamite. The results can be seen most clearly on the east coast of Thailand, where the boom in tourism began first, and where the seas were positively plundered for many years.

Diving Areas

The islands of Ko Larn, Ko Sak and Ko Khrok off Pattaya, with diving to a depth of 20m/65ft, are well known. The small islands of Ko Klung Badan, Ko Man Wichai and Ko Rin are further away. Around Ko Sichang near Si Racha, it is possible to dive to a depth of 40m/130ft and to explore wrecks. The islands Ko Samae San near Sattahip and Ko Chang near Trat have also been popular amongst divers for some time. On the opposite side of the Gulf of Siam and in the Andaman Sea, by contrast, there are still many excellent diving areas. North-west of Phuket is the small and wonderful Similan group of islands, named after Ko Similan at the northern end. Favourite spots here, where divers regularly encounter large

fish such as sharks and rays, include Christmas Point and Breakfast Bend off Ko Bangru and Fantasy Reef. The island of Ko Tachai with the legendary diving area at Richelieu Rock is also a rewarding destination. To the south of Phuket, the best places are Ko Phi Phi Lay and Ko Phi Phi Don, off Ko Lanta Noi and Ko Yao Tal. Shark Point, an interesting underwater reef used by leopard sharks and sting rays as a place to sleep, is close to Ko Dok Mai. The islands around Ko Tarutao, close the border with Malaysia, are also recommended for diving. There are hardly any true insider tips left to be discovered – and if divers hit upon such a secret, they tend to keep it to themselves or at most pass it on discreetly to a few others.

Diving Schools

It is only natural that most diving schools have set up in Thailand's centres of tourism, such as the islands Ko Samui, Ko Phi Phi and Phuket, or in coastal resorts such as Pattaya. From here they make diving excursions to the offshore islands; however, in order to offer the course members a real experience, the distances from port are becoming longer and longer. There are now genuine diving safaris, during which the boats are at sea for several days at a time. The best time of year for exploring the underwater world is between mid-February and early November. In this season visibility under water is at its best, and the peak tourist season, which attracts many thousands of visitors to the beaches of Thailand during other months, is over. However, during the rainy season the sea can be so rough that no Thai skipper will take his boat out. Almost all proprietors of diving schools have a good reputation as far as the quality of their equipment is concerned, as black sheep do not normally stay in business for longer than a single season. Nevertheless, anyone attending a diving school should take a careful look at the equipment: a rusted air cylinder or a rotting diving regulator are alarm signals for every safety-conscious diver. It can be assumed that diving schools offering courses according to international standards (PADI, NAUI or SSI) keep their equipment in good condition. English-speaking instructors and guides are common.

pastime. Boats can put down anchor almost anywhere; restrictions apply mainly to the islands which have been declared national parks. The most beautiful waters for sailing include the islands of **Ko Phi Phi**, **Ko Tarutao** and **Ko Similan**, and there are attractive areas on the east coast near Pattaya. It is essential to have reliable navigation charts which contain details about dangerous shallows and the treacherous currents that occur in the monsoon season. Reputable boat-charter companies provide suitable charts when handing over the ship. It is important to check that the safety equipment on board is complete and in working order. Tourism Authority Thailand has a brochure entitled **Thailand's Marine Wonderland** that contains many useful tips and addresses for sailors (► Infɑrmation).

Every December since 1987 a sailing regatta, the **Phuket King's Cup**, has been held in Phuket to mark the birthday of King Bhumibol. It is attracting more and more international entrants.

Diving   The coast, particularly the outlying islands, is a divers' paradise, even though irresponsible behaviour has destroyed much of the underwater nature. The Thai government has passed restrictive legislation to protect the marine environment, which should be observed. It is

Diving lesson on Khao Lak

strictly forbidden to plunder the coral reefs. Random checks are made on returning boats. Harpooning is also not allowed. There are many **diving schools**. When booking a course, ensure that the teachers possess an international training licence. This particularly applies to beginners who want to acquire a certificate. Only three organizations issue certificates that are acknowledged worldwide: PADI (Professional Association of Diving Instructors), NAUI (National Association of Underwater Instructors) and SSI (Scuba Schools International). It is normally possible to hire diving equipment. Care is needed here: operators not certified by the above organizations sometimes hire out badly maintained equipment that is not fit for use.

Thailand offers many opportunities for fishing. Official permits are not needed. At the beach resorts there are many providers of fishing trips, including ocean fishing for tuna, blue marlin and other large catches. The equipment is provided.

Many owners of boats in Pattaya und Phuket and on the islands in the Gulf of Siam organize trips for ocean fishing, sometimes even with a guarantee of success. With a bit of luck, anglers can catch sharks, rays, tuna, swordfish, pollack, sea perch and mackerel. The best months are January to May. On return to port a big prize can be prepared as a trophy; this takes some days, or even weeks.

Fishing

Time and Date

The time difference to Greenwich Mean Time is seven hours (MEZ + 7 hr). Clocks are not changed for summer time in Thailand.

Time zone

The lunar calendar dictates many traditional and religious festivals, but for other purposes the western calendar is used. On ferry and flight schedule, Monday is the first day of the week.

Lunar calendar

The years, however, are numbered on a different system than in western countries: the year 0 is 543 BC, when Buddha is said to have entered nirvana. 2008 is thus in Thailand the year 2551.

Date: the year

The traditional division of the day into four parts of six hours each, and the use of a number of special expressions for these periods, can also cause misunderstandings. To be on the safe side, state times exactly. »Chao« means »sometime between 6am and 11am«; »klang wan« is noon. »Bai mong« means 1pm, »bai song« 2pm etc. When it becomes cooler in the evening, Thais like to use the word »yen«, which is combined with numbers to denote the time after 6pm. From 10pm the time is stated with »kyn«: midnight is »klang kyn«.

Times of day

Transport

Domestic Flights

Network
The flight network, which is mainly served by the Thai national carrier **Thai Airways International**, is comprehensive. There are flights at least once per day to all domestic airports. The private airline **Bangkok Airways** flies to a number of destinations, and **Air Asia**, a cheap operator with tickets costing up to 50% less than its competitors, has flights to Chiang Mai, Chiang Rai, Hat Yai, Krabi, Narathiwat, Phuket, Ubon Ratchathani and Udon Thani. A further low-cost airline, **Nok Air**, serves Chiang Mai, Udon Thani, Phuket, Hat Yai, Nakhon Si Thammarat and Trang. On domestic routes to the north and south, **Orient Thai** also offers attractive prices. **Phuket Air** is a small outfit flying to only two airports.

Airport duty
On checking in, every passenger must pay airport duty, currently amounting to 500 baht in cash, for connecting and return flights. This duty in included in the ticket price for inland flights; passengers to Ko Samui pay a fee of 300 baht. Airport duty is often included in the price of package holidays.

► AIRLINES FOR DOMESTIC FLIGHTS

► **Air Asia**
www.airasia.com

► **Orient Thai**
www.orient-thai.com

► **Bangkok Airways**
www.bangkokair.com

► **Phuket Air**
www.phuketairlines.com

► **Nok Air**
www.nokair.com

► **Thai Airways**
www.thaiair.com

Rail

Tickets
Fares on the Thai state railways (SRT) are very low. For example, the journey from Bangkok to Chiang Mai costs about £20/US$40 first class (supplement for sleeping car about £10/US$20), from Bangkok to Sungai Kolok around £25/US$50 (supplement for private compartment first class in the sleeping car about £12/US$24). Couchettes cost about half as much. Supplements have to be paid for express trains. Children from three to twelve years of age pay half price ► map p.175.

Air and Rail Connections

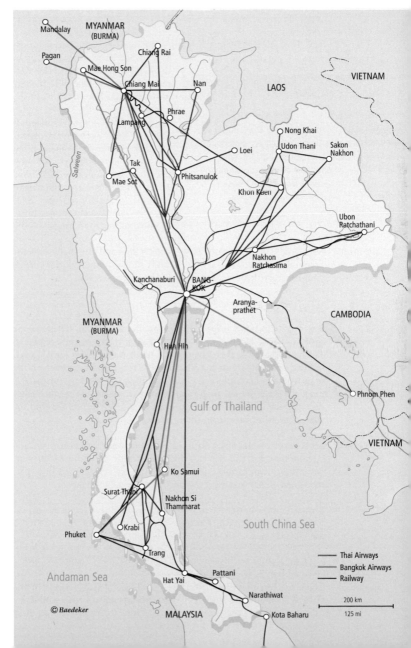

Tickets can be purchased 90 days before the journey at the earliest. It is not allowed to break the journey.

Special Excursions The Thai state railway company organizes frequent special excursions. A popular day trip from Bangkok to Kanchanaburi takes in the River Kwai Bridge and the infamous **»railway of death«** to the terminus at Nam Tok.

All railway stations have information and booking counters (opening times: Mon–Fri 8.30am–6pm, Sat, Sun and holidays 8.30am–noon). To get an impression online of the different routes, stations and schedules available, see www.asia-discovery.com/thailand/trains.htm or www.railway.co.th/Eng/.

! *Baedeker* TIP

Thailand by rail

A good way of getting to know Thailand by rail is to buy the Visit Thailand Rail Pass. Holders are entitled to unlimited rail travel on the whole network for 20 days at a cost of approximately £70/US$140 in second class. The rail pass is for sale only at the main Bangkok station in Hualampong.

Night trains Night trains on all routes have sleeping cars and couchette cars for first and second class (be sure to book in good time). If you change your itinerary or times, new reservations are necessary.

Bus

Most important means of transport Buses are the most important means of transport in Thailand for short and long distances. The connect even the most remote places. They also represent the cheapest way to see the country and to get to know the hospitality of the Thai people. The state bus service on the main routes is complemented by countless private bus companies. Only the state-owned operations run to a reasonable reliable schedule; private companies run buses as required. Their buses stop for passengers who wave from the roadside.

Bus lines Most government buses on fixed routes (rotmee tamadaa) have air-conditioning for the driver, which cools only the front of the bus. For a more comfortable journey, take an air-conditioned bus (rotmee düen). They are more expensive but usually faster.

Tickets Tickets can be bought from bus stations or direct from the driver. Fares are very low (e.g. Bangkok–Chiang Mai, about 700km/430mi, for £7/US$13).

Ferries

Cheap island connection There are ferry services from the mainland to most islands in the Gulf of Siam and the Andaman Sea. They operate all year, with some exceptions during the monsoon season (June to September), as there are then dangerous currents and high waves at times. Some ferries, especially those run by private operators, do not leave until enough passengers have come on board.

Fares are very low and normally no reductions, e.g. for children, apply. Bookings are not taken for local ferries.

Fares and booking

 ## BUS TERMINALS AND FERRIES

BUS TERMINALS

► BANGKOK
Southern Bus Terminal (Dai)
Pinklao-Nakhonchaisi Road
Tel. 02 / 4 34 55 57
Air-con buses: tel. 02 / 4 35 11 99
Buses to Hua Hin, Nakhon Si Thammarat, Surat Thani and Phuket

Northern Bus Terminal (Nya)
Phaholyothin Road
Tel. 02 / 2 71 01 01-5
Air-con buses: tel. 02 / 2 79 44 84-7
Buses to Chiang Mai, Sukhothai, Phitsanulok, Ubon Ratchathani

Eastern Bus Terminal (Ekamai)
Sukhumvit Road
Tel. 02 / 3 91 25 04
Buses to Pattaya, Rayong (then ferry to Ko Samet), Chanthaburi

► CHIANG MAI
Arcade Station
Kaeo Nawarat Road
Air-con buses: tel. 0 53 / 24 26 64
Buses to Bangkok, Chiang Rai, Lampang, Phrae, Nan, Sukhothai, Nakhon Ratchasima

Chuang Puak
Chotana Road
Air-con buses: tel. 0 53 / 21 15 86
Buses to Fang, Hot, Lamphun, Thaton

► HUA HIN
Edge of the town on the Bangkok road
Buses to Bangkok, Nakhon, Si Thammarat, Phuket, Surat Thani, Trat

► NAKHON RATCHASIMA
Bus Terminal 1
Burin Road
Buses to Bangkok, Pak Chong (Khao Yai national park), Surin

Bus Terminal 2
Northern edge of the town
Buses to Chiang Mai, Sukhothai, Phitsanulok, Lampang and Lamphun

► NAKHON SI THAMMARAT
About 1km/0.5mi south of the railway station on route 4015 (pool taxi to the town centre).
Buses to Bangkok, Surat Thani, Phattalung, Songkhla, Phuket

► PATTAYA
Beach Road (between south and north Pattaya)
Buses to Bangkok, Rayong (ferry to Ko Samet), Chanthaburi, Laem Ngob (ferry to Ko Chang), Trat

► PHUKET
Phuket Road
Buses to Bangkok, Surat Thani, Nakhon Si Thammarat, Sungai

Kolok (border crossing to Malaysia), Krabi and Phangnga

► **SURAT THANI**
At Ban Don harbour
Buses to Bangkok, Phuket,
to the ferry for Ko Samui, Ranong,
Phangnga, Prachuap Khiri Khan,
Nakhon Si Thammarat, Ubon
Ratchathani

► **UBON RATCHATHANI**
4km/2.5mi north of the town
(pool taxi to the town centre)
Buses to Bangkok, Mukdahan,
Nakhon Phanom, Nakhon
Ratchasima, Buriram, Surin

FERRIES

► **Hat Yai – Ko Tarutao**
Daily; duration: 2 hr

► **Ko Samui – Ko Ang Thong**
Daily; duration: 1¼ hr

► **Ko Samui – Ko Phangan**
Daily; duration: ¾ hr

► **Krabi – Ko Lanta**
Daily (midday); duration: 3 hr

► **Krabi – Ko Phi Phi**
Daily; duration: 1¼ – 3 hr

► **Laem Ngob – Ko Chang**
Daily (midday); duration: 1 hr

► **Pattaya – Ko Larn**
Daily; duration: ¾ hr

► **Pattaya – Ko Khrok**
Daily; duration: 1 hr

► **Pattaya – Ko Sak**
Daily; duration: 1½ hr

► **Phuket – Ko Phi Phi**
Daily; duration: 1¾ hr

► **Rayong (Ban Phe) – Ko Samet**
Daily; duration: 1½ hr

► **Si Racha – Ko Sichang**
Daily; duration: ½ hr

Car Hire

For calm drivers A journey through Thailand by car can be extremely pleasurable, but only if some pieces of advice are followed. Do not plan to cover more than about 300km/200mi per day, ideally not more than 200km/125mi, in order to have time to appreciate the beauty of the scenery and not to miss cultural highlights that are not directly on the route. Road traffic drives on the left in Thailand. The Asian style of driving and road conditions demand the undivided attention of the driver – and a calm attitude! Those of a nervous disposition should hire a chauffeur; this is less expensive than you would expect, and the Thai drivers have experience of local traffic conditions.

If you hire in Bangkok, collect it from a pick-up point at the edge of the city to avoid driving through the chaotic city traffic. It is relatively inexpensive to rent a minibus with driver. In this way groups of up to eight persons can plan an individual itinerary.

Driving licence Officially an international driving licence must be presented, but most hire companies accept a national driving licence.

⏵ CAR HIRE COMPANIES

▶ **Avis Bangkok**
2/12 Wireless Road,
Bangkok downtown
Tel. 02 / 22 55 53 00-4
Also based in Cha-Am, Chiang
Mai, Chiang Rai, Hat Yai, Hua
Hin, Khon Khaen, Ko Samui,
Krabi, Pattaya, Phuket, Phitsanu-
lok and Udon Thani

▶ **Hertz Bangkok**
87 Wireless Road
Bangkok Downtown
Floor M, Thai Tower
Tel. 02 / 6 54 11 05
Fax 6 54 11 10
Also based in Chiang Mai, Ko
Samui, Pattaya and Phuket

International companies such as Avis und Hertz are represented in Thailand. Their vehicles are in a good and safe condition. There are also numerous regional hire firms, whose vehicles should be inspected to check for damage and whether they are in a safe condition. Ensure that the insurance cover is adequate. The costs of hire are low, but it is highly advisable to take out full insurance cover for damage to the car and accidents. — *Car hire companies*

Those who hire a powerful motorbike in Thailand do so at their peril. They are not normally maintained in such a way as to be safe, and it is easy to misread the road conditions as, for example, the type of road surface can change unexpectedly. For some years now there has been a very high number of serious accidents. The small motorbikes and mopeds that can be hired in Thailand are usually reliable. Note that helmets must be worn on all motorized bikes, mopeds and scooters. — *Motorbikes*

Travellers with Disabilities

The Tourism Authority of Thailand (TAT) (▶ Information) provides information for persons with disabilities who are planning a trip to the country. Some tour operators in Thailand have specialized in organizing trips for people with special needs. The international hotels generally have facilities for guests with disabilities, but getting around can be difficult, as public transport systems are not equipped for passengers with mobility problems. Bangkok is particularly difficult with its high kerbs and busy streets, some of which can only be crossed using bridges. On the positive side, the Thais are extremely helpful, and there is normally access for persons in wheelchairs to the most important sights, such as temples and museums, as well as to most restaurants and bars.

ADDRESSES: DISABILITY ORGANIZATIONS

UNITED KINGDOM

▶ **RADAR**
12 City Forum, 250 City Road,
London EC1V 8AF
Tel. (020) 72 50 32 22
www.radar.org.uk

USA

▶ **SATH (Society for Accessible Travel and Hospitality)**
347 5th Ave, no. 610
New York, NY 10016:
Tel. (21) 4 47 72 84
www.sath.org

Weights, Measures, Temperatures

Linear measures	1 inch (in;) = 2.54 cm	1 mm = 0.03937 in
	1 foot (ft;) = 12 in = 30.48 cm	1 cm = 0.033 ft
	1 yard (yd;) = 3 ft = 91.44 cm	1 m = 1.09 yd
	1 mile (mi;) = 1.61 km	1 km = 0.62 mi

Square measures	1 square inch (in²) = 6.45 cm²	1 cm² = 0.155 in²
	1 square foot (ft²) = 9.288 dm²	1 dm² = 0.108 ft²
	1 square yard (yd²) = 0.836 m²	1 m² = 1.196 yd²
	1 square mile (mi²) = 2.589 km²	1 km² = 0.386 mi²
	1 acre = 0.405 ha	1 ha = 2.471 acres

Cubic measures	1 cubic inch (in³) = 16.386 cm³	1 cm³ = 0.061 in³
	1 cubic foot (ft³) = 28.32 dm³	1 dm³ = 0.035 ft³
	1 cubic yard (yd³) = 0.765 m³	1 m³ = 1.308 yd³

Liquid measure	1 gill = 0.118 l	1 l = 8.747 gills
	1 pint (pt) = 4 gills = 0.473 l	1 l = 2.114 pt
	1 quart (qt) = 2 pt = 0.946 l	1 l = 1.057 qt
	1 gallon (gal) = 4 qt = 3.787 l	1 l = 0.264 gal

Weights	1 ounce (oz;) = 28.365 g	100 g = 2.527 oz
	1 pound (lb;) = 453.59 g	1 kg = 2.206 lb
	1 cental (cwt;.) = 45.359 kg	100 kg = 2.205 cwt

Temperature

Fahrenheit:	0	10	20	32	50	68	89	95
Celsius:	-18	-12	-6.5	0	10	20	30	35

Conversion:
Fahrenheit = 1.8 x Celsius + 32   Celsius = $\underline{5 \, (Fahrenheit - 32)}$

Men's clothing

For men's suits, coats and shirts measurements are identical in the UK and the USA.

Men's shoes:

UK	7	8	9	10	11
US	8	9	10	11	12

Women's clothing: **Women's shoes:**

UK	8	10	12	14	16	18	3	4	5	6	7	8
US	6	8	10	12	14	16	5.5	6.5	7.5	8.5	9.5	10.5

Children's sizes:

UK	3-4 yrs	4-5 yrs	5-6 yrs	6-7 yrs	7-8 yrs
US	3	4	5	6	6X

When to Go

November to mid-February is the best season for people who come from countries with a temperate climate. The weather is then at its coolest (25 30°C/77–86°F), and the humidity is relatively low (65–70%), but prices are at their highest.

For the Thais the main holiday season, and the only time for swimming on the beaches, is from March to the end of May, the period of the school holidays. At this time of year Europeans find Bangkok unbearably humid (95%) and hot, with temperatures exceeding 35°C/95°F. However, the large number of festivals makes this period especially interesting for those who want to discover Thai culture. The period from June until early August is suitable for trips to the south (Malay peninsula). It can be relatively cool in the morning and evening, but when the sun comes out, the temperature reaches 25°C. There are about ten days of rain per month at this time of year.

Mid-August to the end of October is a season worth considering for a trip to Thailand. Flooding may occur at times, but at no other season is the country so green and full of flowers. This is a good time to see the north-east, a culturally interesting region that is not normally attractive in terms of vegetation. It is not necessary to book hotels in advance during this period, as it is in the main season, and low-cost accommodation is available everywhere. It is no longer humid and it rains only once a day, at least in central Thailand, the region around Bangkok: usually in late afternoon for 30 to 50 minutes.

Tours

SHORT TOURS TO GIVE VARIETY TO BEACH HOLIDAYS IN THE SOUTH, LONG EXCURSIONS TO THE EASTERN BORDERS OR THE MOUNTAINS OF THE NORTH: THE MOST BEAUTIFUL PARTS OF THAILAND AND A FEW TIPS ON ORGANIZING YOUR HOLIDAY.

TOURS IN THAILAND

Travellers in Thailand have plenty of options when it comes to shaping their plans according to their own interests within the time available. Relaxation seekers will find a paradise of their own on the beautiful beaches of the south, culture enthusiasts can roam from temple to temple on the trail of the Khmer, and those who like to add cultural spice to their trekking holiday may be tempted by the splendid walks in the far north with the fabulous natural landscape and indigenous hill tribes of the »Golden Triangle«.

TOUR 1   Circuit of north-east Thailand
A tour taking in some of the fabulous cultural highlights in the north-east of the country, a region still unspoiled by tourist development. ► **page 176**

TOUR 2   From Bangkok to Chiang Mai
A tour for holidaymakers with an enthusiasm for art and culture, taking in almost all of Thailand's top cultural attractions. ► **page 179**

TOUR 3   From Chiang Mai to the »Golden Triangle«
Tours though the mountains of the famous »Golden Triangle«, passing through broad poppy fields and magnificent wilderness to the lands of the hill tribes and the national parks near the border. ► **page 182**

TOUR 4   From Bangkok to Phuket
Hugging the coast south to the tropical paradise of beaches on the Andaman Sea. ► **page 183**

TOUR 5   From Pattaya to Trat
Just a short trip along the coast of east Thailand to add a little variety to your beach holiday. ► **page 186**

Country around Chiang Mai
Luxuriant greenery with its own special charm

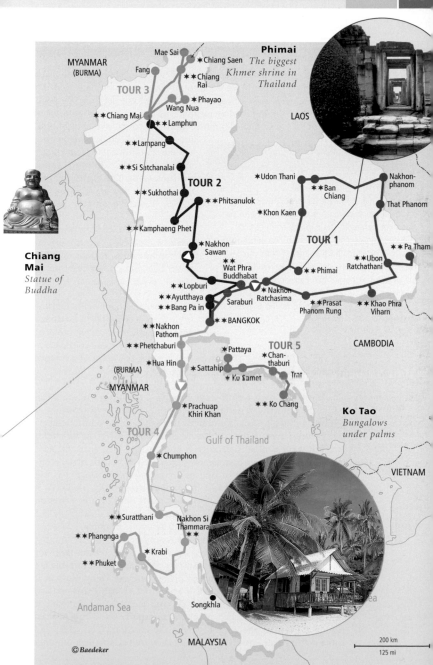

Phimai
The biggest Khmer shrine in Thailand

MYANMAR (BURMA)

Mae Sai
★ Chiang Saen
Fang
★★ Chiang Rai

TOUR 3

★ Phayao
Wang Nua
★★ Chiang Mai
★★ Lamphun

LAOS

★★ Lampang

Chiang Mai
Statue of Buddha

★★ Si Satchanalai

★ Udon Thani
★★ Ban Chiang
Nakhon-phanom
That Phanom

TOUR 2

★★ Sukhothai
★★ Phitsanulok
Khon Kaen

TOUR 1

★★ Pa Tham
★★ Kamphaeng Phet
★★ Ubon Ratchathani

★ Nakhon Sawan
★★ Wat Phra Buddhabat
★ Phimai

★★ Lopburi
★★ Ayutthaya
★★ Bang Pa in
Saraburi
Nakhon Ratchasima
★★ Prasat Phanom Rung
★★ Khao Phra Viharn

★★ BANGKOK

CAMBODIA

★★ Nakhon Pathom
★★ Phetchaburi
★ Hua Hin

TOUR 5

★ Pattaya
★ Chan-thaburi
★ Sattahip
★ Ko Samet
Trat

(BURMA)
MYANMAR

★★ Ko Chang

Ko Tao
Bungalows under palms

★ Prachuap Khiri Khan

TOUR 4

Gulf of Thailand

★ Chumphon

VIETNAM

★★ Suratthani
Nakhon Si Thammarat ★★

★★ Phangnga
★ Krabi
★★ Phuket

Andaman Sea

Songkhla

MALAYSIA

© Baedeker

200 km
125 mi

Travelling in Thailand

No place for speeding Even though there is an extensive road network, Thailand is no place for driving at speed. It would certainly be a waste to hurry past the myriad sights that are often to be discovered not far from the main roads. When driving in the country it is best to aim for an average speed of no more than 40kmh/25mph and to allow plenty of time for sightseeing stops. This applies to the good-quality main roads and even more so to journeys on the back roads. There, buses or lorries and such can be annoying obstacles. Particular care is needed during the rainy season, when back roads and dirt tracks can often become impassable. For driving in the mountainous regions of northern Thailand, it may be better to rent a vehicle suitable for off-road driving.

Since only the main roads are properly lit, it is advisable to avoid **driving at night**. One other problem that might cause some confusion is the variety of spellings for towns and villages, the result of a creative attitude on the part of the sign writers.

! Baedeker TIP

Day trip to Kanchanaburi

Kanchanaburi is the site of the famous »Bridge on the River Kwai« and is within range of a day trip from Bangkok. The experience ought to include the two-hour journey on the notorious Death Railway to the terminus at Nam Tok. Unfortunately, it is only possible to remain there a few minutes before the train departs again. A journey to Nam Tok on Route 323 allows time for the worthwhile two-hour walk to the Erawan Waterfall.

The right means of transport Thailand lends itself well to exploration via **rental car**. All the internationally known car rental companies have their own branches at airports and major hotels. Some of them even offer vehicle reservation before arrival in the country or chauffeur hire. Prices are attractive, but it is essential to arrange comprehensive insurance and accident insurance for all passengers. Care is required with rental companies that are not part of one of the major chains, since it is not unusual for their vehicles to be in less than roadworthy condition. It is not difficult to get used to Thailand's roads, where traffic drives **on the left**. It is advisable, though, to start off slowly and definitely not to take the driving habits of the natives as a good example.

Traffic inspections and radar traps are common all over the country. Speeding can be very expensive, since there is no official tariff for fines, which can be somewhat arbitrary. **Mopeds** and **motorbikes** are often rented out too. Even though helmets are not compulsory, it is vital to wear one. Many back roads are surfaced with gravel and can present a serious accident hazard. Of course, almost all destinations in Thailand can be reached by **public transport**. Buses run to fixed routes and link all the large towns in the kingdom. Timetables and route maps are also available for the major routes, although on other

In the grounds of Wat Umong in Chiang Mai

journeys, bus drivers, especially in the country, may only set out when they feel there are sufficient passengers on board. It is also interesting to travel by rail. Trains are comfortable, with the chance to make contact with the Thais as an added bonus.

The Thai landscape is extremely varied and has an almost astonishing diversity. There are beautiful stretches of scenery in every part of the country, in the northern uplands, for example, where there seem to be more hairpin bends than straight stretches of road, but the reward lies in the multitude of superb views over exquisite landscape. The roads in central Thailand are rather less scenic, the area being dominated by commercial agriculture. In the arid north-east, though, any visitor interested in archaeology can discover a host of treasures. The region boasts innumerable ruins of ancient Khmer temples, bearing witness to a glorious history that reaches back a thousand years. One journey not to be missed in the south is the route between Ta Kuapa and Phang Nga, where endless forests of rubber trees are punctuated by startling limestone peaks.

The most attractive routes

 Toll

■ At present the only toll roads are in the Bangkok area, where many expressways were built privately. There are cashiers at the tollbooths. Pay in cash and have the exact amount ready.

Tour 1 Circuit of north-east Thailand

Length of tour: 2,100–2,600km approx. (1,300–1,600 mi)
Finish: Bangkok

Duration: 8–9 days
Start: Bangkok

This tour explores the north-east of Thailand, a region that remains largely untouched by tourism. The quality of accommodation in the area may not always match up to that in areas more frequented by tourists, but what you do get is an authentic impression of the wonderfully exotic lifestyle in the many towns and villages along the road.

Leaving ❶ ✳ ✳ **Bangkok** and heading northwards on Route 1, drive past Ayutthaya towards ❷ **Saraburi**. From there, transfer to Route 2 in the direction of Nakhon Ratchasima. Initially the landscape is dominated by rice fields which then give way to the typically austere scenery of the north-east. The popular pilgrimage destination of Wat Phra Buddhachai 7km/4.5mi before Saraburi is another worthwhile attraction.

From Saraburi it is worth making a detour 32km/20mi north on Route 1 to ❸ ✳ ✳ **Wat Phra Buddhabat**, the famous temple with the one »authentic« footprint of Buddha in Thailand. About half way to Wat Phra Buddhabat is the cave temple Wat Tham Si Wilai with its magnificent vaulted roof.

Before carrying on to Khon Kaen, an early-morning visit to ❹ ✳ **Nakhon Ratchasima** is recommended. There are not too many attractions to visit on this day apart from one very important diversion to Phimai, but attentive observers will still find plenty to see. Leave Nakhon Ratchasima on Route 2 heading north-east. 4km/2.5mi outside the town is the Khmer temple of Wat Prasat Phanom Wan. The journey continues through a variety of small settlements and some larger towns that demonstrate the bustling life typical all over Thailand.

After 36km/22mi a right turn off Route 2 leads to the notable Khmer temple complex of ❺ ✳ ✳ **Phimai,** where a tremendous restoration effort was made some years ago. ❻ ✳ **Khon Kaen** itself provides few sightseeing highlights. A visit to the National Museum on the mor-

> ! **Baedeker** TIP
>
> **Day trip to Ayutthaya**
> If time is too short for touring in the remote regions of Thailand, it pays to plan at least one day in ►Ayutthaya. Until it was destroyed by the Burmese, Ayutthaya was the capital of the kingdom of Siam and was said to be the most beautiful city in the world. Nowadays, the vast field of ruins is a UNESCO world heritage site and certainly worth a visit even for travellers in a hurry. Ayutthaya can be reached by bus from Bangkok in about two hours.

Rice cultivation ...
... is hard work

Bangkok
*Kinnari in
Wat Phra Kaeo*

Khao Phra Viharn
*Khmer shrine across the
border in Cambodia*

ning of the next day is a must, however (particularly in preparation
for a visit to Ban Chiang on day 4). The museum houses numerous
artefacts from the early history of Thailand, including much pottery
and a grave that was excavated in Ban Chiang.

The short leg from Khon Kaen to ❼ ✳ **Udon Thani** (north on Route
2) is an opportunity to view the scenery or stop off somewhere along
the way to visit a market or one of the many, often simple but generally attractive temple complexes. In order to allow sufficient time
for a visit to Ban Chiang, leave Udon Thani early in the morning (on
Route 22 heading east). ❽ ✳✳ **Ban Chiang** was the site of a sensational archaeological find of pottery and bronze in 1967. It lies 46km/
29mi to the east of Udon Thani. The site itself is signposted from
Route 22 (6km/4mi); the National Museum is 1km/0.5mi from the
site.

Shortly before the village of Ban That Naweng (about 70km/44mi
from Udon Thani) an unpaved road leads from the experimental sta-

tion for rice cultivation to a fascinating Khmer shrine with marvellous sculptures on the door lintels. Continue along Route 22 and turn off to the north-east shortly before Sakhon Nakhon and the Nong Han reservoir to reach **❾ Nakhon Phanom** by evening. The town lies on the Mekong river, which is the border with Laos at this point.

45km/28mi south of Nakhon Phanom on Route 212 is the small town of **❿ That Phanom** with the Buddhist shrine of Phra That Phanom built in Lao style. The river bank opposite the temple is the site of a lively market. About 42km/26mi further in Mukdahan, there are two notable temple complexes built by Vietnamese refugees.

Route 212, which so far has led along the banks of the Mekong from Nakhon Phanom to Mukdahan, now leaves the river. The only sight on the route to the day's destination of **⓫ ✶ ✶ Ubon Ratchathani** is Wat Phra Mongkol in Amnat Charoen with its enormous figure of the Buddha amidst a grove of shady trees. The provincial capital of Ubon Ratchathani is best seen in the early morning and its crowded market, as well several temples, may be of interest. The area around the town is so charming that it is worth spending an entire day there only to return in the evening to the »Royal City of the Lotus Blossom«, the literal translation of Ubon Ratchathani.

i **Drinking water**

■ Care needs to be taken in the more remote parts of Thailand. Even in hotels the water is not necessarily drinkable. Where possible, always drink bottled water.

The next stage takes Route 217 to the east, changing onto road number 2222 beyond Phibun Mangsahan for another 43km/27mi as far as Wat Phokhaokaeo, where there is a very pretty temple made of red clay tiles. On the way to **⓬ Pa Tham** after 7km/4.5mi is the rock outcrop of Sao Chaliang, which has been declared a natural monument. The prehistoric cave paintings of Pa Tham, 12km/7.5mi further along the road, are a further major sight. The town possesses a magnificent view across the Mekong towards Cambodia.

If the political situation allows (obtain information from the TAT bureau in Bangkok or at the latest in Ubon Ratchathani), try to visit the Khmer temple **⓭ ✶ ✶ Khao Phra Viharn**, which is situated across the border in Cambodia and has only been accessible (solely from Thailand) since February 1992. The route does pass close by again on the return to Bangkok but the ideal timing of the journey will not permit a visit (although there may be acceptable overnight accommodation in Surin). The temple can be reached by heading southwest along the local route numbered 2178 that meets Route 221 at Kantharalak.

The penultimate leg of the circuit is rather long but contains two important sights. To ensure sufficient time to see them, an early start will be needed. Starting from Ubon Ratchathani take Route 24 in a south-westerly direction. The road then turns westward. After about 260km/162mi it passes through Prakhon Chai in the province of Buriram. Around 14km/9mi south of Prakhon Chai is the small village of Ban Tako, where a sign indicates the way to Wat ⑭ **✶✶ Prasat Phanom Rung** on a summit 158m/520ft above sea level. One more attraction is at Wat Prasat Muang Tam, another 8km/5mi down the valley. The principal sight there is the extremely imposing main shrine. Returning to Route 24 and after another 130km/81mi, the leg ends at the destination of day two, Nakhon Ratchasima.

On the way back to Bangkok, it is worth taking the opportunity to see ⑮ **✶✶ Ayutthaya**. Arrival there by early afternoon leaves plenty of time to cover the last 60km/37mi to❶ **✶✶ Bangkok**

Tour 2 Bangkok to Chiang Mai

Length of tour : 1,000km/620mi approx.
Finish: Chiang Mai

Duration: 8 days
Start: Bangkok

Thailand's most magnificent cultural monuments are strung almost like pearls on a string along the route from Bangkok to Chiang Mai. To leave enough time to see them all, this route has been planned to limit the driving on any given day to little more than 200 kilometres (125mi).

From Chiang Mai it is probably best to return to Bangkok by plane. Some rental companies offer the option of dropping off rented vehicles in Chiang Mai.

Return journey

Leave ❶ **✶✶ Bangkok** going northward (on Route 1 then Route 32) early in the morning to reach ❷ **✶✶ Ayutthaya** after 76km/47mi. Allow plenty of time to explore the unique ruins at the site. From Ayutthaya continue via Saraburi , stopping off to visit ❸ **✶✶ Wat Phra Buddhabat** before carrying on to ❹ **✶✶ Lobpuri**. If there is not enough time to visit the royal palace and other sights there, then do so on the following morning, since the next leg of the journey to Nakhon Sawan features only one temple visit at Chainat.

Leaving Lopburi, take the road to Singburi, then turn on to Route 311 to Chainat (85km/53mi; near Sanburi). One key sight to take in

Crafts in Chiang Mai

on the short visit there is Wat Thammamun with its statue of the Buddha dating back to the Ayutthaya era. Afterwards, continue along Route 311 via Uthai Thani to the final destination for the day at ❺ ✳ **Nakhon Sawan**. Not to be missed here: Wat Chomkiri Nagaproth, on a hill overlooking the Maenam Chao Phraya, the river that begins here at the confluence of its two tributaries, the Maenam Ping and Maenam Nan. The town itself is situated at the foot of a chain of hills on a plain used intensively for agriculture.

From Nakhon Sawan, national Route 311 heads north towards ❻ ✳ **Phitsanulok**. This particular stage is short in order to leave plenty of time for a visit to Wat Phra Si Ratana Mahathat with its uniquely beautiful Buddha statue, the Phra Buddha Jinarat.

The next leg may seem a little curious, but has been deliberately chosen in view of the lack of desirable overnight accommodation in Kamphaeng Phet. From Phitsanulok take Route 12 to Sukothai, then switch onto Route 101 towards ❼ ✳✳ **Kamphaeng Phet** (103km/ 64mi, 2.5 hours approx.). The major attractions here are the two adjacent temple complexes of Wat Phra Kaeo and Wat Phra That. It is recommended that the return trip to ❽ ✳✳ **Sukhothai** (77km/ 48mi) should not start later than midday in order to leave enough time for sightseeing at the destination.

Follow Route 101 to Sawankhalok first, then carry on to ❾ ✳✳ **Si Satchanalai** (55km/34mi). This town features Wat Chang Lom with its monumental chedi. Afterwards it would be possible to visit the temple of Wat Chedi Chet Theow with its 32 stupas containing the ashes of members of the royal family. From Si Satchanalai take Route 101 until just before Den Chai, then turn onto Route 11, which leads to Lampang after a drive of a good two and a half hours (152km/ 95mi).

A morning in ❿ ✳✳ **Lampang** should be dedicated to visiting as many as possible of the numerous temples. A little outside the town is Wat Phra Kaeo Don Tao, which for more than 32 years was home

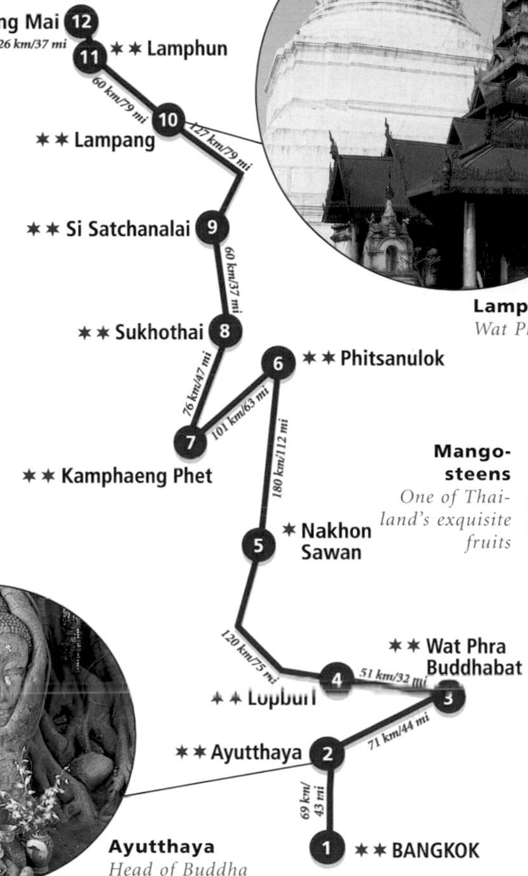

Chiang Mai 12
26 km/37 mi
11 **Lamphun**
60 km/79 mi
10 127 km/79 mi
Lampang

Si Satchanalai 9
60 km/37 mi
Sukhothai 8
76 km/47 mi
6 **Phitsanulok**
101 km/63 mi
7
180 km/112 mi
Kamphaeng Phet

Nakhon 5
Sawan

120 km/75 mi
Wat Phra
Buddhabat
4 51 km/32 mi
Lopburi 3
71 km/44 mi
Ayutthaya 2
69 km/43 mi
1 **BANGKOK**

Lampang
Wat Phra Kaeo Don Tao

Mango-steens
One of Thailand's exquisite fruits

Ayutthaya
Head of Buddha

to the famous Emerald Buddha (actually made of jade). This figure, Thailand's most important sacred relic, is now kept at Wat Phra Kaeo in Bangkok. 18km/11mi outside the town (to the south on Route 1) is another highly notable temple, Wat Phra That Lampang Luang. The last leg to Chiang Mai follows Route 11 via Lamphun, where a visit is planned for the final day.

In order to comfortably see ⑪ ✱✱ **Lamphun** with Wat Phra That Haripunchai and ⑫ ✱✱ **Chiang Mai**, the »Rose of the North« where the tour ends, a whole day ought to be pencilled in.

Tour 3 From Chiang Mai to the »Golden Triangle«

Length of tour: 720km/450mi approx. **Duration:** 3–4 days
Start: Chiang Mai **Finish:** Chiang Mai

This route passes through the unique landscape of northern Thailand with its dense jungle and the high chain of mountains beyond Mae Sai, the northernmost city of Thailand. The frontier to Myanmar (formerly Burma) in this area is still occasionally open to tourists.

From ❶ ✶ ✶ **Chiang Mai,** instead of taking the main road that leads to Chiang Rai (Route 118) it is better to take Route 107, which passes through scenery of quite unparalleled beauty. After about 18km/11mi the road passes through the small town of Mae Rim. 11km/7mi after a left turn onto Route 1096, there is an elephant camp where young animals are trained (a fascinating demonstration takes place every day at 9am). Back on Route 107 the journey passes once again through some dramatic scenery. If time allows, the chance of a visit to the caves at Chiang Dao (61km/38mi from Mae Rim) is not to be missed. Near ❷ **Fang** (155km/96mi) the hot springs of Ban Pin (about 10km/6mi from the town) are also worth a look. After Fang take routes 109, 118 and 1 to ❸ ✶ ✶ **Chiang Rai.**

The small but bustling commercial centre of ❹ **Mae Sai**, 63km/39mi from Chiang Rai, is the northernmost settlement in Thailand (1,010km/628mi from Bangkok) and is situated on the border with Myanmar. The border crossing is the only real attraction apart from the morning market, which is usually over by 9am. Driving back some distance along Route 110, a left turn at Mae Chan after about 70km/43mi leads to ❺ **Chiang Saen**, well known for its individual artistic style. Wat Pa Sak has a lovely site amidst the trees, and the beautiful Wat Chedi Luang should not be missed, in particular for its chedi, which is now 58m/190ft tall but once measured nearly 90m/300ft.
Wat Phra That Chom Kitti with its remarkable crooked chedi lies on a hill a short distance outside the town. Not far from there is the famous beauty spot known (with a certain poetic licence) as the »Golden Triangle«. The confluence of the Maenam Ping river with the Mekong is also worth a look.

The final stage is about 345km/215mi long, making it a little strenuous. One way of easing it is to split the stage into two and spend a night in Chiang Rai. From Chiang Saen take the road back to Mae Chan and ❸ ✶ ✶ **Chiang Rai**, then Route 1, an excellent road that

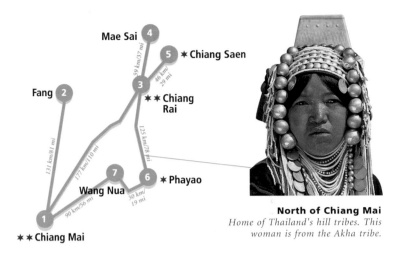

North of Chiang Mai
*Home of Thailand's hill tribes. This
woman is from the Akha tribe.*

leads directly to ❻✶ **Phayao** (162km/101mi). The town is situated
on the shores of a lake some 24 sq km/9 sq mi in size. The Wat Si
Kom Kam temple also lies on its banks. After Phayao, Route 120
runs through a fascinating and unique landscape passing to ❼**Wang
Nua** and ❶✶✶ **Chiang Mai** (182km/70mi). The journey is especially delightful during the rainy season when plants are in full bloom.

Tour 4 From Bangkok to Phuket

Length of tour: 1,250km/780mi
approx.
Finish: Phuket

Duration: 7 days
Start: Bangkok

**This route runs down the coast of the Gulf of Thailand along the
one and only road linking Bangkok with the south of the country.
It is advisable to fly back to Bangkok and usually possible to leave
the rented car in Phuket.**

Leave ❶✶✶ **Bangkok** on Route 4, a good road in the early stages
although it later requires some attentive driving. There are no particularly impressive sights on the way to Phetchaburi (170km/106mi)
apart from the magnificent landscape itself. Once in ❷✶✶ **Phetchaburi**, though, the ascent to Phra Nakhon Khiri, the summer palace built atop a mountain by King Mongkut, is not to be missed. The
62km/39mi from Phetchaburi to ❸✶ **Hua Hin**, where King Bhumibol spends holidays during the hottest months of the year, should be

covered in about an hour and a half. There are a great many hotels in Hua Hin and it is a fine place to spend a short or indeed a longer beach holiday.

Shortly before ❹ ✶ **Prachuap Khiri Khan**, at the 92km/57mi mark, is the narrowest part of the Thai mainland, where the distance from coast to coast is only 13km/8mi. On the left is the impressive backdrop of the hills of Sam Roi Yot (»300 peaks«) National Park. In Prachuap Khiri Khan itself there is not much to see, but there are numerous cave temples around the town.

The journey to Chumphon passes through a varied landscape. Route 4 is never more than a few miles from the Gulf of Thailand. There are no special attractions along the route or in ❺ ✶ **Chumphon** (apart from the little fishing port of Paknam about 10km/6mi east of the town).

From Chumphon take Route 41 down the Gulf of Thailand coast. It is worth stopping off in one of the small fishing villages, where visitors are always warmly welcomed. There should only be about four hours of actual driving, which leaves plenty of time to see ❻ ✶✶ **Suratthani**.

Two roads lead from Suratthani to Nakhon Si Thammarat. Since Route 41 runs inland through a multitude of rubber plantations with no major sights, it is better to take Route 401, which runs along the Gulf of Thailand beyond the town of Sichon. This leg of the tour is

! Baedeker TIP

A relaxing rail journey
One alternative that is worth considering for this route is to forgo the rental car and to make the journey a little less strenuous by taking the train.

quite short and leaves plenty of time to explore ❼ ✶✶ **Nakhon Si Thammarat**, formerly a major port and commercial centre.

Route 401 comes to an end a few miles past Ron Phibun. Thereafter, take Route 41 to Thung Song and head south again on Route 403, which itself joins Route 4 shortly before Huai Yot (turn right). The day's destination, ❽ ✶ **Krabi**, greets the visitor with an impressively exotic coastal landscape including some fabulous beaches. In the past, the entire south was jungle, but nowadays there are row after row of rubber trees. A number of long-disused tin mines will also be noticeable along the way, perhaps the only blot on a flawless landscape.

A few miles west of Krabi on highway 4034 is the 75 million year old »shell cemetery« of Susan Hoi. Back on Route 4, continue past Than Bok Koroni National Park (well worth a brief visit) before arriving in ❾ ✶✶ **Phang Nga**. A boat trip around the bay of Phang Nga with

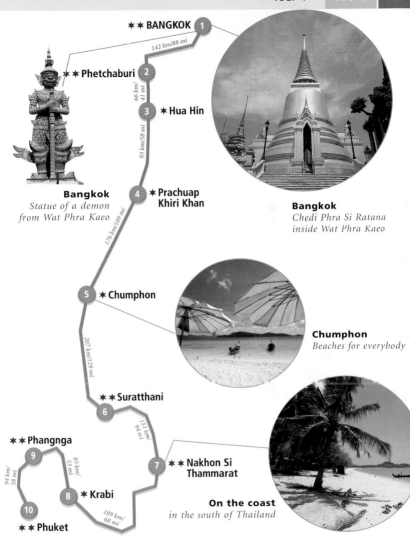

BANGKOK 1

142 km/88 mi

Phetchaburi 2

66 km/41 mi

3 **Hua Hin**

93 km/58 mi

4 **Prachuap Khiri Khan**

176 km/109 mi

5 **Chumphon**

207 km/129 mi

Suratthani
6

151 km/94 mi

Phangnga
9

85 km/53 mi

7 **Nakhon Si Thammarat**

94 km/58 mi

8 **Krabi**

10

109 km/68 mi

Phuket

Bangkok
*Statue of a demon
from Wat Phra Kaeo*

Bangkok
*Chedi Phra Si Ratana
inside Wat Phra Kaeo*

Chumphon
Beaches for everybody

On the coast
in the south of Thailand

the famous rocks featured in the James Bond film *The Man With The Golden Gun* is also a good day trip from Phuket (such a trip can by organized via travel agents or hotels and usually includes a visit to the fishing village of Ko Panyi, built on stilts and populated by Muslims). At the village of Ban Koke Loi take a left turn onto Route 402 over the Sarasin Bridge to the island of ❿ ✶✶ **Phuket**.

40 islands belong to the Ang Thong National Park around Ko Samui.

Tour 5 From Pattaya to Trat

Length of tour: 380–550km
approx. 235–340mi
Finish: Trat

Duration: 1 day or more
Start: Pattaya

This trip can be extended indefinitely by spending the night on the islands of Ko Samet or Ko Chang, and is ideal for a those who are seeking a little change from their beach holiday in Pattaya.

From ❶ ✳ **Pattaya** take Route 3 to the small town of ❷ ✳ **Sattahip** (32km/20mi). 56km/35mi further on Route 3 lies the town of Rayong, which is known in Thailand for processing fish to make the popular fish sauce »nam pla«. At the village of Ban Phe (14km/9mi) turn right towards the sea to reach the harbour, from where there

Ko Samet
Beach paradise

Ko Chang
Picnic under the palms

✳ **Pattaya**

①

33 km/
21 mi　67 km/
　　　42 mi

② ✳ **Ko Samet** ③　　✳ **Chanthaburi**

✳ **Sattahip**　　85 km/53 mi　④　72 km/
　　　　　　　　　　　　　45 mi

Trat　⑤

52 km/
33 mi

✳✳ **Ko Chang**　⑥

are regular ferries to the island of ❸ ✳ **Ko Samet**. Just before Klaeng (30km/19mi from Ban Phe) on the right is the Wat Sukpriwoon temple, a beautiful structure with richly decorated gables showing the Hindu god Indra riding on an elephant.

The town of ❹ ✳ **Chanthaburi** (100km/62mi from Ban Phe) is known for the gem mines in its vicinity, many of which allow visitors. A statue of King Taksin on horseback graces the park, and it is worth visiting Notre Dame, the largest Christian church in Thailand with its Gothic architecture, or the old military defences around Chanthaburi.

From Chanthaburi it is 70km/43mi to ❺ **Trat** and then another 17km/11mi to Laem Ngob, where there is a ferry to the island of ❻ ✳✳ **Ko Chang**. The journey beyond Trat may be hindered by political issues with the neighbouring state of Cambodia. To return to Pattaya, drive to Rayong then take Route 36, which is better surfaced than the coast road via Sattahip.

Sights
from A to Z

BEAUTIFUL BEACHES AND GOLDEN
TEMPLES, ENIGMATIC RUINS AND
BUSTLING METROPOLISES, DARK
RAINFORESTS AND UNDERWATER
CORAL GARDENS – THAILAND HAS
MANY FACES AND IS AN OUT-
STANDING PLACE FOR A HOLIDAY

Ang Thong

D 3

Region: Central Thailand
Altitude: 10m/33ft

Province: Ang Thong
Population: 12,000

The provincial capital of Ang Thong – not to be confused with the Ang Thong archipelago in southern Thailand (▶ Surat Thani) that has now been declared a national park – is not far from the famous ruined city of ▶ Ayutthaya by the Menam Chao Phraya on the central plain of Thailand, in a landscape dominated by broad fields of rice paddies.

Bustling provincial capital
The city itself is somewhat lacking in attractions but in the surrounding region several temple complexes are well worth a look. It is also fun to visit one of the many bustling marketplaces. The best time to do this is in the early morning when business is at its liveliest.

Around Ang Thong

Wat Pa Mok
Wat Pa Mok is 13km/8mi from Ang Thong on the other side of the Menam Chao Phraya. One of the two viharns houses a 22m/72ft-long sculpture of a reclining Buddha in U Thong style (late 14th century). According to one tradition, the legendary **King Naresuen** offered his respects to this Buddha in 1584 before marching his forces

▶ VISITING ANG THONG

GETTING THERE

By car:
From Ayutthaya via Route 309 towards Singburi

By bus:
From Bangkok Northern Bus Terminal or Ayutthaya (several times a day)

By rail:
Closest stations Ayutthaya, Suphanburi and Saraburi (several trains daily from Bangkok Hualampong)

INFORMATION

Tourism Association of Thailand (TAT)
108/22 Moo 4, Tambon Phratoochai
Ayutthaya 13000

Tel. 0 35 / 24 60 76-7
Fax 24 60 78
tatyutya@tat.or.th

WHERE TO STAY

▶ **Budget**
Ang Thong Hotel & Bungalows
60 Ang Thong-Suphan Road
Tel. 0 35 / 61 17 67-8
80 rooms, restaurant, pretty location, well-kept rooms.

CL Garden Inn
42 Mu 3, Pho Phraya-Tha Rua
Tel. 0 35 / 61 26 65-6, 32 rooms

Siam Inn
41/2 Tambon Ban
Tel. 0 35 / 61 20 17, 36 rooms

Rice harvest near Ang Thong

into a decisive battle against the Burmese. The Burmese had attacked and annexed much of the country in 1568, but Naresuen was finally able to defeat them and by 1605 had driven them from the land. In the other viharn there remain some well-preserved murals from the early Ayutthaya period.

From Route 3195 heading towards ►Suphanburi three further temples are within reach. The quite recent **Wat Khun Inta Phra Mun** is a little way from Route 3195, 11km/7mi from Ang Thong and features a massive 50m/164ft-long reclining Buddha in Ayutthaya style that is probably one of the largest such sculptures in Thailand and is certainly highly revered. A pleasant walk away, on a nearby hill, are some remains of an ancient wat.

Wat Kien

The modern building of Wat Kien is surrounded by the frescoed walls of a previous temple. The paintings depict scenes from the Thais' battles with the Burmese. Although conflicts with Burma played a major role in Thai history, such themes are nevertheless rarely found in art.

Wat Luang Suntararam

Near the village of Ban Talat San Djao, about 9km/6mi north of Ang Thong, is Wat Luang Suntararam where the bot features beautiful stucco bas-reliefs from the Ayutthaya period.

Wat Chai Yo Vora Vihara

16km/10mi north of Ang Thong the high, triple-tiered roof of the Ayutthaya-era viharn at Wat Chai Yo Vora Vihara rises above the banks of the Menam Chao Phraya. Its gables are decorated with the most exquisite carvings. Inside the temple, the gigantic statue of Buddha is more recent but no less beautiful.

Ban Bang Phae drum-making village

The small village of Ban Bang Phae is known far and wide across Thailand, because it is the centre of production for what are probably the finest drums for religious use or folk music. The village can most easily be reached by taxi from Ang Thong.

Ban Bang Sadet

The inhabitants of Ban Bang Sadet (also best reached by taxi), too, are known for their handiwork – in this case for their shadow puppets, which are made under the patronage of Her Majesty Queen Sirikit.

★★ Ayutthaya (Phra Nakhon Si Ayutthaya)

D 3

Region: Central Thailand	**Province:** Ayutthaya
Altitude: 4m/13ft	**Population:** 65,000

The former capital of Ayutthaya, now one of the most impressive ruined cities on the Asian continent, is situated in the midst of the broad fertile plain of the Menam Chao Phraya, enclosed within a loop of the meandering river. The city is bordered on practically all sides by the Menam, two other rivers and the canal that joins them all; this makes the city into a strategically defensible island.

History Ayutthaya was the capital of Siam from 1350 to 1767, and enthusiastic western visitors called it »the most beautiful city ever seen«. In the 11th century the **Khmer** had established a small outpost of their empire to the north-east of the present-day railway station near Wat Khudi Dao. When the Thais conquered and started cultivation of the Menam plain, Ayutthaya and Lopburi were incorporated into the U Thong dominion, a vassal state of Sukhothai. In the wake of a dreadful plague in 1347 that killed half the population, the ruler was compelled to flee U Thong. He selected Ayutthaya as the new capital, on a site almost encircled by rivers with an easily defensible core to the south on the Menam. The reshaping of the Siamese kingdom into several principalities after the death of King Ramkhamkaeng also persuaded U Thong to secede from the rule of Sukhothai. In 1350 King Somdet Phra Rama Thibodi (usually called King U Thong) declared his own state, named after his capital. Rama Thibodi claimed himself to be the reincarnation of the god Vishnu and a reborn hero from the Indian Ramayana epic. He legitimated his divine omnipotence through coronation by eight Brahmans from the sacred Hindu city of Benares.

> **? DID YOU KNOW ...?**
>
> ■ Anyone interested in Thai history should visit not only Ayutthaya but also other former capitals in central Thailand, Lopburi and Sukhothai, which are both closely bound up with the history of the country.

Magnificent heyday The history of Ayutthaya unfolded under 33 kings. The city blossomed into a glittering cultural and trading centre, where many European trading companies were represented. The foundations of a Dutch warehouse can be seen to this day along with the restored French cathedral of St Joseph. There were four customs offices, of which the largest was the southern one on the eastern shore of the Menam Chao Phraya. Warships and the royal barge were berthed on the northern shore of the Lopburi river near Wat Tin Tha, opposite

Buddha statue in Wat Yai Chai Mongkol →

▶ VISITING AYUTTHAYA

GETTING THERE

By car:
From Bangkok by National Route 1, after 86km/53mi turn left onto Route 309 near Wang Noi

By bus:
From Northern Bus Terminal (Bangkok) 5am–7pm every 10 minutes daily, air-conditioned buses 6.30am–5pm every half-hour daily

By rail:
From Bangkok-Hualampong (journey time 1½ hrs). Day trips to Ayutthaya are offered by all travel agents.

INFORMATION

Tourism Association of Thailand
108/22 Moo 4, Tambon Phratoochai
Ayutthaya 13000
Tel. 0 35 / 24 60 76-7, fax 24 60 78
tatyutya@tat.or.th

WHERE TO STAY

▶ Mid-range

① *Ayothaya Riverside Hotel*
91 Moo 10, Tambol Kamang
Tel. 0 35 / 23 48 73-7, fax 24 41 39
The best hotel in town, with a view over the Pasak river. Recommended restaurant with terrace.

② *U Thong Inn*
210 Mu 5, Rotchana Road
Tel. 0 35 / 24 26 18, fax 24 22 35
100 rooms
Nicely priced hotel with clean, air-conditioned rooms and restaurant

▶ Budget

③ *Si Samai*
12 Talad Chao Phrom
Tel. 0 35 / 25 12 28, 25 11 04
Well-kept guest house with 58 simple rooms for travellers who are happy with basic accommodation

Long rows of meditating Buddhas flank Wat Yai Chai Mongkol

the royal palace. King U Thong had the city surrounded with earthworks and palisade fencing. It was not until 1549 that it was defended by a brick wall. In 1580 the northern wall was moved closer to the river. Remains of the former defences can still be seen on Pa Maphrao Road. There were six large forts built into the walls, but the only one of which some parts remain is Fort Phom Phet, where the Pasak river flows into the Chao Phraya. After the destruction of Ayutthaya, the stone from other forts and defences was taken away to be used in building a city wall around Bangkok.

The destruction of Ayutthaya in 1767 resulted in the temporary demise of the Siamese monarchy. Rival factions in the royal family had been struggling for power and King Ekatot, the last and perhaps the weakest of the Ayutthaya dynasty, was unable to bring them together. When the Burmese once again appeared outside the city walls, rivals of the king opened the gates to the enemy and allowed the Burmese to occupy the city for more than 15 years.

The end of a struggle for power

The Burmese vandalized the city. No temple was spared and the ancient palace of Wang Luang was razed to the ground. The destruction of thousands of statues of Buddha was symbolic of the final desecration of Ayutthaya. Statues were decapitated to rob them of their »souls«, a monstrous sacrilege to Buddhist believers. Some of these violated statues can still be seen today.

Obliterated temples, ruined Buddhas

Nowadays Ayutthaya is a vast assemblage of ruined temples and palaces. The foundations of some temples have been successively excavated since 1956. Some 100 buildings and ruins have been declared national monuments by the Department of Fine Arts, and others are gradually attaining the same status as their reconstruction or restoration progresses. UNESCO declared the ruins of Ayutthaya to be a World Heritage Site in 1991.

UNESCO World Heritage Site

Tours of the Ayutthaya Ruins

In the core of Ayutthaya alone, on the central island between the rivers, there were as many as three royal palaces, 375 temples, 29 forts and 94 city gates. To get an idea of how massive and beautiful Ayutthaya must once have been, it is worth taking one of the tours that start near the station at Prince Damrong Bridge. A tour takes in ten temples, two museums and two of the palaces. Plan half a day in order to complete it, or longer if you want to spend more time in the museums. It is also possible to take a taxi and ask the driver to stop at the important sights.

🕐
Opening hours:
8am–5pm daily

Cross Prince Damrong Bridge to get to the circular U Thong Road and turn left heading along the road for 700m/750yds. There, ringed by three small ponds, is Wat Suwan Dararam, which was built

Wat Suwan Dararam

Ayutthaya *Plan*

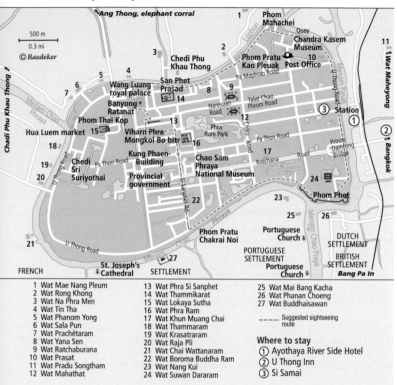

1 Wat Mae Nang Pleum	13 Wat Phra Si Sanphet	25 Wat Mai Bang Kacha
2 Wat Rong Khong	14 Wat Thammikarat	26 Wat Phanan Choeng
3 Wat Na Phra Men	15 Wat Lokaya Sutha	27 Wat Buddhaisawan
4 Wat Tin Tha	16 Wat Phra Ram	
5 Wat Phanom Yong	17 Wat Khun Muang Chai	- - - - Suggested sightseeing route
6 Wat Sala Pun	18 Wat Thammaram	
7 Wat Prachétaram	19 Wat Krasatraram	**Where to stay**
8 Wat Yana Sen	20 Wat Raja Pli	① Ayothaya River Side Hotel
9 Wat Ratchaburana	21 Wat Chai Wattanaram	② U Thong Inn
10 Wat Prasat	22 Wat Boroma Buddha Ram	③ Si Samai
11 Wat Pradu Songtham	23 Wat Nang Kui	
12 Wat Mahathat	24 Wat Suwan Dararam	

around 1700 but has seen much expansion, restoration and adornment numerous paintings during the reign of the Chakri dynasty.
The temple foundations are inclined towards the centre. It is the only
temple in Ayutthaya today that is still inhabited by monks. It is
worth seeing the large bot and its portico, the wooden carvings in
the gables, the frescoes inside that date from the early Bangkok period, the beautiful coffered ceiling and a Buddha statue in the Ayutthaya style. The viharn was built by Rama II (1809–1824) and decorated in 1931 with modern-day murals depicting the history of Thailand.

Fort Phom Phet Leaving the temple compound, the ruins of the one remaining fort,
Phom Phet, can be seen on the opposite bank of the river. Continue
left along U Thong Road as far as Fort Phom Pratu Chakrai Noi
where there is a turn-off north towards the temple of Wat Boroma
Buddha Ram.

Only the walls of Wat Boroma Buddha Ram are left nowadays. It was built in 1683 during the reign of King Narai. The three towers of the bot were decorated with panels inlaid with mother of pearl in around 1740. After the destruction of Ayutthaya, these fabulous works of art were rescued and brought to Bangkok. One of them was installed as a door at Wat Benchama bo-bitr (»marble temple«) and another at Wat Phra Kaeo (in the Grand Palace). The third was altered to become a bookcase and can presently be seen in the ► Bangkok National Museum.

Wat Boroma Buddha Ram

Passing Ayutthaya's local government buildings, the route now leads to the Chao Sam Phraya National Museum established by King Bhumibol in 1961. It contains many valuable pieces in the Lopburi, U Thong and Ayutthaya styles as well as some pieces in Dvaravati and Sukhothai styles. The museum houses archaeological finds from Ayutthaya, bronze and stone sculptures, terracotta artwork, ceramics, wood carvings, paintings, votive tablets and gold jewellery with precious stones. Particular highlights among the early works include a seated Buddha in Dvaravati style (11th–12th century) and a colossal head of Buddha in the U Thong style.

★
Chao Sam Phraya Museum

🕐
Opening hours:
Thu–Sun
9am–noon,
2–5pm
Admission fee

An excellent complement to a visit to the Chao Sam Phraya National Museum is to spend some time in the Ayutthaya Historical Study Center afterwards. Its goal is to allow interested historians from home and abroad to conduct research on the former capital. The building was a joint effort involving Thai and Japanese architects. It holds an exhibition on the life and times of old Ayutthaya displayed on models and panels, as well as reconstructions of both sacred and secular architecture.

Ayutthaya Historical Study Center

🕐
Opening hours:
Wed–Sun
9am–4pm

Turn left on leaving the National Museum to head for the Sanaam Luang fields (also called the Phra Mane Grounds). The western corner is the location of Viharn Phra Mongkol Bo-bitr. Prime Minister Pibulsonggram had the building erected in 1956 in the style and on the site of the original edifice, which burned down at the fall of Ayutthaya, to house the revered and culturally priceless bronze Buddha statue, one of the largest in Thailand, which had previously been kept there in the years following 1603.

Viharn Phra Mongkol Bo-bitr

Little is known of the early history of the statue. Taking into account the features it possesses from both U Thong and Sukhothai styles, it was probably cast during the reign of King Boroma Trailokanat (1448–1488), who introduced the **Sukhothai style** to the Buddha sculptures and chedis in Ayutthaya, supplanting the Khmer style previously used. The statue has undergone frequent restoration, but has changed little from its original appearance. Some years ago several hundred smaller statues were discovered inside it. The ornamentation of the pedestal dates from 1931 and is not as fine as the original work.

Wat Phra Ram	The elephants on the gates of the nearby Wat Phra Ram, which was built amongst ponds from 1369 by King Ramesuen and continually restored and expanded over the centuries, are also impressive. The broad terrace is home to a gallery of nagas and garudas as well as some broken Buddha statues.
Khun Phaen house	Close by is the Khun Phaen house, built in traditional Thai style on a moated island that was formerly the site of the prison. The house is one of the few remaining buildings in this style, having been assembled in 1940 from pieces of previously existing houses (like Jim Thompson's houses in ►Bangkok).
✹ ✹ **Wat Phra Si Sanphet** Details in 3D pull-out, p.200 ►	Follow Si Sanphet Road as far as Naresuan Road and turn left towards Wat Phra Si Sanphet, once the most beautiful and important temple of old Ayutthaya. The temple features three large chedis along a long terrace, and was once the royal temple. It is one of the most impressive sights in the ruined city. The building at the west end of the terrace was once topped by a chedi and has a series of porches, each featuring a small prang. Like the smaller chedis and chapels around the site, these probably contain ashes of members of the royal family.
Royal palaces	Outside the royal temple and across the way is a monument representing King U Thong. Turn left again to reach the royal palace of Wang Luang, known as the »old palace« to distinguish it from the later Chandra Kasem Palace. Of a third palace compound, Klang Suan Luang, by the western wall near the chedi of Queen Suriyochai, no trace is left.

! *Baedeker* TIP

Ayutthaya by boat

There are, of course, many ways of getting to Ayutthaya, but one of the most interesting is by boat along the Menam Chao Phraya. The *Ayutthaya Princess*, for example, embarks from the Oriental Hotel in Bangkok for a return journey. The return leg is particularly beautiful, as the boat arrives in Bangkok at twilight. Bookings can be made from most hotels.

The walls of Wang Luang reach almost to the shore of the Lopburi river, but other than these and some nicely restored foundations there is little to see. This part of Ayutthaya was despoiled and incinerated by the Burmese with particular ferocity so that nothing remains of the original Thai buildings. It is nevertheless possible to get an idea of how large the palace grounds, which included Wat Si Sanphet, once were. They may once have resembled the grand palace compound of Bangkok, since this was built along similar lines to the old Ayutthaya residence, albeit in different style. The destruction of Ayutthaya is considered by the Thais to be the greatest catastrophe in their history. The capital was then moved to Bangkok.

Traditional tour: elephant ride through the ruins →

WAT PHRA SI SANPHET

✶✶ Wat Phra Si Sanphet, also called the royal temple, is originally from the 15th century and was built as the state temple of King Boromatrailokanat. His son Rama Thibodi II added two Chedis, which were intended for the relics of his father and brother. The third Chedi was built after the death of Rama Thibodi II, in order to hold his mortal remains. After the Burmese destroyed it, the ruins were abandoned until they were placed under the protection of UNESCO in 1991.

🕐 Opening times:
9.00-18.00

① Eastern Chedi
King Rama Thibodi II had the eastern-most of the three great Chedis built in 1492 as a mausoleum for the ashes of his father Boromatrailokanat. It is the only one that survived the Burmese invasion intact.

② Middle Chedi
The mortal remains of Rama Thibodi II's older brother rested here.

③ Western Chedi
The ashes of Rama Thibodi II were interred in this Chedi, which was built by his son and successor King Boromaraja IV in the year 1530.

④ Mondhops
The buildings between the individual Chedis were probably libraries (Mondhop).

⑤ Viharn
In front of the terrace in the centre of the temple area are the remains (columns and walls) of the large Viharn, which once contained a 16m/52ft high gilded Buddha figure. The rubble of this statue, from which the Burmese had removed the gold, was placed in Wat Pho in Bangkok by King Rama I.

Burial treasures
All three Chedis were opened and emptied by the plundering Burmese, but they missed hundreds of small Buddha statuettes made of bronze, crystal, silver, lead and gold, which are on display in the national museum of Bangkok today.

Buddha Statues
Other small Buddha statues were placed in Wat Buddhaisawan and in the western Viharn of Wat Pho (both in ►Bangkok).

The three striking Chedis of Wut Phra Si Sanphet still rise up prominently into the sky.

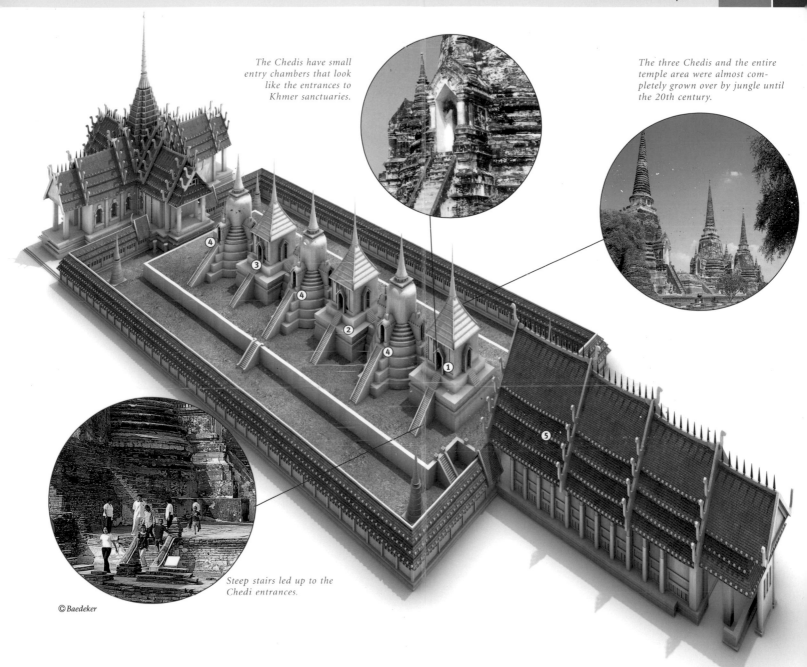

The Chedis have small entry chambers that look like the entrances to Khmer sanctuaries.

The three Chedis and the entire temple area were almost completely grown over by jungle until the 20th century.

Steep stairs led up to the Chedi entrances.

© Baedeker

Wang Luang The old royal palace ▶	The earliest buildings of Wang Luang were erected by King U Thong in 1350, when he declared Ayutthaya the capital of his realm. In 1448 King Boromaraja II added the Sanphet Prasat Palace across the way from Wang Luang. Only a few stumps of columns can now be seen of this. The Somdet viharn was built in 1643 under King Prasat Thong. According to reports from the period, it once had two large tower-like vestibules at the sides and was the first building in Ayutthaya to be covered with gold panels, which led to its being called the Golden Palace. The Chakravat Phaichayon building was also erected under Prasat Thong in 1632. From there the king would begin his processions and military parades. The Banyong Ratanat building (built in the reign of Prasat Thong's son Narai in about 1688 and completed under King Petraja) on an artificial island to the west of the site was the home of King Petraja throughout his reign (1688–1702).King Chulalongkorn had the Trimuk building reconstructed in 1907. It is an open pavilion on a broad terrace, where many kings including the current sovereign King Bhumibol have conducted public ceremonies in honour of the former rulers of Ayutthaya. King Narai the Great was also the builder of the seventeenth-century Suriyat Ainarindra building, of which one high wall still exists. Next to this were once the stables of the king's white elephants.

Wang Luang — *The old royal palace ▶* (as above)

Wat Na Phra Men Inside the bot ▶	Passing by Wat Thammikarat, the overgrown ruins of an unusually large temple (of which some ruined terraces and pillars from the entrance halls remain along with one chedi with a crooked spire), the route leads back to U Thong Road, from which a small bridge crosses the Lopburi to Wat Na Phra Men. This is one of the few temples that was largely spared the vandalism of the Burmese. It is not known when it was constructed. Chronicles merely state that it was restored under King Boromakot (1732–1758) and once again in the early Bangkok era. The bot is a large, imposing structure with beautiful teak wood carvings on the gables and door inlays. The triple-tiered roof and a large portico flanked by two dainty little porches testify to the craftsmanship of the Thais. Inside the bot, two rows of octagonal pillars with capitals shaped like lotus blossoms supporting a beautifully carved ceiling emphasize the height of the building. The great bronze Buddha is wearing a kingly robe, a depiction which is very seldom seen. The small but beautifully proportioned viharn contains a dark green quarzite stone Buddha seated in western fashion as well as one of the best preserved sculptures from the Dvaravati era (6th–10th/11th centuries). According to an inscription in the viharn, the piece comes from Wat Mahathat in Ayutthaya, although it has now been established that it must once have stood in Wat Phra Men in Nakhon Pathom, where the richly decorated stone frame that forms its pedestal originates. Some sections of this frame are in the National Museum in ▶ Bangkok.

Go back across the bridge to the island of Ayutthaya and turn left **Wat Yana Sen** again. About 800m/900yd along the road that follows the Lopburi river is Wat Yana Sen, a temple featuring a tall chedi with several niches. Its fine, well-proportioned design is typical of the Ayutthaya style. From Wat Yana Sen it is already possible to see two of the most important ruined temples in Ayutthaya, Wat Ratchaburana and Wat Mahathat.

Wat Ratchaburana was built by King Boromaraja II (1424–1448) in  memory of his two brothers Ay and Yi, who had killed one another **Wat** in mortal combat for the throne. The wat is supposed to have been **Ratchaburana** built over the site of the battle on two elephants. There are still some pillars and walls belonging to the viharn as well as the ruins of various chedis that surround the prang. Parts of the surrounding wall with lance-shaped portals also exist. The large prang itself is very well preserved. It features many sculpted details showing garudas attacking nagas. The two crypts in the lower part of the prang have some interesting murals. The painters were probably Chinese artists

> **!** *Baedeker* TIP
>
> **»Don't go out in the midday sun«**
> Most organized tours spend only a little time in Ayutthaya itself, often during the hottest hours of the day. The city is, however, at its best in the morning and evening. This is certainly the best time to take photographs.

settled in Ayutthaya, who were able to incorporate a variety of styles such as those of the Khmer and Burmese as well as the Lopburi and Sukhothai styles to create an astonishingly harmonious result. Archaeological excavations of the prang between 1956 and 1958 also turned up more than 100,000 votive tablets. They were sold and the money thus raised was used to fund the building of the Chao Sam Phraya Museum. Votive tablets like this, which were taken on pilgrimages, were mostly made by shaping clay in moulds. They featured depictions of especially holy pilgrimage sites or simply pictures of Buddha. Further discoveries in the prang included wide bracelets encrusted with gems, a head-dress made with filigree gold as well as one solid gold head-dress adorned with precious stones, a five-piece crockery set for betel nuts, two spittoons and gold coins with Arabic inscriptions (most of these finds can be seen in the Chandra Kasem Museum). The Wat Ratchaburana prang is in a mixture of the Sri Lankan and Burmese styles that meld to create a wholly new architectural style. Some of the upper section is been quite well preserved. There was once a square platform with small chedis at every corner. Two more chedis at the crossroads contained the ashes of the two royal brothers, while a third commemorates Queen Si Suriyothai, who rode on an elephant into battle against the Burmese disguised as a man in 1550 and saved the life of her husband, only to perish herself. Close to her chedi, next to the totally obliterated Wat Lokaya Sutha, there is a huge reclining Buddha.

✱
Wat Mahathat

Wat Mahathat is just across the street from Wat Ratchaburana. Some records state that it was built in 1384 by King Ramesuen, who also had the central prang constructed to house a relic of Buddha. Another source claims the first buildings on the site of the Wat Mahathat temple (including the aforementioned prang) had already been started under King Boromaraja I (1370–1388). The 46m/150ft-high prang is one of the most imposing buildings in the old city. The top section collapsed in 1625, and a new section built in 1633 increased the height by a further 4m/13ft. Unfortunately this too fell down, leaving only the corners that can still be seen today. Among the ruins, a secret chamber was uncovered in 1956. It contained gold jewellery, a golden casket with a relic of Buddha as well as some beautifully crafted tableware. The remains of various chedis and prangs are scattered over the temple grounds. One conspicuous chedi is octagonal with a squat spire in the Sri Lankan style. On the ground near Wat Mahathat there is a head from a Buddha statue that is even now treated with great reverence.

Chandra Kasem Museum

🕐
Opening hours:
Thu–Sun
9am–12am,
2–5pm

Return to U Thong Road and follow it along the Lopburi to the Chandra Kasem Museum, which is worth a lengthy visit. It displays Buddha and Bodhisattva statues, gold, jewellery and carvings, gable sections as well as household and religious items from the 13th to the 17th centuries. It is housed in a palace reconstructed by King Mongkut (Rama IV) that was initially used as a residence for the crown prince and later for the monarchs themselves on visits to Ayutthaya. The pieces on display convey only a vague idea of how the early Thai kings sought to demonstrate their status, but a good impression of the lives of Ayutthaya's inhabitants. After exiting the museum, pass Fort Phom Mahachei to reach the wharf then continue down U Thong Road back to the starting point.

Other Sights

St Joseph

If you have a little more time to explore Ayutthaya and learn of its history, a trip across the Chao Phraya to the French cathedral of St Joseph is recommended. The church was built in the 18th century and restored in 1985. It is a reminder of the large community of French settlers in Siam.

✱
Wat Yai Chai Mongkol

At the eastern edge of the town (on the road to Bangkok across the River Pasak and the railway, up a road to the right 300m along) stands the impressive Wat Yai Chai Mongkol with its huge chedi on a square base and four smaller chedis at each corner. The wat was built in 1357 under King U Thong and given over to monks who had been ordained in Sri Lanka and belonged a very strict order. Members of the order are living in the temple to this day. In front of the chedi the stumps of the pillars that held the original temple roof can still be seen.

A corral for elephants was established in the reign of King Rama I 3km/2mi north of the city. Its purpose was to capture, tame and train elephants. It is now the only remaining compound of its type left in the world.

Elephant corral

✶ ✶ Ban Chiang

C 4

Region: North-east Thailand
Altitude: 138m/450ft

Province: Udon Thani
Population: 4,500

The small town of Ban Chiang was known to few people until 1967, when a unique discovery instigated an influx of archaeologists from all over the world to this village of just a few hundred inhabitants. The archaeological finds that sparked the rush were the remains of the most important prehistoric settlements yet found in Asia.

The excavations showed that the region was populated at least 3,800 years before the birth of Christ, when Europe was still at the end of its own Neolithic period. Before these finds came to light, it was believed that the site had first been settled by Lao migrants just 170 years earlier.

History of the ancient settlement

Pottery fragments, iron and bronze tools and even bones had been turned up by peasants working the fields over many years, yet it was not till the American archaeologist Steve Young heard of the finds and made a spontaneous trip to Ban Chiang that scholars in Bangkok took notice of the site. Using thermo-luminescence techniques, the pottery fragments have been dated as being up to 5,800 years old. As well as pottery, bronze tools were also found. They date from a time close to the beginning of the Bronze Age in the basin of the Euphrates and the Tigris in Mesopotamia, and much earlier (2000 BC) than the Bronze Age in northern Europe. This was a sensational discovery, since it was believed until then that the bronze implements from Mesopotamia were

Sensational discoveries: these pottery fragments are almost 5800 years old

► VISITING BAN CHIANG

GETTING THERE

By car:
Ban Chiang is 6km/4mi north of Route 22 and can be reached from Udon Thani in about an hour (56km/35mi).

By bus:
Buses run from Udon Thani and Sakhon Nakhon (Ban Pu bus station)

By air:
The closest airport is Udon Thani (flights once a day from Bangkok)

INFORMATION

Tourism Association of Thailand (TAT)
Mukmontri Road
41000 Udon Thani
Tel. 0 42/ 32 54 06-7
Fax 32 54 08
tatudon@tat.or.th

WHERE TO STAY

In Ban Chiang itself there are no good places to stay. It is better to rent rooms in ►Udon Thani.

the first ever made by mankind. Further excavations funded by UNESCO have confirmed the early finds.

High-quality pottery
Vessels decorated with spirals or hoops (probably not everyday pottery but burial items) display an artistic quality that has not been discovered anywhere else in South-East Asia. The stylized plants and animals, initially painted onto simple rounded pots which later evolved more elegant forms, testify to a high level of culture. The paint was probably applied with fingers using pigments made from flowers.

The pottery vessels date from three distinct periods: during the first phase of the initial period (3600–2500 BC) they are black with decorative bands between their lines; during its second phase (2500–2000 BC) vessels were completely covered with dense patterns; while in a third phase the painting was also enhanced by etched decorative bands. The spiral and hoop ornamentation and the stylized pictures of people and animals are found on vessels made between 2000 and 1000 BC. The characteristic feature of the middle period (1000–300 BC) was the lack of almost any kind of painting, so that the potters' art is confined solely to the form of the vessel. An artistic peak was reached in the most recent period (300 BC – AD 200), from which most of the exhibits at the museum date. They feature the natural brown of baked clay, painted with a red pigment in patterns that display considerable inventiveness as well as an extraordinary feel for the unity of form, pattern and colour. Shortly afterwards (around AD 400) the inhabitants of Ban Chiang appear to have abandoned the site: at least no finds have yet emerged from any later date.

A number of restored and reconstructed vessels can be seen in the small museum. There are models of the excavation work with explanations in English. An interesting book on the history of Ban Chiang is available for purchase at the counter (opening times: Wed–Sun 9am–4pm, admission fee).

★
National Museum of Ban Chiang

About 1km/1000yd from the museum is an open field of excavations that has been left in its original condition, as has the skeleton of a man. A neighbouring reconstructed excavation exhibits pottery finds from this site and other places around Ban Chiang. More pottery has been taken back to Bangkok, where examples can be seen at the Suan Pakkard Palace. All along the main street of Ban Chiang, villagers sell remarkably good imitations of the originals.

★ ★
Original excavation

★ ★ Bangkok (Krung Thep Phra Nakhon)

E 3

Region: Central Thailand
Altitude: 3m/10ft

Province: Bangkok (metropolitan area)
Population: 6.3 million approx.

The pulsating metropolis that is Bangkok is Thailand's only metropolitan province and the administrative and economic focal point of the entire country. The Thais themselves have their own poetic appellation for the city, which they call Krung Thep, »city of angels«. The internationally accepted name of Bangkok probably arose from a series of misunderstandings and westerners' mispronunciation of the name Ban Makok (»village of olives«).

The capital of the Thai kingdom lies more or less in the geographic centre of the fertile delta region of the Menam Chao Phraya river, which flows into the Gulf of Thailand a few miles to the south. The city is far more than just a seat of royalty and government: it is the very hub of the Thai economy. More than half of the gross domestic product and about 90% of foreign trade is generated within the city boundaries. With more than 400 temples, Bangkok is also a centre for religion and art history, in that its multifarious styles are a veritable panopticon of Thai art and culture.

City on the river

> **!** *Baedeker* TIP
>
> **Bangkok Mass Transit System (BTS)**
> Since 1999 many of Bangkok's sights have been accessible by means of an elevated high-speed railway called the Bangkok Mass Transit System (www.bts.co.th).

After the destruction of Ayutthaya, the former capital, by the Burmese in 1767, General Phya Taksin took flight to Chonburi by way of Bangkok, accompanied by some 10,000 soldiers. Having taken re-

History

venge upon the Burmese and driven them out of the country once and for all, he claimed the title **King of Siam** in 1772. One of his first official acts was to declare **Thonburi** (now a Bangkok suburb) as the new capital. At this time Bangkok was known simply as »the place of two citadels« to the Europeans passing through on the way to Ayutthaya. The village was already an important trading centre in a strategic location, although the Europeans initially regarded it as being of somewhat secondary importance.

Since 1782 Bangkok itself has been the **capital of Thailand**, where the government and parliament are based. Rama I (1782–1809), the first king of the **Chakri dynasty** that reigns to this day, moved his royal residence across the Menam Chao Phraya to the opposite bank in the very first year of his reign and thus initiated the rise of Bangkok. The new capital rapidly became the country's major metropolis, as monasteries and temples were built, and important trading organizations set up on the banks of the Menam, transforming the town into an international commercial centre. Bangkok experienced a major boom during the reign of **King Chulalongkorn** (Rama V; 1868–1910;

Highlights Bangkok

Grand Palace
includes highly important shrines.
▶ page 217

Chinatown
One of Bangkok's most vigorous and fascinating districts
▶ page 215

Jim Thompson's houses
A unique monument to Thai art: seven traditional Thai houses once owned by a legendary adventurer
▶ page 231

Wat Arun
This temple prang with its thousands of porcelain decorations is Bangkok's most famous landmark.
▶ page 222

Markets
Always an exotic feast for the scent, sight and taste.
▶ page 215

Wat Pho
A world-famous educational centre for traditional Thai medicine and massage and one of the oldest temples in the capital
▶ page 226

Wat Traimitr
Houses a 3.5m/11.5ft solid gold statue of Buddha that was uncovered wholly by accident.
▶ page 229

Wat Benchama bo-bitr
The »marble temple« of Italian Carrara marble has been in existence a little over a hundred years.
▶ page 223

National Museum
One of the most comprehensive collections in South-East Asia
▶ page 232

*Bangkok is a modern metropolis but there →
remains much that is exotic among the tower blocks*

▶ VISITING BANGKOK

INFORMATION

Tourism Authority of Thailand (TAT)
1600 New Phetchaburi Road
Makkasan, Ratchathewi
Tel. 02 / 2 50 55 00
Fax 2 50 55 11
www.tourismthailand.org
Opening times: 8.30am–4.30pm daily

TAT tourist information office
4 Ratchadamnoen Nok Avenue
Opening times: 8.30am–4.30pm daily

At the airport:
Arrivals terminal, Suvarnabhumi International Airport
Opening times: daily 8am–midnight

WHERE TO STAY

▶ Luxury

① The Oriental
48 Oriental Avenue
Tel. 02 / 6 59 90 00
Fax 6 59 00 00
www.mandarinoriental.com/bangkok
393 rooms, 5 restaurants, coffee shop, 2 bars, swimming pool, fitness centre, spa and much more
A legend has returned to life. After an interruption of some years, in 2005 the Oriental Hotel in Bangkok was once again voted the finest hotel in the world by business travellers. For those who can afford it, the best place to stay is one of the rooms named after famous poets, although the other rooms lack nothing in terms of luxury. The hotel is also beautifully located on the shores of the Menam Chao Phraya.

② The Peninsula
333 Charoen Nakorn Road
Klongsan (Thonburi)
Tel. 02 / 8 61 28 88
Fax 8 61 11 12
www.bangkok.peninsula.com
370 rooms, 3 restaurants, 2 bars, swimming pool, fitness centre. This brand new hotel with highly praiseworthy service and generous-sized rooms stands opposite the Oriental on the Thonburi bank of the Menam Chao Phraya. The upper storeys command a magnificent view of Bangkok and the river.

③ Four Seasons Bangkok
155 Rajadamri Road
Tel. 02 / 2 50 10 00
Fax 2 53 91 95
www.fourseasons.com/bangkok
340 rooms, 4 restaurants, coffee shop, 2 bars, swimming pool, fitness centre, spa and much more
Of the new Bangkok city hotels, the Four Seasons probably has the largest rooms in town. Impressive lobby, large shopping arcade. Good starting point for tours of the city, Skytrain station close by.

④ Banyan Tree Bangkok
27/100 South Sathorn Road
Tel. 02 / 6 79 12 00
Fax 6 79 11 99
www.banyantree.com/bangkok
216 rooms, 4 restaurants, coffee shop, 3 bars, swimming pool, fitness centre, spa.
The newest luxury hotel in Bangkok not only offers large, comfortable suites with a homely atmosphere but unusually also has an open-air restaurant on the roof.

⑤ Royal Orchid Sheraton Bangkok
2 Siphya Road, Captain Bush Lane
Tel. 02 / 2 66 01 23, fax 2 66 83 20
www.sheraton.com/bangkok
740 rooms, 3 restaurants, coffee shop, 2 bars, swimming pool, fitness centre, spa.

The Oriental is not just a hotel, but a legend.
Those who can afford it choose to reside in the Authors' Wing.

The Bangkok outpost of the Sheraton chain has a magnificent garden with a large swimming pool right alongside the Menam Chao Phraya. Many sights such as the Grand Palace or the bustling Chinatown are close by.

▶ Mid-range

ⓖ *Rembrandt Hotel*
19 Sukhumvit Road, Soi 18
Tel. 02 / 2 61 71 00

Fax 2 61 70 42
www.rembrandtbkk.com
407 rooms, 4 restaurants, 2 bars, coffee shop, swimming pool, fitness centre, spa.
This popular hotel has been under Swiss management for many years and is situated on a side street off the main Sukhumvit Road. The rooms are comfortable and the service is attentive.

Centre of Bangkok Plan

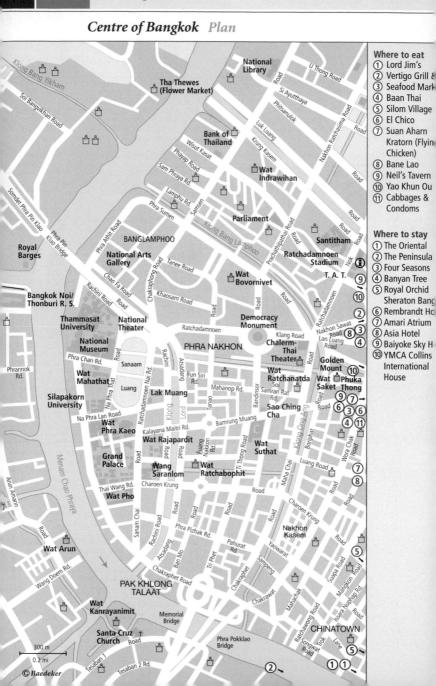

Where to eat
1. Lord Jim's
2. Vertigo Grill &
3. Seafood Mark
4. Baan Thai
5. Silom Village
6. El Chico
7. Suan Aharn Kratorn (Flying Chicken)
8. Bane Lao
9. Neil's Tavern
10. Yao Khun Ou
11. Cabbages & Condoms

Where to stay
1. The Oriental
2. The Peninsula
3. Four Seasons
4. Banyan Tree
5. Royal Orchid Sheraton Bang
6. Rembrandt Ho
7. Amari Atrium
8. Asia Hotel
9. Baiyoke Sky H
10. YMCA Collins International House

© Baedeker

300 m
0.2 mi

⑦ *Amari Atrium*
1880 New Petchburi Road
Tel. 02 / 71 82 00 01
Fax 7 18 20 02
www.amari.com
568 rooms, 2 restaurants, bar, swimming pool, fitness centre.
The central location of this hotel, not far from Sukhumvit Road, means it is always popular, particularly with businesspeople. Tastefully furnished rooms and attentive service.

⑧ *Asia Hotel*
296 Phayathai Road
Tel. 02 / 2 15 08 08
Fax 2 17 01 09
www.asiahotel.co.th
650 rooms, 4 restaurants, bar, swimming pool, fitness centre.
Good mid-range hotel near Ratchathewee Skytrain station. Plenty of shopping in the area.

⑨ *Baiyoke Sky Hotel*
222 Rajprarop Road, Rajthevee
Tel. 02 / 6 56 30 00, 26 56 34 56
Fax 26 56 35 55, 26 56 36 66
www.baiyoke.co.th/baiyokesky
673 rooms, 2 restaurants, coffee shop, bar, observation platform, fitness centre, spa.
The Baiyoke is no longer the tallest hotel in the world since one in Singapore supplanted it. Nevertheless, its 84 storeys rise 343m/1,125ft into the sky (including antennas) and the view from the platform on the 77th floor is fabulous. Large, comfortable rooms.

► **Budget**
⑩ *YMCA Collins*
International House
27, South Sathorn Road
Tel. 02 / 6 77 62 40-5, fax 6 77 62 46-7
http://ymca-hotels.com/thailand/ymca

Y.W.C.A
(Young Women's
Christian Association)
13 Sathorn Tai Road
Tel. 02 / 2 87 31 36, 2 87 31 38
Fax 679 12 80, ext. 519
www.ywcabangkok.com
Both the hostels listed here are genuinely comfortable (early booking is recommended).

WHERE TO EAT
► **Expensive**
① *Lord Jim's*
48, Oriental Avenue
(in the Oriental-Hotel)
Tel. 02 / 6 59 90 00
Possibly the best seafood restaurant in Bangkok – but certainly one of the most expensive. For the money, though, only the highest quality fresh fish is served. Advance booking is recommended.

③ *Seafood Market*
Sukhumvit, Soi 24
Tel. 02 / 66 11 25 29
opening times: 10am–11pm daily
»If it swims – we have it!« is the claim of this unusual restaurant that prides itself on serving anything that the sea can provide. The remarkable feature is that guests can seek out their own ingredients from one of the local markets, then pay and tell the waiter how they wish the meal to be prepared. Caution: sly taxi drivers often maintain that this restaurant has closed down and prefer to drive you to another (where they themselves receive a bigger bonus).

② *Vertigo Grill & Moon Bar*
27/100 South Sathorn Road
Tel. 02 / 6 79 12 00
Opening times: 6pm–midnight daily (except when it rains)
The Vertigo, situated on the roof of

At the Vertigo Grill, the view is thrown in for free.

the Banyan Tree Hotel, is an exclusive open-air restaurant with a wonderful view.

▶ Moderate

④ **Baan Thai**
Sukhumvit Road, Soi 32
Opening times: 11am–10pm daily
High-quality restaurant that puts major emphasis on the freshness of the food.

⑤ **Silom Village**
286, Silom Road
Tel. 02 / 2 35 87 60, opening times: 10am–11pm daily
Although it is not far from the busy Silom Road, the restaurant occupies a pleasant and quiet courtyard. The food is excellent, the prices moderate. In the evenings performances of traditional Thai dance take place.

⑥ **El Chico**
19, Sukhumvit Road, Soi 18
(in the Rembrandt-Hotel)
Tel. 02 / 2 61 71 00, opening times: 11am–10pm daily
This restaurant with its Mexican specialties and music is considered the best of its kind in town. Reservations are essential.

⑦ **Suan Aharn Kratorn (Flying Chicken)**
99/1 Bangna-Trad Road, Bang Na
Tel. 02 / 3 99 52 02

open in the evenings
This has to be seen to be believed. The grilled chicken that is the specialty of the house is placed in a catapult and launched through the air to the waiter who brings it to your table.

▶ Inexpensive

⑧ **Bane Lao**
49 Sukhumvit Soi 36, Naphasap Yaek
Tel. 02 / 2 56 60 96, Opening times: 11am–10pm daily
Very popular with the locals because the food is simply excellent

⑨ **Neil's Tavern**
Ploenchit 58/4, Soi Ruam Rudi, Ploenchit Road
Tel. 02 / 2 56 68 75, opening times: 4pm–midnight daily
Western and international dishes as well as snacks of all kinds, occasionally some live music.

⑩ **Yao Khun Ou**
Petchburi Road, Soi 17
Opening times: 11am–9pm daily
Highly recommended restaurant in a traditional Thai house. It is even nicer, though, to sit in the garden under the open sky. Tasty Thai cuisine at really good prices.

Baedeker recommendation

⑪ **Cabbages & Condoms**
Sukhumvit, Soi 12, tel. 02 / 22 29 46 10
Opening times: 11am–10pm daily
The name represents a kind of philosophy that the owner adopted while he was the cabinet minister responsible for family planning. A free condom comes with the bill, which is always reasonable. It is particularly pleasant to sit in the garden under a myriad lights. The most expensive dish on the menu only costs around £2/US$4.

SHOPPING

Bangkok is a shopper's paradise. By day or by night, it is rare to come home without a bag full of goods. The night markets are delightful, but the shopping complexes filled with hundreds of small shops also provide a huge range of options. Thailand is the land of imitations, however. Most articles are worth no more than their low price suggests.

Mah Boonkrong Shopping Center

444 Phayathai Road (close to Siam Square)

More than 1,500 shops under one roof – where is the like of that anywhere else in the world? The assortment of items on offer is extraordinary. Here, you really can »shop till you drop«.

Siam Center

965 Rama I Road (on Siam Square)

One of the oldest shopping centres in Bangkok, but the shops remain up to date. A few designer boutiques make the Siam Center especially popular with trendy youngsters.

Gaysorn Plaza

999 Ploenchit Road

Plenty of shops purveying authentic art of a quality far in excess of the usual dross, as well as some exclusive boutiques. The top floor houses the Thai Craft Museum Shop with a selection of pretty souvenirs.

Jim Thompson's Thai Silk

9 Surawong Road

Real Thai silk woven to original patterns in the shop that bears the name of the legendary American secret agent and rediscoverer of Thai silk (►see Famous People). There are branches in several of the luxury hotels, including the Oriental Hotel.

World Trade Center

4 Rajadamri Road

No less than 350 shops, two department stores and countless restaurants are to be found in this complex with an almost inconceivable variety of goods. Don't miss it unless you are prone to uncontrolled impulse buying.

MARKETS

In Bangkok, especially in *Chinatown* and its environs innumerable markets take place from dawn till dark. Most of them provide for the local population, selling fresh vegetables and live animals such as chickens and fish, or fabrics and everyday items. In addition to the major weekend market, the smaller markets are also fascinating for their bustle and colour, especially on Fridays and Saturdays, when housewives buy provisions for the weekend. The markets listed below represent only a small selection. Discover more for yourselves!

Weekend Market

For several years Bangkok's regular weekend market has taken place on the northern fringes of the town. In earlier times it was held at Sanaam Luang Park directly in front of the Grand Palace. Despite the move, the market has retained its magical attraction for visitors. The range of goods on offer seems to have no limits. Apart from the stalls there are also food stands and restaurants. Some local traders already make their way there on Friday night by bus, train or car. Take care when buying »antiques«, however, since they are more than likely to be well-made imitations.

Tha Thewes Market

The wide variety of flowers that grow in Thailand is evident at the Tha

There are plenty of markets in Bangkok's Chinatown.

Thewes Flower Market, where people and even children go first thing in the morning to obtain flowers to be made, with typical Thai care and craft, into Thailand's famous lucky garlands. These can then be bought until late the following night for just a few baht from taxi drivers or mobile vendors, who add a little to the income of their families in this way. The flower market is one of the few markets that is still located on the banks of the Chao Phraya. Orchids of unparalleled variety, jasmines, hibiscus and lotus blossoms delight the eye and their fragrance pervades the air throughout the market. Garden greenery and exotic jungle flora lend a verdant backdrop.

Bangrak Market

It is actually possible to see live sheep at Bangrak Market, but only very early in the morning. Even later in the day, though, this extensive market between Sathorn Tai and the Silom Road is always worth a visit, as provides everything the Thais need for their day-to-day existence. Fruit and vegetables are snapped up fast, in particular by the buyers from the big hotels who appreciate the splendid assortment of fresh produce.

Silom Road, Patpong

Every evening Silom Road is transformed into a sizeable all-night market with a huge variety of produce on offer. There are also plenty of food counters and restaurants, where you can eat to your heart's content. Since Patpong, the nexus of Bangkok night life, became a pedestrian zone dozens of traders have set up shop here.

Suan Lum

Sathorn Road/Rama IV Road
The newest night market in Bangkok takes place on a huge paddock with hundreds of small business selling everything you might wish to buy and more. In the middle of the market is a stage for live music and a large open-air restaurant.

► see Famous People). He had wide roads built and a 10km/6mi tramway laid. Under his successors, the city veritably exploded. Even today the city has an unplanned, amorphous feel. Thonburi and Bangkok itself merged into a single urban area, a melting pot in which according to official figures 6.3 million people live on an area of just 6,500 sq km/2,500 sq mi. In the greater metropolitan district there are as many as 10 million inhabitants.

✳ ✳ Grand Palace

One of the most exciting destinations for visitors to Bangkok is the Grand Palace, which includes the highly important shrine of the famous **Jade Buddha** (also known as the Emerald Buddha) in **Wat Phra Kaeo**. Each of the buildings within the compound, which co-

◄ **Location**
Na Phra Lan Road

vers an area of 218,400 sq m/54 acres, expresses one of the stylistic and cultural epochs of Thai history and, in particular, the character of the reigning kings. The buildings in the whole of the consecrated area have retained the style of the age when they were built in spite of repeated restoration. Each of the many renovations has concentrated on preserving the pure essence of the originals, and particularly of the huge murals that have always suffered from severe atmospheric pollution in the ever-expanding city of Bangkok.

> **❓ DID YOU KNOW ...?**
>
> ■ The Thai capital is known to the world as Bangkok but is known locally as Krung Thep. That, however, is not the full extent of the name. The full name is the longest of any city in the world: »Krung Thep Mahanakorn Amorn Rattanakosin Mahintara Mahadirok Popnoparat Ratchathani Burirom Udommahasthan Amornpiman Awathansathit«. This roughly translates as »city of angels, finest depository of divine jewels, great and invincible land of a mighty empire, fabulous royal capital, adorned with the nine heavenly gems, highest seat of kings, home of the gods and domicile of reincarnated souls«.

The **entrance** to the walled palace interior is through the Wissedchairi Gate (»gate of miraculous victory«), from which a wide road leads towards the first outer courtyard. The road is flanked by modern buildings set aside for the officials of government.

Visitors whose clothing is deemed by the guards to be unsuitable are asked to wear a sarong that is provided free, with the person's passport or identity papers being held as a deposit. Admission tickets are stamped at a counter at the start of the road leading to the palace compound proper. The road leads past a modest building that is home to the **museum of royal medals and coins**. Several beautifully carved items of furniture and other indoor fittings can be seen on the first floor.

◄ Make sure you are suitably dressed

🕐 Opening hours:
8.30–11.30am,
1–3pm
(pavilions closed Sat and Sun)

A gate guarded by two fierce demonic statues leads to the consecrated part of the complex, which focuses on the impressive **Wat Phra Kaeo** (Temple of the Emerald Buddha). The guardian figures were

Temple compound

Grand Palace Bangkok

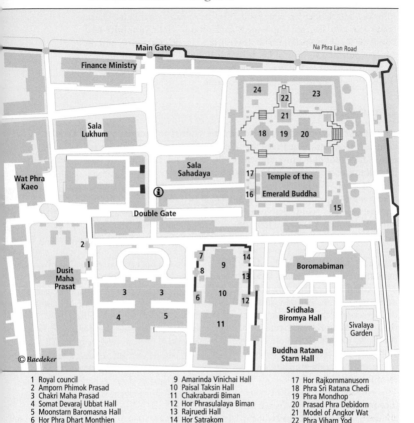

1 Royal council	9 Amarinda Vinichai Hall	17 Hor Rajkornmanusorn
2 Amporn Phimok Prasad	10 Paisal Taksin Hall	18 Phra Sri Ratana Chedi
3 Chakri Maha Prasad	11 Chakrabardi Biman	19 Phra Mondhop
4 Somat Devaraj Ubbat Hall	12 Hor Phrasulalaya Biman	20 Prasad Phra Debidorn
5 Moonstarn Baromasna Hall	13 Rajruedi Hall	21 Model of Angkor Wat
6 Hor Phra Dhart Monthien	14 Hor Satrakom	22 Phra Viharn Yod
7 Dusida Bhiromya Hall	15 Hor Kanthararasdr	23 Hor Monthien Dharma
8 Snamchandr Hall	16 Hor Rajbongsanusorn	24 Hor Phra Naga

sponsored by Chinese merchants and seem a little out of place in a setting that is otherwise dominated by typically Thai architecture. At the entrance gate there are murals depicting the opening of the **Ramakien epic** as well as marble tablets with inscriptions that were put in place by **King Chulalongkorn** (Rama V). Turning to the left, the golden chedi known as **Phra Sri Ratana** comes into view. It rises from a five-tiered base. The relic inside the chedi is said to be a bone or a hair of the enlightened Buddha. The pointed spire of the chedi is typical of the Thai manner of adapting Indian pagodas.

Phra Mondhop Behind Chedi Phra Sri Ratana rises the light and graceful Phra Mondhop, richly decorated with tiny glass mosaics. The four figures at the corners of the mondhop are fashioned in the Borobodur style (14th century). The building looks small compared to the two buildings either side of it, the **pantheon** (Phra Debidorn) and the **relic chedi** (Phra Sri Ratana). Inside it is a black lacquered bookcase with mother-of-pearl inlay in which the holy scriptures, »Tripitaka« (= triple basket) are kept. The floor of the mondhop is pure silver.

The stone model of the temple complex at Angkor Wat that stands on the terrace dates from the reign of **Rama IV**. Although the temple now stands across the border in Cambodia, it was formerly in the tenure of the Siamese kings. Even though it lacks the massive size and imposing jungle setting of the original, the model is still frequently visited by students of history and others.

Angkor Wat (model)

> **? DID YOU KNOW ...?**
>
> ■ The sculptures of elephants alongside the model of Angkor Wat are surprisingly worn around the head and neck. This is due to a popular belief that a return to Wat Phra Kaeo is assured to visitors who first stroke an elephant's head and then their own.

In **Phra Viharn Yod** to the left of the terrace is the oldest feature in the entire palace compound, **the stone throne of King Ramkhamhaeng** (13th century), the founder of Thailand. The throne was discovered by King Mongkut (Rama IV) during his time as a wandering monk and he had it brought back to Bangkok.

The third building on the broad terrace is the Prasat Phra Debidorn, also known as the pantheon. The building is open to the public only once a year on the day of the Chakri festival (6th April). Inside it there are life-sized statues of the first eight kings of the Chakri dynasty (the present King Bhumibol is the ninth of the line).

Prasat Phra Debidorn

Beyond the terrace is Wat Phra Kaeo's »holy of holies«, the **Temple of the Emerald or Jade Buddha**. The bot is entered via one of the portals at the side – the centre gate may only be used by the king himself. Inside the building, upon a high pedestal, stands the Jade Buddha itself, surprisingly small at just 75cm/30in tall and covered by a stepped canopy of nine tiers. It was carved from a single block of jade in Patalibutr (India), according to legend, although some other sources claim it was made in Burma. It arrived in northern Thailand by way of Sri Lanka and Cambodia, and was finally uncovered in Chiang Rai (in 1434), when a camouflaging shell broke open during transport. The Jade Buddha underwent further travels before it finally arrived in Bangkok, where it has remained in Wat Phra Kaeo since 1778. A special celebration is held three times every year, when the king himself changes the Buddha's clothes. The exquisite lines of the statue are best seen during the rainy season (May to October), whereas during the »cold« time of year (November to February) it is almost completely obscured by a golden net.

Bot
◄ No photographs

Work on Wat Phra Kaeo started a couple of years before the French Revolution shook Paris.

An especially notable feature of the bot are its **murals**, although the pictures had to be restored due to their faded condition and are thus no longer wholly original. Above the entrance are scenes from the life of Buddha, whereas the opposite wall depicts images from Buddhist astrology. The paintings on the windows and doors show episodes from the **Ramakien** epic in pictures and in rhyme.

After seeing the temple, it is worth taking in the beautifully tended **Outdoors** outdoor sections of the compound. The graceful gold statues are called **kinnari** (bird women). Pay close attention to the expressive demons that »support« the stepped chedi. Between the bot of Wat Phra Kaeo and the colonnade that marks the edge of the remaining areas of the palace, there are a number of small pavilions. In ear-

✔ DON'T MISS

- Emerald Buddha
- Ramakien corridor
- Model of Angkor Wat

lier times they were given over to the king, who prepared there for ceremonies he was to conduct in the bot itself. Nowadays they simply provide welcome shade to visitors.

The **murals** in the colonnade have been restored with loving care. They too show episodes from the Ramakien as well as scenes from the history of Thailand.

Boromabiman Hall is the official name for the building that stands **Boromabiman** beyond the wide lawn. It used to be the scene of the king's annual **Hall** garden party. Inside it are more **frescoes** depicting the Indian gods Indra, Yahuma, Varuna and Agni as protectors of the universe. Beneath them are some plaques inscribed with Indian texts listing the »ten royal virtues« (liberality, propriety, readiness to make sacrifices, clemency, modesty, conscientiousness, freedom from anger, freedom from suspicion, patience and just dealing). Since Rama VI all the crown princes, including the present king, have grown up here. Nowadays the building is only occasionally used as a guest house for visiting heads of state or Buddhist dignitaries.

West of the Chakri palace is a set of three buildings called the **Mahamontien** (noble residence). The front section (which is accessible to visitors) comprises a single great hall called the **Amarindra Vini-chai** (divine judgement), where King Rama I once accepted obeisance seated upon the great, wide throne. King Bhumibol (who was crowned here on 5 May 1950) also uses this hall, primarily for state receptions, although he usually sits on the throne at the front which allows him to sit in European fashion. On the anniversary of his coronation each year, the king presents medals, not only to public dignitaries and courtiers, but also to men and women from all walks of life who have earned honours for services to society.

After exiting the building, walk around the portico at the front, where the king's regal judgements were once announced. The red-gold pillars were formerly used for tethering the royal elephants.

Grand Chakri Palace   The Grand Chakri Palace is situated within a well-tended garden. The eastern wing was once the residence of the Thai king, while the queen occupied the west wing (no access). Nowadays King Bhumibol, having moved his household to the Chitralada Palace, uses the building to receive delegations and ambassadors from foreign countries. The palace was designed by British architects along Italian Renaissance lines, although at the request of King Rama V it was also given Siamese tiered roofs topped with mondhops. The largest one in the middle contains an urn with the ashes of the eight kings of the Chakri dynasty. All the halls within the palace contain valuable paintings, including portraits of all the Thai kings. Royal proclamations were once read from the balcony at the front. A medallion in the middle shows Rama V, who originally had the palace built.

Dusit Maha Prasat   West of the Chakri Palace is the graceful-looking Dusit Maha Prasat, a palace built in 1789 by King Rama I with four layers of roof that curve one atop the other, decked in red and green glazed tiles. The ground plan is such that the roofs intersect above ornate gables and taper up to a golden mondhop that towers above them like a chedi spire. Four garudas form the base of the mondhop and a harmonious connection between the curved roofs. Garudas are mythical birds that act as steeds for the god Vishnu. One is also depicted on the Thai coat of arms.

The large room inside can also be visited. It once served as the audience hall of Rama I, although the king received visitors not upon the throne seen there today but on one situated behind and above it inside a niche in the wall of the south wing. The murals are from a later date when the hall was used for the lying-in-state of deceased monarchs or other members of the royal family. It was last used in this way upon the death of the king's mother in 1995. The richly decorated divan also dates from the time of Rama I.

Amphorn Phimok Prasat   In front of the building at the exit of the Amphorn Phimok Prasat is a dainty wooden pavilion in which the kings used to change clothes after audiences before venturing out on a litter. Once they had set foot inside, a curtain threaded with gold was lowered between the pillars.

✴ ✴ Wat Arun (Temple of the Dawn)

Location
West bank of the Menam Chao Phraya in Thonburi ▶   As Ayutthaya lay in ashes after conquest by the Burmese, General Taksin undertook to march the remaining survivors »until the sun rises again« and vowed to erect a temple at whatever spot they had reached. The place at which they arrived is now the site of Wat Arun, the temple of the dawn. Initially it was to serve as a palace chapel for Taksin's new abode. The 86m/282ft central prang with four smaller prangs around it has now become Bangkok's leading landmark, even though it actually stands across the river in Thonburi. The outside of

Wat Arun is one of the landmarks of Bangkok. The 86m/280ft prang with its countless ceramic embellishments can be seen for miles around.

the brick building is decorated with thousands of porcelain details that were donated by the people of Bangkok and added at a later date. The construction method of Wat Arun is fascinating. Since the ground beneath it was so swampy, thousands of bamboo stems were laid across one another and the spaces created by this lattice were filled with clay. In this way, a foundation capable of bearing a sufficient weight was created. It is well worth climbing to the top of the prang to experience the fabulous view. On the other side of the river, another wonderful sight can be seen: the setting of the sun over Wat Arun.

✳ ✳ Wat Benchama bo-bitr (Marble Temple)

Wat Benchama bo-bitr, one of Bangkok's most beautiful temples, is also often referred to as the Marble Temple. It was built on the instruction of King Rama V (Chulalongkorn) around 1899 from white Tuscan marble that was brought to Bangkok by ship. Shortly after his 20th birthday in 1873, the already crowned king retreated to the monastery that lay to the south of the modern temple to become a bikkhu (monk) for a period of time. The monastery is popularly known as the »Wat of the Fifth King«.

Location
◄ Suburb of Dusit: corner of Si Ayutthaya Road and Nakhon Pathom Road (south of Dusit Zoo)

Unusually the consecrated area is not accessed via a gate or a viharn. Only a wire fence separates the compound from the street. Behind

Temple compound

! *Baedeker* TIP

Visakha Bucha Festival
The most fascinating time to see the Marble Temple is mid-May, when pilgrims carrying thousands of lighted candles dance three times around the bot on the evening of the Visakha Bucha festival.

the fence is a charming park. The southern boundary between the temple and the monks' quarters is unusual, too: it is formed by a narrow culvert.

The temple has a three-stepped roof made of glazed Chinese tiles. The small pavilions that match the temple in both colour and architecture along with the arched bridges of red and gold make up one of the most successful modern buildings in the Thai style. The king himself provided many of the details, though his half brother Naris was both architect and builder and was almost constantly on site during the construction.

Bot   The bot has a floor plan in the shape of a cross, dominated by simple marble pillars. A colonnade behind the bot, with more than 50 Buddha statues arranged around a courtyard laid with square marble paving, conveys an impression of sublime harmony and symmetry. This further accentuates the curve of the triple roof with its golden naga spires, although this adoption of some of the fanciful features of other, older temple buildings never detracts from the dignity of the building as a whole. The beautifully carved gables depict scenes from the origins of Buddhism, the Hindu god Vishnu riding a garuda and the three-headed elephant Erawan (on the eastern and northern gables). Two white marble lions seated in Burmese fashion guard the entrance to the bot. The temple is usually entered from the courtyard. On the orders of Chulalongkorn the golden Buddha enthroned on the main altar was modelled on the famous Phra Buddha Jinarat (»victorious king«) of Wat Phra Si Ratana Mahathat in ▶ Phitsanulok. The statues of Buddha in the courtyard represent all the styles to have emerged in the development of Buddhist art in Thailand. Marble plaques at the foot of each statue give their dates and the place where they were first erected along with other details (such as whether they are originals or copies).

i Terminology: bot and viharn

■ Bot: the most sacred building in a temple complex, usually accessible only to monks (detailed information: ▶p.68).
■ Viharn: similar to the bot but intended primarily for lay people (detailed information: ▶p.70)

Wat Indrawihan

Location
Wisut Kasat Rd ▶

King Mongkut (Rama IV) had this temple built in the 19th century as a shrine for a relic of Buddha from Sri Lanka. The main attraction of the wat is the monumental 32m/105ft-tall gold Buddha statue.

Monk at the feet of the 32m/105ft Buddha statue in Wat Intharawihan

The massive toes of this modern-day colossus are usually covered with heaps of flowers and other offerings from the faithful (opening times: 8am–5pm). ☉

✶ Vimarnmek Palace

At the back of the park surrounding the National Assembly building (west of Dusit zoo) stands the Vimarnmek Palace, a four-storey building that is supposedly the largest teak edifice in the world. It is home to a huge collection of art belonging to the royal family (including furniture, paintings and jewellery). Much of the collection dates from the time of Rama V (Chulalongkorn; 1868–1910) and was as-

☉
Opening hours:
Mon–Sat
9am–4pm
Admission fee

◀ No photographs

sembled in the wake of his European travels of 1897. Inspired by western architecture, he ordered the building of the palace in 1900. The building was thoroughly restored in 1982 and then opened as a museum.

✷ ✷ Wat Pho (Wat Chetuphon)

Location
Chetuphon Road, south of the Grand Palace ▶

Close to the Grand Palace is the oldest and tallest temple in Bangkok. Wat Pho (also known as Wat Chetuphon or the Temple of the Reclining Buddha) was established by King Rama I. It is said that a small residence belonging to one of the princes of Ayutthaya stood here in the 16th century. Wat Pho has long been known for the hospital that was founded here in the time of Rama III. Wat Pho was also the site of Thailand's first **public university** accessible to all citizens. Nowadays it also houses a world-famous **school for foot reflexology massage**.

Prangs and chedis

A total of 91 prangs and chedis are scattered around the courtyard in front of the shrine. They include the green chedi erected by Rama I in honour of a statue of Buddha that the Burmese had destroyed in Ayutthaya in 1767. Probably the most beautiful of these chedis (the blue-tiled chedi) dates from the time of Rama IV (Mongkut). He

The Buddha in Wat Pho displays the 108 signs of the Enlightened One.

had it built in memory of Queen Suriyochai, who had sacrificed her own life to save her husband from death. The **lion statues** in front of the entrance to the bot were built to a Burmese design, and it is worthwhile studying the marble bas-reliefs from Ayutthaya (depicting scenes from the Ramakien). The tall rectangular hall inside the bot is also impressive with its teak pillars dividing the building into three aisles. The predominant colours of red and gold in the highly decorated ceiling are reflected in the marble floor.

The English name for the Temple of the Reclining Buddha refers to a monumental reclining Buddha statue 45m/150ft long and 15m/50ft high in its own specially built viharn towards the rear of the Wat Pho complex. The remarkable outsized engravings on the jewelled soles depict scenes from the life of Buddha. The room is too narrow to get a full view of the figure so visitors are compelled to concentrate on details such as the fine curves of the face. The hand forming the shape of a lotus bud symbolizes purity and beauty.

Temple of the Reclining Buddha

On the other side of Chetuphon Road, where the entrance to Wat Pho is situated, are the monks' quarters, which are also open to the public. Serious questions about Buddhism can be directed to the monks at any time of the day.

✳ The Giant Swing of Wat Suthat

One of the most eye-catching buildings in Bangkok stands in the middle of a busy intersection in front of the Wat Suthat temple complex. A giant swing that was once central to a religious ceremony hangs from a red teak frame 27m/89ft high. Every December after the rice harvest until 1932, daring competitions were held on the swing, the origins of which are shrouded in prehistoric myth.

Location
◄ East of old Bangkok

Wat Suthat next to the giant swing is one of the oldest temples in Bangkok, as well as being one the most beautiful. Three kings contributed to its construction. Rama I, the founder of the Chakri dynasty started the work after his coronation in 1782, Rama II expanded upon the work and Rama III completed it after a construction period totalling ten years. Apart from the beautiful architecture, the restored murals inside are particularly fascinating. The whole complex covers an area of 40,800 sq m/10 acres and is surrounded by walls stretching 950m/1050yd. It is made up of two separate areas: the temple area itself and the monks' quarters.

✳ Wat Suthat
⏰ Opening hours: Viharn: 9am– 4pm Admission fee

Wat Suthat has had many different names since it was first built. Rama I called it Wat Mahasuthavat, although it became popularly known, on account of the massive Buddha, as the Phra Yai (Great Temple).

The viharn is indisputably superior to the bot in terms of architecture and the beauty of its interior. The almost square building is

Viharn

complemented by splendid vestibules on either side. The splendidly decorated roof gables are supported by six pillars with capitals in the shapes of golden lotus blossoms. Visitors enter the viharn through two massive portals which are decorated with famous carvings (one side of a window was carved by Rama III himself). The room is 30m/100ft high and is separated into 3 aisles by 8 columns. The viharn was specially built for the exquisite 13th-century Phra Buddha Shakyamuni statue that was shipped down the Menam Chao Phraya from Sukhothai to Bangkok by Rama I. When the Buddha arrived in the new capital, Rama I called a celebration that went on for seven days, and the bronze figure was paraded through the streets to its destination as if it were the hero of a conquering army. The king himself joined the great procession in his bare feet. The statue shows Buddha in a pose called the »pang mara vichaya« (victory over the Mara). The bronze body is covered with gold leaf and stands on a decorated stepped pedestal, the lower portion of which contains the ashes of King Rama VIII (Ananda Mahidol), the brother of the present King Bhumibol, who died under mysterious circumstances.

The building is ringed by a double balustrade with 28 Chinese pavilions, handsome bronze horses and Chinese soldiers. Alongside the outer walls are the traditional colonnades with their rows of golden Buddhas.

? DID YOU KNOW ...?

■ At the square with the giant swing, daring teams once gathered regularly after the rice harvest to catapult themselves high into the skies on a narrow board attached to the ropes of the swing. They needed to reach a height of at least 25m/80ft to catch a purse of silver coins that was suspended there. They were expected to grab it with their teeth. As a result of several serious injuries, King Rama VII put a stop to the contests.

Murals At the beginning of the 1980s, considerable effort was put into the full restoration of the frescoes in the viharn. The major problem was that the pictures had become soiled with bat droppings. The damage affected almost half of the murals, which cover an area totalling 2,565 sq m/26,600 sq ft and are considered the finest in Thailand. A tenth was irretrievably lost. Normally those murals that have survived in Thailand depict the life of Buddha, but the frescoes of Wat Suthat are different: they show the lives of the 24 previous Buddhas, as well as three of Buddha's contemporaries. The murals on the pillars show scenes from the Triphum, the Buddhist concept of the universe. We know this from slate tablets that are attached beneath the murals and describe in Pali script the content of each section of the picture. Since these paintings are so different from classical Thai works, and due to the fact that they also display western influences, it is believed that a portion of the murals was commissioned by Rama II (1809–1824), although they may not have been finished until the time of Rama III (1824–1851). Rama VIII was born in Heidelberg and his father Rama VII trained in Germany as a naval officer. For this reason the German government provided financial assistance for the restoration of the paintings.

Wat Traimitr (Temple of the Golden Buddha)

Wat Traimitr's claim to fame arose from a coincidence. Initially it was just one of the hundreds of temples in and around Bangkok and had no outstanding architecture. The story begins when a trading company bought a plot of land and specified as a condition of purchase that a clay statue of Buddha was to be removed from the site. A crane was therefore brought in order to lift the statue. Unfortunately the weight was too much for the crane. The cable broke and the statue fell to the ground. The crane operators gave up their attempts to move it that day and left it unguarded overnight. This was in the midst of the rainy season, and as monks made their way past the toppled statue the following morning, they saw the shimmer of gold glistening through. It was discovered that the clay exterior was merely a shell that covered a 3.5m/11.5ft-high Buddha figure, cast from 5.5 tons of solid gold. It is still not known where this valuable piece originated. Art historians believe it was camouflaged during the Sukhothai period when invaders were threatening the country and its art treasures. Holy items were often disguised in this way at such times.

Location
◄ Chinatown, at the junction of Yaowarat Road with Charoen Krung Road
🕑 Opening hours: During daylight hours

Chitralada Palace (royal residence)

The royal family nowadays lives in the former summer villa of King Chulalongkorn, which lies in about 1 sq km/250 acres of parkland with numerous artificial ponds. It is also the scene of the present monarch's agricultural and scientific endeavours. In 1993 King Bhumibol was the first reigning monarch ever to apply for a patent (for a water treatment plant). The grounds include a cattle farm, an experimental dairy installation, various laboratories and extensive fish farms.

Location
◄ Suburb of Dusit at junction of Rama V Road and Rajawithi Road
◄ No public access

Also domiciled at the Chitralada residence, in quarters befitting their honoured status, are the famous royal »white« elephants, eleven of them. The prestige of a Thai monarch is measured in the number of such beasts he possesses (see►Baedeker Special p.490). King Bhumibol has more white elephants by far than any of his predecessors. No previous ruler was ever presented with so many albino elephants.

White elephants

The man-made canal that surrounds the palace entered history during the student revolts of 1973. Demonstrators outside the fence were driven by the hail of police bullets to seek refuge within – and they found it. King Bhumibol granted sanctuary to those demonstrators who crossed the canal to his residence. This made a major contribution to the high regard in which he is held by his people.

Canal

Wash day on a Thonburi klong

✳ Klongs

Canals   Bangkok no longer has a real »floating market« as it once had. Most of the canals (klongs) that formerly flowed through the capital have been filled in, either due to the risk of epidemic or in order to build roads. Nevertheless some traders still set up stall amid the klongs on the Thonburi side of the river. A **boat trip** on the remaining klongs is still, however, a highlight of Bangkok for many visitors. The best starting place is the jetty near the Oriental Hotel. Many boatmen line up here like Venetian gondoliers to take passengers through the labyrinth of canals and waterways. To see a real floating market, however, as in the old days in Bangkok, the place to go is **Damnoen Saduak** (►Ratchaburi).

Lak Muang

Location
Opposite the south-
east edge of the
Saanam Luang ►

This small building contains a shrine (as well as the reference point for geographical measurements in the country, since it was built around the symbolic foundation stone of the city). According to animists and Hindu believers it houses the spirit responsible for protecting Bangkok. This spirit is revered as the true owner of the land and is represented by two phallic-shaped gilded pillars. At all hours of the day and night, Buddhists laden with flowers and joss sticks bustle around the »lingam« and make offerings seeking to bring fortune in all their earthly endeavours. It is possible to buy birds and set them free from tiny cages, which is said to please the spirit as well as quickening the way to nirvana. Around Lak Muang itself there is plenty of activity. At one corner the Thai dramas that take place there during the day always attract an interested audience. There are also great vats from which the Thais take holy water with lotus blossoms to wash themselves.

Opening hours:
Daily 6am–8pm

Jim Thompson's Houses

The life story of American-born James (Jim) Thompson reads like an adventure novel (►see Famous People), right up to his mysterious disappearance on holiday in Malaysia at the height of his business success in 1967. It was Thompson who made Thai silk famous throughout the world. He left behind a set of beautiful Thai houses that he had discovered in the region of Ayutthaya, where he had them dismantled and shipped by river to be reconstructed in Bangkok. These buildings presently house his fabulous art collection, now the property of a charitable trust.

Location
◄ 2, Soi Kasem San (near Rama I Road)

Opening hours:
Mon–Sat
9am–4.30pm

The seven houses form a unique grouping of a kind that sadly is seldom seen in Thailand nowadays. They contain treasures from every era of Thai art. A visit to Soi Kasem San is a must for any visitor to Bangkok. It is gloriously situated on the banks of a klong where Thompson's silk weavers once exercised their skills. Nowadays the houses are surrounded by a pretty garden. Inside they testify to the good taste of the former owner. Alongside ancient pictures made from real Thai silk, there are Buddha statues from virtually all the recognized eras, along with everyday objects and even more works of art. Jim Thompson obtained the houses only when temple astrologers deemed the moment propitious, but he was not granted much time to enjoy them, since only seven years later he was to leave Bangkok for the last time.

One of the best-kept houses in town formerly belonged to American Jim Thompson.

✳ ✳ National Museum

Location
4 Na Prathat Road,
to the west of Saa-
nam Luang ►

⏲
Opening hours:
Wed–Sun
9am–4pm

No photographs ►

The National Museum in Bangkok offers varied insights into the culture and history of Thailand. At least half the day should be set aside for visiting it. It houses a vast collection, partly because it remained the one and only museum in all Thailand until the mid-1970s. Since then the Department of Fine Arts, the authority responsible for art in Thailand, has established various branches all over the country so that archaeological finds and examples of art can be exhibited as close as possible to their place of discovery.

The **former palace of Wang Na**, built by Rama I, has been preserved almost in its entirety. Chulalongkorn's donations and the splendidly preserved contents of the Wang Na household formed the basis of the collection. It contains religious and ceremonial items, ceramics, games, weapons, musical instruments, the throne of the viceroy and much more.

It is especially worth viewing the collections in the older buildings: gifts presented to Thai kings, the royal barges and insignia, the royal hearses and some other curiosities. The modern buildings house such items as Buddha images from various epochs. The museum also possesses the original stone tablet with the declaration of government by King Ramkhamhaeng (1256–1317, ► Famous People) that was found in ►Sukhothai.

ℹ Tours in English

■ Guided tours of the National Museum in English are on offer every Tuesday, Wednesday and Thursday (starting from the main entrance at 9.30am and lasting one and a half hours). An excellent catalogue of exhibits is available from the main counter, and almost all the items on display have descriptive panels printed in English.

Wat Buddhaisawan

Apart from the later addition of the gable wall with its blue mosaics, the temple of Wat Buddhaisawan within the grounds of the museum dates back to the year 1795. It was built in honour of the finest work of art of the wat, an enthroned Buddha figure under a canopy. This statue is brought out just once every year on the eve of the **Songkhram festival** (Thai New Year ►Festivals, Holidays and Events p.125), when it is carried in procession through the streets of Bangkok. Legend has it that the statue came from Ceylon (now Sri Lanka), but historians have deduced from its style that it was made around 1250 in Sukhothai itself. It is nevertheless likely that, like the Jade Buddha in Wat Phra Kaeo (► Grand Palace), the statue has travelled throughout South-East Asia. In 1795 King Rama I transported it from Chiang Mai to Bangkok.

Even more interesting than the statue itself are the **murals** that adorn all four walls of the bot. Unlike those in Wat Phra Kaeo, they have been preserved in their original condition and are more than 200 years old. They were created using traditional tempera paints made

of pigments from minerals and earth, and depict figures dressed in historic clothing. Some of the paintings show scenes from the earthly life of Buddha.

Red House

The Red House was built by Rama I at the end of the 18th century for one of his elder sisters. It gets its name from a plant-based pigment used to treat the teak from which the house is built. It is no longer in its original location, having been dismantled and re-erected inside the National Museum. In particular, the gilded, wood-carved bed, the dressing table and the towel rail in the bedroom give a good insight into the lifestyle of the royal family. It is also worth mentioning the beautifully decorated, varnished wooden chests in which the splendid gowns were stored. The building also houses Dvaravati sculptures from ►Nakhon Pathom, others in Srivijaya and Lopburi styles (both on the top floor of the south wing) and in the ►Sukhothai style (in the north wing) to name but a few examples.

✶ ✶ Bang Pa In

D 3

Region: Central Thailand
Altitude: 4m/13ft

Province: Ayutthaya
Population: 12,000 approx.

Bang Pa In is the summer residence of the kings of Thailand. It has long been a popular excursion for city dwellers, as it is situated only 60km/37mi north of Bangkok on a natural island in the Menam Chao Phraya.

Summer residence

Bang Pa In had already been chosen as a summer residence by the kings of Ayutthaya. It was initially used as a domicile for the mother of the future king Prasat Thong, who was born there. Nowadays the palace of Bang Pa In and the beautiful parkland around it are open to the public.

After ascending the throne in 1629 Prasat Thong commissioned the Buddhist temple, Wat Chumphol Nikayaram. He expanded a small lake to cover an area of 1.6 sq km/ 400 acres and built a small mansion on its banks, where he and his successors were to spend the summer months. When the more distant Thonburi (now a suburb of Bangkok) became the capital under King Taksin, the buildings fell into disrepair. Later, however, Bang Pa In was rediscovered by King

! *Baedeker* TIP

To Bang Pa In in royal style

It is also possible to travel to Bang Pa In by boat. Bookings can be made with travel agencies in Bangkok or at hotel reception desks. The voyage on the Menam Chao Phraya will mean travelling either there or back on the *Oriental Queen* or *Ayutthaya Princess*, while the other leg is done by bus.

Mongkut. At this time steamships were already plying the Menam Chao Phraya, and the king was able to use such vessels to make the journey. The new palace that Mongkut built to replace the old one was much extended and thoroughly restored by his successors. It was not until Rama VIII selected a new summer residence near the sea at ► Hua Hin that Bang Pa In lost its accustomed status. Nevertheless, the palace is still used by King Bhumibol for state receptions. Most of the buildings that can be seen today in the carefully tended park with its numerous lily ponds date from the time of King Chulalongkorn.

✳ ✳ Palace Grounds

🕐
Opening hours:
Daily
8.30am–3.30pm
Admission fee

Bang Pa In actually consists of two palace complexes, an outer ring and an inner section. The inner buildings were once reserved solely for the royal couple and female servants. The entire complex is surrounded by a high wall, punctuated in many places by massive towers in neo-classical style.

Phra Thinang Aisawan Tippaya Pavilion

The most elegant building on the site is the Phra Thinang Aisawan Tippaya pavilion, which was built in typical Bangkok style in the middle of a small lake by King Chulalongkorn in 1876. It is one of the most beautiful examples of Thai architecture. In actual fact, it is a copy of the Phra Thinang Aphonphimok Prasat pavilion erected in the Grand Palace of Bangkok by King Mongkut. In the middle of the pavilion is a life-sized cast-iron statue of King Chulalongkorn by an unknown artist.

Phra Thinang Warophat Phiman

The hall of Phra Thinang Warophat Phiman displays a mixture of Italian Renaissance and Victorian styles. It is situated north of the boat quay and was used as an audience chamber. Inside it is a magni-

▶ VISITING BANG PA IN

GETTING THERE

Most travel agents in Bangkok offer trips to Bang Pa In.

By car:
From Bangkok on Route 1, turning left after 52km/32mi (see map).

By bus:
From Bangkok every day, every 20 minutes between 5.40am and 7.40pm from the Northern Bus Terminal.

By rail:
Station on the line from Bangkok to Ayutthaya (three times daily from Bangkok Hualampong; approx. 1½ hours travel.).

The pavilion was the prototype for many of the Thai buildings at world fairs.

ficent canopied royal throne flanked by iron parasols honouring the king. On the opposite wall hangs an oil painting of King Chulalongkorn in his state dress. The other walls are hung with images from the Inao, Phra Aphaimani and Ramakien legends. A roofed bridge links the audience hall to a round building with doors that open onto a large terrace; the broad stone steps lead down to the water.

The tall hexagonal tower built of brick in neo-Gothic style is all that remains of the palace of **Uthayan Phumi Sathian**, in which King Chulalongkorn resided. The rest of the palace was built of wood and was destroyed by fire in 1938.

Vehat Chamrun Palace

The Vehat Chamrun palace to the north of the palace compound was built in 1889 and restored in the mid-1990s. It was donated to King Chulalongkorn by rich Chinese citizens from Bangkok who were seeking to gain the king's favour. The fabulous building is modelled on Chinese royal palaces. The colourful glazed roof tiles and decorations, wood carvings and many of the fittings were all brought from China or worked by Chinese craftsmen. Since the palace has glazed windows, it was here that King Chulalongkorn retreated to seek respite from heavy rain. It is worth seeing the beautifully carved bed where rulers once slept, the desk carved in Chinese style that belonged to King Vajiravudh and the bookcases in the study that were made to contain Chinese manuscripts.

Royal observatory

The tower that stands on a small island between the two palaces was erected by King Mongkut, who was a keen amateur astronomer and used the building as his observatory. A stone spiral staircase leads to the observation platform with an excellent view of the surroundings and the palace grounds.

Statue of Queen Sumantha

One of the statues that King Chulalongkorn commissioned to adorn the park was erected in memory of his first wife, Queen Sumantha Kumaritana, who drowned in a boating accident on the Menam Chao Phraya along with her three children. None of the nearby subjects had dared to go to the aid of the drowning family since it was forbidden on pain of death to lay hands on any member of the royal family. In the wake of the tragedy, the king repealed the centuries-old edict that had been introduced by King Rama Thibodi, who had claimed to be a reincarnation of the god Vishnu.

Wat Chumphol Nikayaram
Outside the palace compound proper, on the front portion of the island near the railway station, stands Wat Chumphol Nikayaram, which was built by King Prasat Thong and much altered and refurbished by his successors. It contains murals from the time of King Mongkut that depict episodes from the life of Buddha. The outstanding feature of the two polygonal chedis, which date from the same period, are their lovely proportions.

Wat Niwet Thamapravat
Wat Niwet Thamapravat lies on an island in the river to the south of the royal residence. It was donated by King Chulalongkorn to the monks of the Dhramayutika sect and, unusually, was built in the Gothic style. The largest of the Buddha statues in its bot is a masterpiece by Prince Pradi Vrakarn, who was the court sculptor in the time of King Mongkut and King Chulalongkorn.

Buri Ram

D 4

Region: North-east Thailand
Altitude: 65m/213ft

Province: Buri Ram
Population: 29,000

The provincial capital of Buri Ram, originally a Khmer settlement, is 265km/165mi from Bangkok at the southern edge of the Khorat plateau. The town itself has little of interest to tourists but can be used as a base to reach the important Khmer temples of Prasat Phanom Rung and Prasat Muang Tam.

The poor-house of Thailand
This region on the boundary to the north-east of Thailand has sparse vegetation that turns into mixed woodland as it rises towards the hills.

History
The Khmer peoples spread further and further into Thailand during the 8th century. They had developed their own characteristic way of life, as testified by many of the multitudinous objects that have been discovered from this time. From the turn of the 11th century the principal regions under their control were the Menam basin and the lands in the east. The first seat of the Khmer viceroys was Lopburi. It is not clear why the Khmer erected so many sacred buildings around Buri Ram; the reason is probably geographical, since the region is on a direct line between Angkor Wat and Phimai.

★ ★ Wat Prasat Phanom Rung

Khmer temple complex
Apart from the ruined city of ►**Phimai**, Wat Prasat Phanom Rung is one of the most important Khmer buildings in Thailand. It was a key way-station and religious centre en route from Angkor Wat, the capital of the empire and now within Cambodian territory, to Phi-

mai. The wat itself occupies the summit of a hill that rises to 158m/ 518ft above sea level, with a view to the north over the plain and to the south towards thickly wooded hillsides. The strictly geometric layout of the temple complex testifies to the architects' intention to erect an imposing building for purposes of representation. From the U-shaped Rung Chang Puak building (»stable of the white elephants«), several walls of which remain, a 12m/40ft-wide stone stairway and a road lined with stone pillars lead to another monumental stairway in several flights. The latter was only added in the 12th cen-

Location
◄ 50km/30mi south of Buri Ram

🕐
Opening hours:
9am–5pm daily

Admission fee

Prasat Phanom Rung – an important Khmer shrine

Not to be missed

■ During the Songkhram festival that is celebrated all over the country in April, ritual processions to the temple as well as dance performance and light shows during the night can be seen. Every year on 3 April it is possible to look from the west through all 15 doors of the shrine and see the sun rising in the east.

tury in the reign of the Burmese king Suryavarman II, along with the stone wall that surrounds the site on a square plan. Sculptures depicting scenes from Hindu mythology flank the entrance to the temple. Inside, galleries run along the surrounding wall, from which cross-shaped gateways and windows open onto an inner courtyard. The oldest buildings are three brick prangs (10th century), two of which can still be seen as ruins. Two buildings made of laterite stone on either side of the main entrance were erected in the 12th century. The remains of one small sandstone prang (at the south western corner) featuring some marvellous sculptures were later modified to make a small chapel.

▶ VISITING BURI RAM

GETTING THERE: BURI RAM

By car:
From Bangkok on Route 1 to Saraburi, then Route 2 to Nakhon Ratchasima and finally Route 226

By bus:
From Bangkok Northern Bus Terminal (overnight buses also run).

By rail:
Station on the line from Bangkok to Ubon Ratchathani

By air:
Five times a week direct to Buri Ram

WHERE TO STAY

▶ Mid-range
Wongthong Hotel
512/1 Chira Road
Tel. 0 61 / 25 40
Fax 62 08 60
Popular with indigenous businessmen. Simple rooms, but pleasant service.

▶ Budget
Honey Inn
8/1 Soi Sri Koon
Nang Rong
Tel. 0 62 / 28 25
www.honeyinn.com
Simple guest house with very well-priced rooms not far from the temples.

GETTING THERE: PRASAT PHANOM RUNG

By car:
About 18km/11mi east of the junction with Route 218 (from Buri Ram) the road to the temple leads southwards away from Route 24 at Ban Ta Ko.

By bus:
From Buri Ram to Nang Rong, then to Ban Ta Ko station on Route 24; where you can be picked up by a taxi.

By rail:
The nearest station is Buri Ram on the Bangkok to Ubon Ratchathani line.

Flights of steps lead up to Prasat Phanom Rung

Shrine

The main sanctuary of the temple in its present form is a sandstone prang on a square pedestal that is topped by a smaller prang. This probably dates from the 10th or 11th century. On all four sides of the tower there are **gate towers** (gopuram) that mark the entrance to the sacred compound. The eastern gopura has a corridor that extends to a **hall** (mandapa). It measures 8 x 10m (26 x 33ft) and is open at both ends. Each of the longer sides has a portal and two windows. The **sculptures**(10th–11th centuries) on the gables, door lintels, walls and columns are of the highest artistic quality. The figures represent scenes from Indian (Brahman) mythology. Above the interior doors at the east of the shrine there are sculptures of five hermits, one of whom is particularly emphasized. One legend has it that a highly respected man once retired to the settlement here, and the earliest buildings of Prasat Phanom Rung were erected in his honour. In the grounds of the prasat several important early sculptures were discovered and removed to the nearby museum of Prasat Phanom Rung, which is affiliated to the Department of Fine Arts in Bangkok.

✳ Prasat Muang Tam

Temple complex The partially ruined, yet still imposing Prasat Muang Tam dates from the 10th or 11th century and is enclosed by four laterite walls. For centuries it was overgrown by dense jungle that was only cleared in the mid-20th century. The walls were pierced by three gate buildings (gopuram), each consisting of three sections. The door pillars are quite well preserved in places and feature finely chiselled and therefore highly vivid sculptures with scenes from Brahman mythology. The outer courtyard presents a graceful picture and with a little imagination visitors may get some idea of the former extent of the complex. In each stands a large L-shaped basin bordered by a stone naga with its heads spread apart. Of the galleries that once circled this courtyard, only a few fragments of wall and the entrance portals with their richly decorated door lintels remain.

> ! **Baedeker TIP**
>
> **Best via Prakhon Chai**
>
> Prasat Muang Tam is only 8km/5mi from Prasat Phanom Rung but it is better to make a detour via Prakhon Chai; where Route 2075 leads south to the temple. Look out for the signpost when leaving town.

Shrine In the prasat itself the main shrine stands on a square base. It consists of five brick prangs set in two rows. Only three of the prangs now remain. The main prang has collapsed, leaving only its base. Some beautifully decorated door lintels are either still in place or lying on the ground nearby. One of them shows Krishna as a heavenly shepherd, one of the many manifestations of Vishnu, standing on the head of Kirtimukha. This is a very unusual depiction, since Krishna is usually shown with his beloved Radha.

Chaiya

G 2

Region: Southern Thailand **Province:** Surat Thani
Altitude: 5m/16ft **Population:** 22,000

Chaiya, once an important trading centre, lies on the east coast of the Malayan peninsula, just below the isthmus of Kra. It is worth a visit for anyone interested in history, particularly as part of as tour including Surat Thani, Ranong, Nakhon Si Thammarat and the province of Phang Nga.

History As early as the 5th century Indian merchants from Madras were using the town as a base for their travels along the east coast of Thailand, as various archaeological finds have demonstrated. The **Srivi-**

jaya kingdom (8th–13th centuries.) once encompassed the greater part of the Indonesian archipelago (Sumatra, Java, modern Malaysia) and southern Thailand as far as present-day Hua Hin. At that time Chaiya was an important centre for trade. Some historians even believe that Chaiya rather than Palembang on Sumatra was actually the capital of the kingdom. Nowadays there is little trace of the town's former importance to Indian and Asian trade. Chaiya now lies somewhat inland, as if forgotten. It does still possess the magnificent Wat Phra Mahathat, the one and only well-preserved architectural relic from the Srivijaya period. There were once other such buildings, particularly in Nakhon Si Thammarat, but these have largely been left to ruin.

What to See in Chaiya

Not far from the station in Chaiya is the ruined stupa of Wat Kaeo that dates from the Srivijaya period. In the base of the building a seated Buddha and two smaller statues can still be seen. Close by is **Wat Ratana Waram**, where a large seated Buddha resides in the viharn. Several sandstone steles and a standing Buddha statue are scattered outside.

Wat Kaeo

Wat Phra Mahathat, one of the most revered temples in southern Thailand, lies within its surrounding walls a little way outside the town on Route 4011, which heads west from the station. The oldest part of the temple complex, the central stupa dating from the 8th or 9th century, has twice been restored (in 1901 and 1930) but appears to have retained its original form. It is an excellent example of architecture in the Srivijaya style with its Javanese influence. Like the temple complex of Borobodur on Java, the wat stands on a square base with cornices all around. It has many outbuildings and a three-tiered roof topped with numerous small stupas. The chedi is also interesting, although it probably dates from a later period. Nearby is a

★ ★
Wat Phra Mahathat

▶ VISITING CHAIYA

GETTING THERE

By car:
From Chumphon on Route 41 turn onto route 4112 at Tha Chana or carry on to Pala Ram where a narrow road is signposted to Chaiya (150km/ 95mi).

By rail:
Station on the Bangkok to south Thailand line.

By air:
The nearest airport is Surat Thani (up to four flights daily from Bangkok).

WHERE TO STAY

In Chaiya itself there is little accommodation. It is better to travel a little further to ▶Surat Thani.

small **museum** with copies of statues found in Chaiya, the originals of which are now on view in the National Museum in Bangkok. Also here is the bronze statue, the »Buddha of Grahi« that historians assume to have been constructed over two eras or by two different artists. The Buddha statue itself exhibits Mon influence, whereas the naga snake is clearly cast in the Khmer style.

Wat Suan Mok   The modern Wat Suan Mok, a centre for Buddhist meditation often visited by pilgrims, stands on a small hill a few miles further west. Its bas-reliefs show episodes from the life of Buddha, while the murals inside include a history of Buddhism and illustrations of Aesop's fables. One wall is dedicated to frescoes based on some of the aphorisms of the American Buddhist Emanuel Sherman, who came to Thailand via Japan.

Ban Pou Ma Riang   East of Chaiya is the idyllic fishing village of Ban Pou Ma Riang. The houses of the village are built on stilts and an excellent reputation for silk weaving.

∗ **Chanthaburi**

E 4

Region: Eastern Thailand	**Province:** Chanthaburi
Altitude: 37m/121ft	**Population:** 86,500

Chanthaburi is a rich, bustling and fast-growing town in south-east Thailand near the place where the Menam Chanthaburi flows into the Gulf of Thailand on a verdant plain. A chain of mountains in the country around the town, including the 1633m/5358ft Khao Sai Dhao, marks the border territory between Thailand and Cambodia.

»Thailand's orchard«   The massive plantations around the town grow oranges, pineapples, mangos and the »malodorous« durian. Chanthaburi plays a key role in the Thai jewellery industry. In the shops all along the main street it is possible to see jewellers grinding or sorting the tiny rubies, sapphires and other gems that have been discovered in the local mines. Only experts should attempt to buy here, however.

History   Chanthaburi is probably very ancient. Inscriptions have been found from the Khmer period (9th century) that mention the town as a port and trading centre. In the 14th century the settlement came under the aegis of the Ayutthaya kingdom. When that city was destroyed by the Burmese in 1767, the governor sought to gain independence from the new capital in Thonburi but was defeated by King Taksin and executed. Between 1893 and 1905 the town was occupied by the French. Many of Chanthaburi's inhabitants are of Chi-

▶ VISITING CHANTHABURI

GETTING THERE

By car:
309km/192mi from Bangkok on
Routes 3 and 344, 200km/125mi from
Pattaya on Route 3 or 36

By bus:
From Bangkok Eastern Bus Terminal
(a six-hour journey) or from Pattaya
(about 3 hours). Normally buses stop
a little way outside the town (pick-up
taxis to the town centre). Air-conditioned buses go directly to the centre
of town.

WHERE TO STAY
▶ Mid-range
① *K. P. Grand Hotel*
35/200-201 Trirat Road
Tel. 0 39 / 32 32 01
Fax 32 32 14
202 rooms, restaurant, coffee shop,
swimming pool. The best hotel in
town, featuring comfortable rooms
and a highly recommended restaurant.

② *Chanthaburi Riverside
Hotel & Resort*
63 Mu 9
Tambon Chanthanimit
Tel. 0 39 / 32 40 62
Fax 0 39 / 31 17 26
72 rooms, restaurant, bar, swimming
pool. Good mid-range hotel on the
banks of the river. Nice restaurant
with Thai specialities.

*Durian fruit grows well in the area
around Chanthaburi.*

③ *Chanchaolao Beach Resort*
168 Moo 6, Krongkhud, Thamai
Tel. 0 67 / 3 09 66, 3 33 22
Fax 2 11 96 56
Hotel outside Chanthaburi but right
on the beach with nice rooms and
good service. Own restaurant and
swimming pool.

nese or Vietnamese origin, partly because of the proximity of the
frontier with Cambodia. The town is also home to many Vietnamese
Christians who have fled from oppression in their own country and
has the largest Roman Catholic cathedral in Thailand.

What to See in Chantaburi

Gemstone centre   Everything in Chanthaburi seems to be driven by the jewellery trade. There are whole streets of jewellers in the town. The mines in nearby **Bo Kai** (in Trat province reached via Route 3249), where gemstones (rubies, sapphires and zircons) are strip-mined can be visited as part of an excursion.

Poet's monument   At the northern entrance to the town is a small lake with a monument to the Thai poet **Sunthorn Phu** (1786–1855).

★ Notre Dame Cathedral   The French cathedral of Notre Dame (Church of the Immaculate Conception) was built by Vietnamese refugees in 1898 in historicist style. It is the largest Roman Catholic church in Thailand. It serves a Christian community in Chanthaburi that numbers some 5,000 members. A school for girls run by nuns also produces some pretty wickerwork.

Chantaburi Plan

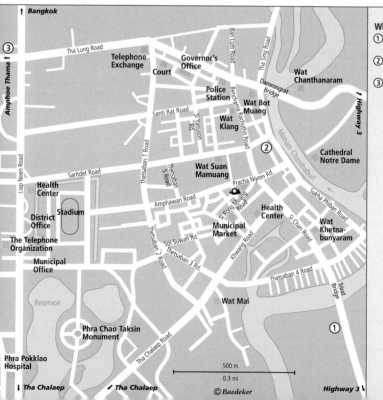

↑ *Bangkok*

Tha Lung Road

Telephone Exchange

Court

Governor's Office

Ban Lum Road

Tha Sing Road

Wat Chanthanaram

Damrongrat Bridge

Police Station

Benchama Rachuthit Road

Wat Bot Muang

Santi Rat Road

Si Yanusorn Rd.

Wat Klang

③ Amphoe Thama ↑

Liap Noen Road

Saritdet Road

Thetsaban 1 Road

Thetsaban 5 Road

Wat Suan Mamuang

② Menam Chantaburi

Highway 3

Cathedral Notre Dame

Health Center

Pracha Niyom Rd.

Amphawan Road

Si Rong Muang Road

District Office

Stadium

Thetsaban 2 Road

Health Center

Si Chan Road

Sukha Phiban Road

The Telephone Organization

Soi Suwan Rd.

Thetsaban 3 Rd.

Municipal Market

Khwang Road

Wat Khetnabunyaram

Municipal Office

Thetsaban 4 Road

Triat Bridge

Reservoir

Wat Mai

①

Phra Chao Taksin Monument

Tha Chalaep Road

500 m
0.3 mi
©Baedeker

Phra Pokklao Hospital

↓ *Tha Chalaep*   ✓ *Tha Chalaep*

Highway 3 ↘

Where to stay
① K. P. Grand Hotel
② Chanthavin Side Hotel
③ Chanchaolao Beach Resor

Relics from the French colonial period include a quadrilateral brick building at the entrance to the town (probably the former customs building) and the city library on the market place, which was previously used as a prison.

Relics of colonial times

Around Chanthaburi

About 5km/3mi south of the town at Khai Nern Wong (»fortress on the little hill«) are some relics of a fortress built by King Rama III in about 1834. The walls are now overgrown but within their bounds is the temple of **Wat Yottanimit**. It was commissioned by King Rama III and also includes a well-preserved prang from the Khmer period (11th century) enclosed by its own wall upon which four (ruined) chedis stand. The shrine itself was erected in 1977 on the foundations of an older temple.

Khai Nern Wong

The harbour of Chanthaburi is about 11km/7mi from the town and no longer has any economic importance since it is too far away from the economic hub of Bangkok. It is still worth paying a visit to the present fishing village, with its houses built on stilts and its idyllic location. It is also possible to travel by boat from here to some of the surrounding islands.

Harbour

The small village of Ban Kacha is 4km/2.5mi north of Chanthaburi where the nearest mine is situated (visitors allowed). A wat featuring a symbolic footprint of Buddha crowns the mountain of **Phu Khao Phloi Waen** (»gem mountain«).

Ban Kacha Mine

The cascades at **Nam Tok Krating** (»waterfall of the bull«), 28km/17mi south-east of Chanthaburi, crash over bizarre rock formations from a height of 400m/1300ft. Another waterfall at **Nam Tok Soi Dao**, which also has a thermal spring nearby, can be reached via

Waterfalls

! *Baedeker* TIP

In search of treasure
Around Chanthaburi there are several gem mines. Anyone can officially register to become a prospector in the mines for a few baht, but there is never much likelihood of actually striking it rich. Whatever you do find as a prospector, however, you may keep and there's always the chance of turning up a small stone or two for a nice ring (information at the TAT office in Chanthaburi).

Route 317, which passes through breathtaking tropical mountain scenery. Another waterfall, a popular place to visit for the locals, is at **Nam Tok Praew** 13km/8mi south of Chanthaburi, where it is even possible to bathe in the pool at the bottom. The entire district is part of the Khao Sor Bab National Park. Minibuses start regularly from the town centre in Chanthaburi.

Wat Tong Tua
On the way to Nam Tok Praew the Khmer ruins of Wat Tong Tua can be visited. Some remarkable 17th-century stone sculptures are kept within this monastery. The plain white chedi at the entrance to the waterfall contains the ashes of Queen Sumantha, who was tragically killed in a boating accident near ►Bang Pa In.

Laem Singh
Further along Route 3, a right turn at the 348km milepost leads to the small fishing village of Laem Singh, which is famous for its dried prawns. The village probably got its name from the island that lies across the bay. Its name is Ko Singh (the ancient Indian word for a lion) since its shape is reminiscent of a lion.

★ ★ Chiang Mai

B 2

Region: Northern Thailand	**Province:** Chiang Mai
Altitude: 310m/3017ft	**Population:** 175,000 approx.

Chiang Mai was once the proud capital of the independent kingdom of Lan Na, the »kingdom of a thousand rice paddies«. Nowadays it is the most important city in northern Thailand and is widely regarded as the most beautiful in the kingdom.

»Rose of the North«
Chiang Mai is the eighth-biggest city in Thailand. It lies in a sheltered basin, a productive agricultural region, at the foot of Doi Pui, at 1685m/5530ft one of the highest mountains in the Indo-Chinese highlands. Irrigation is mainly provided by man-made canals branching off from the Menam Ping.

Traditional and modern
Chiang Mai has long since relinquished its claim to the name »city of the golden temples«, as western visitors once dubbed it. Its teak houses with their gay front gardens have faded away, while sober concrete buildings and good road links have brought much of the modern world into the city. Among the nouveau riche of Bangkok it is thought particularly chic to have a second home in Chiang Mai. This has resulted in creeping development of the land around the town and the loss of some of the traditional feel of northern Thailand. The cultural contrasts could hardly be more stark: only a few miles from Chiang Mai – which is also home to an important

Chiang Mai *Plan*

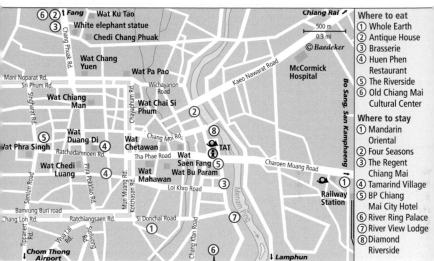

Where to eat
① Whole Earth
② Antique House
③ Brasserie
④ Huen Phen Restaurant
⑤ The Riverside
⑥ Old Chiang Mai Cultural Center

Where to stay
① Mandarin Oriental
② Four Seasons
③ The Regent Chiang Mai
④ Tamarind Village
⑤ BP Chiang Mai City Hotel
⑥ River Ring Palace
⑦ River View Lodge
⑧ Diamond Riverside

university – hill tribes such as the Meo, Akha and Lisu still lead archaic lives.

Chiang Mai is also a mecca for Thai crafts. From here carvings, colourfully painted parasols, batik fabrics, silks and fine silverware are despatched to the tourist havens of the south and exported to all the leading countries of the world. A little known fact is that Chiang Mai is the capital of the Thai jade industry. The coveted mineral is mostly imported (or often smuggled) from Burma.

6th–8th century	Chiang Mai is part of the Mon kingdom of Hariphunchai.	**History**
1281	King Mengrai conquers the Hariphunchai empire and makes Chiang Mai the capital of his Lan Na kingdom.	
1556	The kingdom and its capital fall to the Burmese.	
1767	Chiang Mai is liberated by Taksin, the first Siamese king.	

The original inhabitants of this region were probably the **Lawa**, a people of whom only a few remain in Burma. They were driven out or assimilated by the **Mon**, who spread throughout Thailand between the 6th and the 8th century. The centre of Mon rule was at Lamphun, which was then known as Hariphunchai (as was the kingdom itself). From the 7th century, Thai tribes trickled into the area that

◄ Kingdom of Hariphunchai

▶ VISITING CHIANG MAI

GETTING THERE

By car:
From Bangkok via Route 1 or 32 to Chai Nat, then Route 1 to Lampang and finally Route 11 (750km/470mi approx.)

By bus:
The journey by air-conditioned coach from Bangkok (Northern Bus Terminal) takes about twelve hours.

By rail:
From Bangkok-Hualampong (751km/467mi). Night trains leaving Bangkok in the evening and arriving at Chiang Mai in the morning have comfortable sleeping compartments.

By air:
Several flights daily from Bangkok, approximately 1 hour

INFORMATION

Tourism Authority of Thailand
Responsible for Chiang Mai, Lamphun, Lampang and Mae Hong Son
105/1 Chiang Mai-Lamphun Road
50000 Chiang Mai
Tel. 0 53 / 24 86 04, 24 86 07, 24 14 66
Fax 24 86 05, tatchmai@tat.or.th

WHERE TO STAY
▶ Luxury
① *Mandarin Oriental Dhara Dhevi*
51/4 Chiang Mai Sankampaeng Road
Moo 1
Tel. 0 53 / 88 88 88, fax 88 89 28
www.mandarin-oriental.com
142 rooms, 3 restaurants, coffee shop, bar, swimming pool, spa, shopping arcade, cooking school.
Dhara Devi belongs to the Mandarin Oriental chain and opened in 2005. It covers an area of 22 hectares/54 acres

Luxury in the Lan Na style: a private pool at the Mandarin Oriental Dhara Devi Hotel

and is practically an entire Thai village in its own right. It even has its own rice fields tilled by ox-drawn ploughs. The hotel which was built in the Lan Na style some way from the town centre, has many surprises even for the most spoiled guests. The rooms even contain genuine centuries-old antiques.

② *Four Seasons*
Mae Rim Samoeng Old Road
Mae Rim
Tel. 0 53 / 29 81 81, fax 29 81 90
www.fourseasons.com
82 rooms, restaurant, bar, swimming pool, spa, tennis courts, cooking school.
For those who like to get away from it all, this is the ideal place. Amidst rice fields that are still cultivated, its large comfortable rooms are built into a hillside.

④ *Tamarind Village*
50/1 Ratchadamnoen Road
Tel. 0 53 / 41 88 96 9
Fax 41 89 00
www.tamarindvillage.com
40 rooms, restaurant, coffee shop, bar, swimming pool.

A building in the modern Thai style with plenty of atmosphere. Centrally located in the old town of Chiang Mai but still quiet.

③ *The Regent Chiang Mai*
Mae Rim Samoeng Old Road
Mae Rim
Tel. 0 53 / 29 81 81, fax 29 81 89
www.fourseasons.com
64 suites, restaurant, bar, swimming pool, tennis courts, fitness centre, nearby golf course.
Even the Clintons and other prominent guests have stayed here. The hotel is built in a valley amid lovely natural surroundings. Needless to say, the rooms here lack for nothing.

► **Mid-range**
⑤ *BP Chiang Mai City Hotel*
154 Ratchamanka Road
Tel. 0 53 / 27 07 10
Fax 27 07 09
134 rooms, restaurant, pool.
Recommended mid-range hotel right in the old town, although the rooms are still quiet.

⑥ *River Ping Palace*
385/2 Charoen Prathet Road
Tel. 0 53 / 27 49 32
Fax 27 16 47
10 rooms, restaurant.
This former residence of a well-to-do family is more than 100 years old and its rooms have a charming homely atmosphere. The view from restaurant terrace overlooks the sedately flowing Menam Ping.

► **Budget**
⑦ *River View Lodge*
25 Charoen Prathet Road
Tel. 0 53 / 27 11 09
Fax 27 90 19
www.riverviewlodgch.com
36 rooms, restaurant

Romance by the river: the Riverside Restaurant

⑧ *Diamond Riverside*
33/10 Charoen Phrathet Road
Tel. 0 53 / 27 00 80 85,
Fax 27 14 82
312 rooms, restaurant, coffee shop,
bar, swimming pool.
Very close to Chiang Mai night
market, this charming mid-range hotel
has rooms of an adequate standard.
The swimming pool is situated above
the Menam Ping river.

Guest houses
In and around Chiang Mai there are
hundreds of guest houses with varying
degrees of comfort. A list including
recommendations is available from the
TAT office in Chiang Mai.

WHERE TO EAT
▶ Moderate
① *Whole Earth*
Sri Dornchai Road
Tel. 0 53 / 28 24 63
11am–10pm
Practically an institution, and affiliated
to the eponymous restaurant in

Bangkok. Good vegetarian dishes, and
impressive ambience in a teak-wood
house.

▶ Inexpensive
② *Antique House*
71 Charoen Prathet Road
Tel. 0 53 / 27 68 10, 11am–midnight
Very nice restaurant in an old teak
house with lots of antique furniture.
Tables in the garden restaurant in the
evenings. Specializes in Thai cuisine.

③ *Brasserie*
37 Charoen Rat Road
Tel. 0 53 / 24 16 65, 4.30pm–2am
Thai cuisine and western dishes are on
offer here along with live music every
evening.

④ *Huen Phen Restaurant*
Ratchamanka Road/corner of Jhaban
Road, 11am–10pm
Excellent northern Thai cuisine (beware: sometimes really spicy) with the
appropriate setting of an old teak
building.

⑤ *The Riverside*
9-11 Charoen Rat Road
Tel. 0 53 / 24 32 39
10am–1.30am
Thai cuisine and international specialities. The tables are on two
terraces by the river. Later in the
evening three different bands provide
live entertainment. It is also possible
to book a dinner cruise on the river.

⑥ *Old Chiang Mai*
Cultural Centre
185/3 Wualai Road
Tel. 0 53 / 20 29 93 5
www.oldchiangmai.com
A particular delight for devotees of
original Thai dance. The kantoke
dinner is accompanied by traditional
and highly authentic Thai dances.

now makes up northern Thailand. They came into conflict with both
the Mon and the Khmer, whose dominion was at its peak between
1000 and 1250. In the 11th century northern Thailand came under
the rule of the Burmese king Annarudha of Pagan, whose empire
reached as far as modern-day Cambodia. After his death the eastern
part of his kingdom broke up into small principalities, in which the
first Thai rulers came to power.By this time two other Thai tribes
had crossed the Mekong into north-east Thailand. Among the Thai
potentates, a dominant role was assumed by Mengrai, who was born
Chiang Saen in 1239 and is hailed as the founder of Chiang Rai. He
succeeded in conquering the Mon kingdom of Hariphunchai in
1281, moving the capital to a site near Chiang Mai. He employed
90,000 people to build a wall around the entire area of the city and a

◄ King Mengrai

magnificent new capital, where he
lived until his death in 1317. With
the founding of Ayutthaya in 1350,
the Mengrai dynasty began to lose
influence. When the kingdom of
Sukhothai was annexed, it seemed
to be just a matter of time before
Lan Na was absorbed as well. But
it was the Burmese who conquered
Chiang Mai first, in 1556, bringing
the Lan Na kingdom under their
control, a state of affairs that lasted
more than 200 years.

King Taksin, the first king of the
Bangkok era, forerunner of the
Chakri dynasty and founder of the
first unified Thai state, liberated
Chiang Mai from the Burmese in
1767 and appointed Chao Kawila,
son of the prince of Lampang, to
become prince of Chiang Mai. The
people, however, were worn out by

! **Baedeker** TIP

Plan to stay for several days
Many travel agents offer tours of northern
Thailand using Chiang Mai as the base.
Organized tours have one major disadvantage in
that they only allow for one or two days in
Chiang Mai itself. The city and the fascinating
countryside that surrounds it are worth a much
longer visit, however. There are other places to
see in the area as well, such as:►Lamphun, ►
Mae Hong Son, ►Chiang Dao, ►Phrae, ►Fang,
Mae Sai (►around Chiang Rai) and ►Chom
Thong. All these places are accessible from
Chiang Mai by car, bus or rail. Tours are also on
offer to the Thai part of the notorious »Golden
Triangle« (►Chiang Saen), the location for much
of the opium smuggling that takes place in the
country.

Highlights Chiang Mai

Wat Phra Sing
The largest temple in the city
► page 252

Wat Chedi Luang
The famous emerald is said to have once stood here.
► page 254

Night bazaar
Lively commerce late at night
► page 253

National Museum
Not to be missed by art lovers.
► page 258

the centuries of Burmese oppression and most had abandoned the city. For more than two hundred years, Chiang Mai was almost devoid of people. After 1796 the city once more attracted settlers. It came under the rule of Siam in 1873. Descendents of Prince Chao Kawila still reside in the city.

Chiang Mai played a key role in Siamese art by giving birth to the so-called **Chiang Mai style** that blossomed primarily in the period between 1300 and 1550. The style incorporated influences from the Mon tribes as well as from Burma and the neighbouring kingdom of Sukhothai. For this reason, the temples are nowhere else as colourful, bright and graceful as in Chiang Mai.

What to See in Chiang Mai

City of temples   There are almost 200 temples in Chiang Mai. Most of them are well worth a visit for anyone interested in art. This guide, however, can describe only a few important and beautiful temple complexes that are representative of the artistic and religious creativity of northern Thailand's major metropolis.

City gates   The centre of modern Chiang Mai lies to the east of the city walls near the Menam Ping. Of the five city gates – Tha Phae in the east, Suan Dok (»flower garden«) in the west, Chang Phuak (»white elephant«) in the north, Chang Mai in the south and San Poong to the south west, several have been reconstructed.

Wat Chiang Man   Wat Chiang Man on Ratchaphakinai Road is the oldest temple in Chiang Mai. **King Mengrai** had it built in 1296 even before the town itself had been founded, and this is probably where he lived until his palace was erected. The viharn, which has been restored many times over the course of the years, still exhibits its original form. The double-tiered roof, adorned with winding nagas, curves gently but nevertheless deeply downwards. The most conspicuous feature is the artistically carved gable on the side of the portal. Two lions flank the

! Baedeker TIP

Night market

Every evening the streets between the eastern gate and the Menam Ping are transformed into a gigantic market with countless stalls selling products typical of the region, particularly those made by members of the hill tribes. An abundance of small restaurants, most of them in the open air, provide the opportunity to enjoy the atmosphere. To find out whether the silver bonnets of the Hmong women are really genuine, test their weight. Fake ones are light, cheap dross.

entrance. A plaque in northern Thai script indicates the place where King Mengrai is said to have died. Teak columns divided the inside of the viharn into three aisles. One large gilded Buddha is interesting, as is a bas-relief, is a copy of the holy Buddha Sila. It is under the protection of the abbot of the wat and is displayed to the faithful just once a year at a ceremony. It probably dates from the 8th century and has aspects of Indian styling. It is said to have the power to bring rain. The **Phra Sai Tang Kamani (crystal Buddha)** is also under the protection of the abbot. This figure made of rock crystal has a gold base and may have been a gift to Queen Chama Thevi Queen of Hariphunchai in 663. It was taken as booty by King Mengrai when he conquered Hariphunchai in 1281. Wat Chiang Man also has a chedi with a base featuring 15 sculpted elephants, a small bot and a modern sala.

✷ ✷ Wat Phra Singh

The biggest and most important wat in the city is Wat Phra Singh. It lies on the main street leading right into the broad temple grounds, which were once the centre of the city. The wat was established by King Pa Yo in 1345, and the ashes of his father are housed in the chedi behind the viharn.

Location
◄ Ratchadamnoen Road

The viharn dates from 1518 and has outstanding woodcarving on the gables on either side, which were added at a later date. The small library in front of the viharn to the right is a graceful 14th-century building, a jewel in the crown of Thai religious architecture. The tall white base is decorated with tiny stucco details and the red-gold wooden upper floor has some fine carvings with inlays.

Viharn

Bot The small bot next to the chedi was built in 1600 when the Burmese ruled the city. They were probably also responsible for the lions guarding the entrance to the wat, since this is a typical feature of the Burmese temple style. The well-preserved wall frescoes with their vivid scenes date from the 19th century and tell the story of prince Phra Sang Tong, who was born in a golden sea-shell. The clothes and posture of the people portrayed in the palace indicate Burmese influence.

Phra Singh Buddha The most sacred part of the wat is a small, elegant building behind the bot called Phra Viharn Lai Kam. It was built by King San Muang Ma (1385–1401) for the famous and legendary Phra Singh Buddha statue. It depicts a sitting Buddha making the »gesture of calling to the earth« and is in the Sukhothai style. According to legend it originally came from Sri Lanka and was taken to Ayutthaya, then to Kamphaeng Phet, Chiang Rai, Luang Prabang and back to Ayutthaya. It has been in Chiang Mai since 1767, although it is not actually certain whether the statue is really the original or one of two copies that were made. Identical figures are to be found at the National Museum in Bangkok and in Nakhon Si Thammarat. No expert has yet been able to verify which statue is the original, and all three places therefore claim to have it.

Two other holy statues date from the 15th century: a bronze statue with inlaid gems, and a large statue of Buddha showing the Enlightened One making the earth-calling gesture

✶ ✶ Wat Chedi Luang

Location
Phra Pokklao
Road ►

The oldest part of the extensive temple grounds at Wat Chedi Luang is a brick chedi that collapsed after an earthquake in 1545 but was once 90m/300ft high, as the massive base only hints. The foundations of the building were made of brick and laterite stone, an unusual combination. A small memorial chedi for King San Muan Ma was built on the site in the year 1401, when the king died. His widow and grandson King Tiloka added to the building, using the Bodhgaya pagoda in India as a template. On the terraces and in the niches there are still some lovely elephant heads and Buddha sculptures. The niche on the eastern side of the chedi is said to have once housed the famous **Emerald Buddha** (now in Wat Phra Kaeo in Bangkok).

Viharn The viharn was first built in 1411 and reconstructed 5 times since then. At the entrance to the viharn with its large, three-tiered roof are two impressive cobras with scales of colourfully glazed mosaics. They are said to be the most beautiful of their kind in Thailand. The gaily ornamented gables are also notable. Inside are three bronze statues of Buddha (cast in 1440), several small statues and artistically carved elephant tusks. Most of the finely proportioned chedis in the outer courtyard house the ashes of deceased persons.

A pretty little temple to the east of the entrance (built in 1940) is home to the protector spirit (Lak Muang) of Chiang Mai. It is shaded by a huge rubber tree. It is said that if the tree should topple, a dreadful fate will befall the town.

Lak Muang

Other Sights

Wat Prachao Mengrai, on Ratchamankha Road opposite Wat Chedi Luang, was founded in 1288. A small hall holds a 4.5m/15ft Buddha statue dating from 1920 that is said to represent the city's founder Mengrai. In the viharn note a Buddha statue from Chiang Saen and the lovely lectern.

✱
Wat Prachao Mengrai

The impressive features of Wat Chetawan (in front of the eastern gate) include three richly embellished chedis, their inlaid gold and coloured tiles glinting in the sunlight. Two of the chedis also have fabulous beasts from Hindu mythology. The wood carvings on the viharn are also splendid. Almost opposite the temple on the other side of Tha Phae Road is Wat Mahawan, which has a beautifully structured chedi in the Burmese style. Its spire is gilded and the four corners of the fence are guarded by massive lion statues. The viharn and the small chapel are inlaid with intricate carvings; the towers feature bas-reliefs with scenes from the life of Buddha.

Wat Chetawan, Wat Mahawan

Not far away on Tha Phae Road is the rather inconspicuous entrance to Wat Saen Fang. Flanked by the bodies of two snakes, a narrow alley leads to a picturesque enclosure with beautifully tended gardens and a wonderful chedi in the Burmese style. The façade of the viharn is adorned with gilded carvings.

Wat Saen Fang

A row elaborate gates form the entrance to the magnificent Wat Pha Pong (at the intersection of Suthep Road and Thipanet Road). Various chedis surround a lovely pavilion and steps lead up to a chapel inside the building.
The façade of the rectangular building with its arched windows and columns exhibits Chinese and Burmese influences respectively. The interior has three aisles with murals and statues of Buddha.

✱✱
Wat Pha Pong

To the north of the city (at the end of Rattanakosin Road, 300m/330yd from Chang Phuak bus station) are the ruins of Chedi Chang Phuak and Wat Ku Tao, which has a unique chedi (built in 1613) with a square tiered base. The unusual upper section consists of a series of interlocked spheres diminishing in size (and probably symbolizing begging bowls).The spheres include niches and some have colourful glazed tiles in geometric patterns. A graceful gilded spire tops the unusual and faintly incongruous stupa, which is said to contain the ashes of Burma's Prince Tarawadi. Some old carvings have survived on the gables. The bot was added in the 20th century.

Chedi Chang Phuak

✶✶
Wat Suan Dok

West of the town (on the Suthep Road) is the famous Wat Suan Dok (Dok = flower garden). Its foundation is shrouded in legend and closely connected with Wat Doi Suthep (►p.272). The snow-white, bell-shaped chedi in the Sri Lankan style contains half of a relic no bigger than a pea that is nevertheless claimed to have miraculous powers. A monk by the name of Sumana found it in a small container that was hidden in a set of silver and coral boxes of decreasing size, all enclosed in a bronze casket. The relic underwent a series of travels before it came into the hands of King Kuna (1345–1385) of Chiang Mai, who had the chedi erected for it. In 1383 the relic apparently split into two pieces, yet both fragments miraculously grew to the size of the original. Wat Doi Suthep was then built to house the second relic. In the courtyard various gleaming white chedis of differing shapes and sizes house the ashes of members of the royal family. The bot of Wat Suan Dok has a lovely 6m/20ft-high statue of Buddha in the Chiang Mai style (from about 1550). The viharn takes the form of an open hall and is the largest religious meeting room in northern Thailand. It was built in 1932. Inside are some beautifully decorated columns and ceilings, two Buddha statues that stand back to back and various painted images of the Enlightened One, along with a box in the shape of a palace that contains the ashes of the monk Phra Si Wichai, the driving force behind the building of the viharn.

Wat Umong

Not far to the west along Suthep Road stands Wat Umong amid wooded parkland. King Mengrai had it built for an important monk. The underground vaults were added later under King Kuna (1355–1385) for another monk, apparently so that he could continue his meditation far from earthly matters. There are still traces of some murals on the walls. Since that time the monastery, where a very strict form of Buddhism from Sri Lanka is practised, has served as a retreat for monks electing to live in seclusion. Such monks are identifiable by their dark robes.

Part of the site serves as a meeting place for people of all nations who have an interest in Buddhism. Otherwise there is one collapsed chedi dating back to the time of the foundation, while the remaining buildings (Pali school, monks' quarters and library) are from more recent times.

Outskirts of Chiang Mai

✶
Wat Chet Yot

Wat Chet Yot (off the northern »Super Highway«), sometimes called Mahabodharama or Photharama Viharn, was the most important and magnificent temple in the Lan Na kingdom for about 100 years after its establishment by King Tiloka in 1454. Later, however, the magnificent sanctuary fell into disuse and was in danger of being

The chedi at Wat Suan Dok houses a relic no bigger than a pea. →

swallowed up by creeping jungle. Not until the 1950s was it deemed worthy of restoration. The building was extended and modified several times by Tiloka's successors, so that no one style can be assigned to it. The seven-spired chedi finished in 1455 is a copy of the Mahabodhi temple of Bodhgaya in India, on the site where Buddha is said to have found enlightenment. In the tall central tower there is a stucco Buddha figure and the ground floor contains a room for meditation. The stucco work on the walls is outstanding in its quality and remains quite well preserved. King Tiloka's own ashes are housed in a small rectangular brick stupa with stucco ornamentation that was commissioned by his nephew in 1486.

? DID YOU KNOW ...?

■ In 1477 Wat Chet Yot was the scene of a celebration of 2000 years of Buddhism accompanied by a synod convened by King Tiloka. These celebrations may well have prompted the first building of the temple.

Chiang Mai National Museum

The Chiang Mai branch of the national museum (off the northern »Super Highway«) was opened in 1972 and exhibits many stunning sculptures from all Thai stylistic epochs as well as terracotta pieces from Hariphunchai. A footprint of Buddha with exquisitely intricate mother of pearl inlays is also worthy of note. The top floor of the museum also has tools used by the hill tribes on display (opening times: Tue– Sun 9am–12pm, 1–2pm; admission fee).

University/Tribal Research Centre

In 1965 Chiang Mai University (take the road leading north-west out of town in the direction of Wat Doi Suthep) was opened. It includes the **Tribal Research Centre and Museum**, which is dedicated to studying the hill tribes and is endeavouring to ensure their continued existence and that of their culture. It is also possible to buy genuine hill tribe products here. (opening times:. 9am–5pm daily).

Botanical Gardens and Zoo

Beyond the university lie the city's botanical gardens with a plethora of exotic plants and orchids. Do not miss the nearby zoo which is the largest in Thailand and mainly features animals native to South-East Asia as well as rare birds and butterflies (opening times: 8am–5pm; admission fee).

Craft villages

Chiang Mai is a centre for arts and crafts in Thailand. Dozens of companies have adapted to the tourist boom and offer not only products for sale but the chance to look over the shoulders of local artists as they work. South of the city on Chom Thong Road is the home of the **silversmiths**. They make bowls, tureens and jewellery from pure silver or silver alloys. A little further east in the suburb of Ban Khoen are the makers of **lacquerware** (bowls, caskets and trays). Their black lacquer is applied in multiple coats and polished with ashes or lime. Ornamentation is then etched into the upper coat to be filled with gold or coloured paints. Wulai Road and Ratchangsaen

Road are centres for the **teak carvers**. The products of their economically valuable efforts are exported all over the world. Since the prohibition on the felling of tropical timber in Thailand, the teak is now imported from Myanmar. The **street of the bronze casters**, Chang Loh Road, is also worth a look. Here bells are cast without clappers, their bright sound instead being made by small lead discs strung on a thread. This is also where the solid bronze cutlery is made that is found in practically every shop in the country. North of the city, near the »White Elephant Gate« is the **village of the potters**. All the houses here have rows of pottery outside, which has been put there to dry (or to sell).

Countryside around Chiang Mai

Just off San Khamphaeng Road, lined with the shops of Chiang Mai's manufacturers, is one of the prettiest, yet least known temples in the city. Wat Buakkhrok Luang has a beautiful teak viharn in the Lan Na style from the late 13th century that contains a Buddha statue in the Chiang Saen style. Five rows of teak columns divide the hall into three aisles. The superb murals are from a very early period, as are the magnificently carved doors. There is also a marvellous bot on the left-hand side of the viharn. The temple also inspired a copy that was situated in ►Phayao until it was destroyed by a storm in 1988.
Close to the temple, in a landscape that was left as unspoiled as possible, is the entrance to the Dhara Dhevi luxury hotel belonging to the Oriental Mandarin group.

* *
Wat Buakkhrok Luang

The Old Chiang Mai Cultural Centre does not actually mark the old part of Chiang Mai. In fact it was instituted by a smart entrepreneur who established a village on Route 108 leading south from Chiang Mai itself, where members of the various hill tribes (Karen, Lisu, Akha, Yao) have made homes in replicas of the traditional cottages in which they live up in the mountains. They also wear their traditional dress and work with the tools customarily used in the mountain villages. The craft items that they create, such as jewellery or fabrics, can be bought in the village shops. In the evenings the local restaurant hosts a so-called kantoke dinner, in which a meal of northern Thai dishes is accompanied by traditional dances performed by members of the hill tribes themselves. Visits to the Old Chiang Mai Cultural Centre are offered by many travel agents.

Old Chiang Mai Cultural Centre

Wiang Kum Kam   The ruins of Wiang Kum Kam, about 5km/3mi south of Chiang Mai, were excavated in the mid-1990s. It is believed the settlement was established 700 years before the time of King Mengrai. As few finds were made at the site, there is no dedicated museum. Instead, examples are on show at the National Museum in Chiang Mai itself.

✹ ✹ Wat Doi Suthep

Location and directions
By bus or car 20km/ 12mi along Huai Kaeo Road (1004) heading north-west ►

Wat Doi Suthep is situated amid stupendous scenery at a height of 1053m/3455ft beneath the summit of Mount Doi Pui (1685m/5528ft above sea level). From the car park (where the buses also stop) it is worth making a small diversion to the falls of **Nam Tok Huai Kaeo**, which are surrounding by breathtaking scenery. At the point where the road to the temple steepens sharply, there is a monument to the monk Phra Si Wichai, who was instrumental in inspiring the construction of the first road to Wat Doi Suthep in 1934. He collected money for the purpose from the people of Chiang Mai, some of whom also helped with the actual building. The final stretch can be climbed on foot or travelled in comfort on a short funicular railway. The broad temple terrace itself is accessed via a giant stairway with 306 steps that is flanked by a balustrade made up of the undulating bodies of two seven-headed nagas. From the top there is a fantastic view of Chiang Mai and the surrounding countryside.

The legend   The name of the wat goes back to a monk by the name of Vasuthep who is said to have lived here as a hermit. According to the tale, King Kua was seeking a shrine for the second relic of Wat Suan Dok (see Wat Suan Dok) that had so miraculously replicated itself. Advised by the monk Sumana, who had originally discovered the relic, he had the tiny piece of the relic enclosed in an altar that was fastened to the back of a wild-ranging white elephant. The elephant then climbed the mountain and lay down precisely where Vasuthep the monk was living. When the relic was taken out of the altar, the elephant died. The temple was built where it lay. A small chedi marks the spot nearby where the elephant was buried.

Statue of the earth goddess Thorani   On the first platform, at the bottom of the stairway with the naga balustrade, stands a statue on the right depicting the earth goddess Thorani wringing water out of her hair. The goddess symbolizes the creative potential of the earth. Brahman legend has it that the meditating Buddha was tempted by demons led by Mara (»the evil one«), when Thorani appeared and washed the demon hordes away by wringing the water from her hair.

Temple compound   The entrance to the actual temple compound is guarded by two statues of demons alongside an open spirit house. There are six entrances to the gallery and chedis, but normally only two are open. The gallery features statues of Buddha in the Chiang Mai and Sukhothai styles. Take a good look at the more recent murals showing scenes from the life of Buddha. Within the gallery two viharns that stand one opposite the other are decorated with splendid carvings. The central shrine at Wat Doi Suthep contains a seated Buddha statue, which is highly revered.

The highlight of the complex is the shimmering gold **chedi**, 20m/66ft high and crowned with a five-tiered roof. The chedi is covered with gilded and richly decorated copper plates. At the corners of the surrounding fence there are beautifully sculpted altars and four tall and graceful canopies of gilded copper. To the north beyond the confines of the gallery there is a graceful and richly ornamented chapel. In the courtyard there hangs one large bronze bell surrounded by three smaller ones. It is also worth seeing the small altar that was once carried by the legendary elephant and contained the temple relic. There is also a bust of the hermit Vasuthep. The small **temple museum** at Wat Doi Suthep houses some extremely valuable items as well as some old stamps and coins.

The eye-catching golden chedi

Around Chiang Mai

Following the road from Wat Doi Suthep further up the mountain, a short trip leads to the royal summer palace of Phu Ping (visiting is only allowed when the royal family is not in attendance, and access will also be denied to those wearing inappropriate clothing). The building in the Bangkok style is surrounded by lush gardens.

★
Royal summer palace of Phu Ping

A climb lasting about three hours, through startling countryside, finally leads to the summit of Doi Pui, from where there is a magnificent view of mountainsides and canyons bedecked with dense jungle.

★ ★
Doi Phu National Park

The route passes a Meo village, which has become severely commercialized due to its popularity with tourists. Nevertheless, the colourful traditional clothes and beautifully made jewellery are truly lovely.

Chiang Mai Night Safari

A project started in 2006 called the Chiang Mai Night Safari includes wooded hills, 15 natural springs and five man-made lakes within an area of 130 hectares/320 acres on the edge of the **Doi Suthep Phi National Park**. The park is a half-hour drive (10km/6mi) from Chiang Mai. Within the enclosure are zebras, wild cattle and giraffes imported from Africa. Most of the other animals that it is hoped to establish there, around 1600 of them from 150 genera, will also come from other continents in order to give visitors a sense of the diversity of fauna around the world. The Night Safari is divided into three animal enclosures: the »Jaguar Trail« features small mammals and can be visited by night or by day, whereas the »Predator Prowl« and »Savannah Safari« enclosures provide homes for predators and animals of the savannah and are only open at night. Visiting animal lovers are driven through the enclosures by car (www.chiangmainightsafari.com).

_i_ Beware when trekking!

■ In Chiang Mai plenty of people offer one or more days' trekking in the north of Thailand. Most are reputable, but there are one or two »black sheep« who are seeking only to extort money from tourists. It is also advisable to be careful about the trips on offer to see the hill tribes in the border region between Thailand und Myanmar (Burma). The inflationary trend in prices associated with such trekking tours, which were originally intended to highlight the problems of the Hmong, Lisu, Akha or Karen, has led to visitors being less welcome than in the past. In small villages in particular, inhabitants may even respond with aggression, and nowadays they will at the least demand money for being photographed or may offer goods for sale at ridiculously inflated prices.

Bo Sang

Another place worth a stop is the umbrella-makers' village of Bo Sang, 8km/5mi east of Chiang Mai. Almost the entire population of the village is engaged in stretching silk or lacquered paper made from the bark of the tonsa tree across a bamboo frame. Once the covering is in place, it is varnished then painted with flowers, landscapes or other ornamentation. Even the children design ornate patterns.

San Kamphaeng

How to get there:
east from Chiang Mai via Charoen Muang Road ►

San Kamphaeng was one of the principal centres of ceramic manufacture in Thailand during the 15th century. Ruins of the pottery district lie to the east of the present village. Nowadays Chiang Mai itself has taken on the legacy of San Kamphaeng, but the former heyday of the potters' art has never since been equalled. Nowadays the village is better known for its hand-woven cotton and silk fabrics. Some manufacturers provide a small exhibition demonstrating the manufacture of silk. San Kamphaeng is also the site of the obviously Burmese-influenced temple of **Wat Sai Mon**. Inside the viharn the three aisles are lined by teak columns with ornamental gold insets and countless beautifully made religious artefacts.

One popular destination for weekend excursions is Nong Wua Park, 17km/11mi east of Chiang Mai. The park, with its pond covered in lotus flowers, has been reclaimed from swampland. Restaurants provide nourishment to hungry visitors.

Nong Wua Park

The Mae Sa Elephant Camp near Mae Rim allows visitors to watch the training of elephants. Mae Rim is 20km/12mi north of Chiang Mai and the camp is 7km/4mi further away. Every day guided tours are provided, which do have a serious as well as a rather less serious side. All travel agents in Chiang Mai organize trips to the camp.

Mae Sa Elephant Camp

Since the Thai government issued its complete embargo on the felling of tropical wood in December 1988 in order to prevent further destruction of the environment, the camp at Mae Rim, like all the other elephant camps in Thailand, no longer has any demand for its trained elephants. This means there are several hundred »unemployed« elephants here, for whose upkeep the state provides a subsidy. The main source of income nowadays is clearly tourism, and it is for the benefit of visitors that the training and lives of the elephants, which always played a major role in Thai history, are now put on display.

> ! **Baedeker TIP**
>
> **Afternoon visits**
>
> If you are not particularly interested in watching elephants play football, a pastime not often associated with the lives of the animals in the wild, visit the elephant camp in the afternoon. Countless tourist coaches bringing hundreds of visitors dominate the scene in the mornings, but once they have all departed, it is possible to explore the enormous site at leisure.

Not only elephants are trained for agricultural purposes in Thailand: water buffalo, too, learn to work for man. One training camp for buffalo is situated 18km/11mi north of Chiang Mai near Mae Rim, where shows are given to demonstrate the training of the mighty beasts. There is also an ethnic museum and a traditional house to view.

Thai Buffalo Training Centre

There are also opportunities to ride a buffalo or watch a buffalo race (opening times: 8am–5pm daily, shows daily at 9am, 3pm and 4.30pm; admission fee). ⊙

★ ★
Doi Inthanon
National Park

Day trips and longer tours to Doi Inthanon National Park start from Mai Rim. The park itself is about 80km/50mi to the south west (at ► Chom Tong). Transport is not limited to four-wheel-drive vehicles, as the park can also be visited by elephant. With its rugged canyons, picturesque waterfalls and utterly impenetrable jungles, it is one of the most beautiful nature reserves in Thailand.

Huai Thueng
Thao

Another destination that is popular with the locals is the reservoir of Huai Thueng Thao, about 40km/25mi from the city, where windsurfing and boating are allowed.

★ ★
Landscape
around Chiang
Dao

Follow Route 107 for 72km/45mi from Chiang Mai to the north through a wonderful landscape of thickly forested mountains to the tiny market town of Chiang Dao. It stands atop the Menam Ping gorge on the verdant slopes of the Doi Chiang Dao mountain, which provides a magnificent backdrop with its 2186m/7172ft-high limestone peaks. Close by a **development centre** run by the Thai government is researching the potential for cultivation of coffee and tea and teaching the populace how to farm those products. The objective of the project is to provide the hill tribes with an alternative crop to replace the opium cultivation that has been practised here for centuries. Agricultural scientists travel around the villages of the Meo, Lisu and Karen to assist the people with rice cultivation, husbandry and cattle farming.

Grotto of
Chiang Dao

A road leads north from Chiang Dao for about 6km/4mi to the sacred grotto of Chiang Dao, a cave system 14km/9mi deep. The statues

The fascinating grotto of Chiang Dao

of Buddha ranged inside are bathed in uncanny light that filters through cracks into the caves. The biggest statue is made of white marble Near the entrance there is a large white chedi with many small turrets and a pond filled with sacred fish that is fed from a spring.

* * Chiang Rai

B 2

Region: Northern Thailand   **Province:** Chiang Rai
Altitude: 80m/260ft   **Population:** 62,000

Chiang Rai is named after its founder Mengrai. It is called the »crown of the north«, even though it is relatively lacking in treasures compared to Chiang Mai. However, the town is still worth visiting, mainly for the unique scenery that surrounds it.

Chiang Rai, on the right bank of the Menam Kok, is a good base for excursions into the surrounding countryside. Thanks to good connections to Chiang Mai, Chiang Saen and the slightly more distant Lampang, it is possible to visit many of the most interesting towns of northern Thailand in the course of a tour. The region known as the Golden Triangle between Laos, Myanmar (Burma) and Thailand is the source of approximately one third of the raw opium that is illegally traded around the world today. In the mountains close by live hill tribes whose lifestyles remain largely untouched by civilization, including the Akha, the Lisu and the Meo. Try to visit one of the markets, where men and women of the hill tribes sell their wares dressed in their colourful traditional garb.

Gateway to the »Golden Triangle«

The town is older than Chiang Mai, having been founded by King Mengrai (Meng Rai, 1239–1317) in 1262. He apparently used it as the royal residence in his Lan Na kingdom. Before that, Chiang Rai had for centuries been a place of settlement for the Lawa or Mon peoples, who were attracted by its excellent position on the Menam Kok, a tributary of the Mekong. For many years, the city was under Burmese control, only coming under Thai dominion in 1786, four years after Bangkok became the capital. Although little is known of its earlier history, its development since then has been closely bound to that of Chiang Mai and Chiang Saen, which lies just 60km/37mi away.

History

What to See in Chiang Rai

The famous »Jade Buddha« was found in Chiang Rai. The statue was kept for many years in Wat Phra Kaeo Don Tao and is now in Wat Phra Kaeo within the grounds of the Grand Palace in ►Bangkok). In

*** **
Wat Phra Kaeo Don Tao

▶ VISITING CHIANG RAI

GETTING THERE

By car:
From Lampang on Route 1 (240km/ 150mi), from Chiang Mai on Route 107 until shortly before Fang, then via Route 109 and Route 1 (268km/ 167mi)

By bus:
Daily from Chiang Mai and Bangkok (Northern Bus Terminal)

By air:
Up to six times daily from Bangkok and Chiang Mai

By rail:
The closest station is at Chiang Mai (180km/112mi)

INFORMATION

Tourism Association of Thailand
448/16 Singhaklai Road
57000 Chiang Rai
Tel. 0 53 / 71 74 33, 7 44 67 45
Fax 71 74 34
tatchrai@tat.or.th

WHERE TO EAT
▶ Moderate
① **Aye's Restaurant**
479 Phaholyothin Road
Tel. 0 53 / 72 25 35
Almost unbeatable for its range of dishes ranging from German schnitzels to Thai curry. It caters for well-nigh every taste and also has a wide selection of wines.

② **Muang Thong Restaurant**
Phaholyothin Road
Tel. 0 53 / 71 11 62
Very popular and busy restaurant with attractive Chinese and Thai dishes.

WHERE TO STAY
▶ Luxury
① **Four Seasons Tented Camp Golden Triangle**
Tel. 0 53 / 91 02 00, fax 65 21 89
www.fourseasons.com/goldentriangle
15 tents, restaurant, bar.
For people who are both well heeled and in search of easy adventure. This unusual »hotel« consists of 15 tents, pitched in the open air and accessible only by boat across the Menam Ruak, but nonetheless offering every comfort money can buy. During the day there are excursions by elephant and treks, whilst the evenings revolve around a jungle bar and campfire.

▶ Mid-range
② **The Legend Chiang Rai**
124/15 Kohloy Road
Tel. 0 53 / 91 04 00; fax 71 96 50
www.thelegend-chiangrai.com
78 rooms, restaurant, bar, swimming pool, spa.
This excellent but inexpensive design hotel lies on the banks of the Mae Kok and features comfortable rooms and a highly recommended restaurant that is also open to non-residents.

▶ Budget
③ **YMCA International House**
70 Phaholyothin Road, Rimkok
Tel. 0 53 / 71 37 85-6, 70 27 63-4
Guest house belonging to the internationally known organization for young people, but which in fact caters for guests of all ages.

Chiang Rai Plan

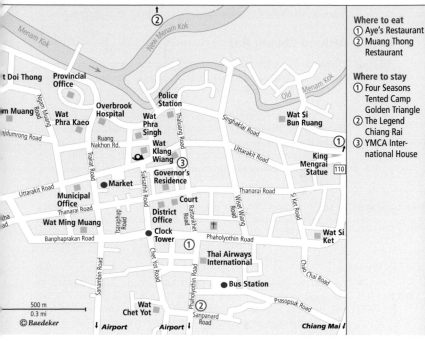

Where to eat
① Aye's Restaurant
② Muang Thong Restaurant

Where to stay
① Four Seasons Tented Camp Golden Triangle
② The Legend Chiang Rai
③ YMCA International House

1434 a chedi at Wat Phra Kaeo Don Tao was hit by a bolt of lightning. Closer investigation revealed a small, somewhat unimpressive figure covered in plaster. However, beneath the plaster a 75cm/30in-tall statue made of jade or nephrite emerged. This soon came to the attention of King Mengrai, the ruler in Chiang Mai. He would have been more than pleased to claim the piece for his own residence, but it was decided to leave the question to the elephant that would carry the statue. At the decisive parting of the ways, the elephant headed in the direction of neighbouring Lampang instead of Chiang Mai. The statue was given a home there in Wat Phra That Lampang Luang, where it remained until 1488. In that year it was brought to Chiang Mai after all, but went on several more travels before finding its way to its present location in Bangkok.

Among the highlights of the wat are the carvings and painting of the wooden facade. Along with the nearby Wat Phra Singh, the temple dates from the 15th century, but both of the complexes have been extensively refurbished and modified.

Wat Ming Muang has a beautifully carved gable and many statues of Buddha in the Chiang Saen style (11th–16th centuries). An elegantly   **Wat Ming Muang, Wat Chet Yot** proportioned viharn and a chedi with seven small towers on a rectangular base are among the remarkable features of Wat Chet Yot.

Around Chiang Rai

Mae Lao reservoir

Thanks to its enchanting location, the Mao Lao dam and its reservoir are a highly popular destination for the locals (Route 1 southwards then Route 109 towards Fang).

Mae Sai

Route 110 leads north to Mae Sai (63km/39mi), the most northerly settlement in Thailand (1,010km/628mi from Bangkok). This small border town with its lively markets was once situated on an important trading route that led all the way to China. It is possible to obtain a one-day visa to visit Myanmar if you leave your passport with the authorities.

Tham Luang cave

Of the four caves that were discovered to the south of Mae Sai some years ago, the largest is the Tham Luang cave with caverns 5–10m/16–33ft in height. The first 1000m/1100yd can be explored fairly easily via stairways and paths. Speleologists with suitable equipment are able to venture a further 6km/4mi.

✳
Wat Phra That Doi Thung

Beneath the summit of Mount Doi Thung, which rises 1300m/4270ft above sea level, is Wat Phra That Doi Thung, an important destination for many pilgrims. In early March, tens of thousands of such visitors flock to the temple by car, bus, motorcycle or on foot. A steep path 17km/11mi long leads up to the wat from Route 110 near the village of Ban Huai Krai. From the top there is a fantastic view of the surrounding landscape of northern Thailand. That alone would make the climb worthwhile. The temple buildings themselves are of limited interest, having been built in recent times. Close to the border with Myanmar near the village of **Mae Chan** is the Mae Chan Community Station, the base for government consultants who advise members of the local hill tribes on the alternatives to opium cultivation.

An unmade road from the community station leads to the **Akha village** of Ko Saen Chai. The wooden swings at the entrance to the village are used for fertility rites. Stilt-built houses with roofs that sweep low towards the ground ac-

Akha woman in Ko Saen Chai

commodate large extended families. There are large rooms for men and for women. Most hill tribes have their own languages and follow animist beliefs. Every aspect of their lives is thought to be animated by spirits. For instance, the belief that water is populated by evil spirits leads them to wash as little as possible (►Facts: Population).

Since 1976 the Thai government has followed a policy of assimilating the **hill tribes** into Thai socie-

> ! **Baedeker** TIP
>
> **Do not visit without a guide**
> It is not advisable at any time to visit hill tribe villages without a guide who is familiar with the locale and language. Difficulties in making oneself understood can lead to misunderstandings and unpleasant incidents. It should not be necessary to mention that great tact and restraint are necessary (especially as regards the taking of photographs).

ty, but progress has proved halting. The Akha living in the mountains around Chiang Rai have so far retained their own cultural identity to a greater extent than the other tribes. They guard their traditional way of life well and express it in the form of artistic craftwork. The government supports several offices of the **Thai Hillcraft Foundation** in Chiang Rai, which organizes distribution and sale of silverwork, tapestry and woven fabrics made by the tribespeople.

Chiang Saen

B 2

Region: Northern Thailand
Altitude: 455m/1493ft

Province: Chiang Rai
Population: 8,000 approx.

The small town of Chiang Saen lies at the very northern tip of Thailand in a broad loop of the majestic Mekong river that forms the border between Laos and Thailand both here and further south.

Chiang Saen, one of the oldest towns in the country, is ringed by tall jungle-covered mountains. Across the river are the hills of Laos.

Border town on the river

Once the capital of what was probably the first Thai principality on territory that is now part of Thailand, Chiang Saen seemed to have descended into a long slumber, even though it did gain some fame as the source of the so-called Chiang Saen style. Recent finds of tools have confirmed the theory that the region was settled as far back as the early Stone Age. The present-day settlement also dates back over 2000 years and was at its peak between the 10th and 13th centuries, especially under King Saen Phu. King Mengrai, who later established capitals in Chiang Rai in 1261 and Chiang Mai in 1296, was born in Chiang Saen in 1238. The countless wars with the Burmese kings and those of Ayutthaya left their mark on the town, which was occu-

History

Chiang Saen *Plan*

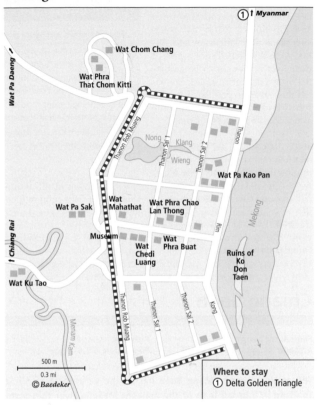

① ↑ *Myanmar*

Wat Chom Chang

Wat Phra That Chom Kitti

Thanon Rob Muang

Nong *Klang*

Wieng

Thanon Sai 1

Thanon Sai 2

Thanon

Wat Pa Kao Pan

Wat Pa Daeng

Wat Pa Sak

Wat Mahathat

Wat Phra Chao Lan Thong

Rim

Mekong

Museum

Wat Chedi Luang

Wat Phra Buat

Ruins of Ko Don Taen

↑ Chiang Rai

Wat Ku Tao

Thanon Rob Muang

Thanon Sai 1

Thanon Sai 2

Kong

Menam Kam

500 m

0.3 mi

© *Baedeker*

Where to stay
① Delta Golden Triangle

pied by the Burmese from the mid-16th until the late 18th century. King Rama I had the entire settlement razed to eliminate it as a target for his enemies. It did not come back to life until the time of King Rama V (Chulalongkorn).

What to See in and around Chiang Saen

City walls   A wall 8km/5mi in length once encircled the town. Some parts of it still stand, and ditches overgrown with grass and trees indicate its course. A few sections have recently been reconstructed, while others remain covered with greenery. The extent of the present town is only a fraction of the area formerly enclosed by the walls. There are countless ruins of temples, some of very old, including many that have not yet been dated. They testify to the former importance of the town.

Wat Pa Sak was founded in the reign of King Saen Phu in 1295 and actually lay beyond the walls. It takes its name from the original enclosure formed of 300 trunks of teak. The lovely surviving chedi was built in the form of a step pyramid to house a Buddha relic that was brought from Pataliputra in the year the wat was established. Twelve large and 16 smaller niches hold some intricately worked Buddha figures in the Sukhothai style, some of which are quite well preserved. At a close look evidence of Srivijaya and Dvaravati influences can also be discerned. Wat Pa Sak is one of the few remaining examples of the highly developed art of stucco and terracotta work.

Poppy harvest in the »Golden Triangle«

Wat Chedi Luang (inside the walls near the western gate) was built in the 13th century. The 60m/200ft tall, bell-shaped chedi (16th century) still has some remains of the original bronze-clad spire. Nowadays the chedi is overgrown with grass.

★
Wat Chedi Luang

The National Museum (a little way in front of the entrance to Wat Chedi Luang) contains several lovely pieces in the Chiang Saen style, including Buddha statues, amulets, silverware and stucco work, steles and demon masks. The stone bas-reliefs from Wat Sang Kha Kaew Don Tun are particularly valuable. They were removed from their original position for security reasons. These do not, however, date

National Museum of Chiang Saen

 ## VISITING CHIANG SAEN

GETTING THERE

A visit to Chiang Saen can be recommended as part of a tour of the region around Chiang Rai. Chiang Mai could serve as the starting point (there are daily bus connections from there and it has the nearest railway station).

By car:
From Chiang Rai via Route 110 to Mae Chan, then Route 1016 (58km/ 36mi)

WHERE TO STAY

► **Mid-range**
① *Delta Golden Triangle*
222 Mu 1, Golden Triangle
Tel. 0 53 / 77 70 01, fax 77 70 05
73 rooms, restaurant, coffee shop, swimming pool, gym.
A hotel very close to the famous (or infamous) Golden Triangle with a fabulous view across the Mekong. Large rooms, nice restaurant with northern Thai specialities.

from the founding of the temple but were created around 300 years ago, as can be determined from the hairstyles and clothing of the figures portrayed. (opening times: Thu–Sat 9am–12am, 2– 4pm; admission fee).

Wat Phra Buat is now an impressive ruin. On one of the collapsed chedis, clear remains can still be seen of a splendid Buddha sculpture. Wat Phra Chao Lan Thong also has one chedi still standing. In a pretty location next to the Mekong stands the more recent Wat Pa Kao Pan, which also includes an older chedi.

Wat Phra Buat

On a hill outside the town (with a great view of the border territory between Burma, Laos und Thailand) are the chedis and ruins of Wat Phra That Chom Kitti which was built in about the 10th century. The spire of the crooked chedi is clad in bronze. A bas-relief of Buddha has also been preserved. Inside niches on each side there are superbly preserved Buddha statues in the Lopburi style. Opposite the wat are the remains of a brick chedi (Wat Chom Chang). A wide stairway with 393 steps leads from here down to the town.

✱ Wat Phra That Chom Kitti

11km/7mi along the Mekong to the north-west of Chiang Saen, a vantage point just below the Delta Golden Triangle Hotel bears the name »Golden Triangle«. At this point the Mae Sai river flows into the Mekong. As the borders of Thailand, Laos and Myanmar meet here, the name is not as misplaced as might first appear. Plenty of souvenir shops have set up along the road, some of them selling products from neighbouring Burma. It is interesting to observe that there is a certain amount of border traffic between Thailand and Laos, even though, officially, only Lao citizens are allowed to cross the river into their country.

»Golden Triangle«

A three-hour boat trip down the Mekong to Chiang Saen in one of the motor boats available here is a memorable experience. Along the river, some people live in boat houses and make a living mainly by means of trade from the limited border traffic between Thailand and its neighbour Laos.

✱ Boat trip on the Mekong

Across the Mekong River opposite Chiang Khong, a lively border town 60km/37mi downriver from Chiang Saen, is the Lao town of Ban Houei Sai with a number of fortifications built there by the French. Fort Carnot is now used by the Lao government as an administrative building. The papers that are needed to undertake the ferry trip across the Mekong can be obtained from the consulate in Bangkok, but it is essential to obtain a second visa for the return trip to Thailand.

Excursion to Ban Houei Sai (Laos)

← *The frontier district between Thailand, Myanmar and Laos is called the »Golden Triangle« as marked by this new gate.*

Chom Tong

B 2

Region: Northern Thailand   **Province:** Chiang Mai
Altitude: 520m/1700ft   **Population:** 6,000 approx.

In the far north-west of Thailand, the broad basin of the Menam Ping widens out to the north and is hemmed in to the south by jungle-covered mountains. Here lies the small town of Chom Thong, which is well known on account of Wat Phra That Si Chom Thong. The highest mountain in Thailand, Doi Inthanon with its summit 2595m/8514ft above sea level, is also nearby.

★★
Wat Phra That Si Chom Thong

Wat Phra That Si Chom Thong dates from the 15th century. The oldest part of the temple is the Burmese-style chedi that was built in 1451. It is said to house a relic of Buddha. In about 1550, when Muang Keos was king, the viharn was built to a cross-shaped floor plan. The tastefully arranged, gilded wood carvings on the side gables, cornices and portals, as well as the ornamentation of the teak columns and beams inside, are of outstanding artistic quality. The viharn also contains a richly decorated altar in the Burmese style with two equally ornate tusks and various statues of Buddha. The seated bronze Buddha is highly revered.

 CHOM TONG

GETTING THERE

By car:
From Chiang Mai by car along Route 108 (56km/35mi).

By bus:
Buses run several times a day from Chiang Mai

WHERE TO STAY

In Chom Thong there is no accommodation that can be recommended. It is better to travel on to Chiang Mai or to make a day trip from there.

A small road behind the monastery leads 9km/6mi to the **Nam Tok Mae Klang** waterfall with its 100m/330ft cascades (bathing is dangerous). From here there is a path onto the rocks. About an hour and a half away on foot is the impressive Borichinda cave.

★★
Doi Inthanon National Park

A trip to the mountain of Doi Inthanon, 2595m/8514ft high and 55km/35mi from Chom Thong, is one of the most exciting excursions it is possible to make, even in a country that hardly lacks breathtaking beauty. The granite massif, a southerly outlier of Burma's Shan Mountains, is the centrepoint of the Doi Inthanon National Park, which covers an area of some 1,000 sq km/400 sq mi (▶ map p.144). Travel agents offer trekking excursions lasting 3 to 5 days on foot or by pony (accommodation in the simple camps of the Wildlife Association). There are also some spartan bungalows at the

In the mountain villages it is as if time has stood still.

national park office (close to the Hmong village of Khun Klang). This national park clearly demonstrates the damage that the Thais have inflicted on their natural environment. Where dense forests were once home to numerous animals, a vast expanse of deforested terrain that has gradually turned to barren steppe now spreads far and wide. The reforestation measures of the government can replace only a fraction of the depleted forest, although efforts are obviously being made.

Other destinations

Route 108 continues to Hot through the narrow valley of the Menam Ping, with craggy rocks on either side leading up to hillsides bedecked by jungle. On the Yanhee reservoir, which lies among stupendous mountain scenery, it is possible to rent a motor boat, or to swim and fish. Close to the reservoir there is a Karen village built on stilts. More Karen villages are to be found on the way to Mae Sariang (105km/65mi from Chom Thong).

★★ Ob Luang gorge

Another natural attraction on the way to Mae Sariang is the Ob Luang gorge, where the Mae Chaem cuts through a towering rock outcrop 30m/100ft high. The gorge can be viewed from above on a bridge that links the two cliffs. Rafting trips on the river are also available. Ask at the Ob Luang National Park office or Mae Sot Conservation Tour (175/18 Ratchadamnoen Rd. Chiang Mai 50000 Tel: 814424, 814505 Fax: 814505).

Chonburi (Cholburi)

Region: Eastern Thailand　　　**Province:** Chonburi
Altitude: 3m/10ft　　　　　　　**Population:** 184,000

The city of Chonburi lies south-east of Bangkok on the Gulf of Thailand. It was founded by one of the kings of Ayutthaya in the 14th century and is nowadays a large and bustling city within the Bangkok commuter belt, inhabited primarily by fishermen as well as merchants and traders.

Provincial capital　Chonburi is the seat of local government for the province of the same name. The province itself has a population of some 840,000 people. The new international **airport at Suvarnabhumi** between Bangkok and Chonburi will, however, probably have a major and lasting effect on the lives of people in the area since thousands of employees are now seeking homes in the region. Another project that stands out in the somewhat dreary landscape of the province is the **Eastern Seaboard Project**, a huge free trade zone with a deep-sea harbour.

What to See in and around Chonburi

Harbour　The harbour of Chonburi is too shallow to become a major trading port. This is probably why it has remained a small and cheerful fishing harbour, from which fishermen put out to sea in the evening dusk. South of the city is the biggest area in Thailand for cultivating oysters.

Sugar cane and cassava are grown in the region, and the sliced corms of the latter are laid out to dry, spreading their acrid smell. The starchy tapioca flour that is made from them is used for baking and for binding. Much of it is exported to a wide range of countries, making it one of Thailand's major agricultural earners.

✷ Wat Sam Yot　Wat Sam Yot stands on a hill near the town centre. It has a statue 34m/112ft high depicting Buddha at the moment of his enlightenment. The view of the city from the hill is excellent.

Wat Intharam, Wat Dhama Nimitr　Chonburi has many temples that are pretty but not influential in terms of the artistic history of Thailand. Only the two oldest, Wat Intharam and Wat Dhama Nimitr, deserve mention. Wat Intharam near the old market in the town centre dates from the late Ayutthaya period and was established under King Taksin. The temple was restored many times during the Rattanakosin (Bangkok) period and its original appearance has been completely lost. The stucco sculptures on the roof are worthy of note, as are the porcelain mosaics on the window arches.

Inside the bot are some very beautiful murals in the early Bangkok style as well as many Buddha statues, some of which are highly unusual.

It is worth paying a visit to **Wat Dhama Nimitr** in the same neighbourhood. Its viharn has a massive statue of Buddha in a boat. Legend has it that Buddha sailed to the Indian city of Pai Salee, where his compassion and empathy healed many people suffering from cholera.

! *Baedeker* TIP

Buffalo races
The festivities for Chonburi's great buffalo races start in the courtyard of Wat Intharam. The event takes place every October and attracts thousands of visitors to the town.

Near Chonburi is the entrance to the Khao Khiew Nature Park, where it is possible to see more than 130 endangered species, including butterflies, monkeys and even leopards in an area covering 145 sq km/56 sq mi. An aviary houses 4,000 Asian birds, including some particularly rare species. The six white tigers in the park were donated by a zoo near Memphis, Tennessee. Part of the park is closed to

Khao Khiew Open Zoo
⏲
Opening hours: 8am–6pm daily
Admission fee

A highly decorated spirit house in Chonburi

► VISITING CHONBURI

GETTING THERE

By car:
From Bangkok on Route 3 (80km/50mi)

By bus:
From Bangkok Eastern Bus Terminal (every hour)

INFORMATION

Tourism Authority of Thailand (TAT)
609 Moo 10, Pratamunk Road
20150 Banglamung, Chonburi

Tel. 0 38 / 42 89 90, 42 87 50, 42 76 67
Fax 42 91 13
tatchon@tat.or.th

WHERE TO STAY

Since accommodation in Chonburi is unattractive, and because it is close to Bangkok and Pattaya, the city is best visited as a brief stop between the two. There are some decent small guest houses on the island of Ko Sichang. Information is available from the TAT office in Chonburi.

the public since it is intended that the animals should be able to range free and unmolested, in the hope that they will breed.

Golf course   The road to the zoo also leads to the charming 18-hole golf course of Bang Saen built on a rocky hill. It is one of the largest and most beautiful courses in Thailand.

Ang Sila   The small village of Ang Sila (stone bowl) is named after a group of rocks that spears into the sea about 7km/4mi south of Chonburi. The village is famous for the production of stone kitchenware, including mortars of various sizes.

Bang Saen   Head south on Route 3 for the resort of Bang Saen. It is impossible to find accommodation here at weekends, when the city dwellers come to its hopelessly overcrowded beaches. 1km/1100 yards inland, on the campus of the Bangkok Education College, is the largest **aquarium** in Thailand (opening times: Thu– Fri 8am–5pm, Sat, Sun

Luk Sam Po ►   8.30am–4.30pm; admission fee). The boat-shaped Chinese temple of Luk Sam Po (best reached via the shore road to the north) was built in memory of a disaster: a boat carrying Chinese immigrants was caught in a heavy storm off the Thai coast and sank. The only survivor endowed the temple as an act of thanksgiving and founded an order of monks living to strict rules. Monks and nuns occupy a group of small houses symbolizing ships' cabins around the central pagoda. The monks' quarters outside the complex are remarkable in that they are shaped like small fishing boats. Inside the monastery there are two smaller copies of the chedi of ►Nakhon Pathom, Thailand's biggest chedi. The complex is open to Buddhists from all over the world for the purpose of meditation. Other visitors are also welcome.

About 20km/12mi south of Chonburi is the up-and-coming town of Si Racha on the Gulf of Thailand. It is known for a very spicy chilli sauce that is made here and used throughout the country. Plenty of restaurants serve excellent seafood. The picturesque peninsula of **Ko Loy**, where there is a small monastery, is worth visiting, especially in the evening.

Si Racha

The fishing harbour of Si Racha is also the starting point for trips to the nearby island of Ko Sichang (six trips a day; lasting about 30 minutes), which actually consists of six rocky reefs. In the 19th century the island was an important trading site, but nowadays Ko Sichang is significant only as a fishing harbour. It is worth viewing the ruined summer residence of King Chulalongkorn (Rama V) on the highest point of the island. Since the island was occupied by the French in 1893, the palace was never completed. A chedi on the southern promontory of the island is all that remains of Wat Asdangnimitr. Two temples are situated on the steep cliffs: the yellow Buddha statue of the first can be seen for miles around, and an excellent view of the busy harbour from the other, a Chinese temple, rewards the climb up 500 steps.

★
Ko Sichang

Chumphon

F 2

Region: Southern Thailand   **Province:** Chumphon
Altitude: 6m/20ft   **Population:** 49,000

Chumphon has the look of a bustling little town and is devoid of major attractions. Tourism has therefore largely passed it by. Nevertheless, the surrounding countryside provides an opulent variety of glorious scenery. To the north of the town the landscape has the character of savannah; the nearby coast is speckled with countless islands and rocky reefs; and inland lie dense rainforests and mountains peppered with caves and grottoes.

Chumphon is at the eastern edge of the isthmus of Kra, the narrowest part of the Malayan peninsula. Kraburi on the Indian Ocean, i.e. on the west coast of the isthmus, is just 40km/25mi distant. Chumphon is famous for its swallows' nests, which are eaten as a delicacy in Chinese cuisine.

Busy provincial capital

What to See around Chumphon

10km/6mi south-east of Chumphon, in the shadow of a wooded hill, is the fishing harbour of Pak Nam, which is particularly lively in the early mornings and late evenings. There is a pleasant walk along the

Fishing village of Pak Nam

▶ VISITING CHUMPHON

GETTING THERE

By car:
Route 4
(460km/286mi from Bangkok)

By bus:
From Prachap Khirikhan or Surat
Thani and Ranong.
By rail: station on the line from
Bangkok to southern Thailand

(485km/301mi from Bangkok, journey
time 8 hours approx.)

WHERE TO STAY
▶ **Mid-range**
Jansom Chumphon
Tha Thapao Road
Tel. 0 77 / 50 25 02, fax 50 25 03
Clean, comfortable rooms and a good
restaurant.

coast to a shrine erected in memory of Prince Chumphon, who took his name from the town, taking in the views of the sea and the tall rocky islands on the way.

Trip to the islands From the harbour boat trips are on offer to the islands of Ko Raet, Ko Mattra, Ko Lawa, Ko Maphrao and Ko Talu, where **swifts** build their nests during the breeding season between March and August. Collectors go in search of the nests are sell them to restaurants. Another island worth seeing is ►**Ko Tao** with its pretty bungalow developments about 80km/50mi from Chumphon.

Paradonpap Beach At the mouth of the Pak Nam Chumphon, 16km/10mi south of Chumphon itself at Paradonpap Beach, are some excellent fish restaurants. 5km/3mi further on is **Ri Beach**, where the torpedo boat *HMS Chumphon* serves as a reminder of the frequent 19th-century conflicts between Thailand and Burma. Not far away is another shrine to Prince Chumphon, founder of the Thai navy. During weekends and holidays the beach is crowded with bathers. In December a light-and-sound festival takes place to honour Chumphon. There is also a herb garden (Mo Phon Traditional Herbal Garden) that is experimenting with the cultivation of numerous healing herbs. 17km/11mi north of Chumphon (towards Bang Saphan) is the beautiful beach of **Thung Wua Laen**.

★ **Khao Kriap Cave** 18km/11mi south of Chumphon (Route 409) at the foot of Khao Kriap mountain, there is an entrance to a cave system that bears the same name. 20m/70ft-tall stalagmites (a torch is needed to see them) represent the biggest attraction. A path leads about 300 yards into the cave.

★ **Landscape** Within range of a day trip from Chumphon there is an almost untouched landscape of dense jungle, impressive caves and waterfalls, beautiful beaches and islands. 21km/12mi north-west of the town, a stairway leads to the imposing Rab Ro system of dripstone caves with statues of Buddha. There is also a fabulous view of the surrounding rice fields.

Fang

B 2

Region: Northern Thailand
Altitude: 655m/2149ft

Province: Chiang Mai
Population: 12,000

The small but growing town of Fang is at the foot of a valley high in the north-west amid a magnificent jungle landscape from which outliers of the Himalayan mountains rise into the clouds. The border with Myanmar, formerly Burma, is just 24km/15mi from Fang.

Little remains to testify to the major role that Fang once played in the Lan Na kingdom as a trading centre and strategic fortress. What does remain, however, is the fascination that surrounds the hill tribes. This makes it rewarding to visit the market in Fang, where the **Akha**, **Lisu** and **Meo** all sell their products. A rather more dubious aspect of Fang is its reputation as the gateway to the Golden Triangle, one of the biggest production centres for illicit drugs in the world.

Gateway to the hill tribes

Fang itself was founded by King Mengrai in 1268. From here the Thais gradually overcame the kingdom of the Mon; only later did the settlement developed into a trading centre. Its inhabitants suffered years of attacks by the Burmese but only surrendered after a long siege in 1732 (Chiang Mai had been conquered as early as 1556). Towards the end of the 18th century, the Thais managed to wrest the town back from its occupiers, and since the 19th century Fang has been part of Chiang Mai province and what is now the Kingdom of Thailand.

 FANG

GETTING THERE

By car:
From Chiang Mai on Route 107 (155km/96mi), from Chiang Rai on routes 1/109 (65km/40mi)

By bus:
Several times daily from Chiang Mai or Chiang Rai

WHERE TO STAY

Due to the lack of accommodation in Fang, the town is best visited on a day trip from Chiang Mai.

What to See in and around Fang

With the exception of a few earthworks, the fortifications that were erected under Mengrai have mostly vanished. King Udom Sin and

Fortifications

his wife are said to have plunged to their deaths in the deep wells in the centre of town to avoid falling into the hands of the Burmese.

Experimental agriculture station

The experimental agriculture station is an interesting place to visit. It lies to the north of Fang (head from Fang towards Tha Thon, then turn left just before Ban Mae Ai and follow the road about 15km/9mi to Doi Pha Hom Pok, the second highest mountain in Thailand) and serves as a school of agricultural techniques. It belongs to the **Tribal Welfare Committee** and is part of an attempt by the government, involving large financial subsidies, to wean the hill tribes away from opium cultivation to alternative crops. The station provides education in the cultivation of fruit, vegetables, wheat, tea and coffee.

Hot springs

About 50 hot springs with sulphurous water, some of which are permanently active, can be found near the village of Ban Pin about 10km/6mi outside the town. To get there, take Route 1089 northwards as far as Ban Pin, then follow the signs to the hot springs.

✶ ✶
River trips on the Menam Kok

The river trip from the border town of **Tha Thon** (24km/15mi north of Fang) on the Menam Kok is an unforgettable experience. Lined by steep cliffs, the river winds its way over many rapids down to Chiang Rai. In Tha Thon it is possible to hire a raft that accommodates up to six passengers, who sleep and eat on board. The journey to Chiang Rai can take from two to six days, depending on the time of year and the strength of the current. A local boatman guides the raft downstream and will even stop off at some of the many hill-tribe villages along the route. The services of a local guide (and a suitable off-road vehicle) are also advisable for a trip through the mountains around Fang. Members of the **Lisu**, **Haw**, **Meo**, **Akha** and **Yao** tribes inhabit the mountains, in conditions that seem archaic to westerners. Linguistic barriers and traditions that go back centuries still define the lives of these peoples. It is hoped that modern agricultural methods will supplant the slash-and-burn culture that has hitherto prevented permanent settlement among the hill tribes.

Karen woman

Hua Hin

E 2

Region: Western Thailand   **Province:** Prachuap Khirikhan
Altitude: 3m/10ft   **Population:** 42,000

The oldest seaside resort in Thailand is the summer residence of King Bhumibol, since the royal family moved here from Bang Pa In. The main attraction of this otherwise quiet town is its 3km/2mi-long beach of fine white sand.

Hua Hin (»starry head«) is 232km/144mi south of Bangkok on the Gulf of Thailand. For those who find the bustle of Pattaya on the other side of the gulf unattractive, Hua Hin is the perfect place. A number of quiet hotels and holiday villages along the coast are particularly well suited for a family holiday.

Holiday homes

The growth of Hua Hin is closely linked to the completion of the railway to southern Thailand in 1910. Before that time Hua Hin was an unimportant little town, until it was discovered by the Bangkok elite, especially Prince Nares, son of King Chulalongkorn, who was the first of the royal family to establish a summer residence here (Saen Samran House). Subsequent princes and princesses added more bungalows and parks. While the residence of King Rama VII is open for tours of the rooms and parkland, the residence currently used by King Bhumibol at the western end of the town is off limits.

> **? DID YOU KNOW ...?**
>
> ■ The Thai royal couple has the deserved reputation of being in touch with the people. It is even possible for ordinary tourists in Hua Hin, where King Bhumibol and Queen Sirikit take their summer holidays, to find this out for themselves. The best chance to see the king close up is when sailing, a passion that Bhumibol carries on in even his old age. It is not possible to come too near to the monarch, but it is something to be able to say, »Look who's sailing over there, it's the king of Thailand«

What to See in Hua Hin

The lively fish market at the northern end of the town is always worth a visit, especially in the mornings. Hua Hin has the second-biggest fishing fleet in Thailand. Tons of fish are landed every morning and delivered to the processing plants.

✶ Fish market

The royal palace was built in the style of European mansions and was given the name Klai Klangwan (»away from it all«) by King Prajadibok (Rama VII). The palace was completed in 1910 and is surrounded by a splendid park that stretches all the way to the sea. At the southern end of the sandy beach is a large rocky outcrop that looks a little like a man's head; this gave the village its name.

✶ Royal palace

► VISITING HUA HIN

GETTING THERE

By car:
From Bangkok on Route 4 or Route 35 via Samut Songkhram

By bus:
From Bangkok Southern Bus Terminal (journey time about 3 hours)

By rail:
Station on the line from Bangkok to the Malayan peninsula (229km/142mi from Bangkok, journey time 6 hours)

By air:
Once a day from Bangkok and Ko Samui

WHERE TO STAY

► Luxury
Sofitel Central Hua Hin
1 Damnernkasem Road
Tel. 0 32 / 51 20 21 38, fax 51 10 14
www.sofitel.com
154 rooms and 64 villas, 2 restaurants, coffee shop, 2 bars, 3 swimming pools, spa, shopping arcade.
Guests with an eye for tradition can now stay in this elegant hotel where the staff of the Thai railway company were once accommodated. The former »railway hotel« is still the top hotel in Hua Hin, in spite of many newly built competitors. Apart from the rooms in the main building there are also 64 small luxury suites. It goes without saying that every part of the hotel provides the utmost level of comfort. The kitchen is run by a star chef.

Anantara Resort & Spa
43/1 Phetchkasem Beach Road
Tel. 0 32 / 52 02 50, fax 52 02 59
www.anantara.com
187 rooms, 2 restaurants, coffee shop, swimming pool, spa.

New luxury resort in splendid gardens but right on Hua Hin beach. The rooms are equipped with every conceivable comfort and the spa has an outstanding reputation.

Hua Hin Marriott Resort & Spa
107/1 Phetchkasem Road
Tel. 0 32 / 51 18 81
Fax 51 24 22
www.marriott.com
216 rooms, 3 restaurants
Just 10 minutes from the centre of Hua Hin, another luxury resort set in beautiful gardens. The buildings imitate the traditional Thai style and the rooms are very well equipped for the price.

► Mid-range
Lunar Resort
80/1 Takeap Road
Tel. and fax 0 32 / 53 68 02
lunarhut@hotmail.com
Pretty hotel, not exactly close to the beach but always praised for its excellent service.

► Budget
City Beach Resort
16 Damnoen Kasem Road
Tel. 0 32 / 51 28 70
Fax 51 24 48
162 rooms, restaurant, bar, shopping arcade.
A budget hotel which nevertheless offers a mid-range level of comfort. Not far from the Hua Hin night market and just a short walk to the nearest golf course.

WHERE TO EAT

Good, affordable restaurants serving seafood fresh from the ocean line the main street.

The strenuous climb to Wat Khao Lad is rewarded with a fabulous view.

Wat Khao Lad, situated on an outcrop not far from the town, has a glorious view of the sea, the mountains in the east and the village of Khao Takiap. To reach it means climbing a steep stairway with many steps. Buses run from Hua Hin every 20 minutes.

✳ Wat Khao Lad

The market that takes place every night on Dechanuchit Road is not to be missed. Apart from the traders' mobile stalls there is also a wide range of restaurants and snack bars.

✳ Night market

The station at Hua Hin has become the final resting place for a beautifully restored steam locomotive. Steam trains were in service on the State Railway of Thailand (SRT) until 1975. Since then they have been supplanted by diesel locomotives, and some lines have been electrified. The royal waiting room at the station is also very pretty.

Railway station

Around Hua Hin

The limestone mountains around Hua Hin have dozens of accessible caves (worth a half-day visit). Some can be found for example, at the **Tham Dao temple**, **Tham Mai Lab Lae**, **Tham Kai Lon** and **Tham Kai Fa**, where there are several appealing statues of Buddha, though none that are particularly significant from an artistic point of view.

Caves

Khao Takiap Bay In a bay about 6km/4mi south of Hua Hin lies Khao Takiap with an especially fine sandy beach and several good fish restaurants. An imposing, snow-white statue of Buddha stands on the neighbouring mountain; a troop of wild monkeys lives behind the associated temple.

★
Khao Sam Roi Yot National Park

On the way to the town of Pranburi, some 25km/16mi to the south, the road initially passes a number of quiet bays that are great places for a swim. South of Pranburi a massive limestone massif rises along the coast. Its host of peaks gave it the name Khao Sam Roi Yot (»mountains of the three hundred summits«). It forms the central part of a national park covering an area of 130 sq km/50 sq mi. The mountains are riddled with caves and canyons and are part of the **central Cordillera** that runs from northern Thailand down to the Malay peninsula. The most prominent geological features are the often bizarre-looking limestone monoliths that sometimes rise as high as 600m/2000ft above a smooth, flat plain.

Although this part of the national park is easily explored, the area of dense vegetation that lies to the west is uninviting and inimical to cultivation. There are no signposted footpaths and any attempt to explore it without guides is ill advised. The section of the park lying to the west of Pranburi, however, is linked by a road and various forest trails. Nowadays it is possible to see many birds, but the shrimp farms that were set up on the plain in the 1980s are no adornment to the park. They are evidence of one struggle between environmentalists and business that the nature lovers lost.

★ ★ Kamphaeng Phet

C 2

Region: Northern Thailand
Altitude: 47m/154ft

Province: Kamphaeng Phet
Population: 44,000

The landscape around Kamphaeng Phet is jungle-covered mountain, while the town itself and its impressive ruins are sited on the banks of the Menam Ping. This was once the site of one of the richest towns in the Sukhothai kingdom. The few remains from that time only hint at the glory that must once have been.

Provincial capital with roots in the Sukhothai kingdom Not far from Kamphaeng Phet the edges of Thailand's last remaining teak forests stretch far to the north. Since the total embargo on the felling of tropical wood that was passed in 1988 and announced by the king in the wake of disastrous flooding, no more teak logs have floated down the Menam Ping to Bangkok.

History King Liu Thai (1347–1368) had the city built as a bulwark of the Sukhothai empire to replace the older town of Chakang Rao on the other side of the river, of which little remains today. As the Sukhothai kingdom lasted only until 1376, the heyday of Kamphaeng Phet was short-lived. Nevertheless, further temples were established in the 15th and 16th centuries, and building only ceased when the Burmese attacked at the end of the 16th century, plundering the town and destroying large parts of it.

What to See in Kamphaeng Phet

Where Route 1 comes into Kamphaeng Phet from the north, it passes the ancient town of Chakang Rao just before the bridge over the Menam Ping. The town is identifiable by the remains of the laterite-built fort Phom Thung Setti and four elegant chedis that have been restored. The large chedi with niches in the sides to the left of the road was probably based on Burmese models and formed part of the former Wat Boromathat. The wrought-iron canopy that tops it dates from the 20th century. The chedi was built during the early Bangkok period over three chedis from Sukhothai era, which can still be seen inside (the chedi is open to the public). Over the bridge and to the right is the new town; on the left is the old walled region where remains of earthworks that once stood 6m/18ft high are still visible.

Chakang Rao

If you have not previously visited Sukhothai, first pay a visit to the museum alongside the ruins. It contains numerous finds from Kam-

Museum

Ruined chedi at Wat Phra Kaeo in Kamphaeng Phet

▶ VISITING KAMPHAENG PHET

GETTING THERE

By car:
From Bangkok via Route 1 (360km/ 224mi), from Phitsanulok on Routes 117/115 (102km/63mi), from Sukhothai Route 101 (76km/47mi)

By air:
The nearest airport is Phitsanulok (several flights a day from Bangkok)

WHERE TO STAY

▶ Budget

Phet
189 Bumrungrat Road, Soi 3
Tel. 0 55 / 71 28 10-5
Fax 71 29 27
phethtl@phethotel.com
220 rooms, restaurant, bar, night club. Best hotel in town with clean and comfortable rooms (all with air conditioning). Very good Thai restaurant.

---

phaeng Phet. The elegance and harmony of the Sukhothai style is plain to see in many of the exhibits. The museum also houses sculptures and bronzework from all the eras of Thai art, including several masterpieces, such as a seated bronze Buddha in the U Thong style, bronze figures from the 13th century and works in the Lopburi and Dvaravati styles.

★ ★
Wat Phra Tat

Opposite the museum are the ruins of Wat Phra That, the second most important monastery in the town. The bell-shaped form of the central chedi on its square base shows Sinhalese influence. When it was built, the strict form of Buddhism that is still practised in Sri Lanka was widespread. The chedi is surrounded by columns and once contained a relic, the whereabouts of which are no longer known. Only the foundations and the parts of one rectangular pillar remain of the viharn.

★ ★
Wat Phra Kaeo

Wat Phra Kaeo stands right next to Wat Phra That in the former palace grounds. It was the royal wat rather than an ordinary monastery. The various Buddha statues that stand forlorn amid the ruins are particularly impressive. The huge statue on the high terrace of the former bot in front of a collapsed bell-shaped chedi has lost its face due to erosion. In the centre of the former viharn is another massive statue of Buddha that has also suffered weathering of the face. It is surrounded by many smaller statues arranged in a rectangle that resemble modern sculptures. The shapes of the bodies, heads and limbs are now thoroughly abstract in appearance, since their stucco exteriors have crumbled away and left only the laterite torsos. A reclining Buddha statue with an elegant head featuring lovely, well-preserved facial features is also of note. On the base of the large bell-

The Buddha statues of Wat Phra Kaeo are truly impressive. →

shaped chedi, some fragments remain of what were once 32 sculptures of lions. Some of the 16 niches in the upper section still contain Buddha statues. At the edge of the compound there is a symbolic footprint of Buddha made of brick.

Lak Muang North of Wat Phra Kaeo is the foundation stone of the city, the highly revered Lak Muang, with two long ponds that surround a third round pond.

Other ruins The finest and most important ruin is beyond the city walls in a beautiful park (follow signs to Arunyik Area). In the woods north of the city, monks of a strict Buddhist sect built magnificent monasteries in the Sukhothai style featuring strong Sinhalese influence.

Wat Phra Meud, Wat Phra Non Here are the ruins of Wat Pu Mud Nok and the small Wat Phra Meud. Further on is the much larger Wat Phra Non, the »temple of the resting Buddha«. The first of its buildings is a large bot, of which some pillars and walls that are still standing display the narrow vertical window openings typical of the Sukhothai era. Behind it is the viharn, a square building with four rows of four massive pillars. It once housed a statue of a reclining Buddha, but only some sections of the long base remain. Of the two chedis in the temple grounds, the one behind the viharn was the larger. It was bell-shaped with an octagonal pedestal resting on a square base.

✳ Wat Si Iriyabot The mondhop of Wat Si Iriyabot once housed statues showing Buddha in all four basic postures, (sitting, striding, walking and resting). It was from these that the temple got its name: si = four, iriyabot = postures. A colossal statue of a standing Buddha, one of the most beautiful sculptures in the Sukhothai style, has survived. Some remains of the striding Buddha are still to be seen, but the other two have crumbled away.

Wat Chang Rob The impressive ruins of Wat Chang Rob lie on a hill. There was once a tall bell-shaped chedi but nowadays only the foundations and some of the fine stucco ornamentation (running birds) are left. 68 stone elephants, whose upper bodies still rise out of the stonework, supported the chedi. Between them the walls are decorated with stucco trees and porcelain demons. Steps lead to the upper section of the chedi.

Wat Chao Arwat Yai The deep water-filled basin next to Wat Chao Arwat Yai was once a quarry from which the stone used to build this temple was excavated. A low double wall with an entrance that is graced by two small chedis encloses the compound, at the centre of which it is still possible to identify the remains of the viharn. The small chedis on either side of the courtyard are ruined, but one large chedi with a stepped base is still well preserved (apart from the broken spire).

In Wat Chang Lom (on the hill) relics of a bell-shaped chedi on a square base remain. The elephant sculptures that once supported the upper section have not survived, apart from two examples that now stand in front of the entrance to the Kamphaeng Phet branch of the National Museum.

Wat Chang Lom

✶ ✶ Kanchanaburi

D / E 2

Region: Central Thailand
Altitude: 74m/243ft

Province: Kanchanaburi
Population: 738,000 (province)

Kanchanaburi province has long been regarded as the perfect place for a holiday, thanks to its charming countryside and proximity to Bangkok. Excavations have shown that the province was already settled in prehistoric times and that even then the rivers that flow out of the mountains to the west were an important part of the trade route from the Indian hinterland to what is now Cambodia.

The Three Pagodas Pass near the source of Menam Kwai Noi was all too often the route taken by invading Burmese hordes, most recently in 1767, when they attacked Ayutthaya and razed it to the ground. The provincial capital of Kanchanaburi thus grew in a strategically important location, where the Kwai Yai (familiar as the River Kwai) and Kwai Noi rivers merge to become the Mae Klong and leave the deeply gorged mountains to flow across the wide plain to the Gulf of Thailand. This was a favourable site for the Siamese armies to foil enemy attacks. The extremely fertile soil of Kanchanaburi may already have attracted settlers in these times. Sugar cane, tobacco, cotton, maize and cassava are all grown in the area, although most of the cultivated land is given over to rice. The many gemstone mines (including spinel and sapphire mines) in the area also contribute a to the local economy.

Gateway for the Burmese

Highlights Kanchanaburi

Bridge on the River Kwai
Experience the history of the Second World War up close, even though the famous film was made elsewhere.
► page 292

Via the Death Railway to Nam Tok
Vertiginous excitement as the train hugs the sheer cliffs
► page 296

Erawan waterfall
Perhaps the most beautiful waterfall in all Thailand – and swimming is allowed too
► page 299

Wat Pha Luang Ta Bua
Where monks and tigers live together in peace and harmony
► page 295

Kanchanaburi *Plan*

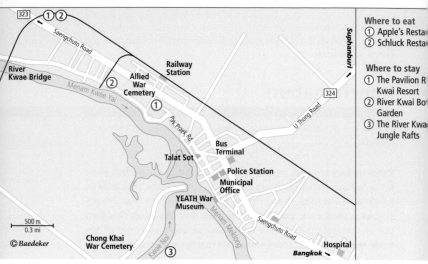

Where to eat
① Apple's Resta...
② Schluck Resta...

Where to stay
① The Pavilion R...
   Kwai Resort
② River Kwai Bo...
   Garden
③ The River Kwa...
   Jungle Rafts

Caves Among the dense rainforests covering the limestone mountains close to Kanchanaburi, which extend far into the country and attain heights of 1800m/5900ft, many marvellous caves and grottoes are hidden. In Kanchanaburi itself, though, there is little to see other than the bustling life of the city.

History The first systematic research was made under the leadership of the Dutch archaeologist Dr van Heekeren, who as a prisoner of war was forced to work on the building of the River Kwai bridge (▶Baedeker Special p.296) and remained in the country after the war. In the 1950s his investigations began with finds of prehistoric stone tools, e.g. in Bo Phloi (north Kanchanaburi) and Sai Yok (to the west). In Sai Yok two caves on the banks of the Kwai Noi revealed tools that were dated to the Neolithic period. One Bronze Age grave has been preserved in its entirety. The burial technique it displays is still practised in Kanchanaburi today, with the face directed toward the north, the legs bent and the body held down with a stone, apparently to keep the ghost of the deceased in the grave and not to disturb the living.

What to See in and around in Kanchanaburi

Note Kanchanaburi's main attractions are spread far and wide. For that reason it is probably best to rent a car or a taxi.

★★
The Bridge on the River Kwai The most popular destination for a day trip is the notorious Bridge on the River Kwai, which was made famous in the eponymous novel by Pierre Boulle (1956) and the spectacular film (made in 1958 in

► VISITING KANCHANABURI

GETTING THERE

By car:
From Bangkok via Nakhon Pathom on Route 4 (130km/80mi approx.)

By bus:
Regular buses from Bangkok Southern Bus Terminal

By rail:
From Bangkok to Thonburi several times a day. There are regular special services to the terminus at Nam Tok (information from the station).

INFORMATION

Tourism Authority of Thailand
Saengchuto Road
71000 Kanchanaburi
Tel. 0 34 / 57 72 00, 51 25 00, 62 36 91
Fax 51 12 00, tatkan@tat.or.th

WHERE TO EAT

► Inexpensive
① *Apple's Restaurant*
Mae Nam Khwae Road
Tel. 0 34 / 51 20 17
Excellent food, available to non-residents as well as those staying at the attached guest house.

② *Schluck Restaurant*
Mae Nam Khwae Road
Western dishes and thick steaks for everyone who feels like a change from the local fare.

WHERE TO STAY

► Mid-range
① *The Pavilion Rim Kwai Resort*
79/2 Ladya-Erawan Road
Tel. 0 34 / 51 38 00, fax 51 57 74
www.pavilionhotels.com
194 rooms, restaurant, bar
Very pleasant hotel with modern and well-kept rooms right on the River

Kwai and just a few miles from the town centre. Nice and quiet.

② *River Kwai Botanic Garden*
14/7 Moo 1, Tambol Bankao
Tel. & fax 0 34 / 64 50 88
www.botanic.co.th
72 rooms, restaurant, wide range of excursions.
The most attractive rooms are in the rustic-style bungalows amid a typical Thai landscape. An evening meal in the floating restaurant is warmly recommended. The management also organizes river excursions on a bamboo raft.

Baedeker recommendation

► Budget
③ *The River Kwai Jungle Rafts*
Tambol Tasao, Amphur Saiyoke,
Kanchanaburi, tel. 02 / 6 42 63 61 2
(bookings). www.riverkwaifloatel.com
100 rooms, restaurant, bar.
Very comfortable hotel on the River Kwai Noi, constructed almost exclusively with local building materials. Large range of sports and excursions.

The bridge over the River Kwai - one of the most famous bridges in the world

Morning breaks over houseboats on the Kwai

Sri Lanka rather than at the original location). The girder bridge that can be seen today is actually a second bridge on the site. It was erected by forced labour, including many prisoners of war, after the construction of a provisional wooden bridge. The remains of the wooden bridge can still be seen when the water level is low.

Mangkorn Thong cave The Mangkorn Thong cave is reached by a boat ride of about half an hour down the Kwai Noi. Boats can be rented in Kanchanaburi. More than 95 steps lead up to a temple within the cave; then a tunnel under the summit of the mountain leads to another cavern with beautiful stalactites.

A trip to Wat Pha Luang Ta Bua, better known as the Tiger Temple, is a nerve-tingling visit. Monks currently live in the temple along with 16 tigers, as well as other animals such as monkeys, horses, peacocks and water buffaloes. The story of this cohabitation of man and tiger starts in 1999. Some local inhabitants found an orphaned tiger cub and brought it to Abbot Phra Acharn. In spite of the great care lavished upon it, the animal died, but just a few weeks later two more wounded tigers were found in a poacher's trap. Three more tigers were brought in over the course of time, and since then a number of tigers have been born at the temple itself. Every day they are allowed to run free in a basin that was blown out of the rocks, where it is possible to stroke them. The serious nature of this project, now famous the world over, is proven by the close cooperation offered by an animal behaviour researcher from Bangkok. The expert opinion is that, since the tigers have never learned to hunt, they would be unlikely to survive in the wild. The temple is about 40 km/25mi from Kanchanaburi on Route 323. The best time for a visit is early afternoon.

★ ★
Tiger Temple Wat Pha Luangta Bua

> **? DID YOU KNOW ...?**
>
> ■ Tigers, the largest cats on earth, are an endangered species. One reason for this is that parts of their body are considered to be aphrodisiacs and are often purchased as such in China. Nowadays there may be no more than 7,000 tigers left in the world, half of them living in India. The number of wild tigers living in Thailand is estimated at about 600, although just a few decades ago there were more than 8,000. One of the most dedicated figures in the movement to protect the species was the former Indian prime minister Indira Gandhi, who put much effort into setting up tiger reserves in her country.

Ban Kao on the Kwai Noi is one of the most important archaeological sites in Kanchanaburi province. The finds (including tools, animal bones, ceramic pots and the complete grave mentioned above) are now on display at the National Museum in Bangkok, now also home to statues in the Lopburi style that were found in Prasat Muang Singh, the »city of lions« (34km/21mi from Kanchanaburi). This town, too, was built as a bulwark against the Burmese. The rectangular walls once enclosed an area of 1,000 x 600m (1,100 x 650 yd). Some parts remain, along with a shrine and four gopuram (gate towers). The well-preserved shrine has a brick prang, and many inscriptions were found within the library.

Archaeological excavation at Ban Kao

The cave at Tham Keng Lawa is truly stunning. It is located in a beautiful landscape of rugged outcrops, jungle-covered mountains and deep gorges with waterfalls, and has many caverns with impressive stalactites. The largest cave in the area is about 75km/47mi from Kanchanaburi on the banks of the Kwai Noi river.

Tham Keng Lawa cave

The original of the famous bridge was made of wood.

The railway journey through fabulous scene on the way to Nam To is a thrilling adventure For gazing down from the bamboo trellises th cling to the cliffs, it is best to have a good hea for heights.

THE DEATH RAILWAY TO BURMA

The fate of British, American and Australian prisoners of war, who died during the building of the famous Bridge on the River Kwai during the Second World War was immortalized in the eponymous film of the novel by Pierre Boulle.

The spectacle is repeated every day, for a fixed price that includes a soft drink and a sandwich. Close to two hours into a journey that begins early in the morning from Bangkok, the driver of the Thai State Railways diesel reduces speed before passing between the sober steel girders of the bridge that crosses the river Kwae Noi. Dozens of camera shutters click before the eyes of the tourists behind them. An old man quietly whistles the first few bars of the River Kwai march that gained fame back in the Fifties.

Prisoners of War

The men who made this bridge one of the most famous, yet most poignantly tragic on earth had no reason for whistling. They were prisoners of war from Britain, Australia, the USA and the Netherlands, who numbered some 61,000, plus an estimated quarter of a million more Asian prisoners from Burma, Malaysia or Thailand, and even some from Japan itself. What is nowadays a tourist magnet with hotels, restaurants and souvenir shops was an indisputable hell at the time of the Japanese concentration

camps. Countless men were overcome by the unbearable heat and the inescapable mosquitoes. Many died of starvation or from the violence and bullets of their guards. Not to be forgotten either are those that died in the allied bombing raids. Their story was told in the novel *Bridge on the River Kwai* by Pierre Boulle, which gained still greater fame and notoriety after the book was made into a film starring Alec Guinness, even though the movie was actually filmed in Ceylon, as the island was then called.

Wooden Bridge

The bridge over the minor river Kwae Noi was part of a strategic railway that was to cross the Three Pagodas pass and link Thailand to Burma, with the objective of securing military supply lines. The 415km/257mi line quickly earned the appropriate moniker »Death Railway«. The work took 13 months to complete, constantly interrupted by allied air raids. What remains is no longer the original construction of that time. The »real« bridge was largely made of teak (and another provisional bridge about 100

yards upstream that can still be seen in the dry season was made only of bamboo). Not until after the war were the present concrete piles set and the modern steel construction spanned between them.

Journey to Nam Tok

Once the train has passed the bridge it picks up speed again, but only for a few miles before the brakes go on once more. At that point, the journey continues to Nam Tok over bamboo trellises attached perilously to vertiginous cliffs. Anyone who dares to look down from the train window stares into a gaping abyss cut by the Kwae Noi river. Looking inwards at the mountain, the train continually passes small caves where many of the prisoners of war were once compelled to sleep. Nam Tok is nowadays a terminus. The rails that once led deep into Burma were ripped up after the war. By the shores of the Mae Klong in Kanchanaburi, a small museum, the **JEATH War Museum**, recalls the men who built the line (opening times

8am–6pm daily, no photographs). It consists primarily of three leaf-built huts like those in which most of the prisoners were housed. The exhibits include old photographs, pictures painted by the prisoners themselves depicting the life in the camps and improvised surgical instruments that the imprisoned doctors were forced to make with their own hands in order to treat their stricken comrades.

After the War

The end of the war in Thailand did not spell freedom for most of the surviving prisoners. The Japanese deported them once again, this time to the mines of Nagasaki, where many more were to die in appalling conditions. Do not miss the opportunity to visit at least the smaller of the two soldiers' cemeteries that are accessible by boat from the bridge. Amid the beautiful and verdant scenery are the graves of 1,700 men.

At the bridge itself there is a memorial plaque and an old locomotive on display.

Peasants threshing rice

More excitement is to be had on a boat trip over the rapids between high cliffs to the **Sai Yok Yai waterfalls** (2km/1.5mi from Nam Tok railway station). A mountain stream plunges over multiple cascades into the Kwai Noi – a particularly impressive sight during the rainy season.

From the Sai Yok Yai waterfalls a path leads through almost untouched jungle to the **Three Pagodas Pass**, where hill tribes eke a living by means of slash-and-burn agriculture. The pass gets its name from three pagodas that are situated along the route. It reaches a height of 1400m/4600ft, while the highest mountain in the region is 1950m/6400ft high. Nowadays the pass is a popular smuggling trail between Burma und Thailand (you are advised not to attempt the walk).

Hellfire pass, only 73m/80yd long and 25m/27yd wide, is a cutting through the mountain that was made as part of the Death Railway during the Second World War. Prisoners were forced to labour on this cutting and another one 450m/500yd further along, working 18 hours a day under inhuman conditions.

Hellfire Pass Memorial Museum

The events that took place at Hellfire Pass are recalled by a museum that has been partially financed by the Australian government, since many of the prisoners were Australian. The museum, 80km/50mi north-west of Kanchanaburi on Route 323, exhibits many of the original tools along with photographs depicting the tragic history of the workers on the line. (opening times: 9am–4pm daily; admission fee).

Mines of Bo Phloi

Some of the wealth of the Kanchanaburi province derives from its productive mines and quarries, some of which are still worked (e.g. at the village of Bo Phloi, 48km/30mi north of Kanchanaburi). Gold, silver, tungsten and tin are all found here. There are also many gem mines where blue sapphires, star sapphires, rubies and semi-precious stones such as garnet and amethyst are found. In Bo Phloi it is possible to buy cut or uncut stones as well as finished jewellery cheaper than anywhere else in Thailand.

About 95km/60mi from Kanchanaburi (Route 3199 north, then a left turn at Ran Nong Preu) there are two fascinating caves. A large number of objects found in the first, Tharn Lot cave, indicate that there were already settlements here in prehistoric times. Within the high and wide caverns many stalactites can be seen. The second cave, Talad Yai (»large cave«), about 2.5km/1.5mi beyond the waterfall at Nam Tok Trai Treung, is home to two hermits.

Tharn Lot cave, Talad Yai cave

Good places to visit in the valley of the Kwai Yai include **Wat Kanchanaburi Khao**, a temple on the site of the old town of Kanchanaburi where a chedi and a prang from the Ayutthaya period are still preserved, and the Erawan waterfall (55km/34mi from Kanchanaburi by car on Route 3199 or a three-hour boat trip). The water splashes from basin to basin in 15 cascades. The falls are supposed to resemble the three-headed elephant of the god Indra, which is how they got their name.

★
Erawan waterfall

! Baedeker TIP

Don't forget your swimwear

The basins of the Erawan falls are an inviting place for a dip, so don't forget your swimwear.

Covering an area of 2,024 sq km/780 sq mi, Khao Salop National Park gained protected status in the 1990s. Further along lies **Thung Yai National Park**. The best time to visit the parks is during the week, since they are popular destinations for the inhabitants of Bangkok at weekends.

Khao Salop National Park

East of Kanchanaburi on Route 323 towards Nakhon Pathom (probably the course of an ancient trade route) is the famous archaeological site of Pong Teuk. Excavations here have revealed the foundations of several buildings that probably once belonged to a temple complex. One sensational find was made here in 1928: a bronze Roman oil lamp that was probably cast in Alexandria in Egypt during the 2nd century. This discovery proved the existence of trade between South-East Asia and the Roman Empire.

Pong Teuk

Other attractions include the teak-built temple of Wat Dong Sak, which has some particularly fine carved gables and a 6th-century Vishnu statue. Some of the finds from the Pong Teuk archaeological excavation site are also on display here. At **Wat Phra Taen Dong Rang** (reached via Routes 323 or 324), according to legend Buddha lay down in a niche to enter nirvana. Another shrine on a mountain not far from here is traditionally believed to have been the place where Buddha's earthly body was cremated.

Wat Dong Sak

Khao Lak

G 2

Region: Southern Thailand
Altitude: 2–25m/6–80ft

Province: Surat Thani
Population: 175,000 approx.

Khao Lak was long held to be a secret quiet spot for holidaymakers seeking to get away from the bustle of Phuket. With the tsunami of 26 December 2004, however, Khao Lak was suddenly thrust into the public eye. Nowhere in Thailand were the consequences of the disaster as pitiless as here.

Floods With all the brutal power of the ocean, the waves washed over seven miles of beach, damaged or destroyed practically all the hotels and took many human lives. It is a testament, however, to the resilience and entrepreneurship of the Thais that only a few weeks after the disaster they had set to work rebuilding, so that now practically all the accommodation has been fully restored.

What to See in Khao Lak

Holiday district Khao Lak is not a town or a village but the name of a region that stretches along the coast about 80km/50mi north of Phuket. Rocky promontories jutting out into the sea divide the 12km/7mi of beach in Khao Lak into several smaller sections: Khao Lak Beach (south), Sunset Beach, Nang Thong Beach, Bang Niang Beach, Kukkak Beach and Coral Cape along with the small fishing village of Ban Pramong.

Takua Pa Takua Pa has the best claim to being the main town in the Khao Lak region. It is a busy settlement of about 20,000 inhabitants on the river of the same name, 134km/83mi from Phuket. There is no accommodation here that can be recommended, but a visit to the market in the early morning, or at least before noon, does give a good idea of the commercial nature of the Thais.

Takua Pa has a very mixed history. There is clear evidence of a settlement here as early as the 3rd century BC. Various discoveries have been made from this time, including pottery, jewellery and statuettes that have mainly been found in the river itself. A large number of gravel pits, large and small, are dotted around inland and testify to an important economic past, when the local tin industry, here and on the island of Phuket, was of great importance. In the **old quarter** of Takua Pa there are still some fine examples of domestic and commercial buildings in the Chinese style, but unfortunately their owners pay little attention to the upkeep and some of them look rather shabby. In one small park three **statues** of Indian provenance represent the four-armed Hindu god Brahma; Phra Luk, Rama's brother from the Ramayana epic; and Nang Srida, Rama's wife, who is revered as a helper in times of need.

▶ VISITING KHAO LAK

GETTING THERE
By car:
From Phuket via Route 4 (80km/50mi approx.)

By bus:
Several good connections daily from Phuket and Surat Thani

WHERE TO STAY
► Luxury
Mukdara Beach Villa & Spa Resort
26/14 Moo 7, Kukkak, Takua Pa
Tel. 0 76 / 42 99 99
Fax 42 00 99
www.mukdarabeach.com
148 rooms, 3 restaurants, coffee shop, 2 bars, 3 swimming pools, spa.
A hotel in exquisite Thai style with tasteful rooms and generous gardens right next to the sea.

► Mid-range
Similana Resort
4/7 Moo 1 Kuk-Kak, Takua Pa
Tel. 0 76 / 42 01 66-8, fax 42 01 69
www.similanaresort.com
71 rooms, restaurant, swimming pool, bar, beach.
This lovely, largely wooden hotel lies in a natural setting at the end of the long bay of Khao Lak. It has pleasant, spacious rooms just a few metres from the beach in chalet bungalows built on stilts that have been completely renovated since the tsunami.

Khao Lak Seaview Resort & Spa
18/1 Moo 6, Petchkasem Road
Tel. 0 76 / 42 06 25, fax 42 06 26
www.khaolak-seaviewresort.com
197 rooms, 2 restaurants, coffee shop, bar, spa.
After a complete reconstruction made necessary by the tsunami, this hotel near the small village of Ban La On

Formal Thai meals are always a feast for the eyes

has comfortable rooms with every amenity. Splendid location next to the beach.

► Budget
Khao Lak Resort
158 Sritakuapa Road
Tel. 0 76 / 42 00 60, fax 42 06 36
www.khaolakresort.com
95 rooms, 2 restaurants, bar, swimming pool, gym, spa. Attractive hotel in nicely laid-out gardens. The rooms are tastefully furnished and have a view of the sea.

Baedeker recommendation

The Sarojin
60 Moo 2, Kukkak, Takua Pa
Tel. 0 76 / 42 79 00-4, fax 42 79 06
www.sarojin.com
56 rooms, 2 restaurants, bar, swimming pool, gym, spa, excursions.
The day before the luxurious Sarojin hotel was to open, the tsunami struck and completely flooded the large section of the hotel next to the beach. It took a further six months for the hotel to open its doors. It has comfortable, well-furnished rooms in a timeless modern style and very friendly staff.

The coast near Kao Lak

Khao Sok National Park
About 4km/2.5mi beyond Takua Pa, along a right turn leading towards Surat Thani, lies Khao Sok National Park. The scenery in the park is typically varied and hilly with several beautiful waterfalls. Part of the park has been declared a special protected area since it contains the last remains of the tropical rainforest that once covered the region. The highest point in the park, 960m/3150ft above sea level, rises out of a landscape that is tangled with jungle growth. There are some rather modest guest houses at the entrance to the park.

Similan Islands
Takua Pa is an ideal base for a trip to the offshore marine national park of the Similan Islands. The islands probably have the finest coral reefs in Thailand, which have largely survived even the tsunami with their original beauty intact. The Similans are among the best and most popular destinations for underwater sports enthusiasts from all over the world. They consist of nine individual isles that have retained their character as a tropical paradise. Travel agents and diving schools offer excursions. To get there without booking an organized trip, drive the 104km/65mi north from Phuket to Thap Lamu and take the ferry. Except in the monsoon season, boats also travel from Patong Beach on Phuket to **Ko Similan** (journey time about 5 hours). From Khao Lak the journey only takes about 2 hours. On the main island there is plenty of simple accommodation and bases for diving.

★ ★ Khao Phra Viharn

D 5

Region: North-east Thailand   **Province:** Si Saket
Altitude: 172m/564ft

The most important shrine testifying to the splendour of Khmer culture, for which the province of Si Saket is famous, is the rock temple of Wat Khao Phra Viharn. Along with the temple complex in ▶Phimai and Prasat Phanom Rung, it is regarded as being the finest and most important example of the superb religious art of the Khmer.

In Cambodian territory

According to a judgement of the International Court in The Hague, Khao Phra Viharn is situated on Cambodian territory, yet its site on a rocky plateau makes it accessible only from Thailand. It was not until 1989, two decades after it was rediscovered, a period during which the temple was left to decay, that the then prime minister Choonhavan agreed with the head of the Cambodian government Hun Sen that this unique cultural monument should once again be made accessible to the public.

? DID YOU KNOW ...?

■ A small but accurate copy of Khao Phra Viharn can be viewed at the Ancient City open-air museum in Samut Prakan.

Temple complex

With its length of one kilometre (1100 yards), Khao Phra Viharn is one of the largest temple complexes of the Khmer. It was probably built under King Jayavarman II in the 11th century, around the same time as the famous Angkor Wat in modern-day Cambodia. It follows Indonesian models and was built to honour the Hindu god Shiva. The entrance towers, called gopuram (the singular is gopura), mark the access points to all four levels of the temple. From the lowest level a partially intact stairway inset with nagas leads though several

 ## VISITING KHAO PHRA VIHARN

GETTING THERE

By car:
From Surin via Route 226 (120km/75mi; from Nakhon Ratchasima 270km/168mi) to Si Saket. From Si Saket Route 221 leads to Khao Phra Viharn (100km/60mi approx.).

By rail:
From Bangkok-Hualampong (515km/320mi)

By bus:
From Bangkok (570km/354mi), Surin and Ubon Ratchathani

WHERE TO STAY

The nearest accommodation is to be found in ▶Surin.

The gate to the second prasat at Khao Phra Viharn is especially well preserved.

more levels up to the main temple. On the second level there remains a cross-shaped pavilion (prasat) that once matched another on the third level. The ponds for holy water have long since dried up and are overgrown with grass. The temple has largely collapsed. It was overgrown by dense jungle for many years and has only been cleared in recent years. One mondhop has survived. Like most of the complex, it was built in the early Baphuon style. In the case of some buildings only the foundations of the walls can be seen, so that it is difficult to visualize the original extent of the site. Countless Buddhas carved out of stone and several bas-reliefs have been wholly or partly preserved. The pavilions with their beautifully made lintels and the remains of the enclosing walls are particularly interesting.

i According to legend ...

■ Like many temples in Thailand, the foundation of Khao Phra Viharn is associated with a legend. An avaricious married couple living on the Mekong had devised a new kind of angling gear, with which they sought to become the richest fishers in the region. Their pretty daughter Pin, who was not in sympathy with this aim, secretly gave the money to the poor. Her deeds came to light and she thereby won the heart of a local prince, who became her husband. To atone for the sins of her parents and thus smooth their way to nirvana, Pin commissioned the building of Khao Phra Viharn.

There is an excellent view of the temple complex and the neighbouring countryside from Mor Daeng Cliff (look at the beautifully preserved bas-reliefs and the rock drawings, which are quite easy to see in places).

Mor Daeng Cliff

Around Khao Phra Viharn

From Si Saket (Route 2076) it is easy to visit Prasat Kamphaeng Noi just 8km/5mi away. On the site one unadorned prang still stands. Inside the well-preserved perimeter wall, some fragments of beautifully sculpted door lintels and columns have survived.

Prasat Kamphaeng Noi

Further along Route 2076, then left at the junction with Route 226, are the impressive ruins of Prasat Kamphaeng Yai. Particularly noteworthy features are the gigantic portal at the entrance, two brick buildings upon which fine decorative sculptures have partially been preserved, the remains of three prangs and the almost entirely complete inner wall. Apart from the well-preserved cornices, windows and door lintels there is also a bas-relief showing the god Shiva riding an elephant above the grimacing face of a demon. The origin of one armless bronze statue is not known. It probably once depicted Vishnu.

★
Prasat Kamphaeng Yai

★ ★ Khao Yai National Park

D 3

Region: Central Thailand
Area: 2,168 sq km/840 sq mi
Altitude: Up to 1350m/4430ft

Provinces: Nakhon Nayok, Nakhon Ratchasima, Prachinburi, Saraburi

Khao Yai National Park opened in 1962 and is the oldest national park in Thailand. The tallest peaks in the park, some of which are still covered with original rain forest, reach as high as 1350m/ 4430ft. The picturesque waterfalls and idyllic lakes are as popular with native Thais as with visiting tourists.

Dong Phayayen lies inside the national park and was additionally declared a UNESCO protected area in 2005 due to its remarkable variety of wildlife, including tigers and leopards, gibbons and the increasingly rare hornbills. It is best to avoid the park on weekends or holidays since it can get very crowded.

Dong Phayayen

The highest mountains are in the eastern part of the park: Khao Laem (1328m/4357ft) and Khao Khiau (»green mountain«, 1350m/ 4429ft). Both command magnificent views and can be climbed as part of a day trip. There are some lovely waterfalls at **Nam Tok Haeo**

★ ★
Diverse jungle landscape

! *Baedeker* TIP

Rip-off

Be careful if offered very »cheap« prices for taxi journeys in the park. The price may only be valid for a single stretch of the journey. If in doubt, it is better to rely on the travel agents in Pak Chong, Saraburi or Nakhon Ratchasima or the guides at the Khao Yai Garden Lodge.

Suwat, **Nam Tok Pa Kluai** (»orchid falls«, where the rocks are entwined with orchids) and **Nam Tok Kong Keo**. The international-class eighteen-hole golf course is beautifully located. The park itself is home to elephants, bears, tigers, tapirs, buffalo, monkeys, deer and wild boar. The game can be watched from the tower at Nong Pak Chi in the mornings and evenings. The park administration provides a map showing in detail a total of eleven walks of varying degrees of difficulty. The official routes are well marked. It is also possible to rent mountain bikes at the park base station.

Bat caves A large cave in the limestone rock about 2km/1.5mi north of the park entrance is home to hundreds of thousands of small bats. The place is most impressive shortly before sunset when the animals leave the protection of the cave and fly off in search of food.

▶ VISITING KHAO-YAI-NATIONALPARK

GETTING THERE

By bus/car:
Many buses run from Bangkok Northern Bus Terminal to Khao Yai National Park (journey time about 4 hours). Drivers should take Route 1 from Bangkok to Saraburi, then Route 2, turning right just before Pak Chong onto Route 2090, then follow the signposts.

By rail:
Pak Chong station is on the line from Bangkok to Nakhon Ratchasima.

WHERE TO STAY
▶ **Budget**
Khao Yai Garden Lodge
Tel. 0 44 / 36 51 78
www.khaoyai-garden-lodge.com
The German owner of the lodge has lived in Khao Yai National Park for many years and often offers tours through the park lasting one or more

days. Highlights include the guided tours given by Peter Boy, who has discovered 35 species of insects that now bear his name. The rooms are furnished in rustic fashion and there is also a restaurant and a bar.

On the north-eastern edge of Khao Yai National Park, about 180km/110mi north-east of Bangkok, lies the small town of **Pak Chong** right at the foot of the mighty mountain range that separates the Menam basin from the Khorat plateau. It is worth strolling through the lively daily market, with plenty of wares that attract people from all over the surrounding countryside.

Khao Yai National Park *Map*

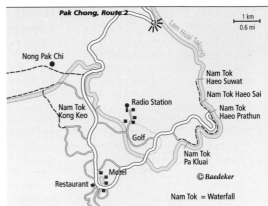

About 15km/9mi east of Pak Chong, not far from Route 2, is the broad valley of the lovely **Lam Takhong reservoir** that supplies the people of Bangkok with water.

Khon Kaen

C 4

Region: North-east Thailand
Altitude: 155m/509ft

Province: Khon Kaen
Population: 141,000

The city of Khon Kaen is about 380km/236mi north-east of Bangkok in the region where the rather barren landscape of the Khorat plateau gives way to the fertile land to the north. After Nakhon Ratchasima it is the most important administrative and commercial centre of north-eastern Thailand

Khon Kaen is the only university town in north-east Thailand. The economic development of the town has been boosted by the »Friendship Highway« (Route 2) built by the Americans, for whom it played a major role in supplying the forces stationed in north-east Thailand during the Vietnam war. Apart from the famed National Museum there is not much else to see in and around the town.

University town

★ ★ National Museum

The museum on the northern edge of the city (Lang Soon Ratchakarn Road) contains some of the astonishing discoveries from ▶Ban Chiang: pottery painted with geometric patterns, leaves and flowers or animals. The pieces have been dated to a period between 4500 BC

🕐
Opening hours:
Wed–Sun
9am–12pm,
1–4pm
Admission fee

▶ VISITING KHON KAEN

GETTING THERE

By car:
From Bangkok on Route 1 or 2 (440km/273mi; 190km/118mi from Nakhon Ratchasima), from Phitsanulok by Route 12 (300km/186mi)

By rail:
Station on the Bangkok – Nakhon Ratchasima – Udon Thani line (450km/280mi from Bangkok, journey time 7 hours approx.)

By air:
Daily from Bangkok

WHERE TO STAY

▶ Budget
Sofitel Raja Orchid
9/9 Prachasumran Road
Tel. 0 43 / 32 21 55
Fax 32 21 50
www.sofitel.com
292 rooms, 2 restaurants, bar, night club, swimming pool, gym.
The best hotel in town with large, comfortable rooms at a surprisingly good price. A major entertainment centre. The beer in the restaurant is brewed in the hotel's own micro-brewery.

and 3500 BC, although little more is known about their origins. One of the graves that was excavated in Ban Chiang is also on display here. On the ground floor there is an extensive exhibition of Thai folk art and a collection of prehistoric finds. Temporary exhibitions on various themes are also held.

The sandstone tablets on the ground floor and in the large gardens include some finely delineated bas-reliefs with scenes from the life of Buddha. They were done in the Dvaravati style of the 8th to 10th centuries, along with some Khmer elements. Some of them came from **Muang Fa Daed** (▶Ban Sema).

Among the works of art on the upper floor, it is worth noting the large and beautiful statue of the seated Buddha in the Sukhothai style, an artistically worked lintel (11th century, showing the god Indra riding an elephant) as well as a bronze sculpture of the god Shiva (12th/13th century). There are also some notable sculptures in Dvaravati style and bronzes in Chiang Saen style.

To the east of the National Museum is a pretty, palm-fringed lake with a small restaurant.

Around Khon Kaen

✳
Ubol Ratana reservoir

The Ubol Ratana reservoir, 80km/50mi long and named after a daughter of King Bhumibol, lies 55km/34mi north-west of Khon Khaen. It irrigates the somewhat barren land and is a popular spot for a day trip among local tourists. At the entrance to the **Phu Phan Kum National Park** steps lead up the mountain Phu Phan Kum, from which there is a fantastic view of the reservoir.

The village of Ban Sema near Yang Talat, around 60km/37mi east of Khon Kaen, holds a major attraction. Between the 9th and 11th centuries this was the site of the Dvaravati town of **Muang Fa Daed**, which was surrounded by two moated walls. Many items of importance for the development of Thai culture were found here from the era between the 6th and 13th centuries. An interesting aspect here is the mixture between native art and that of the neighbouring peoples such as the Khmer.

★★
Ban Sema

Two beautifully shaped boundary stones from the site show Buddha being worshipped by the royal couple (a tablet that is now kept in the monastery buildings of **Wat Po Chai Semaran**) and an illustration of the story of Buddha returning to his own family (in the museum at Khon Kaen). More stone tablets are exhibited in the grounds of the wat.

North-west of the temple compound there are ruins of several chedis from the Dvaravati period, including a well-preserved example of elegant lines with some original stucco decoration still apparent on the lower part of the building. The building in the middle has been restored more recently and a spire added that shows the unmistakeable characteristics of the Ayutthaya style.

Dvaravati chedis

Between Yang Talat and Kalasin on the road near **Ban Nong Wang Noeng** there are some interesting examples of Dvaravati stone artwork: three gilded bas-reliefs showing a reclining Buddha which date from the period between the 8th and 10th centuries.

Dvaravati bas-reliefs

★★ Ko Chang

E/F 4

Region: South-east Thailand
Altitude: 3–744m/10–2440ft
Province: Trat
Population: 14,000

Ko Chang, »Elephant Island«, between Phuket and Ko Samui is Thailand's second biggest island. It and 46 smaller and mostly uninhabited islands in the proximity were declared a nature reserve in 1982 under the name Ko Chang Marine National Park.

The island of 3,500 inhabitants is about 29km/18mi long, 8–14 km/5–7mi wide and has retained some of its original charm thanks to its national park status. For many years the accommodation in the region was rather spartan, but since than a large number of bungalow developments and small hotels have been built, some of which are very comfortable. Since the Trat province has attracted the presence of several international companies, Ko Chang has become a very popular place for weekend trips by employees.

Former backpackers' paradise

► VISITING KO CHANG

GETTING THERE

By car:
75km/47mi from Chanthaburi to Trat via Route 3

By bus:
Regular connections from Bangkok, Pattaya and Chanthaburi

Picnic in the bay of Ao Klong Phrao

Ferry:
Regular sailings from Centerpoint Pier not far from ►Trat, every 20 minutes from 8am to 7pm. Cars and motorcycles can be taken on board. Another route exists from Laem Ngop (every weekday at 1pm, returning from Ko Chang around 4pm).

By air:
From Bangkok to Trat via Bangkok Airways, up to three times daily depending on the season. The airport is not far from the ferry terminals.

WHERE TO STAY
► Budget
Sea View Resort
Mu 4, Kai Bae Beach
Ko Chang
Tel. 0 39 / 59 71 43
Fax 02 / 4 11 46 62
52 rooms, restaurant. Well-kept rooms in a nicely laid out garden – a quiet alternative to the White Sand Beach hotel.

Ko Chang Resort
12/3 Mu 1
Klong Prao Beach
Tel. 0 39 / 59 70 28
Fax 02 / 2 77 09 75
60 rooms, restaurant, bar, swimming pool. Relatively expensive rooms, but pleasant and clean. Lovely beach.

Plaloma Cliff Resort
White Sand Beach, 11/2 Moo 4
Tel. 0 39 / 55 11 19
Fax 55 11 18
www.plaloma-cliff.thai.li
18 rooms, restaurant, swimming pool. A popular destination for many years for those seeking to get away from it all. Nice garden above the beach. Swiss management.

The natural beauty of some of the landscape is practically unspoiled, with thickly wooded hills that rise to 744m/2440ft above sea level. The interior of the island is dominated by dense rainforest, where monkeys, snakes and some wild boar roam. **Nam Tok Tham Mayom** is the largest waterfall on the east coast. Not far away is the **Nam Tok King Rama** waterfall. There are a number of walks by which the interior can be explored, although they are not particularly well signposted.

✶ ✶
Unspoiled nature

The largest settlement on Ko Chang is the fishing village of Klong Son. From the jetty boats ply the route to Laem Ngop (17km/11mi from Trat). Some of the houses are built on stilts. The inhabitants' main sustenance comes from the extensive coconut and rubber plantations and from fishing. Lately, however, tourism has also played an important role.

Klong Son fishing village

At 2km/1.5mi **White Sand Beach** is not the longest beach on Ko Chang but it is the one most frequented by tourists. Past failings have been cast aside by replacing simple huts with comfortable hotels, which are actually supported by loans from the government. The small fishing village of Ban Hat Sai Kaeo is sited right in the middle of the beach. The best view is to be had from a hill at the southern end of White Sand Beach upon which there is also a Chinese temple. The remaining beaches on the island are **Klong Phrao Beach**, **Klong Makok Beach**, **Kai Bae Beach**, **Thanam Beach** and **Bailan Beach**. These also offer a wide range of accommodation. The beaches on the east coast of Ko Chang are less recommended, as there is little good accommodation there and, in particular, they tend to be crowded with Thai holidaymakers.

✶
Beaches

✶ Ko Lanta

Region: Southern Thailand
Altitude: 0–488m/1600ft

Province: Rayong
Population: 20,000

The islands of Ko Lanta Yai and Ko Lanta Noi lie about 50km/30mi south of Krabi in the Andaman Sa. Ko Lanta is the name normally used for both islands, though in fact they consist of a large (yai) and a small (noi) isle separated by a narrow strait.

Parts of Ko Lanta Yai and some of the nearby islands have been included in the Koh Lanta marine national park that was established in 1990. Ko Lanta itself is very hilly: the highest peak in the southern part of the Ko Lanta Yai island rises to 488m/1600ft above sea level. Until a few years ago the islands were known as a refuge of globe-trotting backpackers, but when word spread about its attractions,

Marine national park

▶ VISITING KOH LANTA

GETTING THERE

Ferry:
There are express boats from Krabi, Ko Phi Phi and Trang to Ban Saladan, the island's main settlement, once or twice daily depending on the weather. During the monsoon period the ferry service hardly runs at all.

By air:
The nearest airport is at Krabi, from where the islands are reached by boat.

WHERE TO STAY

▶ Luxury
Pimalay Bay Resort & Spa
99 Moo 5, Ba Kan Tiang Beach
Lanta Yai, tel. 0 75 / 60 79 99
Fax 60 79 98, www.pimalai.com
86 rooms, 3 restaurants, swimming pool, spa and base for diving excursions.

This new hotel on a broad, curving bay 900m/1000yd long has all the comforts of home. The associated diving station provides lessons for beginners according to the PADI system that is used throughout the world.

▶ Mid-range
Sri Lanta
111 Moo 6, Klongnin Beach, Lanta Yai
Tel. 0 75 / 69 72 88, fax 69 72 89
www.srilanta.com
49 rooms, restaurant, bar, swimming pool. Lovely hotel with villas furnished in rustic style and equipped with all comforts.

▶ Budget
Plenty of bungalows directly on the coast not far from the main town of Ban Saladan offer varying degrees of comfort.

A street in Old Lanta

including sandy beaches that were almost totally unspoiled, bungalows started sprouting almost at once. Some of them are now very well appointed. The inhabitants' success in protesting against government plans to declare a nature reserve now allows the development of tourism, which will doubtless continue over the next few years. During the busy season between December and February, accommodation is mostly expensive and often fully booked. Only a few of the inhabitants of Ko Lanta currently make a living from tourism. The main sources of income remain the coconut plantations and countless shrimp farms.

What to See on Ko Lanta

Neither Ban Saladan on the west coast nor Ban Ko Lanta on the east coast have any particular sights, but both are charming places and worth a visit when the markets take place (usually in the mornings). »Old Lanta«, the oldest settlement on the island, has some interesting houses and a few outstanding fish restaurants. **Markets**

About 2km/1.5mi west of Ban Saladan is the Kaw Kwang peninsula with the beach of the same name, from which steps lead up to a lookout point on the hill. There is also a small sandy beach where swimming is possible (at high tide only). **Kaw Kwang peninsula**

The beaches of Ko Lanta are not as beautiful or well kept as those in some other parts of Thailand, but it is always possible to find a good spot on them. The nicest beaches (**Klong Dao** and **Long Beach**) are to be found along the 22km/14mi of road that lead along the south coast, where most of the bungalows and hotels have been built. The beaches on the eastern side are rather flat by comparison. **Beaches**

✴ Ko Pha Ngan

Region: Southern Thailand **Province:** Surat Thani
Altitude: 0–627m/2057ft **Population:** 8,000 approx.

The island of Ko Pha Ngan with its jungle landscape is dominated by a limestone mountain ridge that comes right down to the beaches in places. The inhabitants mainly live from fishing, although tourism is increasingly becoming an extra source of income. Ko Pha Ngan has some excellent beaches, but few other attractions beyond the impressive jungle scenery.

The island is 19km/12mi long and 12km/7mi wide and lies about 16km/10mi north of Ko Samui, for which it has long served as an overflow resort when Ko Samui is full up. **Thong Sala** is the only real **Next door to Ko Samui**

► VISITING KOH PHA NGAN

GETTING THERE
Ferry:
From Don Sak (Surat Thani) usually with an intermediate stop at Ko Samui, from Ko Samui and Nathon

WHERE TO STAY
► Mid-range
Santhiya Resort & Spa
Thong Nai Pan Beach
Tel. and fax 0 77 / 23 83 33
www.santhiya.com
Rrestaurant, bar, swimming pool, water sports,
shopping arcade.
Probably the most attractive accommodation on Ko Pha Ngan at the moment. Comfortable bungalows built in Thai style. Intoxicating location with fantastic views next to a broad sandy beach.

► Budget
First Villa Bungalow
Ban Tai Beach
Tel. 0 77 / 37 72 25
Fax 23 83 52
www.firstvilla.com
Pleasant accommodation with restaurant, bar, swimming pool, jeep and motorcycle hire plus water sports.

Hansa Resort
Ban Tai Beach
Tel. 0 77 / 37 74 94
Fax 37 74 95
www.hansaresort.com
4 rooms und 10 bungalows, restaurant, bar, water sports.
Pretty and nicely tended bungalow complex with comfortable rooms.

The beaches of Ko Pha Ngan are among the most beautiful in Thailand.

Ko Pha Ngan Map

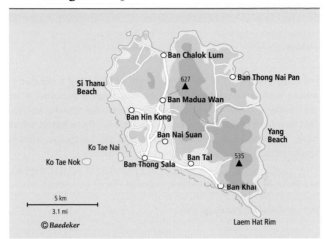

Ban Chalok Lum

Si Thanu Beach

627 ▲

Ban Thong Nai Pan

Ban Madua Wan

Ban Hin Kong

Ban Nai Suan

Yang Beach

Ko Tae Nai

Ban Tal

535 ▲

Ko Tae Nok

Ban Thong Sala

Ban Khai

5 km
3.1 mi

© *Baedeker*

Laem Hat Rim

settlement on Ko Pha Ngan. There used to be just a few fishing families here, but nowadays the village is the centre of island life and has all the necessary facilities for tourists. The jetty for boats from Ko Samui is also in Thong Sala.

It is worth visiting the meditation temple of Wat Khao Tham at Ban Tal, which also features a footprint of Buddha. Those interested in Buddhism can take part in the English-language meditation courses that take place here.

Wat Khao Kam

Ko Pha Ngan has more than 17km/11mi of beaches, which remain among the most beautiful in Thailand. Most are very small but idyllic. Pick-up taxis take visitors there and back in no time at all. There is plenty of simple accommodation but no comfortable hotel. On some beaches the sand flies can be a nuisance.

★★ Beaches

Fabulous **boat trips** to the islands of the **Ang Thong Archipelago** (► Surat Thani) reveal a fascinating sub-tropical world with some beautiful beaches. Many of these islands remain uninhabited, although there are a few bungalow developments on Ko Khanom und Ko Sichon.

! *Baedeker* TIP

Dance beneath a full moon

The full moon parties, which have been taking place for a few years now on Ko Phang Ngan on the first night of the full moon, have become legendary. They attract thousands of young people to the island, who dance with abandon before the massive speaker stacks. Beware of undercover agents posing as dealers, who may offer to sell drugs. It is quite common for such dealings to end in a jail sentence.

✳ ✳ Ko Phi Phi

H 2

Region: Southern Thailand
Altitude: 2–744m/6–2441ft

Province: Rayong
Population: 3,500

For many years the Phi Phi islands south of Krabi had a reputation among backpackers as an out-of-the-way tropical paradise. Since then many a travel company has discovered the islands, and the first huts have given way to bungalows and finally to hotels, which have, however, been skilfully slipped into the landscape without spoiling much of the original flavour of the islands.

Koh Phi Phi Don
Of the many small islands in the 390 sq km/150 sq mi **Hat Noppharat Thara Marine National Park**, only Phi Phi Don is inhabited. Its incomparable scenery features truly exquisite, exotic beaches with fine sand and crystal clear water.

✳ ✳
Trip around the island
Many trips around the island of Phi Phi Don by long-tailed boat are on offer starting from **Ton Sai Bay** or from many of the hotel jetties. Intermediate stops for snorkelling or swimming are often included.

Phi Phi Lay
The island of Phi Phi Lay just a few kilometres away is uninhabited but often visited by divers or holidaymakers seeking peace and quiet.

Exotic beaches and a picture-postcard landscape can be found on the island of Ko Phi Phi Don.

► VISITING KO PHI PHI

GETTING THERE
Ferry:
There are regular ferries from Surat Thani, Krabi and Phuket (journey time between 1.5 and 3 hours) to the main settlement at Ton Sai Bay. Between May and September ferries may sail rarely or not at all, depending on the weather. Hotel guests travel on to their final destinations by long-tailed boat.

WHERE TO STAY
► Luxury
**Holiday Inn Resort
Phi Phi Island**
Laem Thong Beach
Tel. 0 75 / 62 13 34
Fax 67 63 17
www.phiphi-palmbeach.com
80 bungalows, 2 restaurants, bar, swimming pool, water sports. The Phi Phi branch of the international hotel chain. Very comfortable rooms, well-tended premises and attentive service. Large sandy beach.

P. P. Natural Resort
Laem Thong Beach
Tel. 0 75 / 61 30 10
Fax 61 30 00
www.phiphinatural.com
77 rooms, restaurant, bar, swimming pool, water sports centre. Attractive hotel built in extensive gardens with individual wooden bungalows. Broad sandy beach.

► Mid-range
Andaman Beach Resort
Hin Kom Beach
Tel. 0 75 / 61 80 60
Fax 61 80 18
www.andamanbeachresort.com
82 bungalows, restaurant, swimming pool.

This pretty hotel is near the quay. It has air-conditioned rooms and excellent service, plus a highly recommended restaurant.

Paradise Pearl Resort
Long Beach
Tel. 0 75 / 62 21 00
ax 35 48 82
www.ppparadise.com
80 bungalows, restaurant, bar, swimming pool, diving base, day trips. Hotel open all year round with tastefully furnished bungalows. Restaurant right on the beach (partially open-air).

► Budget
Since the tsunami, visitor numbers for Ko Phi Phi have been well under the numbers that were common before the disaster. Even hotels that escaped the flooding have suffered from this. It is therefore worth trying to negotiate discounts, even in the better hotels. There is also a good range of well-priced guest houses.

WHERE TO EAT
For those who prefer not to eat in hotel restaurants, there are plenty of alternatives in the main settlement of Ton Sai Bay. The only problem is that some of the more remote beaches are accessible only by boat.

► Inexpensive
Thai Cuisine
Ton Sai Bay
Simple but busy restaurant in the main town. All kinds of good Thai dishes and an excellent breakfast are available.

i **Since the Tsunami**

■ Phi Phi island was one the areas of Thailand worst hit by the tsunami of 26 December 2004. 691 died in the flooding according to official estimates and several hundred are still missing. More than 200 bungalows and other buildings were swallowed by the sea and the whole infrastructure was destroyed. In the meantime, practically everything has been rebuilt and only a few places still give a hint of the damage that took place.

Nevertheless, Phi Phi Lay also has economic importance, as whole families earn commission from the holder of the concession by collecting **swallows' nests** from the numerous caves and grottoes. They clamber precariously up scaffolds made of bound bamboo canes or lianas. The nests are a rare and popular delicacy in Chinese cuisine. 1kg/2lb of nests can fetch as much as US$2,000 in Hong Kong. It is not the nest themselves that are eaten, but the threads of spittle that the birds use to hold the nests together. They need to be softened for a long period, after which they are cleaned and cooked to make bird's nest soup.

✶✶
Coral reefs

Off the coast of Phi Phi Lay there are many beautiful coral reefs, some of which go down to depths of 25m/80ft. The undersea world around the reefs is varied and colourful. Phi Phi Lay was also the location for the film *The Beach* with Leonardo Di Caprio.

! *Baedeker* TIP

Climb to View Point

The best view of Phi Phi Don can be enjoyed from the so-called View Point. A climb lasting about 20 minutes starts just behind Ton Sai Bay

On the northern side of the island Phi Phi Lay there are cave paintings which remain a mystery to scholars. They are often called Viking paintings, but the ships por-

✶✶
Cave paintings

trayed can hardly have been painted by the Norsemen. Many other caves, some of them considered sacred, are the impressive result of natural processes that have continued for millennia.

Ko Samet (Ko Kae Phisadan)

E 3

Region: South-east Thailand
Altitude: 2–105m/6–345ft

Province: Trat
Population: 2,500 approx.

Ko Samet was one of the first of Thailand's islands to attract tourists from all over the world with its wonderful beaches, crystal-clear water and luxuriant vegetation. Even its status as a national park has not stemmed the influx of visitors. Dozens of bungalow developments have been built, and the beaches are not at all as clean as they once were.

In spite of some unsolved problems – built-up beaches, rubbish, lack of drinking water – a prohibition on overnight stays that was placed on the islands in 1990 was lifted two years later after protests from businesspeople and locals. Thousands of Thai holidaymakers come from Bangkok, especially at the weekends. Most stay at **Hat Sai Kaeo Beach** on the east coast in the north. The leftover debris of wild parties may be the final nail in the coffin of the once-healthy island environment.

! Baedeker TIP

Beware mosquitoes!

As there is occasionally a risk of malaria on Ko Samet, preventive measures such as daily application of mosquito cream are essential. At night it is vital to use the mosquito nets provided in every bungalow.

The island is nowhere wider than 800m/900yd and measures a mere 200m/220yd at its narrowest point. It is 5km/3mi in length. The west coast consists mainly of cliffs; only in the north are there sandy beaches from which the fabulous sunsets may be enjoyed. On the eastern coast several long sandy beaches can be reached by well-sign-posted paths or pick-up taxis.

Holidays Crusoe-style

Trips to the Mainland

Rayong The lively town of Rayong is a typical middle-sized settlement 140km/90mi south-east of Bangkok on the Gulf of Thailand. The oldest part of town is the fishing harbour at the mouth of the river, which can be very lively, especially in the afternoons. Rayong is famous for **»nam pla«** fish sauce, a Thai speciality that is used to flavour many meals instead of salt. The town also produces a shrimp paste called **»kapi«** as well as dried fish that are sold all over the country. Outside the town sugar cane, cassava and pineapples are **Beaches ►** cultivated on extensive plantations.Along the coast between Pattaya and Rayong there are some lovely beaches. Some attractive hotels for a holiday by the sea, including the quiet Rayong Resort, can be found near Rayong. East of Rayong the bathing resort of Suan Wang Kaeo and the beach at Tha Rua Klaeng also deserve mention.

Khao Chamao National Park The establishment of Khao Chamao National Park north-east of Rayong, with its headquarters 9km/6mi beyond the village of Klaen,

 ## VISITING KO SAMET

GETTING THERE

By car:
From Bangkok by Routes 34/3/36 (180km/112mi) to Rayong

By bus:
From Bangkok Eastern Bus Terminal (journey time 4 hours approx.). From Rayong (minibuses from the clock tower) by Route 3 to Ban Phe; and by ferry from there (the ferry travels on demand, last trip around 5pm).

Ferry:
The main quay on the island is in the fishing village of Samet. When the sea is tranquil, boats travel around the western promontory to the beaches where they put in at temporary landing jetties.

WHERE TO STAY
► **Mid-range**
Ao Prao Resort
Paradise Beach (Ao Phrao)
Tel. 0 38 / 61 68 80

Fax 61 68 85, www.aopraoresort.com
About 60 rooms, some of them in bungalows, restaurant, bar, shopping, diving base. One of the few hotel complexes on Ko Samet worth recommending. Very well-kept development, good service and a PADI diving base with lessons in English and other languages.

Le Vimarn Cottages
Paradise Beach (Ao Phrao)
Tel. 0 43 / 97 71-2 (in Bangkok)
Fax 9 03 52
www.aopraoresort.com
As above: recommendable hotel in a pleasant garden above the beach with well-appointed bungalows.

► **Budget**
Candlelight Beach
Ao Thian
Tel. 01 / 2 18 69 34 (mobile telephone)
21 bungalows (no air-conditioning)
For travellers on a low budget, simply furnished but cosy.

can be traced back to the uninhibited logging of tropical rainforests that once blighted Thailand. By declaring the 15 sq km/6 sq mi area a national park it was possible to protect one last outpost of forest from logging and create a reserve for various species of wildlife and especially birds. Obviously the fauna and flora in the park are not entirely free from interference, since the area is a popular destination for local families to visit. Not far from the park headquarters there are two waterfalls at **Nam Tok Khao Chamao** and **Nam Tok Chong Laep**, as well as a popular picnic site. A stiff climb led by a local guide who can be hired at the entrance to the park leads to two impressive caves, **Tham Samit Cave** and **Tham Lakhon Cave**.

✶ Ko Samui

G 2/3

Region: Southern Thailand
Altitude: 2–635m/6–2083ft

Province: Surat Thani
Population: 36,000 approx.

Ko Samui is part of the Ang Thong Archipelago north of Surat Thani, along with about 40 other, mostly uninhabited islands. Until the 1980s the islands were seen as a refuge for backpackers and a little-known, secret haven of delightful, near-empty beaches. The charms of Thailand's third-biggest island did not escape the attentions of the travel companies for long, however, and when Bangkok Airways built a private airport there in the late 1980s nothing stood in the way of continuous development of the tourist infrastructure.

Since Ko Samui has managed to retain a good deal of its charm in spite of the rapid development, the islands are still among the most popular places in Thailand for a beach holiday. Even though the cheap and cheerful accommodation of the past is on the decline, it is still possible to get a room for as little as 200 baht or not much more. For those who prefer more comfort, there are a great many hotels ranging right up to the most luxurious category. The explosion in visitor numbers has undoubtedly benefited the economy of the island, if little else. As far as the downside of development is concerned, the natural environment has taken the brunt of it. An overall planning strategy for hotels bungalows and other tourist facilities has been put in place only recently – too late to rectify the sins of the past.

Island for beach holidays

Ko Samui provides all types of water sports, diving, snorkelling, windsurfing, etc. The island is ringed by a good coast road that offers access to practically all tourist facilities. Apart from taxis (mostly pick-up taxis, known locally as songthaos), visitors can get around by hiring motorbikes or cars.

Water sports

Ko Samui Map

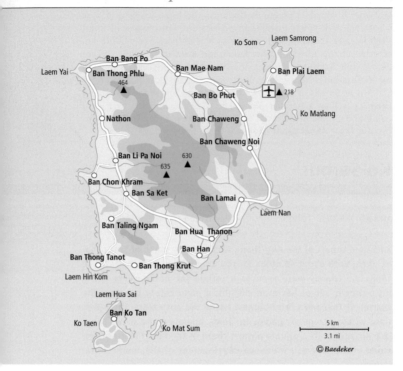

Ban Nathon The boats from Surat Thani or Phuket dock at Ban Nathon, the main town on the island. Nathon itself offers little in the way of attractions but it does have plenty of restaurants, travel agents and souvenir shops as well as the island's small hospital.

Fishing villages The main attractions of Ko Samui are its picturesque fishing villages, giant coconut and durian plantations and the waterfalls that are tucked away in the jungle amid 600m/2000ft-high mountains.

Big Buddha Beach This bay gets its name from a huge statue of Buddha which is 12m/40ft in height, along with a recent temple. It is a busy, cheerful place not far from Ko Samui airport and well worth a visit.

Bay of Chaweng On the 6km/4mi-long Bay of Chaweng it is easy to see at a glance some of the environmental sins that have been committed on Ko Samui. For years there were only two small hotels here, but then the small town exploded: souvenir shops, restaurants and other tourist facilities appeared in no time at all. Since then Chaweng Beach has become the real centre for tourism on Ko Samui. A deterioration in the state of the long sandy beach and the water quality went hand in hand with the improvement of the tourist infrastructure. The building of sewage plants has at least dealt with the problem of water quality. Chaweng Beach is geographically split into two parts: Chaweng Yai Beach und Chaweng Noi Beach. Both are densely built up, although Chaweng Noi Beach is a little quieter and more relaxed. It is also a good place for snorkelling outside the monsoon season.

The 4km/2.5mi of **Lamai Beach** (about 22km/14mi from Nathon) is very touristy but not as crowded as Chaweng Beach. Reefs lie offshore on the eastern and northern parts of the bay and are sometimes

Lamai Beach

exposed at low tide. The level of prices for restaurants and accommodation is somewhat lower here than at Chaweng Beach. An interesting rock formation between the two fishing villages of Ban Hua Thanon and Ban Lamai is open to a variety of interpretations. The natives call it »Mummy and Daddy Rock«.

Wat Hin Ngu stands on steep cliffs next to the village of Ban Hua Thanon. A market that takes place here every year in mid-March is **Wat Hin Ngu**

linked to a religious celebration at the temple and attracts thousands of people from all around the district.

The cheapest accommodation on the island can be found at **Mae Nam Beach** in the north of Ko Samui. There are numerous bungalow developments, some of them a bit spartan and reminiscent of the early days of tourism on Ko Samui.

Between Chaweng Noi and Lamai Beach lies **Thon Ta Khian Beach**, which is surrounded by beautiful scenery but almost completely co-

! Baedeker TIP

Wear a helmet!

Motorcycling on Ko Samui can be fun. There are dozens of rental companies. Unfortunately an increasing number of serious accidents are occurring, most of which involve tourists. The reasons include the fact that driving on the left is unfamiliar to some, and the state of repair of the rented bikes. When renting a motorbike, check to see that the vehicle is safe (check the lights and brakes in particular). Also, riding without a helmet means running the risk of serious head injuries on what are often only gravel roads.

▶ VISITING KO SAMUI

GETTING THERE

By air:
From Bangkok via Bangkok Airways (about 1hr flying time)

By rail:
From Bangkok to Surat Thani (Phun Phin station) then by taxi to the ferry quay (15 hours total)

WHERE TO STAY

► Luxury

Amarin Victoria Resort
12/71 Moo 1, Tumbol Mae Nam
Tel. 0 77 / 42 56 10-5, fax 42 75 52
www.amarinsamuiresort.com
46 rooms, 2 restaurants, bar, swimming pool. Very tasteful rooms in a modern style that lack no comforts. Only 15 min. away from the sparkling night life of Chaweng Beach. A golf course is close by and Mae Nam Beach only five minutes away.

Le Royal Meridien Baan Taling Ngam
295 Moo 3, Taling Ngam Beach
Tel. 0 77 / 42 91 00, fax 42 32 20
www.kohsamui.lemeridien.de
71 rooms, 3 restaurants, 2 bars, swimming pool, gym, water sports centre.
It would not be difficult to spend hours in the swimming pool just

Spa for the privileged few: the view from Tongsai Bay Hotel

admiring the view of the sea and the islands off Ko Samui. The rooms have every comfort known to man. The hotel is situated a little off the tourist track.

Imperial Boat House
83 Moo 5, Choeng Mon Beach
Tel. 0 77 / 42 50 41-52
Fax 42 54 60
www.imperialhotels.com/boathouse
210 rooms, 2 restaurants, 3 bars, swimming pool, fitness centre, water sports centre (photo ▶p.326)
The hotel has a certain originality: in addition to its ordinary rooms it also offers special accommodation in boat-shaped buildings. They are on dry land but retain something of a maritime atmosphere.

The Tongsai Bay
84 Moo 5, Bo Phut
Tel. 0 77 / 24 54 80
Fax 42 54 62
www.tongsaibay.co.th
83 rooms, restaurant, 2 bars, swimming pool, private beach. For peace and quiet or getting away from it all, the Tongsai Bay is the perfect spot. The hotel has its own beach, though a rather stony one. Apart from the rooms in the main building, there are also cottages with a stunning view of the sea.

▶ Mid-range
The Fair House
124/1-2 Moo 3, T. Bophut
Tel. 0 77 / 42 22 55-6
Fax 42 23 73
www.fairhousesamui.com
130 rooms, restaurant, coffee shop, bar, swimming pool, water sports centre.
This hotel in the upper mid-range has been a recommended address for many years and lies a little distance from the tourist centres. The broad, clean beach makes it perfectly suited for families.

Health Oasis Resort & Healing Child Center
Tel. 0 77 / 42 01 24, 23 62 55
Fax 42 01 25
www.healthoasis.com
36 bungalows, vegetarian restaurant, bar, swimming pool.
Why not combine a holiday on Koh Samui with a health and fitness program? This is just the place, and even stressed-out children can join in (e.g. with health diets or reiki courses). Attractively furnished rooms and pleasant grounds.

▶ Budget
The days of cheap and cheerful accommodation on Koh Samui are long gone. Any sort of decent room involves shelling out between 600 and 1500 baht per night (about US$20–50/£10–25). For this sort of outlay, however, there is an abundance of acceptable places to stay near any of the beaches.

WHERE TO EAT
Dozens of restaurants with menus ranging from Thai to Italian, German, Mexican, Indian or entirely international fare line the approaches to the beaches. No recommendations can be made here, if only because the restaurants seem to change names, owners and staff overnight.

SHOPPING
A gigantic assortment of shops, from souvenir kiosks to bespoke tailors, is also to be found on the beach approaches. The main shopping district is Chaweng Beach, where there is something to please everybody.

A unique way to spend a holiday: bungalows at the Imperial Boat House Hotel on Ko Samui

vered at high tide. **Phangka Beach** in the south west of Ko Samui takes some finding, as no public transport runs here. About 20km/12mi from Nathon is Set Beach with some interesting rock formations.

Ko Samui Aquarium ⏱ All those reluctant to venture into to the sea to explore the varied underwater world can gain a good impression of the island's marine beauty by visiting Ko Samui Aquarium (in the Samui Orchid Resort hotel; opening times: 9am–6pm daily; admission fee).

Samui Snake Farm ⏱ There is little danger of encountering snakes on Ko Samui, except inland or at the Samui Snake Farm (2km/1.5mi north west of Ban Thong Tanot). Tours are given twice daily(11am and 2pm) – with a shudder included in the price.

✴ Ko Tao

Region: Southern Thailand
Altitude: 2–379m/6–1243ft

Province: Ranong
Population: 600 approx.

The small island of Ko Tao, not discovered by tourists until the 1980s, is one of the Gulf of Thailand's little jewels. The best time to visit Ko Tao is between December and April or from August to September.

Ko Tao is only 8km/5mi long and no more than 3km/2mi wide. It is also a considerable distance (38km/24mi) from the mainland. The island nevertheless gets very crowded, especially during the Thai summer holidays (end of April to the middle of May) when many take their vacations here.

»Turtle island«

 ## VISITING KO TAO

GETTING THERE
Ferry:
The standard ferry ride from Chumphon takes about 6 hours, the express boat only 2 hours. Another express boat plies the route twice a day from Thong Sala on Ko Pha Ngan (2 hours), and a further boat runs from Ko Samui.

By air:
The nearest airport is on Ko Samui.

On Ko Tao there are few motor vehicles but the distances are short enough to be covered easily on foot.

WHERE TO STAY
► Luxury
The Seaview Villas
Sairee Beach North, Koh Tao
84280 Surat Thani, Thailand
Tel. 0 99 / 09 92 55, fax 0 77 / 48 47 22
www.kotaoseaview.com
3 villas, restaurant, bar, swimming pool, private jacuzzi. Probably the most exclusive accommodation in Ko Tao at the moment. It has just 3 villas

that lack for nothing in terms of comfort.

► Mid-range
Villa Lipanaa
Sairee Beach
Tel. 0 99 / 09 92 55
www.lipanaa.com
This pleasant and highly recommended development is not directly on the beach but does have large and comfortable bungalows at a nice price.

► Budget
Grand Sea Resort
Nai Wok Bay
Tel. 0 77 / 3 77 77 76
www.phangan.info/grandsea
26 rooms, restaurant, bar, swimming pool, herbal sauna. This is the result of transposing the Lan Na style of northern Thailand into a southern setting: a pretty teak villa, a little way from the beach but comfortably appointed in a charming, lovingly tended setting.

Ko Tao has about 600 inhabitants, mainly concentrated in the villages of **Ban Mae Hat**, **Ban Hat Sai** and **Ban Chalok**, the first of which has the largest population. In Ban Mae Hat, a beautiful spot ringed by granite cliffs, there are plenty of facilities for tourists including restaurants and a bank. This is also where the ferries dock.

Whereas a few years ago harassed city dwellers once felt like Robinson Crusoe and could rely on having the **beautiful beaches** of Ko Tao practically to themselves, nowadays there are hosts of bungalow developments. The prettiest beaches in the west of the island are easier to reach than the rather narrow beaches of the east and south.

Paradise for divers   Ko Tao is still a good place for divers and snorkellers as its underwater beauty is practically untouched. One particularly attractive destination consists of three small islands off the north-west coast which together go by the name of **Ko Nang Tuan**. On Kao Tao itself there are about a dozen diving schools that will rent out the necessary equipment or provide lessons according to the PADI method.

Palm-lined beach on Ko Tao

★ Ko Tarutao

H 2

Region: Southern Thailand
Altitude: 2–713m/6–2340ft

Province: Satun
Population: 500 approx.

Ko Tarutao is largest of a total of 51 islands that were assimilated into a national park as early as 1974. The archipelago was once a haunt of pirates and smugglers.

National park

The area covered by Ko Tarutao National Park close to the border between Thailand and Malaysia is about 1,400 sq km/540 sq mi. Most islands in the region are uninhabited. Between 1939 and 1947 they were used to house political prisoners who were persona non gratis on the mainland (the remains of the prison walls can be seen at Talu Wao Bay in the east of the island).

For the protection of the unique island environment **a headquarters for the nature conservancy authorities** has been established at Punta Bay on Ko Tarutao. This should be the first port of call for all visitors to the park, because anyone failing to pay the 50 baht admission fee that is currently charged risks a fine of 20 times that amount. The rangers will also be able to arrange for boats to take visitors to Crocodile Cave, for example, with its awe-inspiring stalactites and stalagmites. The slide shows that are sometimes given at the visitor centre reveal the diverse natural environment of the islands.

Walks

Officially there are some paths that lead through the interior of the main island Ko Tarutao, but most are quickly overgrown by jungle. Even for experienced jungle trekkers it is then almost impossible to walk the trails. On those trails that are passable, however, langur monkeys, loris, pythons, monitor lizards, shrimp-eating macaques and more than a hundred types of nesting birds can be seen. The flo-

 ## VISITING KO TARUTAO

GETTING THERE

Ferry:
From Pak Bara Harbour (about 65km/40mi north of Satun) ferries cross to the main island of Ko Tarutao twice a day during the busy season from November to April.
During the other months there is practically no service due to the monsoon weather and all accommodation closes down.

WHERE TO STAY

On Ko Tarutao visitors have the choice of staying in bungalows, small cabins and bamboo houses.
On the neighbouring island of Ko Adang only bamboo houses are available.
Camping is allowed in some places.
Further information is available from the national park administration office in Bangkok, tel. 02 / 5 79 48 42 or 5 79 52 69.

ra is just as rich in species. Botanists have recorded no less than 869 flowering plants on the island. Marine turtles lay their eggs on the beaches between the months of May and September.

✶ ✶
Beach

One fabulous tropical sandy beach not far from the large bungalow development on Ko Tarutao is an inviting place for swimming and snorkelling. A walk on the narrow path that circles part of the island leads to even more beaches.

✶
Ko Ladang

Trips to the islands of Ko Ladang are an exploration of glorious tropical scenery: rocky islands covered in dense vegetation, tall limestone mountains and clear waters with coral reefs.

Trips to the Mainland

✶
Satun

Satun, the most southerly town in Thailand, lies on the Andaman Sea about 800km/500mi from Bangkok as the crow flies. It is situated at the foot of the steep Tenasserim Mountains at the mouth of the Menam Satun amid an exotic, almost unpeopled landscape with dark green rainforest and rugged mountainous ridges. Many islands and coral reefs lie off the coast, which has wonderful beaches with crystal-clear water. The remote town near the border has an old-fashioned charm. Its inhabitants live from fishing and trade with Malaysia. Two lively fishing harbours stand out in the middle of the otherwise quiet town.

Dusan reservoir

Dusan reservoir, close to Route 406 22km/14mi north of the town, has an idyllic situation; a towering rocky outcrop and a surrounding park make for an impressive backdrop.

✶ Krabi

G 2

Region: Southern Thailand
Altitude: 12m/40ft

Province: Krabi
Population: 24,000

The harbour of Krabi lies opposite the island of Phuket on a strip of land at the mouth of the river of the same name. In the background bizarrely shaped limestone mountains rise out of the luxuriant vegetation. Inland the scene is marked by seemingly endless rubber plantations, only occasionally broken by patches of jungle. White, palm-fringed beaches line the coast.

Beach resort

After the first backpackers discovered Krabi in the mid-1980s, the town's reputation as a paradise practically unspoiled by tourism lasted for some years. However, this ended in 1999 with the opening of an airport served by regular flights of Thai International Airways. Se-

► VISITING KRABI

GETTING THERE

By car:
Route 4 (210km/130mi from Surat Thani, 230km/143mi from Nakhon Si Thammarat, 870km/540mi from Bangkok)

By bus:
From Bangkok Southern Bus Terminal (13 hours)

By air:
From Bangkok 814km/506mi (daily flights lasting about 40 minutes)

WHERE TO STAY

► Luxury

Central Krabi Bay Resort
334 Moo 2, Ao Nang, Muang
Tel. 0 75 / 63 77 89
Fax 63 78 00, 75 63 82 32
www.centralhotelsresorts.com
191 rooms, 3 restaurants, 2 bars, swimming pool, spa, various water sports.
The hotel was built in 2006 in front of a bizarre limestone rock formation, primarily using local building materials. The »smallest« rooms measure 77 sq m/830 sq ft. Each has a terrace with a view of the sea as well as all the comforts of home.

Rayavadee
214 Moo 2. T. Ao Nang
Tel. 0 75 / 62 07 40, fax 62 06 30
www.rayavadee.com, 103 rooms, restaurant, coffee shop, bar, spa.
This pleasant development was built in the midst of a large grove of palms alongside one of Thailand's most beautiful beaches and its startling limestone rock formations. The rooms are provided with all amenities, and the spa has good facilities for recuperation.

Sheraton Krabi Beach Resort
155 Moo 2, Nong Thale
Tel. 0 75 / 62 80 00, fax 62 80 28
www.sheraton.com
246 rooms, 3 restaurants, 2 bars, swimming pool, fitness centre, shopping arcade and much more.
New hotel in 16 ha/40 acres of gardens right next to the sea. Lovely and luxurious rooms.

► Mid-range

Pakasai Resort
88 Moo 3, T. Ao Nang
Tel. 0 75 / 63 77 77, fax 0 75 / 63 76 37
www.pakasai.com, 77 rooms, restaurant, coffee shop, bar, spa. If the five-minute walk to Ao Nang Beach is not too much, this is a comfortable but inexpensive place to stay.

► Budget

Maritime Park & Spa Resort
1 Tung Fah Road
Tel. 0 75 / 62 00 28, fax 61 29 92
www.krabi-hotels.com/maritime
221 rooms, restaurant, coffee shop, 2 bars, swimming pool, fitness centre. Fair room prices and a highly recommended restaurant make this development not too far from the centre of Krabi an alternative to the luxury hotels listed above.

veral highly luxurious hotel developments were already in existence for guests who appreciated the glorious white sandy beaches. The beaches have lost the air of solitude that they once had. The beaches at **Ao Nang** and **Rai Leh** are particularly busy during the months November to April.

What to See in and around Krabi

Phra Nang Beach
Phra Nang Beach, west of Krabi, was once a well-kept secret that one globetrotter passed on to another, but once the early bungalows gave way to permanent buildings offering superior comfort, it was only a matter of time before the large hotel chains took notice of the fabulous bay. The small fishing village that the town once boasted is also a thing of the past, and the inhabitants now make their living primarily from tourism, e.g. in the Dusit Rayavadee luxury hotel. The beach in front of the hotel remains accessible to all and there are even adequate toilet facilities

Phra Nang Cave
It is worth taking a boat to see the cave of Phra Nang at the south-western end of Phra Nang Beach, which opens right onto the sea and has some imposing, age-old stalactites.

Ban Thong Agricultural Station
About 22km/14mi north-west of Krabi, Route 4 runs past Ban Thong Agricultural Station, where new types of rubber tree, tea and coffee plants are being grown (open for visitors). What becomes of the plants can be seen in the aforementioned rubber plantations on the way back to Krabi. In front of the mostly wooden houses, white latex mats are hung out to dry. This is the one of the intermediate steps in making rubber from the sap of the trees, which is collected in containers that hang from the branches. Raw rubber from Thailand is exported to many countries throughout the world and makes a major contribution to the balance of payments.

Hat Noparat Thara Beach
4km/2.5mi south-east of Ban Thong station, Routes 4033/4034/4202 fork to the right. The road runs through a series of villages and some diverse scenery to the wonderful beach of Hat Noparat Thara to the south. Alternatively, the beach is only 500m/550yd from Ao Nang and as yet relatively undiscovered. The beach is of fine white sand sprinkled with tiny shellfish. Opposite are a few small islands that can be reached on foot at low tide.

A cave can be visited at one end of Phra Nang Beach. →

★★
Susan Hoi shell graveyard

8km/5mi further to the east (Routes 4203/4204) is one of the most popular attractions in the region, the 75 million-year-old shell graveyard of Susan Hoi (a deposit of fresh-water shellfish). Unfortunately the petrified limestone remains, one of only three such deposits in the world, are visible only at low tide.

Khao Phanom Bencha National Park

The peak of Khao Phanom Bencha, 1350m/4430ft high and thickly wooded, is situated about 22km/14mi north of Krabi. To get there, it is best to take a taxi from Krabi. The mountain is visible for miles around and is the key landmark in the national park that bears its name. The park, which was established in 1981, stands out for its wide diversity of flora and fauna (32 mammal species and 162 birds have been recorded in this small area alone) and can be explored quite easily thanks to the well-marked nature trails. The second trail leads to the unique **Nam Tok Huay To** waterfall, where swimming is allowed in the basin. A map of the trails is available from the visitor centre near the waterfall.

★★ Lampang

B 2

Region: Northern Thailand	**Province:** Lampang
Altitude: 242m/794ft	**Population:** 52,000

The provincial capital of Lampang lies on the broad plain of the Menam Wang and is surrounded by the typical wooded, mountainous landscape of northern Thailand. Lampang still has a small-town character but has gained increasing economic importance in recent years. The economy is dominated by agriculture, as the fertile plain is cultivated for rice, maize and cotton.

History

In about the 7th century the Mon founded the principality of Lampang, which was originally part of the **Hariphunchai kingdom** and was annexed to the Khmer empire in the 11th century. It was brought into the Lan Na kingdom by King Mengrai, but overrun in the 16th century by the Burmese, who had already taken Chiang Mai and Lamphun. They left traces that are still visible to this day.

What to See in Lampang

Burmese influence

There is little trace nowadays of the old town of Lampang apart from an octagonal tower that was once part of the fortifications. The remaining sights mainly date from the time subsequent to the Burmese conquest, and many of the highlights display a Burmese artistic signature. To get an impression of the famed but lost governor's residence of **Ho Kham** (gilded hall), for example, it is necessary to go to Ancient City near ▶Samut Prakan where there is a faithful model of the original. Individual discoveries over the past few years suggest that many more secrets may be hidden beneath the ground. One particularly interesting find was the discovery of several stone bas-reliefs in the Dvaravati style, which gave the first indications of the artistic quality of the buildings.

★ ★
Wat Phra Kaeo
Don Tao

Wat Phra Kaeo Don Tao was built in 1680 and is one of the most revered temples in Thailand. It stands on a highly picturesque site next to the Menam Wang. The small chapel that was built around 1800 is particularly interesting. It is one of the finest examples of classical Burmese architecture with its excellent wood carvings around the arched openings, the fine tendrils that adorn the columns, not to mention the imaginative and colourful bas-relief decorations and the magnificent coffered ceiling with mother-of-pearl, enamel and glass inlays. The colours and shapes of the ornaments are perfectly at one with the proportions of the architecture. The copper figure of Buddha is also interesting. The neighbouring staircase building dates from a later period (the Bangkok era) but is distinguished by its beautiful wood carvings inlaid with blue ceramic tiles. In the chapel a little way from the main buildings there is a Buddha statue in the Chiang Mai style. The exhibits in the museum near the entrance include some excellent carvings.

The clay elephant in the garden commemorates events surrounding the famous Jade (or Emerald) Buddha. After the statue was found in Chiang Rai in 1434, Sam Fang Kaen, the king of Chiang Mai at the time, is said to have ordered that it be carried in a procession to his

Wat Phra Kaeo Don Tao *Lampang*

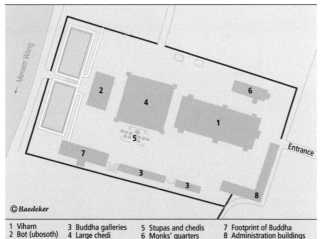

1 Viharn	3 Buddha galleries	5 Stupas and chedis	7 Footprint of Buddha
2 Bot (ubosoth)	4 Large chedi	6 Monks' quarters	8 Administration buildings

© Baedeker

▶ VISITING LAMPANG

GETTING THERE

By car:
Route 1 from Tak (158km/98mi), from Chiang Mai or Lamphun (76km/47mi) or by the scenic route from Chiang Mai on Route 11

By rail:
Station on the line from Bangkok to Chiang Mai (642km/399mi from Bangkok, journey time 13 hours)

By bus:
From Bangkok Northern Bus Terminal five times daily

By air:
Twice weekly from Bangkok and Phitsanulok

WHERE TO STAY
▶ Budget
Lampang Wiengthong Hotel
138/109 Phaholyothin Road
Tel. 0 54 / 22 58 091
Fax 22 58 08
surapa@success.net.th
227 rooms, coffee shop, bar, swimming pool. Good mid-range hotel conveniently situated in the centre of Lampang.

residence. Unfortunately the elephant chosen for the task went astray and headed towards Lampang. Afterwards the statue was kept at this wat for 32 years until 1468, when it was again moved to a temporary home in ►Chiang Mai. After many more travels, the statue finally arrived in ► Bangkok, where it has since been revered in Wat Phra Kaeo as one of the most holy items in Thailand.

There is some attractive carving on the gables and columns of the interesting Burmese-style Wat Si Rong Muang (Takrao Noi Raod).

Wat Si Rong Muang

Another good and well-preserved example of the Burmese style situated amid the rice fields in the north of the town is Wat Chedi Sao. Its 20 white chedis, beautifully proportioned and adorned with reliefs and a small golden roof, are unique.

★ Wat Chedi Sao

Around Lampang

About 18km/11mi south-west of Lampang near the town of Ko Kha stands Wat Phra That Lampang Luang, one of the most beautiful temples in Thailand. Its exquisite ornamentation probably comes from the time of Princess **Chama Thevi** (AD 650–700), who is said to have founded the complex. The wat may have acted as a refuge for the people during the course of its long history when invaders, primarily from Burma, were terrorizing the land, setting fires and plundering settlements.

★ ★ Wat Phra That Lampang Luang

← *Chedis at Wat Phra Kaeo Don Tao*

The evidence for this is the thickness of the enclosing walls, which give the temple something of the air of a fortress. In the north and east long stairways lead to the gateway, their balustrades made up of the serpentine bodies of the seven-headed naga, an unmistakeable hallmark of Burmese architecture. More or less in the centre of the 16th-century temple compound there is a hill surrounded by mature trees upon which stands a chedi, structured by cornices and topped with a long gilded spire. The centre is covered with gilded copper plates and surrounded by a bronze balustrade. There are also delicate copper canopies at each of the corners. The decoration of the viharn is quite magnificent, with exquisite woodcarvings of flowers, leaves and fine creeping plants. On the inside of the portal is a »wheel of life«, and the columns, façades and portals sparkle with fantastic decoration. There are two Buddha statues in Chiang Saen style inside the viharn. In the open sala, which has a triple-layered roof covered in glazed tiles, there is a beautiful altar decorated with relief sculptures in the Burmese style and surrounded by carved insignia (thongs) that hang from poles. The tiles are not original.

Viharn ►

Reclining Buddhas at Wat Phra That Lampang Luang

Nestling almost inconspicuously in one corner of the compound is ◄ Teak temple
the teak-built temple that actually houses Wat Phra That Lampang
Luang's most sacred relic. The little Buddha behind its heavy grille is
said to have been hewn from the same block of jade as the famous
Jade Buddha in Wat Phra Kaeo in Bangkok. It may, however, actually
only be a copy of the original, which has been in Bangkok since 1778
although it was previously kept for some time at Wat Phra Kaeo Don
Tao.

Close by is a temple museum with some splendid exhibits, including **Temple museum**
bookshelves made of red-painted wood, Buddha statues inset with ⊙
gems, a head of Buddha in the Chiang Saen style, wood carvings of Opening hours:
animals and several thongs. The Buddha figures in the colonnade Wed–Sun
along the inner wall are also very good. 9am–12pm,
1–5pm

Wat Mon Cham Sin is also worth seeing, partly because of its three **Wat Mon Cham**
lovely chedis in Burmese style, yet even more so on account of the **Sin**
impressive views of the varied landscape. The wat is situated on a
small hill close to the road on Route 1 heading towards Chiang Mai.

Wat Phra That, 16km/10mi north-east of the town, dates from the **Wat Phra That**
early period of the Lan Na kingdom (14th century) and is built in
Chiang Mai style. The large viharn (17th–18th centuries) with its triple-layered roof looks as though three houses had been stacked one
inside the other.

A dense, mountainous and virtually untouched region of forest, ✹ ✹
punctuated by canyon-like valleys and surmounted by rugged rocky Scenery
outcrops, stretches away from Lampang towards the north. The
summit of Doi Khun Tan rises to a height of 1348m/4423 ft and can
be seen easily from Route 11 on the way to Chiang Mai or from the
railway. Route 1 between here and Chiang Rai suddenly narrows
after about 50km/31mi, so that both sides are lined by steep and imposing cliffs. This part of the route is known as **Pratu Pa** (»doorway
to the forests«) and is said to be watched over by a protective spirit,
to whom a nearby small temple is dedicated (another »pratu« can be
found a few miles outside Lampang on the road to Chiang Mai).

The Thai Elephant Conservation Centre 28km/17mi beyond Lamp- ✹
ang (follow the signposts) constitutes recognition of the fact that ele- **Thai Elephant**
phants are now among the endangered species of South-East Asia. **Conservation**
Furthermore, since the complete embargo on felling tropical timber **Centre**
in Thailand's few remaining rainforest regions, many hundreds of
trained elephants have entered the ranks of the »unemployed«. The
tricks that the elephants have learned since then are purely intended
for the entertainment of tourists. The results can be seen here. Shows
are given every day at 9.30am, 11am and 2pm, starting in the morning with a communal bath for both elephants and drivers in the

nearby river. After every show, visitors are permitted to ride the elephants. The grounds also encompass a hospital for sick or injured elephants that gained world fame when the elephant cow Motola came there in 1999 after treading on a mine (▶ Baedeker Special p.36). In spite of all their efforts the vets at the hospital were unable to save the elephant's front leg. Instead it was decided to provide Motola with a custom-built false leg.

> **!** **Baedeker TIP**
>
> **Adoption**
>
> It is possible to adopt an elephant. Information can be obtained from Friends of the Asian Elephant, 36/15 Moo 2 Ram-Indra Road, 10220 Bangkok (www.elephant.tnet.co.th)

✷
Tham Pu Thai cave

Another 10km/6mi along Route 1 is the cave of Tham Pua Thai, one of the largest and most interesting caves in Thailand with stalactites and stalagmites.

✷ ✷ Lamphun

B 2

Region: Northern Thailand	**Province:** Lamphun
Altitude: 295m/968 feet	**Population:** 43,000 approx.

Lamphun is 24km/15mi south of Chiang Mai on the right-hand bank of the Menam Kuang, a tributary of the Menam Ping. Since the building of a through road past the town, it has been somewhat off the beaten track, allowing it to retain much of its typical northern Thai ambience.

Peaceful town on the river

The peaceful impression that the town exudes is particularly obvious when approaching via the older Route 106 rather than Route 11. For mile after mile magnificent old trees of all kinds line the road. The temples old and new that are strung out along the road like pearls on a string are notable for the quality of their architecture. The residents of Lamphun primarily live from agriculture and the products of the extensive orchards and plantations, as well as from the hand-woven silk for which the town became famous. It is also known for its traditional silver-work. The weaving of cotton is also practised here, especially at **Pa Sang** (about 10km/6mi from Lamphun).

> **?** **DID YOU KNOW ...?**
>
> ■ The residents of Lamphun are traditional speakers of the northern Thai dialect, which is almost an independant language with many Mon elements. This dialect was banned at times under King Rama V, but today it is even taught in some schools.

Lamphun was once the capital of the **Hariphunchai kingdom** and al-   **History**
so retained its importance in the Lan Na kingdom founded by King
Mengrai at the end of the 13th century, which was itself part of the
Mon empire. The dignified aura of the town has barely altered right
up to the present day. According to local legend, Wat Phra That Hariphunchai was built initially to house a relic of Buddha, but a fortified town grew up around the temple very quickly. The Hariphunchai kingdom lasted for about 600 years until it was ended by **King
Mengrai** (1281). At that time the city was burned to the ground. The
first capital of the new Lan Na kingdom was at Kum Kam (now Saraphi) between Lamphun and Chiang Mai. A number of archaeological discoveries were made at Saraphi around 1980; some of the most
important pieces can be seen in the National Museum at ▶ Chiang
Mai . Mengrai did not remain at this capital for long, since it suffered from serious flooding of the Menam Ping several times a year.
Legend has it that this was the reason for King Mengrai, along with
the monarchs of the neighbouring kingdoms, King Ramkhamhaeng
and King Nareng Muang, to climb a nearby mountain in order to
pick out a capital for all three of them to share. In 1556 the Burmese
conquered both Chiang Mai and Lamphun, and it was not until
1775 in the reign of **King Taksin** that the two towns were liberated
from foreign occupation. The former Lan Na kingdom was not assimilated into the kingdom of Siam until 1873, in the reign of King
Rama V. The name of Hariphunchai mutated into Lamphun, now
the capital of a province that is home to some 400,000 inhabitants.

✱ ✱ Wat Phra That Hariphunchai

The temple of Wat Phra That Hariphunchai is greatly revered   **History**
throughout the land. It nestles amid the grounds of the former royal
palace that stood outside the city walls, of which some remains are
still to be seen. The history of the wat goes back as far as 867, when
the Mon king Atityaraj had a mondhop erected for a relic of Buddha.

The temple faces the river and is best entered from that side. The   **Temple**
first things that come into view are two immense lion statues, indica-   **compound**
tive of the Burmese influence on the temple architecture. In front of
the temple proper there is a relatively small and unadorned viharn
with a reclining Buddha 15m/50ft in length. As an enlargement of   ◀ Chedi
the original building, a chedi was built. It has been altered and made
taller over the course of the centuries, and attained a height of 51m/
167ft by the 16th century. The elaborately designed base and the
upper section are covered with decorated and gilded copper plates.
The spire has a nine-tiered canopy on top. The chedi is ceremonially
washed with holy water once a year in the course of a grand procession. East of the chedi, there is a bell tower in Burmese style that
contains one of the biggest gongs in the world. The present temple   ◀ Viharn

Wat Hariphunchai *Plan*

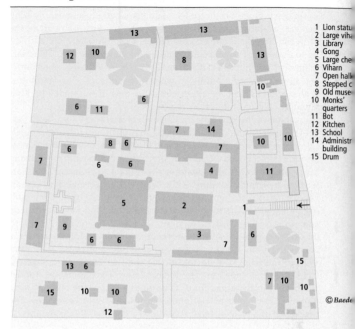

1 Lion statu
2 Large viha
3 Library
4 Gong
5 Large che
6 Viharn
7 Open hall
8 Stepped c
9 Old muse
10 Monks'
   quarters
11 Bot
12 Kitchen
13 School
14 Administr
   building
15 Drum

© Baede

buildings were almost all built during the 20th century – the viharn, for instance, in 1925. Its façades, doors and windows are all decorated with marvellous carvings. Inside the focus is upon a statue of Buddha in the Chiang Saen style, as well as the beautifully ornamented pulpit and the artfully constructed wooden ceiling. The murals in the interior and around the entrance were recently renovated. The graceful wooden library pavilion to the left of the viharn is also worthy of note. It was built on the site of an earlier building from the 19th century. The upper section with its tiered roof is decorated with carvings and inlays and rests atop a massive base. The antique bookcases inside contain valuable manuscripts written on palm leaves (lontare). Pass the large viharn to the right to see an 8th-century brick chedi that once contained 60 Buddha statues, although few of them now remain. On the front of the square base there are three Buddha figures in the Chiang Saen style.

Temple museum   Towards the rear of the extensive grounds is a small temple museum with some quite remarkable Buddha statues from various eras, many in the Chiang Mai style with some clear features of the Dvaravati

Canopies to honour Buddha flank the chedi at →
Wat Phra That Hariphunchai

▶ VISITING LAMPHUN

GETTING THERE

By car:
From Chiang Mai on Route 11 or the more scenic journey on Route 106 (about 26km/16mi to the south). Taxi from Chiang Mai.

By bus:
Several buses a day from Chiang Mai.

By rail:
Station on the Bangkok – Chiang Mai line (729km/453mi from Bangkok)

WHERE TO STAY

The small number of guest houses in Lamphun offer rather a meagre degree of comfort. Chiang Mai has plenty of accommodation and is not far away.

Opening hours:
Wed–Sun
9am–12pm,
1–4pm

style. There are also several ancient stone tablets with bas-reliefs as well as various bookcases, votive tablets, manuscripts and pots made of both silver and gold. The latter are used for the ceremonial washing of the chedi. Several other viharns and monastery buildings (including an open pavilion with four symbolic footprints of Buddha) complete the complex. In passing it is worth looking at the shutters of one otherwise bare building. They feature some of the lacquerwork so typical of northern Thailand.

Around Lamphun

Wat Kukut

The second important temple in Lamphun is about 1km/1100yd outside the town. Wat Kukut is often called Wat Chama Thevi after the original queen of Lamphun. The son of Chama Thevi, King Mahandayok, had the wat built in the early 8th century. The temple is worth a visit for its two chedis alone, splendid examples of Mon architecture. The larger, at 21m/69ft high, is the more important, although its spire has been lost to a lightning strike. Upon its immense, square, stepped base there are five tiered storeys. Smaller chedis emphasize the transitions between storeys. On each side there are three richly decorated niches each containing a plaster Buddha. Altogether 60 statues of Buddha are scattered through the site, some making the gesture of dispelling fear, and Khmer influences are highly prominent. Although the bodies of the statues are original, the heads of almost all of them have been replaced or restored. This chedi holds the ashes of Queen Chama Thevi.

The smaller chedi in the Mon style also takes the form of a stepped pyramid with niches for Buddhas, and features some giant demon statues.

Wat Phra Yun

One other temple of interest is Wat Phra Yun, 2km/1.5mi north of the town on the opposite bank of the Menam Kuang. It was built in 1369 by King Kuna for the monk Sumana. King Kuna summoned

Sumana to his kingdom from Sukhothai in order to spread the teachings of Theravada Buddhism. This form of Buddhism gradually superseded the hitherto prevailing Mahayana Buddhism that had been practised by the Mon, among others. Sumana also brought with him the relic that had miraculously reproduced itself, which was later transferred to Wat Suan Dok in ▶Chiang Mai. In the 16th century a chedi was built over the ruins of the mondhop that had once housed the relic. The Buddha statues in the niches of the upper section are mostly reproductions of the crumbled originals. A sandstone tablet in the courtyard has an inscription in Pali and Thai announcing the arrival of Sumana. The viharn, with its three 16th-century standing Buddhas, the bot with its beautiful gilded carvings and the elegant library were built around 1900.

Wat Saphoen

Wat Saphoen is distinguished by the fine gilded carvings on its gable and by mighty teak pillars and elegant wooden beams inside.

Wat San Kamphaeng

Wat San Kamphaeng is another temple decorated with beautiful carvings. The atmosphere inside the viharn is characterized by the colours red and gold. The chedi in the courtyard shows distinct Burmese influence.

Karen village of Ban Kon Tang

About 11km/7mi beyond the village of Bang Hong, about 40km/25mi from Lamphun on Route 106, is the Karen settlement of Ban Kon Tang. Its inhabitants still wear their colourful traditional costumes and sell their craft products.

＊ ＊ Lopburi

D 3

Region: Central Thailand
Altitude: 30m/100ft

Province: Lopburi
Population: 54,000

Lopburi, a city with a famous and magnificent past, lies on the river of the same name at the northern edge of the central Thai plain. It is the capital of a growing province in which the inhabitants primarily live from the produce of the fertile farmland. In the north the fabulous scenery is dominated by Khao Wong Phra Chan, easily identified by the three jagged spikes on the summit.

History

Lavo, as the city used to be called, was supposedly founded in AD 468 by King Kalavarnadis of Taksila. Until about 950 it was the capital of a large Mon kingdom that stretched from the Menam plain north-eastwards to the banks of the Mekong, and lasted until the 11th and 12th centuries. Inscriptions on coins and tablets, some in Sanskrit, others in the local Mon alphabet, indicate that the name of the kingdom was Dvaravati. At the beginning of the 11th century the

Lopburi Plan

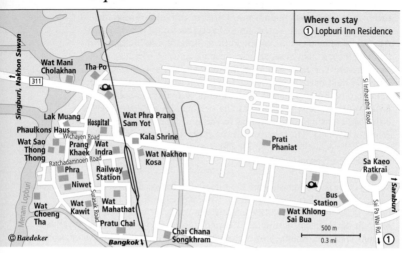

Where to stay
① Lopburi Inn Residence

Khmer under King Suryavarman I (1002–1050) conquered large
parts of what is now Thailand. Lopburi became a fortress of the
Khmer empire and the residence of its provincial governor. The
Khmer style was dominant in architecture and sculpture until the
15th century, yet the intermingling of Khmer and Dvaravati styles in
Lopburi produced a new, mixed artistic paradigm that is called the
Lopburi style. With the decline of Khmer rule the lands to the south
of the Menam basin came under the control of the Thai king Si
Dharmatraipitok. For about 100 years, kings made Lopburi their
capital and ruled the land from there. Later, however, it passed into
the hands of various rulers, including Burma's King Annarudha and
the Thai king U Thong. When the latter moved his own residence
from the town of U Thong to Ayutthaya in 1350, he made his son
Prince Ramesuen governor of the Lopburi state. The city played a
major strategic role in conflicts with the kings of Sukhothai. When
in 1376 Sukhothai became a vassal state, and later an integral part of
the Ayutthaya realm in 1438, the town declined in importance. It
was not until the reign of King Narai (1656–1688) that Lopburi was
to experience a new era of glory as the secondary capital to Ayutthaya. Narai chose Lopburi as his second seat of government partly
because it was safe from flooding and secondly because the river provided fresh water for the city and the palace. When the Dutch were
threatening to attack Ayutthaya, Narai temporarily moved his own
residence further away from the Gulf of Thailand to Lopburi and
had palaces erected, even adopting western styles for some (as in
Phetchaburi). It was also Narai who opened up Thailand to Europe
and established diplomatic ties with the French royal family. He received a delegation from King Louis XIV led by Chevalier de Chau-

mont, who was to write a report of his travels that provides much of what we know today about Lopburi at that time. Narai also named the Greek Constantine Phaulkon (►Famous People) as his adviser. After the death of Narai (1688), Phra Petraja (Luang Sorasak) took the throne and had many of his predecessor's supporters executed (including the French diplomats and merchants in the town). He disliked Lopburi and moved back to Ayutthaya. The royal residence fell into disuse and its buildings became ruined. Only in the reign of King Mongkut (1851–1868) was the one relatively well-preserved building remaining on the palace site, the Chanthara Phisan Pavilion, restored along with the walls and gates. New palace buildings were then erected, some of which are still in existence; a few have been made into interesting museums.

What to See in Lopburi

Route 1 entering Lopburi passes the monument to King Narai (Sa Kaeo Ratkrai) alongside the first roundabout. He was the most important king in the history of the city. A little further, down a side-road to the right, it is possible to see remains of the city walls and one of the old gates, called Pratu Phaniat. This was once the site of an elephant corral where King Narai showed the French delegation under Chevalier de Chaumont how elephants were trained.

Monument to King Narai

By the third roundabout, a short distance before the railway line, are the ruins of the Kala temple, a Hindu shrine from the 10th century.

Kala temple

 VISITING LOPBURI

GETTING THERE

By car:
From Bangkok on Route 1. The road makes a large sweep taking in Saraburi and Wat Phra Buddhabat (155km/96mi) but it is well worth going the long way round. The alternative is to go via Ayutthaya on Route 32 until just before Singburi, then take Route 311 to the east.

By rail:
Station on the Bangkok – Chiang Mai line (133km/83mi from Bangkok)

By bus:
From Bangkok Northern Bus Terminal

INFORMATION

Tourism Authority of Thailand
Ropwat Phrathat Road
15000 Lopburi
Tel. 0 36 / 42 27 68-9
Fax 42 40 86 tatlobri@tat.or.th

WHERE TO STAY

► **Budget**
① *Lopburi Inn Residence*
180 Cholpatan Cannel Road
Tel. 0 36 / 61 34 10
Fax 61 34 04
130 rooms, 2 restaurants, coffee shop, bar, swimming pool.
Centrally located mid-range hotel with pleasant, comfortable rooms.

The most beautiful temple in Lopburi is Wat Phra Prang Sam Yot.

The huge base of what was once a very tall prang built of laterite bricks still remains in existence, although the temple above it is of a later date. The reliefs on the door lintels are worth seeing. They depict Vishnu lying on a snake. The new temple from 1953 that stands on the base contains statues of two Hindu gods. In the banyan tree (ficus indiaca) with its intertwined roots above the ground and in the streets around the temple, hordes of monkeys have made their home, apparently undisturbed by the heavy traffic around them.

There are only a few remains of the beautiful, brick-built, Khmer prang of **Wat Nakhon Kosa** (turn left down the road just before the Kala temple). It was probably once part of a Hindu shrine before being converted to a Buddhist wat during the Ayutthaya period. A chedi in the Ayuttaya style and the remains of a viharn are also notable. To the west stand the ruins of Wat Indra, which probably dates from the Ayutthaya period.

★★
Wat Phra Prang Sam Yot

The three prangs atop the interlinked chapels of Wat Phra Prang Sam Yot (»temple of the three towers«) on Wichayen Road are probably the most impressive ruins in Lopburi and are a fine example of the architecture of the Lopburi period. The three chapels are built with a cross-shaped floor plan; each of them has a door on every side. A roofed corridor once linked them to a long brick building, formerly covered with stucco. Remains of ornamentation can be seen in many places, along with the grimacing faces at one corner of the walls. The rooms and towers have corbel vaults. Inside them are some fragments of old Buddha statues and one well-preserved figure of a seated Buddha from the Sukhothai era. The building was probably dedicated to the three Hindu gods Vishnu, Shiva and Brahma but was later reconsecrated as a Buddhist temple.

Wat Phra Si Ratana Mahathat in the west of the city on Nakala Road was already an important shrine when it was built by the Khmer in the 12th century. In the centre of the complex is a large, slender prang made of laterite bricks (Lopburi style) with lovely stucco work. The main entrance to the prang is emphasized by a small porch topped with a tower. The viharn, which is still in existence, is incorporated into it and leads on to another gallery in a most unusual style with arched windows, which probably goes back to the time of King Narai. In the second courtyard there are still some chedis, large and small, from various eras but mostly from the Ayutthaya period. Some of them have niches with statues for veneration. The temple compound was redesigned several times, particularly during the reigns of the Ayutthaya kings.

Wat Phra Si Ratana Mahathat

✸ ✸ Royal Palace of Phra Narai Ratcha Niwet

The main entrance to the »Palace of King Narai« (named by King Rama IV, who commissioned a major restoration in the 19th century) is on Surasak Road but can also be entered from the direction of the river. This was once the site of a quay where kings moored their boats, their most common means of travel to Lopburi. The sightseeing route described here approaches from that direction.

Opening hours:
8am–6pm daily

Phra Narai Ratcha Niwet Lopburi

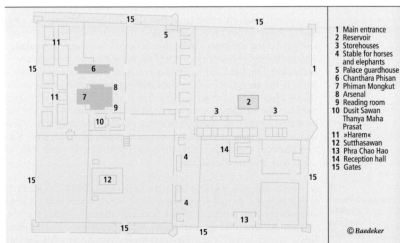

1 Main entrance
2 Reservoir
3 Storehouses
4 Stable for horses and elephants
5 Palace guardhouse
6 Chanthara Phisan
7 Phiman Mongkut
8 Arsenal
9 Reading room
10 Dusit Sawan Thanya Maha Prasat
11 »Harem«
12 Sutthasawan
13 Phra Chao Hao
14 Reception hall
15 Gates

© Baedeker

i City of monkeys

■ No other city in Thailand has such a population of monkeys – at least, nowhere else are monkeys so commonly seen as in Lopburi. It is essential to be wary of them, however, as they can become quite aggressive, especially if they can clearly see food that is not given to them. The loss of a pair of glasses is one of the more harmless things that could happen. For this reason the advice to tourists is to keep a careful distance from the animals, unlike the Thai boy in the picture.

Tour

Gated walls separate the palace compound into various courtyards. The most interesting sights nowadays are in the inner courtyard. The rectangular complex is surrounded by colossal walls, their mighty gates topped with crenellations. Large parts of the site date from the 17th century and were built to the designs of King Narai. The later, more modern buildings gained their frontages in the time of King Mongkut, who had most of the buildings demolished and replaced apart from the Chanthara Phisan Pavilion, which was in good enough condition to allow for restoration. The compound can be entered via the entrance on Surasak Road. This is where Narai's Greek adviser Constantine Phaulkon is supposed to have met his fate – he was arrested and later beheaded. His residence is a further attraction in Lopburi. On the way to the second courtyard, separated from the first by a magnificent gate, are various buildings. It is said that the king, while on his death bed, demanded some particularly fine clothes that were brought to him from these twelve halls, which may therefore have been treasuries. On the right behind them are the old brick-walled water tanks that were fed from springs on a hill east of the town. In order to transport water to the palace, a French and an Italian engineer were commissioned to design a hydraulic system that apparently only worked after ten years of intense experimentation. Opposite the water tank, set back a little in a well-tended park, is the reception hall for foreign dignitaries (Phra Khlang Supharat). Just before the second gate it is possible to see traces of walls marking the building where the royal elephants were kept. On the lawn behind the gate stand some statues in the Dvaravati style. They do not all come from Lopburi, but have been brought here from various places in the surrounding territory. There are still some ruins of water tank and an arsenal here.

★
Chanthara Phisan Pavilion, National Museum

In the second courtyard, to the right of the Chanthara Phisan Pavilion, stands the former residence of King Narai. It was built in 1665 and now houses a branch of the National Museum. From the balcony at the front, King Narai once greeted his guests. The pavilion has a throne inside it and its walls were once lined with mirrors brought to Thailand by Chevalier de Chaumont, the ambassador of King Louis XIV. The building originally had just one room and was split into two only during Mongkut's renovations. The second room contains an oil painting by an unknown artist depicting the arrival of the French delegation. The larger room, the reception hall itself, has two magnificently decorated wooden thrones and some elegantly carved and gilded bookcases.

To the left of the Chanthara Phisan Pavilion is the three-storey Phra Thinang Visuthivinitchai temple erected by Mongkut. The western part was the Phiman Mongkut Pavilion. Its upper storey contained the king's private quarters (large bedroom, reading rooms and arsenal), while the ground floor had workrooms and an audience hall. The pavilions are now set up as a museum containing sculptures, votive tablets, weapons and faience porcelain.

Opening hours:
Wed–Sun
9am–4pm
Admission fee

★
**Phra Thinang
Visuthivinitchai**
Opening hours:
Wed–Sun 9am–4pm

The small houses in an enclosed court behind the king's chambers were home to the many wives and children of the sovereign (nowadays it is a museum with exhibits of agricultural tools). This part of the complex was only accessible to a chosen few during the time of Mongkut. At that time it was still entirely forbidden to lay hands on any member of the royal family. This law was only repealed by King Chulalongkorn (Rama V).

»Harem«

On the left of the Phiman Mongkut Pavilion are the ruins of the Dusit Sawan Thanya Maha Prasat, the royal audience hall surrounded by its high walls. Fragments indicate that the frontage was dominated by European design (e.g. the Gothic arches above the doors) whereas the rear featured classical Thai architecture. It was probably the tallest building on the palace grounds and, according to reports from the time, it once had a pyramid-shaped roof. The walls of the hall were lined with mirrors presented by King Louis XIV. The inside of the hall must have been magnificently furnished. Nicholas Gervais, a member of the French delegation, told of many murals, floor mosaics, Chinese crystal and porcelain and of a glorious raised throne at the end of the hall that the king reached by climbing a marble stairway.

Royal audience hall

In the neighbouring, extensive gardens the foundations of Sutthasawan Hall can be seen, the former residence of King Narai, where he died on 11 July 1688. Some of the large laterite blocks were brought to Bangkok in the early 1800s and used in the building of Wat Sakhet. According to Nicholas Gervais, the roof was covered with yellow glazed tiles and the roof pillars were decorated with large amounts of gold. Around the building there were four ponds, in which the king liked to swim. If the sun was shining, large canopies were stretched over them. Next to one pond, Narai had a small grotto built. In the courtyard to the south-east there were two more private reception halls and the Phra Chao Hao building dating from

Sutthasawan Hall

Narai's time, which is still in quite good repair. Granaries, stables and quarters for the guards were all situated here as well as several ponds.

Other Sights in Lopburi

Wat Sao Thong Thong

Just to the north of the palace compound next to the bank of the river behind a modern wall is Wat Sao Thong Thong, which was built in the early Ayutthaya period. The viharn on its tall base with long narrow windows in the shape of a lotus blossom was a Christian chapel in the time of King Narai, and the large statue of a seated Buddha inside still wears a Christian cross. The columns are adorned with leaf capitals and the wall niches hold statues of Buddha in the Lopburi style. The pavilions alongside the monastery buildings were built by King Narai as quarters for his foreign guests.

✱ Phaulkon's Palace

🕐 Opening hours: 8am–6pm daily

North of Wat Sao Thong Thong, on Wichayen Road near the river, is the site of Phaulkon's, palace, so named although some buildings had already been erected for Chevalier de Chaumont. The palace is a large three-storey building in a mixture of Siamese and European styles. The compound was ringed by a wall 2m/6ft in height and included a kitchen (to the left at the rear), stables (to the right) plus baths, a church with a house for a Catholic priest and a free-standing bell tower, and a single-storey audience pavilion. All of these are now in ruins. The three massive gates in the southern wall once formed the entrance to the palace and are well preserved. The middle one leads to some well-kept grounds.

Fortifications

Of the strong fortifications that once encircled Lopburi, only Fort Tha Po in the north-west, Fort Chai Chana Songkhram and the Pratu Chai gate in the south still remain. French engineers were also responsible for building the dams and sluices for a large reservoir to the north of the city that has since been filled in. King Narai had one other summer residence, the Phra Thinang Yen Kraison Sahavarat Pavilion, or Yen Pavilion. It was built on an island in the middle of the reservoir. With a little imagination, the ruins can still give some impression of the former beauty and exquisite proportions of this building.

Around Lopburi

Singburi

Singburi lies north-west of Lopburi, 25km/16mi along Route 311 on the right bank of the Menam Chao Phraya, at the intersection of several important roads. The town is right in the midst of the central plain with its virtually endless rice plantations.

✱ Wat Phra Nou Chak Si

5km/3mi south-west of Singburi (2km/1.5mi along Route 309 or Route 3032) is Wat Phra Nou Chak Si with its gigantic, 40m/130ft-long statue of a reclining Buddha, the biggest in Thailand. Its artistic quality, however, has been diminished by repeated restoration attempts.

On a hill close by is an Ayutthaya-style prang with lovely stucco ornamentation which, apart from a few ruins of some other buildings, is all that remains of Wat Phra That. The three niches in the prang are occupied by statues of Buddha, and there are more attractive Buddha statues inside.

Ayutthaya Prang

Route 3032 leads to the walled town of Bang Rachan. On the way there (32km/20mi) it passes the partially restored ruins of Khai Bang Rachan. The monks of Wat Po Kao Ton played an important role in the wars with the Burmese. Their temple has two viharns, one old, one new, and some ancient chedis.

Bang Rachan

✦ ✶ Mae Hong Son

B 1/2

Region: Northern Thailand
Altitude: 160m/525ft approx.

Province: Mae Hong Son
Population: 15,000 approx.

The attraction of the small town of Mae Hong Son, far in the north near the Burmese border, is primarily the fascinating mountain scenery with its verdant tropical vegetation.

The region known as the »Golden Triangle« has one claim to fame that the Thai government would prefer to be a thing of the past. It is one of the world's major areas for the cultivation of drugs. Since this district in the province of Chiang Rai has been increasingly targeted by police, the drug dealers have retreated to smugglers' trails in the mountainous border regions between Mae Hong Song and Myanmar.

In the shadow of the »Golden Triangle«

Sights in and around Mae Hong Son

The mountainous landscape around Mae Hong Son is among the most naturally beautiful in Thailand. Its magnificence can be seen clearly during the journey to the town. Mae Hong Son makes a good base for day trips or longer treks through the countryside. Such journeys are offered by many travel agents; the adventurous can equally well strike out on their own and enjoy river rafting on the Pai River, the Phra Bong reservoir and several national parks.

Scenery

✔ DON'T MISS

■ For breathtaking scenery it is well worth taking the more difficult mountain route around horseshoe bends from Chiang Mai via Hot and Mae Sarieng, a distance of around 380km/236mi.

> ### ! Baedeker TIP
>
> **The ordination of the loving sons**
> The festival of Buat Luk Khaeo, »the ordination of the loving sons«, is celebrated elsewhere in Thailand, but nowhere is it as colourful and joyous as in Mae Hong Son, where it is actually called the Poy Sang Long festival. During the ceremony, which takes place from March to April in Wat Chong Kham, boys between 10 and 13 are ordained as novice monks (»nakh«). The procession on the first day is a particularly exciting affair, in which the boys are carried to the temple on the shoulders of the men, rocking rhythmically (►Baedeker Special p.356).

Especially during the hours when the markets are doing business (5.30am–9am every day), there is a good chance of encountering many members of the **hill tribes**, colourfully dressed Meo, Karen, Lawa, Lisu and Lahu, mostly offering handmade goods and foodstuffs for sale, along with some of the produce of the fertile land, such as chillis, tobacco, betel nuts, fruit and vegetables.

★ Wat Chong Kham, Wat Chong Klang

The Burmese-style temples Wat Chong Kham and Wat Chong Klang stand close together on the shore of the small lake in the middle of the town. The viharn of Wat Chong Klang has more than 30 statues that were brought here from Burma in around 1860.

★★ Mount Doi Kung Mu

The mountain of Doi Kong Mu towers some 250m/820ft above Mae Hing Son. At its summit, just a half hour's walk from the western edge of the town, await the Burmese-style chedis of Wat Phra That Doi Kong Mu, which are also spectacular at night when they are lit up. The climb is an experience; it involves ascending an overgrown stairway in the midst of tropical jungle until, in the last few metres, two massive stone lions in the Burmese style rise up before the summit. From here there is a fantastic view of the town and the surrounding country.

Fish cave

17km/11mi north of the town (on Route 108) in Tham Pla Forest Park there is a cave with a pond that is home to many different kinds of exotic fish. Water from a nearby river feeds the pond.

Shan villages

The Shan have been fighting for decades for independence from Burma and Thailand, so far without success. Any attempt to visit this warlike people should only be attempted in the company of a local guide who is known to be welcome amongst them.

Mae Hong Son *Plan*

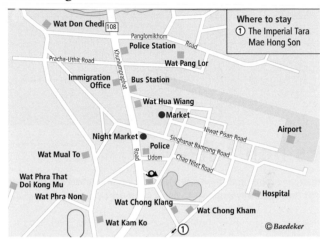

Where to stay
① The Imperial Tara Mae Hong Son

Wat Don Chedi 108
Panglomikhom
Police Station   Road
Pracha-Uthit Road   Khunlumphat
Wat Pang Lor
Immigration Office   Bus Station
Wat Hua Wiang
● Market
Airport
Night Market ●   Niwat Pisan Road
Wat Mual To   Police   Singhanat Bamrung Road
Udom   Chao Nitet Road
Wat Phra That Doi Kong Mu
Wat Phra Non
Hospital
Wat Chong Klang   Wat Chong Kham
Wat Kam Ko   ①
©Baedeker

About 20km/12mi north-west of Mae Hong Son via Route 108 lies a village populated by members of the Kuomintang that is now known as **Mae Aw**. The direct ancestors of its people were soldiers of the Chinese general Chiang Kai-shek. After their defeat at the hands of the Mao Tse Tung's People's Liberation Army, they did not follow their leader to Formosa (modern-day Taiwan) but fled to Burma. From there they migrated across the Thai border, where they currently remain with the permission of the Thai government. The men of the Kuomintang often work as policeman or officials for the government and many are involved, for example, in guarding the border with Myanmar.

Kuomintang village

An hour and a half's drive north-west from Mae Hong Son, just 3km/2mi from the Burmese border, is the village of the Pradong.

Pradong village

 VISITING MAE HONG SON

GETTING THERE

By car:
From Chiang Mai north on Route 107, turning off just before Mae Taeng north-west along Route 1095 (130km/81mi) or from Mae Sarieng on Route 108 (170km/106mi)

By air:
Several flights a week from Chiang Mai (flight time 45 minutes)

WHERE TO STAY

► **Mid-range**
① *The Imperial Tara Mae Hong Son*
149 Moo 8, T. Pangmoo
Tel. 0 53 / 61 10 21, fax 61 12 52
www.imperialhotels.com
104 rooms, restaurant, bar, swimming pool, fitness centre, sauna. Slightly outside the town centre on the river, the hotel has a lovely garden and a good restaurant.

Thai believers spend up to three months in a monastery

MONKS DON'T BEG

Monks with orange robes and shaven heads are a common feature of daily life in all parts of Thailand. They continue to enjoy immense reverence throughout the land.

Practically every male Buddhist in Thailand spends at least one period of his life in a monastery. Until 1945, the minimum period for such a stay was 3 months, but nowadays a few weeks' attendance is considered enough for young men to immerse themselves in the teachings of Buddha. In many temples it is possible to see ten- to twelve-year-old boys who are starting their schooling at the monastery. They will then be taken on as novices at the age of 15. Many boys also attend the monasteries during the school holidays.

Monastic Rules

In Thailand as a whole there are 3,000 temples and an estimated 200,000 monks. Even as novices, the boys endeavour to absorb the three most important rules of monastic life: a monk must be poor, must never do harm to any other person and must forego all sexual pleasure. During his life as a monk, a novice may possess only eight objects: the three components of his monk's robe, a needle and thread, a cut-throat razor to shave his head, a sieve, a bowl for alms and a string of 108 meditation beads. Early in the mornings, monks with their orange robes (kasaya) and shorn heads dominate the scene in all the major cities of Thailand while they are collecting food for the day. In this respect, the idea that they **»beg« is completely wrong**. On the contrary, the faithful give their offerings of food to the monks with great humility, hoping thereby to have contributed to the health of their own soul, and always thank the monk by pressing their hands together in a respectful »wai«.

The custom that monks are not permitted to accept anything that has been touched by a woman's hands was not instituted by Buddha himself, but emerged long after his death. Nevertheless, monks will still refuse to accept food or money from a woman. However, the monasteries themselves are also home to so-called Mae Ji, women who live by equally strict but differing rules to the monks. As they are permitted to handle money, these women are largely responsible for running the establishments.

Young monks studying Pali scriptures

Ordination

One of the key events in a man's life is his ordination as a monk. This is celebrated by his family and neighbours as well as being marked by a religious ceremony. Days before the ordination, the young men visit each of their relatives and neighbours to beg forgiveness for their »sins«. On the eve of the event the whole community and all their kin gather together. They bring an orchestra with them, or maybe two, one featuring adult musicians while the other is made up of the monk-to-be's own contemporaries, who may play jazz and pop in addition to the familiar Thai repertoire.

While the youngsters stroll the streets to the light of lanterns and partake freely of the rice and desserts that are made available from giant cauldrons, older relatives and neighbours assemble in the parents' house around the day's new »Siddharta«, who is attired like a prince and lies on the floor before a white-robed Brahman. The Brahman lists once more the good things that the boy's parents have done for him. Relatives and neighbours will already (for a fee) have given ceremonial recitations events from his own life. Particularly praiseworthy deeds will cause the elders to punctuate their smoking, tea-drinking or chewing of betel nuts

with a loud cheer and the young man will often break down in thankful, or sometimes rueful, tears. The ceremony lasts for several hours until midnight.

The room is adorned with an altar upon which there will be flowers, joss sticks, a statue of Buddha and colourful paper nagas. »Naga« was the snake god who once protected Buddha from a heavy rainstorm by spreading his seven heads over the meditating monk, for which he asked to be included in the Enlightened One's fraternity. The request was refused but thereafter every monk was to take the snake's name on the day before his ordination.

The ceremony takes up where it left off on the following morning. The celebrating family and friends form a colourful procession towards the temple, marching and dancing to the beat of drums. A horse fit for a prince is provided for the initiate, or if no suitable beast is available, the young naga rides on the shoulders of his peers. Others carry gifts piled high on silver platters. In the temple itself there is a ceremony in which the boy's head is shaven, and on the third day the young man finally receives the saffron monk's robe from his future monastic brothers. For the family, the celebration nevertheless goes on, even without the new novice.

Preparing for a photo-shoot: a Pradong girl near the Burmese frontier

The existence of this mysterious hill tribe was little known until a little over twenty years ago, when a community of 50 or so Pradong moved over the border from Myanmar to Thailand and at last came to the public eye. It is not known for sure where the Pradong stem from, but their dress, customs and rituals suggest a northern Burmese origin. The Pradong start putting golden rings around the necks of their young girls when they are about four years of age. The rings are regularly added until the girls reach an age of about 25, when they may have as many as 25 of them. Visiting their village as a »tourist attraction« may cost quite a lot of money. The very reason the »long necks« crossed the border was that they had heard about the money to be made from tourists in Thailand. Apart from levying an admission fee to enter the village, they also charge extra for the taking of photographs.

✷ ✷ Nakhon Pathom

E 3

Region: Western Thailand
Altitude: 8m/26ft

Province: Nakhon Pathom
Population: 63,000

Only history relates that Nakhon Pathom was once on the Gulf of Thailand. The network of rivers running through the central plain has deposited such quantities of sand and silt over the years that the sea has retreated by as much as 50km/30mi. Nakhon Pathom has nevertheless remained a burgeoning trading centre in spite of this change to its geographical status. Furthermore, within its walls is the holiest Buddhist building in all of Thailand, Phra Pathom Chedi.

Nakhon is certainly one of the oldest settlements in Thailand. In the **History** 3rd century BC, King Ashoka (273–231 BC) was the ruler of a great Indian empire. Having converted to the new Theravada Buddhism, he sent monks as missionaries to the area where the town now stands. It is from this period that the forerunner of its most imposing building, the Phra Pathom Chedi, is said to date. Definite proof of settlement at Nakhon Pathom currently goes back no further than AD 675, however. At this point the city became the capital of King Chaisiri and the eponymous kingdom. Most of the population was of Mon stock but their culture, as confirmed by archaeological finds of the time (include stone wheels of life and images of Buddha), was heavily influenced by Indian Buddhism in the Gupta style. Nakhon Pathom became the successor to U Thong as the capital of the powerful Dvaravati kingdom. The wealth of the city can be determined from the coins minted there: silver coins from the 7th and 8th centuries show symbols of riches (a cow and calf or a vase of flowers) while the reverse has the Sanskrit inscription »credit to the Dvaravati kings«. The city was probably destroyed either by King Suryavarman I (1002–1050) or Jayavarman VII (1181–1218). After that Nakhon Pathom was largely forgotten. Most of its inhabitants left and founded a new city called Nakhon Chaisi on the right bank of the Ta Chin river, which remains to this day. Phra Pathom Chedi was gradually swallowed up by the jungle. It was not until the time of King Mongkut (Rama IV), who had made a pilgrimage to the chedi during his time as a monk, that anyone recognized the importance of the location. When he ascended the throne in 1851, he immediately ordered its restoration. Since the old shrine was badly ruined,

▶ VISITING NAKHON PATHOM

GETTING THERE

By car:
From Bangkok on Route 4 (Petchkasem Highway, 54km/34mi).

By rail:
From Bangkok-Hualampong

By bus:
From Bangkok Southern Bus Terminal. Nakhon Pathom is a good place for a day trip from Bangkok. Travel agents often offer tours, some of which include a visit to the floating market at Damnoen Saduak (► Ratchaburi) and the Rose Garden.

WHERE TO STAY

▶ **Luxury**
Antique Thai Teak Houses
Pet Kasem Road, km 32,
Sampran, in the Rose Garden
Tel. 0 34 / 32 25 44
Fax 32 27 75
www.rose-garden.com
This traditional Thai-style hotel amidst beautifully tended parkland offers a fine alternative to accommodation in Bangkok. A less expensive option is the Riverside Hotel, which is also located in the Rose Garden.

Nakhon Pathom *Plan*

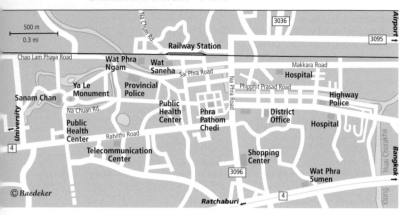

however, he initially had a chedi built over what was left of the dagoba that dates from the Khmer period. The building was not finished until the time of Mongkut's successor Chulalongkorn, since part of the building had collapsed during a storm.

Prang Approaching along Route 4 from Bangkok, a whitewashed prang on a square base is immediately conspicuous. It is alleged to be the oldest Buddhist edifice in all of Thailand, older than Phra Pathom Chedi. Nearby, foundations and the terrace of a sacred building have been found along with fragments of wall friezes adorned with statuary and various Buddha statues.

✷ ✷ Phra Pathom Chedi

Opening hours:
8am–5pm daily

Phra Pathom Chedi, »the first and holiest chedi«, is the **tallest Buddhist building on earth** at 118m/387ft (127m/417ft with terraces), bigger than the famous Shwe Dagon, the golden pagoda in Rangoon (which is 99.36m/326ft high and was completed in 1773).

One statue in the viharn to the north of the compound is said to depict King Phya Kong, who features in the legend of how the chedi came to be built. An astrologist told him that his son would one day kill him. Believing this, he abandoned the boy in the forest, but a woman found him and brought him up under the name Phya Pan. When he grew up, he entered service with the king of Ratchaburi, whose land was a fiefdom of the neighbouring kingdom of Nakhon Chaisi. Phya Pan's intelligence and discretion became famous far and wide and, for this reason, he was adopted by the king. It was Phya Pan who persuaded his adopted parent to rise up against his feudal master, and in the ensuing battle Phya Pan did indeed slay his own father. After his triumph, he demanded to take the queen of the defeated king as his wife, as custom decreed, but in doing this, he learned of his origins and discovered that she was his own mother. In penance, he allowed a dagoba to be built. It became the forerunner of the Phra Pathom Chedi, but is now concealed beneath the current building.

The sacred precinct forms a square enclosed by a wire fence. The main entrance is on the northern side, where a broad stairway leads to an initial terrace surrounded by a balustrade. The balustrades are decorated with all manner of adornment, including seven-headed nagas, and have faience inlays. There are several buildings on the terrace. In the bot to the south of the eastern entrance stands one of the finest Buddha statues, made of light-coloured quartzite and partially covered in gilt and paint. It is in the Dvaravati style and shows Buddha seated in the European manner (»the future Buddha«). Three exact copies of this statue are known to exist. All of them used to belong to **Wat Na Phra Men** in Nakhon Pathom, of which only a few brick-built remains can now be seen. Another copy now resides in Wat Phra Men in Ayutthaya, while the other two are in the National Museum in Bangkok. Above the circular foundations rises a great dome (98m/322ft in diameter) in the shape of a bell or an alms bowl of a Buddhist monk. Decorated cornices tapering towards the top put the finishing touch to the base.

The chedi at Phra Pathon is the tallest Buddhist edifice in the world

Above that is a square section, which is interpreted as a sanctuary that rises above the world. The final element is a round tower that tapers to a point, the canopy that symbolizes the dignity of Buddha. Around the base of the chedi there is an columned arcade punctuated by four symmetrically arranged viharns.

Temple museums
🕑
Opening hours:
Tue–Fri
9.30am–4pm

The viharn to the north of the east entrance houses the old temple museum, which houses stucco and stone sculptures. Some stone wheels of life outside the museum by the southern stairway, dating from the earliest days of Nakhon Pathom, should not be missed. Inside are some Buddha statues, stone and terracotta sculptures and items of daily life. Also at the southern end is a model of the Khmer prang, over the ruins of which King Mongkut had the present chedi built, along with a copy of the famous chedi at Wat Mahathat in Nakhon Si Thammarat. The northern stairway continues to an upper terrace where there are two salas in Javanese style and a columned gallery with by four viharns. Red-painted moon gates lead to an inner terrace with 24 small towers containing bronze bells. Both terraces feature Chinese stone statues, many finds from the temple site and several salas. This is also the way to the monks' quarters at the south-east of the temple compound.

! *Baedeker* TIP

Temple fair

Every year in November Nakhon Pathom plays host to a huge temple fair that attracts pilgrims from all over the country. Theatre performance are given on the temple terraces along with shadow plays and other spectacles. A market is built at the foot of chedi, which itself is strung with garlands of lights.

Viharn
The four viharns consist of an open porch and an interior room. In the porch of the northern viharn an impressive gilded statue of Buddha in the Sukhothai style stands 8m/26ft tall. Its hands and feet come from a stone statue unearthed in Sawankhalok near Sukhothai around 1915. The body was cast in bronze in Bangkok. An inscription on the wall of the viharn says that the ashes of King Mongkut are kept in the base of the statue. Two statue tableaux are to be found in the viharn, one depicting a scene in which two princesses pay homage to the newly born Siddharta (Buddha), while the other shows a key scene from the life of Buddha, where animals brought food to him after he had fasted for forty days. The southern viharn contains some wonderful stone sculptures, and one small niche in the wall houses a figure of Phya Pan from the 6th or 7th century. The reclining Buddha in the porch of the western viharn measures 9m/30ft in length.

Other Attractions

Palace of Sanam Chan
In the north-west of the city, King Rama VI had the Sanam Chan palace built amid extensive parkland in 1901, before he was made king. A broad avenue leads there from the west gate of the chedi. Some of the buildings are highly interesting, including architecture in a mixture of European and Thai styles and an audience hall in the Bangkok style. There is a shrine for the worship of the Hindu god Ganesha with his elephant's head and his immense human body with

multiple arms. One curiosity is the statue of a dog that stands before a building bearing the name Chali Mongkol Asana. This probably represents Ya Le, King Rama IV's favourite hound. The building is now used by departments of the local government.

West of Nakhon Pathom station is Wat Phra Ngam, built in the Bangkok style by King Chulalongkorn on the foundations of a shrine that dates from the Dvaravati period.

Wat Phra Ngam

The Rose Garden park, 32km/20mi south-west of Bangkok on the way to Nakhon Pathom is a draw for those wishing to get away from the city as well as for golfers (it has an 18-hole course). The gardens are mainly designed in an Italian style. Open-air restaurants on the Menam Chao Phraya serve Western, Chinese and Thai cuisine. There are bungalow hotels with swimming pools and tennis courts. Particularly during the Christmas and Easter holidays, it is worth making early reservations. An hour-long show held every afternoon at 2.45pm features rustic and family Thai ceremonies as well as working elephants, historical Thai dances and traditional sports and games. After the show guests can ride the elephants.

✱
Rose Garden
☉
Opening hours:
8.30am–5pm
www.rose-garden.com

Nakhon Phanom

C 5

Region: North-east Thailand
Altitude: 138m/453ft

Province: Nakhon Phanom
Population: 31,000 (in the town itself)

Nakhon Phanom, capital of the province of the same name, lies amid bald landscape in the far north-east of Thailand along the Mekong river, close to the border with Laos. On clear days it is possible to see beyond the tree-lined banks across the river to the town of Thakhek in the Lao mountains.

During the Vietnam war, tens of thousand of refugees sought sanctuary here. About 40,000 have remained in and around the town. 12km/8mi to the west, Nakhon Phanom was a US base and interrogation station. Apart from two lively markets there is little to see in the town itself, but due to its high-quality hotels (some of which were built during the period when the American base was in existence) Nakhon Phanom makes a good starting point for excursions into the surrounding country.

Sanctuary for refugees from the Vietnam war

Around Nakhon Phanom

That Phanom also lies on the Mekong about 45km/28mi south of Nakhon Phanom. The town's centrepiece is its most outstanding building, a prang that was built in the grounds of Wat Phra That

✱ ✱
Wat Phra That Phanom

Buddha at Wat Phra That Phanom

Phanom on the western bank of the Mekong in around 900. The prang has been restored several times over the centuries and is said to house a relic of Buddha. The first building on the site was erected just eight years after the death of Buddha by five kings of the Si Gotapura kingdom. During the Lan Chang period in 1614 the perimeters of the shrine were realigned and a wall built around them. The prang took on more or less the shape is has today around the year 1690, when the monk Phra Khru Luang Phonsamek had it extended to a height of 47m/154ft, adding much ornamentation and a pointed canopy made of 16kg/35lb of pure gold. The sculptures and floral ornamentation on the sides were added around 1901 during the Bangkok period. The prang was restored in 1941, reaching its present height of 57m/187 feet, then a second time in 1979. Outstanding bas-reliefs in the Khmer style adorn the square base. They show scenes from Brahman mythology; homage being paid to Buddha by the four guardians of the world and the entrance of the Enlightened One into nirvana. In front of that there is a multi-tiered pedestal with a Buddha statue under a canopy. The other temple buildings are from recent times. A colonnade surrounds the courtyard and has some well-preserved murals around the doors. Its pretty trees, bushes and flowers make it look like a neat garden.

! Baedeker TIP

Phansa festival

Every January Wat Phra That Phanom attracts a host of pilgrims for the celebration of the Phansa festival. Many events take place in and around the temple at this time (including folk dances, markets and boat races on the Mekong).

About 7km/4mi north-west of That Phanom is the silk weaving village of **Ban Renu**. Shops are strung out all along the main street for the sale of the beautifully dyed silken fabrics in both traditional and newly designed patterns. The tiered tower of **Wat Phra Renu** is also interesting. It is covered from base to spire with expressive and brightly painted bas-reliefs. The designs show a sure feel for perspective. The realistic figures, including the child Buddha riding a horse and an elephant, emerge from beautifully intertwined threading. The method of depiction shows modern influences amid the traditional way of thinking.

★
Lake Nong Han

About 80km/50mi south-east of Nakhon Phanom a broad, low plain that is relatively well watered from Lake Nong Han stretches to the Mekong on one side and is bordered by thickly wooded mountains to the south-west. Lake Nong Han, the largest inland lake in Thailand, is rich in fish.

Sakhon Nakhon

The sleepy town of Sakhon Nakhon on the south-west shore of the lake attracts very few tourists. Those that do get here can see some high-quality and well-preserved relics of Khmer art and the badly ruined Khmer shrine of **That Dum**. The new white prang of **Wat Phra Cheung Chum** was planted on top of a 16th-century Khmer prang that is still visible inside. The viharn has a statue of a sitting Buddha.

★
Wat Phra That Narai

West of Sakhon Nakhon is Wat Phra That Narai, a shrine that was built in the 11th century. The well-preserved and beautifully sculpted door lintels depict scenes from Brahman mythology (including the gods Vishnu and Krishna).

▶ VISITING NAKHON PHANOM

GETTING THERE
By car:
From Kalasin on Routes 213/22 (98km/61mi)

By bus:
From Bangkok North-Eastern Bus Terminal (727km/452mi) and Kalasin

By air:
Daily from Bangkok

INFORMATION
Tourism Authority of Thailand
184/1 Suntornvijit Road
48000 Nakhon Phanom

Tel. 0 42 / 51 34 90-1, fax 51 34 92
tatphnom@tat.or.th

WHERE TO STAY
▶ **Budget**
Mae Nam Khong Grand View Hotel
527 Sunthon Wichit Road
Tel. 0 42 / 51 35 64
Fax 51 10 37
112 rooms, restaurant.
Rather small rooms. The best accommodation is in the deluxe wing. The hotel does have a spectacular view of the Mekong, and its restaurant is reputed to be one of the best in Nakhon Phanom.

Phu Pan National Park Route 213 towards Kalasin leads through the Phu Pan National Park, its mountain slopes covered in luxuriant monsoon forest. In the absence of a guide, the park along with its view point, waterfalls and caves is quite difficult to find.

✳ **Nakhon Ratchasima** (Khorat)

D 4

Region: North-east Thailand	**Province:** Nakhon Ratchasima
Altitude: 222m/728 feet	**Population:** 207,000

Nakhon Ratchasima is on the south-western edge of the Khorat plateau and has developed in recent decades into a major supply centre for a region that suffers from the poorest infrastructure in all Thailand. It is here, however, that the railway lines from the north and east intersect.

Outpost against the Khmer The town was probably established in the 13th century by the Thai principalities as an outpost against the Khmer. Some remains are still to be seen of fortifications built later under King Narai (1656–1688). Chronicles report an attack by Khmer troops in 1826, which is commemorated by the Khunying Mo monument in front of the western gate.

What to See in Nakhon Ratchasima

Fortifications The wide moats and restored gate of **Pratu Chumphon** give an impression of the former extent of the fortifications. Upon a plinth in front of the gate stands the bronze monument to Thao Suranari (Khunying Mo), honoured as a national heroine. When the Khmer army under King Anu attacked the town in 1826, the wife of the garrison commander and other townspeople threw a huge drinking party for the occupiers outside the town. Then the woemen ambushed them when they were drunk. After a month, the Khmer were driven away.

? DID YOU KNOW …?

■ The inhabitants of Nakhon Ratchasima pay special reverence to the national heroine Thao Suranari and have adopted the following motto in which she is honoured: »Town of the woman who showed great bravery, of fine silk, korat noodles, and great old stone buildings that are known far and wide. The unique Dan Kwian earthenware made of special clay is a speciality of the town.«

✳ **Wat Sutthachinda** Wat Sutthachinda is surrounded by lovely gardens. The small viharn guarded by two lions is particularly pretty, as is the dainty bell tower. Note the richly decorated gables of the viharn and the superbly carved windows on both sides of the shrine. Inside the beautifully proportioned viharn are three Buddha statues covered by five-tiered canopies. The largest of the statues displays the gesture of forgiveness, one of the five classic gestures of Buddha. Alongside the temple is a crematorium, where Buddhist cremation ceremonies are carried out (Opening times: 9am–4pm daily)..

Close to the large and enjoyable markets on Mukkhamontri Road is the extensive Wat Phra Narai Mahathat on Prajak Road, where there are several sculpted sandstone tablets, originally from Khmer temples, and one highly revered Vishnu statue in a small Hindu temple.

✱ Wat Phra Narai Mahathat

Temple-goers at prayer with burning joss sticks

Around Nakhon Ratchasima

Silk-weaving villages
The province of Nakhon Ratchasima is one of the main centres of Thai silk production, producing both yarns and fabrics. In the silk-weaving village of **Pak Thong Chai** (33km/21mi from Nakhon Ratchasima south-west then on Route 304 towards Kabinburi) it is possible to view the whole process of silk production starting with the worms. Some producers provide guided tours of their production facilities and sell silk items at low prices. There are many small silk weavers all along the main street.

Wat Prasat Hin Noen Ku
Old Khorat has an interesting Khmer temple in Wat Prasat Hin Noen Ku in the place now known as Muang Khorakhopura (37km/23mi west of Nakhon Ratchaburi). The building atop its large square terrace is flanked by two smaller buildings and exhibits some fine sculptures from the mid-10th century.

Wat Prasat Muang Khaek
Close to Wat Prasat Hin Noen Ku are the ruins of Wat Prasat Muang Khaek, with its prang and porch that are particularly renowned for their elaborate and finely hewn sculptures on the door lintels, gable

► VISITING NAKHON RATCHASIMA

GETTING THERE

By car:
From Bangkok via Route 1 to Saraburi, then Route 2 (»Friendship Highway«; 265km/165mi)

By rail:
Station on the Bangkok – Ubon Ratchathani and Bangkok – Udon Thani lines

By bus:
Several times a day from Bangkok North-Eastern Bus Terminal

By air:
Daily from Bangkok

INFORMATION

Tourism Authority of Thailand
2102-2104 Mittraphap Road
30000 Nakhon Ratchasima
Tel. 0 44 / 21 36 66, 21 30 30
Fax 21 36 67, tatsima@tat.or.th

WHERE TO STAY

► **Budget**

① *Sri Pattana*
346 Suranari Road
Tel. 0 44 / 25 53 49
Fax 25 16 55
212 rooms, restaurant, bar, swimming pool, fitness centre. Very agreeable, spacious and comfortable rooms. The pool is open to people who are not staying at the hotel on payment of an admission fee.

② *Sima Thani*
2114 Mittraphap Road
Tel. 0 44 / 21 30 00
Fax 21 31 21
www.simathani.com
265 rooms, 4 restaurants and bar, coffee shop, swimming pool, fitness centre, sauna.
Comfortable rooms at a nice price, right next door to the TAT office.

Nakhon Ratchasima *Plan*

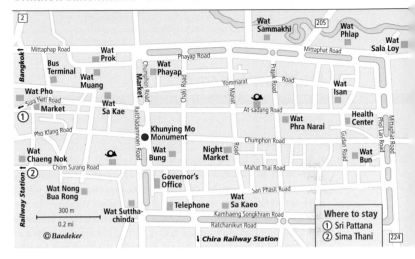

Wat Sammakhi | 205 | Wat Phlap | Wat Sala Loy
Mittaphat Road
Mittaphap Road | Wat Prok | Phayap Road
Bus Terminal | Wat Phayap | Market | Yommarat
Wat Muang | Chumphon Road | Chao Phaya Road | Prajak Road
Wat Pho | Sura Nati Road | Wat Sa Kae
Market | Pho Klang Road
Wat Phra Narai | Wat Isan | Health Center
At-sadang Road
Khunying Mo Monument | Chumphon Road
Wat Chaeng Nok | Chom Surang Road | Wat Bung | Night Market | Gudan Road | Wat Bun
Mahat Thai Road | Phol Lan Road | Mittaphat Road
Railway Station | Wat Nong Bua Rong | Governor's Office | San Phasit Road
300 m | Wat Suttha-chinda | Telephone | Wat Sa Kaeo
0.2 mi | Kamhaeng Songkhram Road
© Baedeker | Ratchanikun Road
Chira Railway Station | **Where to stay** ① Sri Pattana ② Sima Thani | 224

ends and pillars (mostly showing motifs from Brahman mythology). Some beautifully made 10th-century stone sculptures were also discovered in the temple.

★ ★
Wat Prasat Phanom Wan

Although the Buddha statues in the old Wat Prasat Phanom Wan, about 14km/9mi north-east of Nakhon Ratchasima (on Route 2 turning right after about 10km/6mi, then a further 4km/2.5mi to the village of Ban Kho), are still revered by many worshippers and are honoured with regular devotional gatherings, the small but outstandingly preserved Khmer temple is quiet and almost forgotten. Some newer monastery buildings have been put up on the foundations of older buildings, but the 11th-century shrine has survived. As the ornamentation indicates a period as far back as the 10th century, there may have been an even older building on the site. The rectangular perimeter wall with galleries on the inside was pierced by a beautifully decorated gate on each of the four sides. In the courtyard, ruins of prangs and many door lintels are still preserved. The shrine is a rectangular compound with a prang of greyish sandstone that has had porches added on all four sides. From the eastern porch a covered way lit by windows leads to a 10 x 3m (33 x 10ft) hall (mandapa) with a tiered roof. The Buddha statues, many of which are gilded, derive from later periods.

Ruins of Muang Sema

A field of ruins about 40km/25mi west of Nakhon Ratchasima near the village of Muang Sema possibly indicates the site of an important Mon city that must have stood here between the 6th and 11th centuries. Results of research into the site have not yet been released.

Tip   56km/35mi north-east of Nakhon Ratchasima are the famous Khmer temples of ►Phimai. The superbly preserved Khmer buildings of ► Prasat Phanom Rung and Prasat Muang Tam near Prakhon Chai are also accessible as part of a day trip (about 130km/80mi away).

✹ Nakhon Sawan

D 3

Region: Central Thailand	**Province:** Nakhon Sawan
Altitude: 28m/92ft	**Population:** 91,000

Nakhon Sawan, formerly known as Paknam Po, is about 240km/ 150mi north of Bangkok where the confluence of the Menam Ping and Menam Nan rivers forms the great Menam Chao Phraya, which provides water for the entire central plain before flowing into the Gulf of Thailand. Nakhon Sawan has been a thriving town for many years, but the embargo on the felling of tropical wood imposed in 1989 has hit it hard, since it was formerly the terminus for the great log rafts from the north.

Trading centre   Trading in wood still dominates the brisk commercial life of the town. Jute, maize and peanut plantations are characteristic of the landscape. The mighty mountain range of Khao Pathawi towers to the west.

What to See in Nakhon Sawan

✹
Wat Chomkiri Nagaproth   Little remains of the old town of Nakhon Sawan. The wat that stands on a nearby hill across the Menam Chao Phraya dates from the Su-khothai era and has a footprint of Buddha that is accorded particular reverence. More important is Wat Chomkiri Nagaproth, on a hill

▶ VISITING NAKHON SAWAN

GETTING THERE
By car:
From Bangkok on Routes 1/32/1 (about 240km/150mi)

By rail:
Station on the Bangkok – Chiang Mai line

By bus:
From Bangkok Northern Bus Terminal

WHERE TO STAY
▶ **Budget**
Pimarn Hotel
605/244 Asia Highway Road
Tel. 0 56 / 22 20 97, fax 22 12 53
124 rooms, restaurant, bar, discothe-que, swimming pool, fitness centre, shopping arcade.
Centrally located for the attractions of Nakhon Sawan with nicely furnished rooms.

across the Menam Chao Phraya to the south of the town. Here two rows of semas flank the bot of the Sukhothai-era temple. Inside, a beautiful statue of a sitting Buddha in the Ayutthaya style is a highlight. Buddha's throne is borne by demons. Behind the statue there is another Buddha and a footprint. More Buddhas in the Ayutthaya style surround a large seated Buddha in the viharn, and in the courtyard a large, intricately engraved bell from 1870 hangs between two stone columns. The many lively markets in the vicinity are also worth a visit.

Nature enthusiasts should not miss Lake Boeng Boraphet east of Nakhon Sawan. One of the largest inland lakes in the country, it reaches its fullest extent at the end of the monsoon season when it has a length of 20km/12mi. The lake is rich in fish and is home to many species of waterfowl. Part of the large swamp region has long been declared a nature reserve for bird life.

✹
Lake Boeng Boraphet

About 6km/4mi south of Nakhon Sawan is the small village of Phayuha Khiri, home to numerous ivory carvers. Here you can watch carvers making beautiful works of art, although nowadays it is rare for genuine ivory to be used. Substitutes are used since elephants are now protected under the Washington Convention on trading in endangered species.

Phayuha Khiri

★ ★ Nakhon Si Thammarat

Region: Southern Thailand
Altitude: 13m/43ft

Province: Nakhon Si Thammarat
Population: 118,000

The town of Nakhon Si Thammarat on the Malay Peninsula, just a few miles from either coast, has a long history. Beyond the fertile coastal plain, mountains decked with verdant growth gently rise to the 1835m/6020ft-high summit of the Khao Luang massif.

Fruit cultivation and mining made the city rich but the niello technique that was perfected here has made it a centre for Thai crafts. Its magnificent past has given the city a dignified grandeur that is still perceptible to this day.

Centre of Thai arts and crafts

The city was once known by the Malay name of Ligor and has been a major stop on the trading routes from Europe, Africa and India since ancient times. Over 1500 years ago Nakhon Si Thammarat is

! *Baedeker* TIP

Full moon festival
Every year thousands of white-clad pilgrims flock to the full moon festival (February/March) at the imposing chedi of Wat Mahathat. They circle around the building draping saffron cloths over it.

said to have been the capital of a principality bearing the name Tambralinga that lasted until 1360. What is certain is that Nakhon Si Thammarat was in existence in the 8th century under the dominion of the Srivijaya kingdom that encompassed Sumatra and large parts of the Malay peninsula. A stone tablet claims that around 775 a temple was built to spread the message of Mahayana Buddhism. At the end of the 10th century, a ruler of the Tambralinga region conquered the Mon kingdom of Lopburi, which had already become part of the Khmer empire, and declared himself king of Angkor Wat under the name Suryavarman I. In 1292 King Ramkhamhaeng of Sukhothai overcame Tambralinga, which later became a vassal state of the Ayutthaya kingdom along with Sukhothai in the 14th century before being absorbed fully into the kingdom. King Rama Thibodi II (1491–1529) allowed the Portuguese to establish a trading base in Ligor in 1516. When Ayutthaya was destroyed in 1767, Tambralinga briefly became independent again before King Taksin absorbed it into his new empire.

Art and crafts   The town played a key artistic role and was the home of many well-known artists who were famed for the quality of their Buddha images.

Nang theatre   Nang shadow plays originated in Indonesia and are common in Thailand only in the south, especially in Nakhon Si Thammarat, where they are most often performed during Buddhist festivals. Some shops sell the shadow figures cut from heavily tanned buffalo hide.

What to See in Nakhon Si Thammarat

The old city   The city previously lay directly on the coast, which is now 26km/16mi away. The long main street still follows the line of the old coast road. Nowadays the city has expanded towards the north beyond its ancient boundaries, and the old town and its attractions have become something of a suburb. In the midst of it, some partially reconstructed remains of the old walls can be seen.

Wat Maheyong   Heading south along Ratchadamnoen Road with its pretty wooden houses, the road passes Wat Maheyong before it reaches the old city

Buddhist monks studying Pali scriptures →

walls. The wat contains a lovely bronze Buddha in the Nakhon Si Thammarat style.

Wat Sema Muang ✳

Wat Sema Muang, also on the right-hand side of Ratchadamnoen Road, was founded in 775 and is the place where the aforementioned stone tablet was found. No remains of the building can now be seen, however. Only a few steps further are two Brahman temples covered with red roofs from the Srivijaya period. In the shrine on the right there are a few lingas (phalluses, symbols of the god Shiva).

Ho Phra Sihing ✳✳

Ho Phra Sihing, a small chapel in the courtyard of the Thai-styled prefecture (in the centre of town near the junction of Route 4019 to Thung Song), houses a famous statue called the Buddha Phra Sihing (in Sukhothai style). Both the National Museum in Bangkok and Wat Phra Singh in Chiang Mai have an identical copy, all of which are claimed to be authentic. The original probably came from Ceylon (Sri Lanka as it is now known). The two Buddha statues covered in silver and gold are also worthy of note.

Wat Mahathat ✳✳

Wat Mahathat on Ratchadamnoen Road is the most famous temple of Nakhon Si Thammarat and one of the oldest in Thailand. It can be distinguished from some distance by its 74m/243ft-tall chedi, which has a spire made of 216kg/4.25cwt of pure gold. The precise date of the temple foundation is unknown; it was probably in the 10th century. A thorough rebuilding program that left little of the original complex was undertaken between 1157 and 1257.

Temple complex ►

A colonnade covered with glazed, coloured tiles encloses the extensive grounds of the wat. In the courtyard there are 156 large and small chedis, in both bell-shaped form and in the form of stupas.

Wat Mahathat *Nakhon Si Thammarat*

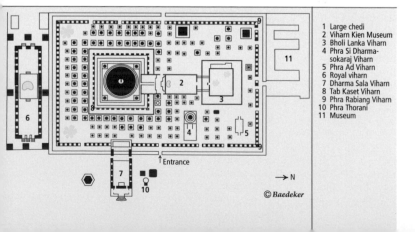

1 Large chedi
2 Viharn Kien Museum
3 Bholi Lanka Viharn
4 Phra Si Dharma-
   sokaraj Viharn
5 Phra Ad Viharn
6 Royal viharn
7 Dharma Sala Viharn
8 Tab Kaset Viharn
9 Phra Rabiang Viharn
10 Phra Thorani
11 Museum

Entrance

→ N

© Baedeker

VISITING NAKHON SI THAMMARAT

GETTING THERE

By car:
From Bangkok on Routes 3514/41/ 401; from Surat Thani heading south or initially eastward along the coast

By rail:
Two trains a day in either direction from Bangkok-Hualampong direct to Nakhon Si Thammarat (832km/ 517mi taking about 14 hours); otherwise to Thung Song then change

By air:
The airport at Nakhon Si Thammarat is served by Thai Airways daily from Bangkok.

INFORMATION

Tourism Authority of Thailand
Ratchadamnoen Road
80000 Nakhon Si Thammarat
Tel. 0 75 / 34 65 15-6
Fax 34 65 17, tatnksir@tat.or.th

WHERE TO STAY

► **Budget**
Grand Park Hotel
1204/79 Pak Nakhon Road
Tel. 0 75 / 31 76 66
Fax 31 76 74
129 rooms, restaurant, bar, swimming pool.
Highly recommended hotel east of the town centre. Well-kept rooms and attentive service.

Khanom Golden Beach Hotel
59/3 Moo 4, Nadan Beach
Khanom
Tel. 0 75 / 32 66 90
Fax 52 92 25
www.khanombeach.com
70 rooms, 2 restaurants, bar, night club, swimming pool, beach. Some way outside the town but with very nice, modern and spacious rooms. Very good restaurant.

Even the central chedi, the foundatio2ns of which date back to 757, is surrounded by a covered gallery housing 172 Buddha statues. The main shrine lies to the north in front of the chedi. From there a wide stairway guarded by lions and yaks leads up to a terrace of the chedi. Two chapels lie along the steps. The left one holds a statue of Buddha in the Sukhothai style and stucco reliefs in both the Srivijaya and Ayutthaya styles. The right-hand chapel has a Buddha statue in Ayutthaya style and stucco reliefs on its altar. The small temple museum in Viharn Kien contains many fine exhibits as well as fine silverware and faience porcelain from China and Sawankhalok. Special mention should be given to two valuable and wonderful pieces, a sitting Buddha in Srivijaya style and a standing Buddha in Dvaravati style.

◄ Temple museum
🕐
Opening hours:
Daily 8am–12pm, 1–4pm

At the Viharn Luang (royal viharn) next to Wat Mahathat the sharply inclined pillars both inside and outside (typical of the Ayutthaya period) catch the eye. Diagonally opposite Wat Mahathat on the other side of the street in Wat Na Phra Boromathat are the monks' quarters.

Viharn Luang

★★
National Museum

⏱ Opening hours:
Wed–Sun
9am–noon,
1–4pm
Admission fee

No photographs ▶

The local branch of the National Museum on the main street was opened in 1974 and is well worth seeing for its fine collection of art in various styles. Note the three 9th-century stone images in the Indian Pallava style that show Vishnu and two worshippers (a man and a woman). Finds from the Neolithic period (stone chains), pots and cooking implements from the 3rd century and the splendid gable fashioned in 1769 for Wat Sa Riang are among the other attractions. One statue of Vishnu is unique. It is the oldest such statue in Thailand and dates from the 5th century. Upstairs there are agricultural implements and domestic items. The courtyard has an exhibition of coaches and litters, while a side room features elaborately ornamented sticks that were once used for defence against snakes.

★
Wat Phra Du

The northern edge of the city, in a side street that leads away from Ratchadamnoen Road near the station, is the site of another fascinating temple called Wat Phra Du. It is said to contain the grave of King Taksin who, in contrast to the conventional story, supposedly escaped execution in 1782 to spend his final years in a cave in the mountains near Nakhon Si Thammarat.

★
Animal market

The animal market that takes place regularly near the bus station is an unusual sight. Monkeys, elephants, snakes and occasionally even wildcats are sold.

Around Nakhon Si Thammarat

Close to the town

Nakhon Si Thammarat has extremely varied surroundings. Inland the scenery is dominated by broad rubber plantations, the coast has several fabulous beaches and in the mountains near the town there are numerous caves such as the **Taksin cave** (Route 4015 towards Lan Saka). Not far from there is **Wat Khao Khun Phanom**, a temple surrounded by magnificent jungle scenery with several fine Buddha statues and a statue of King Taksin. The **Phrom Lok waterfall** (north-west on Route 4016) is also worth a look; swimming is allowed in its basin.

★
Khao Luang National Park

30km/21mi west of the town (northwards on the road to Chawang) is the 1834m/6017ft mountain Khao Luang, from which the surrounding national park gets its name. The park was opened in 1984 and is reached by driving to Ban Ron village and following signs from there. One particular attraction is the **Karom waterfall** that cascades in several stages from a height of 40m/131ft. It is the starting point for a trail that leads through a fascinating jungle landscape past another 19 waterfalls.

The park is home to a wide range of wildlife. If you are lucky you could see tapirs, Macaque monkeys, porcupine, leopard, barking deer, panthers, tigers or wild pigs as well as a great variety of birds. Or enjoy looking for some of the 300 different types of orchids.

✶ ✶ Nan (Nang)

Region: Northern Thailand
Altitude: 200m/656ft

Province: Nan (Nang)
Population: 22,000

Nan lies amongst high mountains near the border with Myanmar in the valley of the Menam Nan, one of the major tributaries of the Menam Chao Phraya. The difficulty of the terrain ensured the continuation of a small kingdom until well into the last century. The town has some important temples and the surroundings are a delight to nature lovers. Nan's sweet tangerines are famous too, as are the artistic craft creations in cane, made at home by women and children.

Traces of settlement in the province of Nan go back to around 1280. From the beginning of the 15th century Nan was part of a kingdom ruled by King Boroma Trailokanat (1448–1488). At some point the kings of Nan paid tribute to those of Chiang Mai. For 200 years they were vassals of the Burmese empire, then later of Ayutthaya. Nevertheless, the kings of Nan always enjoyed certain privileges. It was not until 1931 that Nan became part of the kingdom of Siam.

History

What to See in Nan

The oval-shaped city walls in the Mon style were erected in 1857 after the old fortifications had been destroyed by repeated flooding of the Menam Nan.

City walls

The architecture of the early period of Nan shows features of both Mon and Chiang Saen styles, but later on it was influenced by the

✶ ✶
Wat Phumin

⏵ VISITING NAN

GETTING THERE

By car:
From Phrae on Route 101 (125km/78mi), from Chiang Rai on Route 1 as far as Ngao then Route 103 to Rhong Kawan and finally Route 101

By bus:
Regular buses from Chiang Mai, Chiang Rai, Phrae and Phayao

By air:
From Bangkok via Chiang Mai or Phitsanulok

WHERE TO STAY

▶ **Budget**
Grand Mansion Hotel
71/1 Mahayot Road
Tel. and fax 0 54 / 75 05 14-5 57
rooms, restaurant, bar.
The best hotel in town with spacious, comfortable and clean rooms.

Sukhothai style. The town's famous Wat Phumin temple, south of the provincial government building on Suriyaphong Road, dates from 1596 and includes elements of all the styles mentioned above. It has a cross-shaped floor plan and triple-tiered roofs sweeping up to a graceful intersection crowned with a dainty canopy. The four symmetrically arranged entrances, approached via short but elegantly sweeping flights of steps guarded by lions, have wonderfully embellished carved portals. Four seated bronze lions in the Sukhothai style flank the cube of the altar inside. Columns and a beautiful construction of beams support a coffered ceiling. The murals date from the 19th century and depict, in vivid pictures with unusually bright colours, scenes from the history of the country, particularly battles, as well as episodes from the earlier lives of Buddha (the »Jataka«). They simultaneously describe the life of the people in northern Thailand.

✳
Elephant's tusk

One of the government buildings contains a 300-year-old tusk. It is shorter and thicker than most tusks and its ivory colour has faded over the years to a blackened yellow.

✳
Wat Chang Kang

The »temple borne by elephants« is the literal translation for the name of the wat that lies opposite the government buildings. Its characteristic feature is its beautiful chedi from the 15th or 16th century on a base supported by the statues of 28 elephants. The two shrines contain several outstanding Buddha sculptures in the Sukhothai style, including a sitting Buddha and a standing Buddha with extended arms and open hands in one shrine, and a solid gold striding Buddha in the other. This last Buddha was hidden for many years under a disguise of thick plaster, which came away when the statue was being moved. According to the inscriptions on the pedestal of the first two Buddhas, King Ngua Pha Sum 1426 had five such statues made. The other two of these life-size statues, perhaps the most beautiful of the set, now reside in Wat Phaya Phun.

Wat Suan Tan, Wat Ming Muan

In Wat Suan Tan at the northern end of Pakwang Road, a temple founded in 1456 by the wife of the of first king Nan, a sitting Buddha in the Sukhothai style with some elements of the Chiang Mai style and a prang-like chedi that towers to a height of 40m/130ft deserve mention. Wat Ming Muang was established in 1999 and is decorated on the outside with masses of plaster ornamentation, while the inside features colourful frescoes that depict in very clear fashion the former lives of the peasants and rulers.

National Museum
🕐

The small branch of the National Museum on Pa Gong Road has several excellent exhibits that mainly highlight the various ethnic groupings around the region of Nan (opening times: Tue–Sun 9am–4pm; admission fee). Many of the exhibits also have English descriptions. The house was the palace of the last feudal ruler of Nan and then donated to the government.

Around Nan

Two miles south-east of the town atop a bank on the opposite side of the Menam Nan stands the picturesque Wat Phra That Chao Meng. It is said that Buddha himself visited the site and prophesied that relics would be found here and a temple built for them. Two wide paths flanked by nagas lead up to the entrances of the wat, which was established in 1300 and renovated in 1476. The elegant chedi is 56m/184ft high and covered with gilded copper plates, decorative turrets and lion statues. The viharn clearly displays the Lao style.

Wat Phra That Chao Meng

A hard-earned living extracting salt near the Lao border

South of the town, beyond Route 101 **Wat Phaya Phun** stands on a mountain. Its chedi takes the form of a pointed step pyramid with niches. It has not yet been determined whether it dates from no later than the 18th century, or whether like its Buddha statues it was built in the 14th century, when Theravada Buddhism was reintroduced after years of domination by the Hinayana sect and animist beliefs were foresworn.

Wat Phra That Khao Noi About 2km/1.5mi further along the same road is Wat Phra That Khao Noi with its Chiang Saen-style chedi. The mountain of Khao Noi commands an extensive view of the plain and the city of Nan.

★★ Scenery Branching off from Route 101, Route 1026 leads away from the village Sa, 24km/15mi south of Nan, towards Ban Na Noi. Three groups of uncannily towering rock outcrops mark the gorge-like landscape of this area: **Nom Chom**, **Sao Dip** and **Sao Nin**.

★ Wat Bun Yeun The small village of Sa is famous for its hand-woven silk and cotton fabrics with modern and traditional patterns. The temple of Wat Bun Yeun beautifully illustrates the Lao style. The wonderful carved door of the harmoniously designed viharn depicts a deity. The Chiang Saen-style chedi is also worth a mention.

★ Narathiwat

H 3

Region: Southern Thailand	**Province:** Narathiwat
Altitude: 3m/10ft	**Population:** 42,000

From Narathiwat, Bangkok is 1530km/950mi distant, whereas the Malaysian border is only 67km/42mi away. Malay styles and Malay ways of life are prominent everywhere and a large proportion of the population speaks the language of the neighbouring country. Alongside Buddhist temples, muezzins can be heard calling the Islamic faithful to prayer and the markets offer both pork and lamb.

Colourful mix of peoples The inhabitants of the town have come to an accommodation, even if some few still demand to be part of Malaysia. Apart from Moslems, Narathiwat is also home to countless Chinese. The Thai royal family has built a palace in Narathiwat that serves as a residence on their annual tours of southern Thailand.

History The southern provinces were added to the Thai kingdom only in the 18th century. This is one reason why many of the inhabitants feel they really belong to Malaysia. Cultural bonds that had taken centuries to develop were not torn asunder when the border was drawn

▶ VISITING NARATHIWAT

GETTING THERE

By car:
From Songkhla on Routes 408/43/42
(200km/124mi)

By bus:
From Pattani, Betong and Songkhla

By rail:
The nearest station is at Songkhla

By air:
From Bangkok via Air Asia
(once a day)

INFORMATION

Tourism Authority of Thailand
102/3 Moo 2
Narathiwat-Takbai Road
96000 Narathiwat
Tel. 0 73 / 52 2 4 13, 51 61 44,
52 24 11
Fax 52 24 12
tatnara@tat.or.th

WHERE TO STAY

▶ Mid-range
Royal Princess
Phichit Bamruang Road
Tel. and fax 0 73 / 51 50 41
rsvnctr@dusit.com
117 rooms, 2 restaurant, coffee shop,
bar, swimming pool.
The hotel opened in 1997 and is part
of the Dusit chain. Its rooms provide
every comfort and it has a very good
restaurant (specializing in seafood).

▶ Budget
Tanyong Hotel
16/1 Sopapisai Road
Tel. 0 73 / 51 14 77
Fax 51 18 34
84 rooms, restaurant, bar, swimming
pool.
Comfortable hotel in a quiet location.

between Thailand and Malaysia in 1786. The Malaysian government,
however, has little interesting in absorbing these lands. Younger Moslems in particular are inclined to sympathize with separatist movements and some are not averse to troublemaking. Visitors are unlikely to experience this, but are well advised to avoid large gatherings of people.

The town The onion-shaped domes of the mosques, the Malay-style houses
and the colourfully dressed populace give the town its character. The
markets and the lively fishing harbours are also interesting places to
visit.

Around Narathiwat

★ Scenery The intensively cultivated region around Narathiwat is an attractive
area for a round tour. The extensive coconut plantations play a major role in the local economy. Trained monkeys are often used to
pick the fruit. The coast has plenty of fine, sandy beaches with some

A small country shop

bungalow developments. About 25km/17mi north (on Route 42, turning off after 73km/45mi) there is a beautiful waterfall at **Nam Tok Bacho**.

Pattani   Even 80km/50mi north in Pattani most of the population is Moslem. Some of them seek secession from Thailand. In the 15th century an independent city state was established, ruled by the Moslem rajas. However, they were compelled to recognize the rulers of Srivijaya, then those of Sukhothai and Ayutthaya as their sovereigns. In the early 16th century, trade with Europe, India and China began to blossom. The Portuguese and Dutch established trading bases. In 1619 Dutch and English warships fought a battle in the harbour that was won by the Dutch. Ruins of the old raja palace are still in existence but the most magnificent building in the town now is the mosque with its twin domes. The Chinese temple dates from the late 18th century. Inland from Pattani is a mountainous landscape covered in jungle, but the coastal region is varied and fascinating. The people of Pattani are passionate fans of a form of bullfighting where animal is pitched against animal. The Thai fondness for betting provides the main attraction of these events – the actual fight is almost irrelevant.

✳ Nong Khai

C 4

Region: North-east Thailand   **Province:** Nong Khai
Altitude: 160m/100ft   **Population:** 60,000 approx.

What draws visitors to the town of Nong Khai is its proximity to the border with Laos and its capital city of Vientiane (formerly Viangchan). The view across the mighty Mekong is truly impressive. The river is the longest in South-East Asia and the eighth-longest in the world.

In 1994 a bridge 1174m/1384yd long, the »Friendship Bridge«, was opened as the first-ever bridge across the lower Mekong. It was a joint project between Thailand, Laos and Australia and is important not only as a traffic link but as a symbol for the economic reform intent of the Lao government. Thailand has been the major trading partner of Laos for many years. This bridge means there is now a through road connection all the way from Singapore to Peking.

Friendship Bridge

i Visas

- For trips into Laos, it is necessary to obtain a visa from the Lao embassy in Bangkok. A re-entry visa to get back into Thailand is also required.

Around Nong Khai

A few miles from the town, still on the Thai side of the Mekong, is Wat Kaek, where a great many statues are exhibited, although in a seemingly unplanned way. Below them is a colossal statue of a meditating Buddha with a gaily ornamented pointed headdress, along with a four-armed statue of the Indian god Ganesha riding on a rat.

✳
Wat Kaek

▶ VISITING NONG KHAI

GETTING THERE

By car:
From Udon Thani via Route 2 (53km/33mi)

By rail:
Terminus of the line from Bangkok to north-east Thailand

By air:
The nearest airport is at Udon Thani (50km/30mi with a connection by bus)

WHERE TO STAY

▶ **Budget**
Pantawee Hotel
1049 Haisoke Road
Tel. and fax 0 42 / 41 15 68
www.pantawee.com
120 rooms, restaurant, coffee shop, bar, swimming pool.
The best accommodation in Nong Khai with large and comfortable rooms. The hotel can arrange excursions.

Pastry for spring rolls is dried on tall bamboo trellises near Nong Khai.

Animal figures some 20m/65ft in height and made of concrete represent a parody of human society. The complex was established in 1975 by a Lao who had been forced to flee his country.

Across the border to Laos Ferries to Laos can be found close to the station. The actual **border crossing point** for pedestrians is in the town centre. The crossing to Tha Deau in Laos takes just a few minutes.

★★ Vientiane The town of **Vientiane** is 24km/15mi away (the only way to get there is by taxi). Sights to see in Vientiane include **the royal palace, Wat Phra Kaeo** which has an interesting museum, the triumphal arch and **Wat That Luang** with its famous pagoda. The numerous markets in the town are also of interest.

★ Nonthaburi

E 3

Region: Central Thailand
Altitude: 18m/59ft

Province: Nonthaburi
Population: 40,000 (in the town)

The town of Nonthaburi is about 20km/12mi north of Bangkok on the banks of the Menam Chao Phraya. Dozens of waterways and picturesque klongs run through and around the town, sometimes in straight lines and sometimes on a meandering course to the great river. Much of the life of the town takes place on the water. Along the banks of the klongs, lined by lush vegetation and houses on stilts, there are several interesting temples.

What to See in Nonthaburi

The old city hall of Nonthaburi was built during the reign of King | **Old city hall**
Rama VI in European style and is decorated with beautifully carved
teak.

Wat Chaloem Phra Kiat, which lies on the opposite bank of the Me- | **Wat Chaloem**
nam from Nonthaburi and a little way upstream, can be reached ei- | **Phra Kiat**
ther by renting a boat in the town or by means of the regular ferry.
The wat was built in the early 19th
century and is enclosed by two
rings of high walls, the first crenel-
lated, the second marked by Chinese towers. The elegant proportions of the highly decorated main
temple and the chedi delight the
eye. Two other buildings are now
only to be seen as ruins.

! *Baedeker* TIP

By water

The nicest way to get to Nonthaburi is along the
Menam Chao Phraya from Bangkok (regular
boats from Oriental Pier).

Take the boat further then turn into Klong Bang Yai to the village of | ✳
Bang Yai, around which a number of klongs flow. A waterway going | **Bang Yai**
south leads to **Bang Kruai** and passes several interesting and prettily
located modern temples. Wat **Prang Luang**, on the right-hand bank
beyond Bang Yai, dates back to the Ayutthaya period. Its beautifully
shaped prang is in a good state of preservation.

Ko Kret is a tiny island in the middle of the Menam Chao Phraya, | **The island of**
accessible by boat from **Wat Sanam Nua**. The island is home to de- | **Ko Kret**
scendants of the Mon people, who work as potters. A fine surface
with a reddish-black shine and sophisticated design are typical of
their work. Worth seeing are **Wat Poramai Yikawat**, the main temple, and **Wat Chimplee**. Thais come to Ko Kret to sample dishes
unique to the island.

⏵ VISITING NONTHABURI

GETTING THERE

By car:
From Bangkok on Samsen Road,
which intersects with Songkhram
Road at Phibul, then following the
banks of the Menam Chao Phraya
(about 20km/12mi)

By bus:
Several buses a day from Bangkok
Southern Bus Terminal

WHERE TO STAY

▶ **Budget**
Golden Dragon Hotel
20/21 Ngam Wong Wan Road
Tel. 02 / 5 89 01 30
Fax 5 89 83 05
114 rooms, restaurant.
Simple but well-run hotel with good
service in the centre of Nonthaburi.

Wat Prasat   Wat Prasat, set a short distance from the right bank of the klong (built in 1700) is a further Ayutthaya-style temple The huge main temple has two pillared porches and is magnificently decorated with sculptures and carvings in the typical Nonthaburi style. Bold brush strokes, a characteristic of the early Bangkok period, lend the frescoes inside a very vivid appearance. The ruins of two more temples on the right bank as well as Wat Chalo at Bang Kruai all date from the late Ayutthaya period.

✔ **DON'T MISS**

■ A boat trip through the many klongs west of the Menam Chao Phraya, for example to Bang Bua Thong, is a truly exotic experience.

Around Nonthaburi

Pak Kret   Pak Kret is about 8km/5mi north of Nonthaburi near a loop in the Menam Chao Phraya. The fascinating boat trip from Nonthaburi to this old Mon settlement takes just 20 minutes. The region around Pak Kret and the village itself are still inhabited by descendants of the Mon, although they have largely been assimilated into Thai society nowadays. The pottery in Pak Kret has a long tradition. The items made in workshops all along the river for exhibition and sale are characterized by a consummate sense of form.

**✱
Wat Chim Phli**   The elegant Mon-style temple of Wat Chim Phli lies at the southern tip of Pak Kret island. Boats tie up right in front of it. Inside there is a lovely Buddha statue from the Ayutthaya period.

✱ Pathum Thani

Region: Central Thailand	**Province:** Pathum Thani
Altitude: 7m/23ft	**Population:** 14,000

The region around Pathum Thani, the provincial capital not far to the north of Bangkok, is typical of the southern part of the central plain, which is dominated by the delta of the Menam Chao Phraya. Countless klongs and tributaries of Thailand's most important river allow for intense cultivation of the land.

History   Pathum Thani is one of the settlements established by King Taksin (1768–1782) for Burmese Mon, who had emigrated from Burma and who still retain their original language today. The modern name, which means lotus town, was granted as a gesture of thanks by King Rama III, since he was always presented with garlands of lotus whenever he visited the town.

What to See in Pathum Thani

The town's major attraction is Wat Pai Lom, a temple on the far bank of the Menam Chao Phraya. A rented boat (5 minutes journey) ✶ **Wat Pai Lom**
or river taxi from Bangkok are the best ways to reach it. The wat is interesting not for its architecture, but because its grounds are home to thousands upon thousands of **openbill storks** (anastomus oscitans). Their numbers have increased ten-fold in recent years due to the protection they receive here. No weapons or hunting are allowed within the compounds of Thai temples. The Wat Pai Lom complex was probably established during the Ayutthaya period, i.e. long before the founding of Bangkok. The name means »bamboo temple«; possibly because the original temple was made of bamboo, or on account of the thick bamboo forest that once surrounded the temple site. Storks' favourite food is snails, which they can find in the nearby rice fields during the flood season. They leave the temple early in the morning in search of food then return in the afternoon. The trees in which they nest have entirely lost their leaves due to over-fertilization by bird

▶ PATHUM THANI

GETTING THERE

By car:
From Bangkok via Route 1

By bus:
From Bangkok Northern Bus Terminal

By rail:
Station on the line from Bangkok Hualampong towards the north

By boat:
The distance is much shorter by river along the Menam Chao Phraya. Boats leave regularly from the Oriental Pier.

Storks are normally monogamous birds, but the male storks here often have several »wives« that sometimes have to share the same nest.

droppings. The excess population of birds has also benefited the giant lizards. If a stork makes a mistake when building its nest, the eggs fall to the ground where they are quickly snapped up as a delicacy for reptiles. The breeding season in March is the most interesting time for stork-watching. Elevated hides have been built to allow visitors a close-up view of a kind that is very rare. Photographers will still need a telephoto lens, however, because the storks are frightened very easily.

✳ **Pattaya**

E 3

Region: South-east Thailand
Altitude: 3m/10ft

Province: Chonburi
Population: 300,000

Sun, sand and sea are the essential assets of this, the largest and perhaps the most popular seaside resort in South-East Asia. Its expansion is no longer confined to the bay, as the explosive growth of recent times has seen Pattaya extend far inland as well.

Tourist stronghold
Between the beach and the countless hotels runs a busy, 6km/4mi-long promenade. The area to south around Jomtien Beach is also highly tourist-oriented.

History
Pattaya was a sleepy little town for many years. A few visitors came from Bangkok, mainly at weekends, but it was the US troops stationed at the U Tapao Air Force Base near Sattahip during the Vietnam war who really discovered Pattaya. Suddenly, in the 1970s the small town grew rapidly to become a both a seaside metropolis and a mecca for sex tourists. The withdrawal of the US forces in the late 1970s left a gap that was primarily filled by European tour operators, especially those in Germany, Switzerland and Austria.

Now Pattaya faces major problems that have directly stemmed from mistakes made during the recent period of explosive growth. An extensive programme of action has been put in place to improve the somewhat dubious reputation of the town and to attract family tourism. The opening of a large sewage treatment facility in 1992 markedly improved the quality of the sea water and ensured that the water supply remains reliable even during the dry season.

! **_Baedeker_ TIP**

No place for seekers of peace and quiet
If you are planning a relaxed seaside holiday, the Royal Cliff Beach Resort or the newly built Sheraton Pattaya next door may be able to provide just that, but if these are out of your price range it may be better to head for a destination in southern Thailand like Hua Hin or Ko Samui.

Pattaya *Plan*

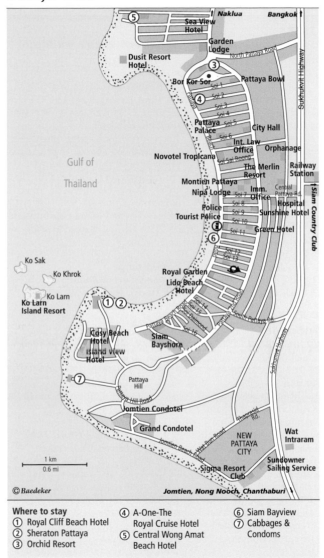

Where to stay
1. Royal Cliff Beach Hotel
2. Sheraton Pattaya
3. Orchid Resort
4. A-One-The Royal Cruise Hotel
5. Central Wong Amat Beach Hotel
6. Siam Bayview
7. Cabbages & Condoms

Night life

Pattaya only really comes to life after dark. During the day the centre is almost sleepy. The biggest attraction of the town, for better or worse, is its night life, unparalleled the world over and the very

▶ VISITING PATTAYA

GETTING THERE

By car:
From Bangkok on Route 34/3 (150km/93mi)

By rail:
From Bangkok Hualampong to Pattaya. There is a shuttle bus from the station into the town and to the various hotels.

By bus:
Plenty of buses every day from Bangkok Eastern Bus Terminal

INFORMATION

Tourism Authority of Thailand (TAT)
609 Moo 10, Pratamunk Road 20150
Banglamung, Chonburi
Tel. 0 38 / 42 89 90, 42 87 50, 42 76 67
Fax 42 91 13, tatchon@tat.or.th

WHERE TO STAY

▶ **Luxury/mid-range**
① *Royal Cliff Beach Resort*
353 Phra Tamnuk Road
Tel. 0 38 / 25 04 21, fax 25 05 11
www.royalcliff.com
Here are actually four hotels south of Pattaya in a single complex that has for many years been one of the prime places in town. The largest hotel is the Royal Cliff Beach (527 rooms). The Royal Cliff Terrace (88 rooms) is also comfortable, the Royal Cliff Grand (372 rooms) has magnificent views and the Royal Wing & Spa (85 suites) is luxurious and exclusive. All four hotels offer everything that could be desired and are not far from the bustle of Pattaya itself.

▶ **Luxury**
② *Sheraton Pattaya Resort*
437 Phra Tamnak Road
Tel. 0 38 / 25 98 88, fax 25 98 99
www.sheraton.com
156 rooms, 3 restaurants, coffee shop, 2 bars, swimming pool, fitness centre, spa, private beach. A hotel that opened in 2005, built on several levels upon a steep cliff. The architecture is ambitious, the rooms are modern in a timeless style and furnished with every comfort, and on occasion the hotel attracts the Thai aristocracy.

▶ **Mid-range**
③ *Amari Orchid Resort*
240 Moo 5, Pattaya-Naklua Road

Tel. 0 38 / 42 81 61, fax 42 81 65
176 rooms, 3 restaurants, 2 bars, swimming pool, tennis court (floodlit), spa. A hotel that has been particularly popular with families over many years and is situated in attractive gardens. Quiet in spite of its proximity to the centre of Pattaya.

④ *A-One The Royal Cruise Hotel*
499 North Pattaya Beach Road
Soi 2, Pattaya City
Tel. 0 38 / 42 48 74, fax 42 42 42
a-onehotel@a-onehotel.com
465 rooms (264 in the new wing), 3 restaurants, coffee shop, 2 bars, swimming pool, fitness centre, sauna, spa, Thai cooking courses. Originality of design right next to the main beach in Pattaya: the hotel was built in the shape of a boat. Comfortable rooms with every amenity. Suitable for families.

► Budget

⑤ *Central Wong Amat Beach Resort*

277-8 Moo 5 Naklua
Tel. 0 38 / 42 69 90-9, fax 42 85 99
www.centralhotelsresorts.com
137 rooms, 2 restaurants, bar, 2
swimming pools, fitness centre, tennis
courts, spa.
A little way outside Pattaya near the
neighbouring town of Naklua, but
excellent for families. Well-tended
gardens, rooms of an adequate
standard and attentive service.

⑥ *Siam Bay View Resort*

Pattaya Beach
Tel. 0 38 / 42 38 71, fax 42 38 79
www.siambayview.com
270 rooms, 3 restaurants, 2 bars,
swimming pool, tennis courts.
Right in the heart of Pattaya but
separated from the beach by a couple
of busy roads. Comfortable rooms at
a reasonable price.

⑦ *Cabbages & Condoms*

Hu Gwang Bay (am Asia-Hotel)
Tel. 0 38 / 25 05 56
Fax 25 00 34
www.cabbagesandcondoms.co.th
50 rooms, restaurant, bar, swimming
pool, private beach.
Affiliated to the near-legendary restaurant in Bangkok, this hotel is
situated near a beach a little way
outside Pattaya. Very suitable for
families.

SHOPPING

The heart of Pattaya is Beach Road,
also dubbed in recent times »Pattaya
Walking Street«. It stretches north
from the main beach and really comes
to life in the evenings. Everything that
money can buy is on offer here, with
bespoke tailors cheek by jowl and one
jeweller after another. Between the
shops there are countless restaurants
and bars. Second Road behind it has
also developed into a shopping centre
with any number of shops. It is worth
noting, however, that it is usually
cheaper to buy outside the main
shopping centres and that a bit of
haggling is always expected.

The most popular attraction in Pattaya is still the night life on Beach Road.

source of Pattaya's international fame. Countless bars, night clubs, discotheques and other places of amusement crowd the sides of both the main streets. The cultural and historical attractions are few and far between in Pattaya; a couple of internationally renowned drag shows are the local substitute for conventional cultural highlights.

What to See in Pattaya

View point One of the few daytime attractions other than the beach are two relatively new temple buildings that sit atop a couple of hills to the south of the town. One of them has a Chinese garden, the other a gigantic statue of Buddha. A major reason to visit them is for their magnificent views over Pattaya.

»Believe it or not« Another highly entertaining place to visit is the **cabinet of mysteries**, »Believe it or not«, a branch of America's Ripley chain of museums in South Beach Road. Laser Trek next door is a chance to fight with virtual weapons, whilst the Motion Master Moving Theatre offers a simulated flight through a three-dimensional world of film (opening times: 10am–12am daily; admission fee).

Underwater World The sea-water aquarium Underwater World is also a major attraction. More than 4,500 fish and other marine species can be seen on a tour that leads through underwater tunnels made of a special plexiglass. (Sukhumvit Road; opening times: 9am–6pm daily; admission fee).

Water sports All kinds of water sports are very popular in Pattaya, including surfing, diving, motor boating and even parasailing (which is rather expensive). Pattaya is not particularly exciting for divers, however, since the coral reefs have deteriorated over a long period. Nor are the diving ranges near the offshore islands particularly inspiring. But there is a tourist submarine to take guests further offshore to see the corals. There are also numerous boats that offer trips of different lengths, most leave from Bali Hai pier.

Practically every hotel has its own **tennis courts**, some of which are floodlit for use in the evenings. **Golf courses**, some of international standard, are situated at the Asia Pattaya Hotel, a little way outside of town at the Siam Country Club and in Sattahip. Two **go-kart tracks** are a boon to fans of motor sport.

! **Baedeker TIP**

Jeep tours

Admittedly Pattaya's beaches are inviting spots simply to take it easy, but it is still worth rising, for a day perhaps, from a lazy place in the sun to explore the villages further along the coast to the south. There are plenty of jeep hire companies all over Pattaya. Don't forget your swimwear, because the other beaches on the way might tempt you to spend a little more time in the sun after all.

Around Pattaya

If the dolce vita of a beach holiday is not enough, there are plenty of opportunities for excursions to places around Pattaya. The coral islands of **Ko Larn**, **Ko Lin** and **Ko Khrok** off the coast have their own attractive beaches and can be reached by boat from the main beach in Pattaya. Many boat owners run day trips to the islands.

Islands

»Thailand in miniature« might be the slogan of Mini Siam on Sukhumvit Road. As at Ancient City (in ► Samut Prakan) all of Thailand's major landmarks are on view here, reproduced on a 1:25 scale. It is pleasant to visit the park in the evening when the 80 exhibits are lit up (opening times: 7am–10pm daily; admission fee.).

Mini Siam

Close to the motorway heading for Bangkok is the orphanage set up by the Irish Redemptorist priest **Ray Brennan** (► Famous People), which is partly devoted to coping with the »side effects« of sex tourism. Visitors interested in seeing a side of life that lies behind the façade of »pleasure city« are welcome at any time if they make an appointment (tel. 0 38 / 71 66 28)

Pattaya orphanage

Market in Naklua

THE »OLD FLOOZY« GETS RESPECTABLE

»Once upon a time, there was a pretty little fishing village in the tropical paradise of Thailand's southern coast ...« This could be the beginning of the story of Pattaya. The tale could start another way, however. If you have come to Pattaya to experience Thailand, you are in the wrong place. This is a town full of contradictions.

Pattaya was »discovered«, so to speak, by American soldiers stationed a few miles to the south at the air base of U Tapao. From here during the 1960s, B52 bombers would set out on missions to drop their deadly cargo over southern Vietnam. Places like Pattaya were known as »R and R« centres, places of rest and recreation. They kept coming even when the war was over, and when an aircraft carrier was docked in the bay with a dozen grey frigates in tow, then it was time for the »high life« on Beach Road. »Welcome to the US Navy« read the neon signs welcoming not only the sailors but also their well-filled purses.

In the wake of the marines, other tourists flooded in, Americans, western Europeans and many more ...
Along Pattaya Beach Road, one hotel after another shot up and restaurants offering menus from all the leading countries opened their doors. The dubious reputation of the town, however, undoubtedly stems from the innumerable bars of a seedier quality, with scantily dressed girls and expensive Singha beer. Pattaya attracted people whose lives were, to a greater or lesser extent, scuppered, who came to indulge immoral penchants in louche establishments. Many of these reckoned without the Thai

police and found themselves deported forthwith to their own countries, where they were received in handcuffs.

Light on the Horizon

All the time there were decent, and even outstanding, individuals whose names became inseparable with the history of Pattaya and thus merit mention here.

Among them were the Dutch traveller Dolf Riks, who opened a restaurant offering possibly the finest Indonesian rice dishes west of Sumatra. Here, a »community« would meet every evening, not just to enjoy a magnificent meal but to air its discontent about the annually increasing tourist horde. Another individual who made his mark on Pattaya was a Swiss citizen named Alois X. Fassbind, who arrived in the town to become general manager of the Royal Cliff Hotel, which he transformed into one of the finest beach hotels in South-East Asia. Also, since it did no harm to distance his establishment from the Gomorrah that was Pattaya, he carefully changed the advertising for the hotel, so that it merely claimed to be »near Pattaya«.

The third key figure was Father Brennan (see Famous People), the founder of the local orphanage, where many of the »unintended by-products« of fleeting holiday liaisons ended up being cared for by the Irish Redemptorist priest. Until well into the 1980s, the Thai tourist industry continued to make money from the dubious image of Pattaya, but then a change of heart began. Instead of »the old floozy«, as some almost lovingly called the resort, it was to become a respectable place of recreation. There was to be an official crack-down on prostitution, and some of the most disreputable joints were closed by the authorities. Nevertheless, a certain ambivalence still remains about the place. Some even say Pattya is no different to any resort on the Mediterranean coast, even if it actually lies at 12° 55' N, 100° 52' E...

Nong Nooch Village

Nong Nooch village (15km/9mi south-east of Pattaya and pronounced »nung noot«) is not unlike the Rose Garden in Nakhon Pathom. It has 400 hectares/1000 acres of parkland and illustrates the lives of country folk. There are Thai boxing matches, cock fighting and an elephant show. The gorgeous orchid garden is not just for plant lovers, and the zoo with its typical local animals is not just for children.

Wat Tansangwararam

Just before the road to Nong Nooch turns off Route 3, another road leads to Wat Tansangwararam, which was built in 1988. Along the way there is a lake to the right with pretty Chinese pavilions and other buildings. The approach to the hill-top temple of Wat Tansangwararam consists of 299 steps flanked by naga serpents. Where the site levels out into well-tended parkland, there are several buildings including a round viharn and a wing of monks' quarters.

Elephant corral

About 6km/4mi from Pattaya is an elephant corral that demonstrates work with elephants on a daily basis. The tours are in English. After the programme of events, it is possible to ride the elephants. Another elephant corral lies 5km/3mi from Sukhumvit Road near the Reo Ranch.

Pattaya Park

About 8km/5mi from Pattaya (take Cliff Road southwards and follow the signs) is the Pattaya Park leisure centre with large pools and **four giant water-chutes**. There are restaurants as well as a holiday village and a hotel.

Pattaya Park Tower

One of the landmarks of Pattaya is the 250m/820ft-high Pattaya Park Tower with two revolving restaurants on the 52nd and 53rd floors, both with fabulous views of Pattaya and the coastal landscape.

Market in Naklua

In the morning when the fish market takes place or in the evening when the night market begins, it is worth travelling the 12km/7mi to Naklua. There are several good fish restaurants around the market. The short journey is probably best made with a pick-up taxi from Pattaya.

Sanctuary of the Truth

The Sanctuary of the Truth has been in existence near Naklua since 2004. The wooden building took more than 20 years to build. Its centre point is a 100m/330ft-tall pavilion decorated with both religious and secular images (opening times: 8am–5pm daily, admission fee).

Excursions

Many places of interest are in easy reach of Pattaya, in particular ► Chanthaburi, ► Trat (to the south) and ► Chonburi (on the way to Bangkok). As an alternative, take a trip to the islands of ► Ko Samet, Ko Sichang (near ► Chonburi,) and ► Ko Chang. Many trips to ► Bangkok are also on offer in Pattaya.

✶ ✶ Phang Nga

G 2

Region: Southern Thailand
Altitude: 6m/20ft

Province: Phang Nga
Population: 11,000

The town of Phang Nga lies on the river of the same name, which flows down from 1000m/3300ft-high mountains. The landscape along the Andaman Sea is full of surprises: white mountain tops rise out of the intense green of the jungle, picturesque villages cling to the slopes and a boat trip through the bays between Phang Nga and Ao Luk is one of the greatest experiences of nature that can be had.

From the lower elevation of the Chinese quarter, where there are still many older houses, the surrounding cliffs seem even steeper. They form sharp silhouettes against the sky.

Chinatown

Around Phang Nga

Though the town of Phang Nga itself offers little to see, the surrounding limestone mountains are peppered with caves, the resting places of countless bats, some containing fabulous stalactites and stalagmites. One of the best-known caves is Tham Reussi, the »hermit's cave«, which is close to the town near the custom house. It is a laby-

✶ ✶ Tham Reussi Cave

An unforgettable encounter with nature on a boat trip around Phang Nga Bay

▶ VISITING PHANG NGA

GETTING THERE

By car:
From Krabi or Phuket on Route 4 (both 85km/53mi), from Surat Thani on Routes 401/4040/4 (195km/121mi). Route 4 from Phang Nga leads through fantastic jungle scenery.

By rail:
Nearest station Surat Thani

By bus:
From Bangkok Southern Bus Terminal

By air:
Nearest airports at Phuket and Surat Thani, several flights a day from Bangkok

WHERE TO STAY

▶ Budget
Phang-Nga Inn
2/2 Soi Lohakit, tel. 0 76 / 41 19 63
phang-ngainn@png.co.th
42 rooms, restaurant
Small and well-kept guest house with tastefully furnished rooms.

---

rinth of curiously shaped caves filled with stalactites and stalagmites. One stalagmite resembles the shape of a man, so that the local populace have associated it with a long-dead but miracle-working hermit. It is highly revered and offerings including little gold plates are made to it every day. Around the entrance to the cave a small park has been laid out with ponds.

Wat Tham Pong Chang
From here a tunnel leads about 500m/1640ft to the shrine of Wat Tham Pong Chang (»temple cave in the elephant's belly«), deep inside Khao Chang mountain, the »mountain of the elephant« (named because of its shape). Inside it there are three statues of holy elephants.

Tham Suwan Kutta
An avenue lined with palms indicates the entrance to the cave temple of Tham Suwan Kutta (13km/8mi from Phang Nga on Route 4 towards Khok Kloi, follow the signs). The temple has a number of different Buddha statues. The cave system behind the temple cavern has several beautiful dripstone formations. 17km/11mi further on is the pretty village of Ban Koke Loi at the foot of the mountains. From here, a bridge leads to the island of ▶Phuket.

Ta Kuapa
About 75km/47mi north of Koke Loi (120km/75mi from Phang Nga) the town of Ta Kuapa lies on the Andaman Sea. There are many attractive, sandy beaches in its vicinity. However, the tsunami

The limestone Ko Tapu outcrop that towers upwards from the bay of →
Phang Nga featured in a James Bond film and has been called the
»James Bond rock« ever since.

of 26 December 2004 caused huge damage, most of which was put right in an amazingly short time. Ta Kuapa itself was a stop for Indian traders in the 1st century BC. They either travelled further down the coasts of the Malayan peninsula or set out from here towards Cambodia and China. Three Pallava images (9th century BC), found in the region of Ta Kuapa are now on view in the national museum at ► Nakhon Si Thammarat. The remains of an ancient settlement have also been discovered. From Ta Kuapa Route 401 leads through a valley towards ► Surat Thani on the Gulf of Thailand.

Khao Sok National Park

About 4km/2.5mi inland from Ta Kuapa by a milestone marked 145.5 km, a turning leads to a fantastic landscape around the mountain of Khao Sok. The mountain forms the centre point for the 646 sq km/259 sq mi region of Khao Sok National Park, which is under special protection as the remnants of tropical rainforest still exist here. Unfortunately the forest is by no means the kind of rainforest that has evolved over millennia, being exclusively secondary forestation. Nevertheless, this too is several centuries old and gives a good impression of the original nature of the rainforest. The national park provides a refuge for monitor lizards, snakes, birds, bears and elephants, and there is a good chance of seeing some of these animals. The landscape is rich in caves and grottoes, with several impressive waterfalls. The most distinctive of them is **Nam Tok Sip-et-Chan** (waterfall of the eleven elephants), where the water cascades down eleven drops. It is possible to raft or canoe on the **Menam Sok**, the river that flows through the national park. There are a few rather spartan places to stay in the park; many of the owners offer trekking tours lasting one or more days. At the park visitor centre an informative brochure is available that maps and describes the clearly waymarked trails.

Than Bok Koroni Nature Park

The entrance to the Than Bok Koroni Nature Park, one of the finest in Thailand, is near Ao Luk (42km/26mi east of Phang Nga). Magnificent plants, tall rock cliffs and a river that plunges into the ground and re-emerges magically amid the rocks are the remarkable features of the park. The bay of Ao Luk with its steep, towering cliffs is a fantastic backdrop.

Phang Nga Bay

Boat trips around the bay of Phang Nga start from a jetty on the river Klong Khao Thalu (5km/3mi on Route 4 towards Phuket and turn left at the sign). The trip first weaves through mangrove forests before it reaches the beautiful bay of Phang Nga after about half an hour. There the boats head for the rocky cave of Khao Khien with its famous cave paintings. They depict crocodiles, fish, dolphins and other marine creatures surrounding a man, a vividly depicted hunter. The colours are a brownish red, ochre and black. The passage under the Tam Lod arch, with stalactites that hang down all the way into the water, is unforgettable.

Panyi, home to Moslem »sea gypsies«

At the mouth of the Phang Nga off the rocky island of Ko Panyi lies the **Moslem village** of Panyi, a settlement of houses built on stilts with about 1400 inhabitants, who mostly live from tourism nowadays. The white-and-green mosque is conspicuous from some distance away. There are several restaurants and plenty of shops to welcome visitors. The boat travels through spectacular scenery, as densely overgrown rocky outcrops in the most fantastic shapes, the impressive result of weathering by ocean and weather over the course of centuries, rise steeply out of the sea. Many of them have caves, others their own tiny beaches with crystal-clear water. The most tempting places to swim are **Ko Mak**, **Ko Chong Lat** and **Ko Klui**

✦ ✦
Ko Panyi

One remarkable attraction is the bay of Khao Ping, which was seen in the James Bond film, *The Man With The Golden Gun*. Many of the film's location shoots were made here and after it was released, the limestone rock of Ko Tapu that rises almost vertically out of the middle of the bay was popularly named the »James Bond rock«. The best view of the rock and the surrounding bay is from the narrow path that leads steeply up from the right of the beach where the boat lands. On the beach itself souvenirs are offered for sale and there are several refreshment stalls.

✶ ✶
Khao Ping Gun
◀ James Bond rock

✳ **Phattalung**

Region: Southern Thailand   **Province:** Phattalung
Altitude: 32m/105ft   **Population:** 42,000

Phattalung lies amid typical south Thai scenery at the southern tip of the Tenasserim range and is separated from the Gulf of Thailand by a large fresh-water lake that is gradually drying out. Visitors will experience an impressive landscape of thick jungle and steep rocky cliffs populated by a variety of animals and plants. Some temples in the area are fine examples of Thai architecture. The inhabitants of Phattalung are mainly Moslem and of mixed race through inter-breeding between Thais and Malaysians.

✳ **Wat Khuha Suwan**
Via Route 4018 northwards towards Khuan Khanum ▶

Wat Khuha Suwan at the foot of a steep, conical outcrop is one of the prettiest temples in Phattalung. The beautifully decorated gables and the ornamentation in the viharn are especially fine. Behind the wat, a stairway leads to a grotto. Enough daylight enters the large rocky cavern to illuminate the many statues of reclining and sitting Buddhas, some covered in gold. A bodhi tree towers above them, its leaves made of copper. The small cave was once the home of a hermit who left many of the statues behind when he died. From a chedi up on the rocks there is a marvellous view of the town and the lake of Thale Luang.

✳ **Wat Wang**

About 8km/5mi east of the town is Wat Wang, the palace temple. The elegant chedi has some splendidly preserved frescoes from the late 18th century (early Bangkok period).

Ban Lam Pam

Another 7km/4mi east lies the fishing village of Ban Lam Pam close to the banks of Lake Songkhla, of which the northern part is called Thale Luang. A boat ride lasting some 15 minutes leads out to the **Tham Malai cave**, situated between two distinctive rocks on the plain of Phattalung. The rocks are popularly known as the »mountain of the pierced heart« (the vertically rising rock has a deep hole in it) and the »mountain of the severed head«. Legend has it that they are the petrified remains of two women who fought each other out of jealousy. A small shrine stands on the hill at the entrance to the dripstone cave.

✳ **Thale Noi National Park**

34km/21mi north-east of Phattalung is the Thale Noi National Park. This swamp and jungle environment has been left in its natural state. Its flooded fields are home to 220 species of birds. Between January and March migratory birds, such as white ibis, storks, cormorants and grey herons can also be seen. Bird-watching is mainly done from boats here. No admission fee to the park.

30km/19mi south of Phattalung it is possible to bathe in the **hot springs** of Khao Chai Son which reach a temperature of 52°C. Bathing facilities with scoop showers and Thai saunas are among the delights.

About 55km/34mi west of Phattalung lies the provincial capital of **Trang** on the river of the same name, just 20km/12mi from the Indian Ocean. Extensive rubber plantations cover the gently undulating landscape and are the basis of the town's wealth. Trang is inhabited by the Chinese and Malays who give southern Thailand its typical colour. A large park with pretty lotus ponds and towering trees and palms is situated off Phattalung Road. 3km/2mi to the north there is the Chinese temple of Kwan Tee Hun with its colourful and imaginative roof decoration.

Child of mixed Thai-Malay stock

A further 10km/6mi along Route 4 a road branches off to the cave temple of Khao Pina, where it is possible to see Thai-Chinese traditional art and some handsome stalactites and stalagmites. **Khao Pina**

▶ VISITING PHATTALUNG

GETTING THERE

By car:
From Nakhon Si Thammarat on Route 401 to Ron Phibun, then Route 41 (about 120km/75mi). From Songkhla on Route 407 to Hat Yai, then Routes 43/4 (140km/460mi).

By rail:
Station on the Bangkok – Malaysia line

By bus:
Buses run from all the places named above

WHERE TO STAY

▶ Budget
Lampam Resort
88 Mu 6
Tambon Lampam
Tel. 0 74 / 61 14 86
17 rooms, restaurant.
This small hotel is about 8km/5mi east of the town. In Phattalung itself there is nowhere to stay worthy of recommendation. The guests here sleep in lovely, air-conditioned bamboo bungalows and the restaurant provides outstanding Thai cuisine.

Beaches The Indian Ocean is fringed with sandy beaches. One of the best, reached via Routes 4046/4162 (about 40km/25mi), is the beach at **Pak Meng** where the sand is particularly fine. From here it is possible to visit the islands of Ko Ngai, Ko Muk, Ko Libong and ►Ko Lanta.

＊ Phayao

B 2

Region: Northern Thailand	**Province:** Phayao
Altitude: 67m/220ft	**Population:** 21,000

Phayao is in the far north of Thailand on the eastern bank of a picturesque lake, overlooked by striking mountains. The drive to the town passes through glorious scenery. Formerly the capital of a small sovereign kingdom contemporary with the Lan Na kingdom into which it was absorbed in 1338, Phayao is now a small and relatively insignificant town.

History The town was founded in the 11th century on the foundations of a much older settlement that was defended by walls and ditches and entered via eight gates. It may be that this town existed as early as the Bronze Age, but archaeological excavations have so far been unable to confirm this.

What to See in Phayao

Kwan Phayao Phayao is on the banks of the Kwan Phayao lake, which is so shallow that in the months of low rainfall its margins dry up. A modern temple and many small restaurants next to the lake are popular among the local inhabitants in the evenings and at weekends.

 VISITING PHAYAO

GETTING THERE

By car:
From Lampang (145km/90mi) or Chiang Rai (95km/ 59mi) on Route 1. An alternative road from Lampang is Route 1035 heading north as far as Wang Nua, then the new Route 1882 to the west. This is a longer journey but the wonderful scenery makes the detour rewarding.

By rail:
Nearest station Chiang Mai

By air:
Nearest airport Chiang Mai.

WHERE TO STAY
► Budget
Gateway Hotel
7/36 Pratu Klong 2 Road
Tel. 0 54 / 41 13 30, fax 41 05 19
The best hotel in Phayao: friendly staff and well furnished, but the rooms are still affordable.

Only a few sparse ruins remain of Wat Ratcha Santhan, a teak-built 12th-century temple. In 1988 this excellent example of Thai temple architecture collapsed in a storm. In its place is an almost unadorned building. Even the two cobras that once reared up either side of the entrance stairway have been reduced to rubble. Looking closer, however, it is possible to see the wooden beams of the old temple, which have been reused in the new viharn. Inside there is still a statue of Buddha in the Sukhothai style. The modern bot with its pretty carvings on the gables is also worth a look. Interestingly, there is an almost identical building in ► Chiang Mai called Wat Buakkhrok Luang.

Wat Ratcha Santhan

At the northern edge of the town lies Wat Si Kom Kam, with a viharn that was specially erected in recent times to house a giant 16m/52-ft statue of a standing Buddha. The carefully gilded carvings of the viharn façade are particularly notable.

✱ Wat Si Kom Kam

A visit to the Doi Luang National Park north-west of Phayao is worthwhile for the waterfall of **Pu Kaeng** alone. This is fed by what, at first glance, seems to be a quite unspectacular stream, but which then plunges down nine cascades over a distance of 1.3km/1400yd (although only after it has been raining, at which time it is also possible to swim in the basin). There are several picnic sites, since the national park has become a popular place to visit among the locals.

✱ Doi Luang National Park

✱ ✱ Phetchaburi

E 2

Region: Western Thailand
Altitude: 6m/20ft

Province: Phetchaburi
Population: 42,000

This provincial capital surrounded by impressive mountain chains is located near the place where the Phetchaburi river flows into the Gulf of Thailand. Khao Khlang mount, with King Mongkut's palace at its summit, dominates the skyline. The temples in the valley bear witness to a long history, the Chinese quarter to the fact that Phetchaburi was once a centre for overseas trade. Several lovely, quiet beaches are only a few miles away.

The »city of diamonds« was probably founded in the 8th century by Mon peoples, but there had already been an important trading centre here for commerce between Europe and China via India. In the 11th and 12th centuries, the Khmer took command of the city and established a religious centre here. Around 1350, Phetchaburi became part of the Ayutthaya kingdom. In 1610 it was briefly controlled by Japanese pirates, whose leader declared himself an inde-

History

pendent ruler of the district. This was not to the liking of the kings of Ayutthaya, who were open to outsiders and permitted numerous European traders to set up subsidiaries in the country, but this situation did not last. Various conflicts ensued and in 1688 King Petraja 1688 had the »farang« (foreigners) expelled from the country, which then remained closed for 130 years.

✷ ✷ Royal Palace of Phra Nakhon Khiri

🕐
Opening hours:
Tue–Sun

9am–4pm
Admission fee

Atop the 95m/312ft summit of Khao Khlang the royal palace of Phra Nakhon Khiri looks down over the town. King Mongkut (Rama IV; ▶Famous People) had the palace built in European neo-classical style in 1860. The architect Thuam Bunnak, who later served as deputy defence minister, had travelled in Europe and taken an interest in the architecture of the ruling classes there. The palace expresses, as no other building in Thailand, the cosmopolitan outlook and lifestyle of the Thai monarchs. Phra Nakhon Khiri was built on a hill with two summits that are connected by footpaths. From the road that runs to the north of the hill, the palace compound on the north-western summit can be reached via a stairway lined with nagas or by a funicular railway that runs as long as the palace is open. On the way are the remains of some forts and several buildings erected for the royal guard. The palace compound itself is open to the public if no member of the royal family happens to be staying there. Its broad terraces command an excellent view of Phetchaburi.

> ❗ **Baedeker TIP**
>
> **Beware of monkey bites**
> Dozens of monkeys live around the hill with the royal palace. Sometimes they can be quite aggressive. Keep your distance!

Phra Thinang Phetphum Phairot

The foundation stone for Phra Thinang Phetphum Phairot was laid in 1859. It is the largest building on the site and was built in pure neo-classical style. It originally served an audience chamber but was later converted into accommodation for visiting guests of state, for which it is still used following an extensive renovation. Points of interest inside include many fine pieces of furniture, such as a bed that belonged to King Chulalongkorn.

Phra Thinang Wichien Prasat

One particularly fine example of Thai religious architecture is Phra Thinang Wichien Prasat, a highly evocative building in spite of the simplicity of its design. On its roof four small but richly decorated towers surround a symbolic prang, while the base is enclosed by a balustrade that runs all the way around the building. Inside the building a seven-tiered canopy covers a statue, in front of which is a bust of King Mongkut. The bust was made by a French sculptor, who initially worked from a photograph. King Mongkut was not happy with the result, so he commissioned a bronze statue to be cast

Phra Nakhon Kiri *Phetchaburi*

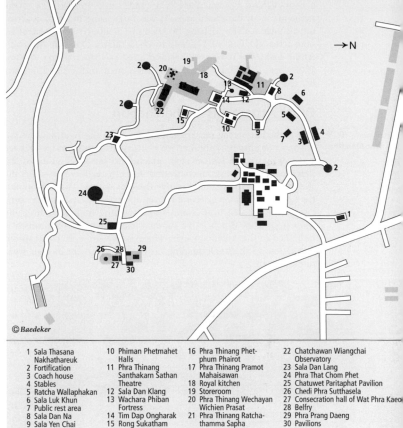

© Baedeker

1 Sala Thasana Nakhathareuk	10 Phiman Phetmahet Halls	16 Phra Thinang Phetphum Phairot	22 Chatchawan Wiangchai Observatory
2 Fortification	11 Phra Thinang Santhakarn Sathan Theatre	17 Phra Thinang Pramot Mahaisawan	23 Sala Dan Lang
3 Coach house		18 Royal kitchen	24 Phra That Chom Phet
4 Stables	12 Sala Dan Klang	19 Storeroom	25 Chatuwet Paritaphat Pavilion
5 Ratcha Wallaphakan	13 Wachara Phiban Fortress	20 Phra Thinang Wechayan Wichien Prasat	26 Chedi Phra Sutthasela
6 Sala Luk Khun	14 Tim Dap Ongharak	21 Phra Thinang Ratchathamma Sapha	27 Consecration hall of Wat Phra Kaeo
7 Public rest area	15 Rong Sukatham		28 Belfry
8 Sala Dan Na			29 Phra Prang Daeng
9 Sala Yen Chai			30 Pavilions

by a local artist. The latter, however, used the Frenchman's effort as his template. The bronze had not been completed when Mongkut died. Note, too, the building that houses the royal observatory (Chatchawan Wiangchai) with its glass roof and pretty ornaments as well as the three buildings that make up Phiman Phetmahet; the king made his religious devotions in the largest of them.

The walk from the north-western to the south-eastern summit takes twenty minutes. The most important building there, Wat Phra Kaeo, is startlingly reminiscent of its prototype in ▶Bangkok. The ordination hall (bot) with its gaudily decorated gables and beautifully carved doors formerly housed a crystal Buddha, which was trans-

Wat Phra Kaeo

ported back to Bangkok upon Mongkut's death and replaced here by a copy. Behind the hall there is a chedi some 9m/30ft tall by the name of Chedi Phra Sutthasela. It was built using material quarried on the island of Ko Sichang (▶Around Chonburi) and brought by boat across the Gulf of Thailand to Phetchaburi. Opposite this ordination hall stand three pavilions and a red sandstone prang. A 40m/130ft chedi that King Mongkut commissioned on the site of an earlier chedi occupies the main hill.

Other Attractions in Phetchaburi

Wat Mahathat

✳

Wat Mahathat on the market place dates from the Ayutthaya period but was not finished until the 19th century. Its dominant features are a tall prang in the Khmer style attached to the gatehouse and the four smaller prangs grouped around it. In the gallery that skirts the site there are many small, attractive Buddha statues. The large viharn has some fine stucco decoration on its exterior and inside some beautifully restored murals and various sitting Buddha statues, the most notable of which is the topmost statue on the altar, which is fashioned in the Ayutthaya style. There is also some excellent stucco decoration on the small building next to the viharn in its own separate courtyard.

Bas-relief at Wat Phra Song in Phetchaburi

▶ VISITING PHETCHABURI

GETTING THERE
By car:
From Bangkok on Route 4 (170km/106mi) or via Route 35

By bus:
From Bangkok Southern Bus Terminal

By rail:
Station on the line from Bangkok to Southern Thailand

INFORMATION
Tourism Authority of Thailand
500/51 Phetkasem Road
76120 Cha-Am, Phetchaburi

Tel. 0 32 / 47 10 05-6
Fax 47 15 02
tatphet@tat.or.th

WHERE TO STAY
▶ **Budget**
Rabieng Guesthouse & Restaurant
1 Chisa Road
Tel. 0 32 / 42 57 07, fax 41 06 95
17 rooms, restaurant.
The hotel occupies the pretty rooms of an old teak house. Since it is right alongside the road, it can be rather noisy in the evenings. The restaurant is recommended and the owners offer tours of Kaeng Krachan National Park.

Of the many interesting temples in Phetchaburi, Wat Yai Suwannaram to the east of the town centre is one of the loveliest. It dates from the 17th century and its oldest buildings exhibit exemplary Ayutthaya styling. The viharn has some outstanding murals, primarily featuring horizontal friezes of deities paying homage to Buddha. The fine quality of the colouring, the sureness of touch in delineation and the careful attention to detail are immediately apparent. The splendid coffered ceiling and a sitting Buddha statue are also worthy of mention. During the reign of King Chulalongkorn a gallery was added, adorned by sculpted lintels. Of the two wooden libraries, one dates from the time of the temple foundation, the other from the late 19th century. Note also the large sala with its jewelled ornamentation and bold proportions. Further north is the small but atmospheric **Wat Phra Bat Chai** with its splendid carved doors.

Wat Yai Suwannaram

Wat Ko Kaeo, on the eastern bank of the river in the south of the town, was built at the start of the 18th century and is famous for the outstanding murals on the walls of the bot. The vivid scenes from the life of Buddha are distinguished by sure brushwork and an unusual and remarkable triangular framing motif on which the most acute angle of the triangles points downwards. The spaces between these triangles form upward-pointing triangles that recall the shape of a chedi. Most of them include Jataka scenes (episodes from Buddha's 500 previous lives). The mural behind the altar for offerings shows Buddha's temptation by and victory over the Mara.

★
Wat Ko Kaeo

Buddha statue in the Tham Khao Luang cave near Phetchaburi

Around Phetchaburi

✱
Tham Khao
Luang Cave

Of the many caves and underground systems in the vicinity, the most famous is the Tham Khao Luang cave, which is also a Buddhist shrine. Follow Route 4 westward then take a right turn onto Route 3173 (9km/6mi). The cave system itself comprises caverns of differing height and breadth. Various Buddha statues have been placed near the entrance. Some steep stairs lead down to one very large cavern with stalagmite formations and Buddha statues, where daylight filters through crevasses and holes in the ceiling to create a magical effect.

✱
Khao Yoi

Another 18km/11mi north along Route 4 leads to Khao Yoi, the »stalactite mountain« that features several caves, some of which are kept as shrines and are adorned with Buddha statues.

Reservoir

✱
Kaeng Krachan
National Park ▶

South of Phetchaburi a road branches off Route 4 near Tha Yang and passes through cotton fields and sugar cane plantations to the Kaeng Krachan reservoir with its spectacular mountainous backdrop. The reservoir supplies water for irrigating the fields below as well as drinking water for Phetchaburi. Stretching away to the south is one of the finest national parks in Thailand, which has not attracted large numbers of visitors as yet. An admission fee is payable to enter the park. Overnight accommodation is available in bungalows alongside the park administrative offices (ask at the entrance to the park). Kaeng Krachan is Thailand's largest national park, covering an area of almost 3000 sq km/1160 sq mi. The near-inaccessible region close to the Burmese frontier is covered with thick rainforest and home to wild elephants, tigers and Malay bears. Trekking tours or rafting excursions should only be undertaken with the assistance of a guide. The **waterfall of Pala U** is popular with locals.

✶ ✶ Phimai

D 4

Region: North-east Thailand
Altitude: 240m/787ft
Province: Nakhon Ratchasima
Population: 15,000

Phimai is situated amid the sparse vegetation of the Khorat plateau. It was founded by the Khmer. Its temple precinct is not only Thailand's largest but also one of the best preserved testaments to the art of the Khmer on Thai soil. . It came into existence only a few years after the magnificent temple of Angkor Wat, which is now situated in Cambodian territory. The temple of Phimai is much smaller than Angkor Wat, but is the equal of its model in terms of the artistic quality of its pure and exquisite Khmer style.

Discoveries of pottery fragments and jewellery have shown that Phimai was already settled in the Neolithic period, but it was not till the 11th century that the Khmer fortified the town and made it a key centre of their empire. Phimai, ► Buri Ram, Chaiyaphum and ► Lampang all lie on the route that linked Angkor to the provinces. The distance from Phimai to Angkor was about 240km/150mi. Phimai must have also been a major religious centre at this time. In the 14th century when Ayutthaya's first ruler, King Rama Thibodi I (1350–1369), conquered Angkor, Phimai declined in importance and many its splendid buildings fell into decay. After the destruction of Ayutthaya by the Burmese in 1767 and the accompanying dissolution of the kingdom, Phimai initially emerged as the capital of an independent principality, but as early as 1768 King Taksin defeated the town's ruler Phiphit of Phimai and absorbed it into the new kingdom of Siam. The ruins of Phimai were painstakingly restored in the 1980s and opened to the public under the name of **Phimai Historical Park**.

History

 ! **Baedeker TIP**

Phimai boat race

Every year in the second week of November at the time of the Loy Krathong Festival, which is celebrated all over Thailand, an international boat race takes place on the Mun river alongside the ruins of Phimai, accompanied by a light-and-sound presentation.

● VISITING PHIMAI

GETTING THERE

By car:
From Nakhon Ratchasima via Route 2 as far as Talat Khae (44km/27mi) then right onto Route 206 (signposted for total journey of 56km/35mi)

By bus:
Buses run to Phimai from Bangkok North-Eastern Bus Terminal and from Nakhon Ratchasima

By rail:
Nearest station Nakhon Ratchasima

By air:
Nearest airport Nakhon Ratchasima (daily from Bangkok via Thai Airways)

WHERE TO STAY

▶ Budget
Phimai Hotel
305, Haruthairom Road
Tel. 0 44 / 47 13 06
20 rooms, restaurant.
Simple hotel but recommendable on account of its friendly staff and nice clean rooms.

The town   Modern Phimai occupies only a small part of the lands formerly defended by walls, dykes and moats. The original area was some 1030 x 565m/1130 x 620yd. Some traces remain of the 4m/13ft-high sandstone walls along with one of the pavilion-like gates, the south gate. This portal once welcomed the Khmer rulers and their entourage from Angkor. From here a street lined with shops led right to the temple compound. One parallel road to the right passes the hill of **Meru Boromathat**, where it is said that the cremation of King Boromathat took place, although the brick building in which the ceremony was conducted is now a ruin. A smaller hill that faces it was probably the site for the cremation of Boromathat's wife. Phimai was strategically located on an island between the Menam Mun and Khlong Chakrai, one of its tributaries. The two rivers encircled most of the town and a linking canal that no longer exists closed off the rest.

✳ ✳ Ruined City

⊙
Opening hours:
Daily 7.30am–6pm
Admission fee

The temple sanctuary of Phimai dates from the 11th and 12th centuries and was dedicated to Hindu gods as well as Buddha. However, the temple was built on the foundations of a much older sanctuary, the origins of which are unknown. The shrine and the town around it took their name from the Buddha Vimaya. Just a few yards to the left of the south gate, some remains of the **Khlang Ngoen** can be seen. This may have been a royal guest house or possibly a hospital for the populace. The pavilion was probably built at the time of King Jayavarman VII (about 1200). The well-preserved south gate in the second of the three perimeter walls gives access to the temple com-

TOUR ▶

pound. The outer courtyard was adorned with large ponds at all four corners, although nothing remains of these but the stone edges. They were created to symbolize the four holy rivers of India and were filled with rainwater that was poured over the lingam (the phallic symbol of Shiva) and other deities. Two buildings made of laterite and sandstone near the western gate were also built during King Jayavarman VII's reign and probably served as libraries or possibly as residences for the Khmer kings. To the right of the south gate are the remains of a terrace, upon which a wooden building is likely to have stood. Some bas-reliefs are placed there now, as their original location was unsafe. The four gatehouses in the gallery (12th century) are aligned to the points of the compass and laid out in the shape of a cross. They and the porticos stood on massive square pillars, of which parts remain. To the left of the inner courtyard, which covers an area of 86 x 64m/94 x 70yd, is the red sandstone prang of Hin Daeng. The building beyond it is thought to have been a Hindu shrine (although it may have been a treasury or library) and to the right stands the laterite-built Meru Boromathat prang. Here, an outstanding statue of King Jayavarman VII was discovered that is now displayed in the National Museum in Bangkok.

Main temple

This complex was erected by the 11th- and 12th-century kings Jayavarman VII and Dharaindravarman I. It is built of fine grey sandstone and is the finest example of Khmer architecture outside Angkor Wat, exquisitely proportioned and sparingly but artistically decorated. The main sanctuary is crowned by a handsome and spectacularly tiered prang and has stepped porticos on all four sides with beautifully sculpted superstructures and side doors. The southern portico is attached to a long building lit through door openings in the sides and at the main entrance through windows with stone balustrades. A row of lotus buds decorates the roof. The pyramid-shaped tower of the sanctuary, also topped by a lotus bud, is supported by garudas and sculpted with nagas, gods and demons. The artistic quality of the lintels and gables of the porch and prang is outstanding. They display scenes from Khmer history as well as images of Buddha and the holy figures of Mahayana Buddhism. Another area shows scenes from the Ramayana epic. Five-headed nagas border the gables on both sides while the sills of the base and the columns on both sides are decorated with bas-reliefs. The tower has false vaulting of protruding stones and once contained the most important Buddha statue in the temple. This figure and others were used by priests in ceremonies attended by the people of the city, at which the statues were sprinkled with rainwater from the four ponds of the outer courtyard. The opening for the water pipe and its metal base are still visible on the eastern side of the tower. In the outer courtyard close to the ruined northern entrance, remains of the perimeter wall for the temple of Wat Doem can be seen. This temple was also built on the foundations of an earlier shrine.

RUINED CITY OF PHIMAI

✱ ✱ Phimai clearly shows the influence of Kmer architecture on this part of the country. The buildings have been dated at about the 11th century, when this area still belonged to the Khmer kingdom. Phimai was conceived as a sister city of Angkor. The temple complexes from this time are still well-preserved and are being restored true to detail.

⊙ Hours:
daily 7.30am-6pm
Admission fee

① Dancing Vajrasattva
A beautifully formed Varjasattva can be seen in the pilaster of the southern entrance to the temple.

② Mandapa
The architectural historians call the main entry hall the Mandapa.

③ Prang
The characteristic blossom formed tower could have been the model for the architecture of Angkor Wat.

Ruins of Phimai

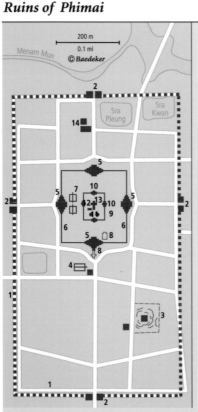

1 Outer perimeter wall
2 City gates, southern gate: Pratu Chai (victor's gate)
3 Meru Boromathat
4 Khlang Ngoen (treasury)
5 Portal buildings (gopuram)
6 Middle perimeter wall
7 Royal pavilions
8 Terraces
9 Inner perimeter wall (gallery)
10 Portals
11 Shrines
12 Hindu shrine (»library«)
13 Main shrine
14 Wat Doem

④ **Northern entry hall**
The lintel of the door is especially worth noting here, which is also decorated with dancing Varjasattva as well as the depiction of a gracefully dancing group of girls.

⑤ **Depiction of Buddha**
Under the Prang in the northern entry hall there is an especially beautiful reproduction of a Buddha protected by the Naga snakehead from the 13th century (Ill. foldout).

The inner surrounding wall is dominated by gate constructions.

The ruined city of Phimai is guarded by fabled creatures.

© Baedeker

The dancing Shiva and the steer Nandi can be seen at the southern gable of the Mandapa.

In a scene from the Ramayana on the northern gable Vishnu is depicted with a shell, lotus, discus and club.

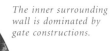

★★
National Museum of Phimai

A small building to the right of the bridge over the Menam Mun (when heading north-west out of the town) houses the National Museum of Phimai. Exhibits include wonderfully sculpted lintels from Khmer temples in the region and Buddhas, including one under the umbrella formed by a seven-headed naga. The coiled body of the snake forms the base. This particular depiction of the Enlightened One is typical of Khmer sculpture (opening times: Tue–Sun 9am–4.30pm, admission fee; no photographs).

★★
Banyan tree

Beyond the bridge, a right turn leads off towards a small reservoir. About 1km/1100yd further on there is a botanical curiosity, a giant banyan tree (ficus indiaca) with a leafy canopy that measures all of 85m/280ft in diameter. Although it has a multitude of roots that creep over the surface under the tree, it still needs concrete pillars for support. The shade of its leaves makes it a popular place for families to relax. The tree is situated on an island where a number of restaurants on the banks are a pleasant place to sit.

Around Phimai

Chaiyaphum

Take Route 2 northwards from Phimai then Route 202 north-west to Chaiyaphum (or Jayabhumi). The town now has a population of some 26,000, but in Khmer times it was a major waystation on the route from Angkor Wat to Si Thep, one of the other main cities of their empire. From here, it is possible to visit the following two important religious centres.

★★
Wat Prang Ku

The temple of Prang Ku, about 2km/1.5mi outside the town, was built in the reign of King Jayavarman VII (1181–1201). Its quite well-preserved sanctuary has a number of good sculptures on the gables and lintels. Inside there is a sitting Buddha statue in the Dvaravati style and another in the Ayutthaya style. There is also a standing Buddha in the same Ayutthaya style. A second but sadly ruined building retains one fine and well-preserved lintel with depictions from Hindu mythology.

★
The hill of Buddha

The »hill of Buddha« is about 30km/19mi from Chaiyaphum (Route 201 northwards for about 13km/8mi then turn left and drive another 17km/11mi). Seven Buddhas in the Dvaravati style have been carved into one of the many sandstone blocks on the hill. They attract many pilgrims every year, as does the 2m/6ft Buddha that sits on another of the blocks.

Prasat Phanom Wan

Follow the road from Phimai and a few kilometres before Khorat there will be a sign for Prasat Phanom Wan. It is not nearly as well preserved as Phimai, but for that quieter and without the usual tourist souvenir and food stands. It is dated to the 10th-11th century and might originally have been a Hindu temple.

✶ ✶ Phitsanulok

C 3

Region: Northern Thailand
Altitude: 50m/164ft

Province: Phitsanulok
Population: 84,000

Phitsanulok, the neighbour city of Sukhothai, is situated in the northern part of the central plain drained by the Menam Nan river. It is surrounded by rice fields. A fire destroyed practically all of the old city but it has now become a modern business centre and trade focus, and its former importance is just a memory.

From the bridge over the Nan river or the avenues that lead along the banks, it is possible to get a good idea of the bustling atmosphere on the river and surrounding the buildings that rise from its banks on stilts. A visit to Phitsanulok fits well into a mini-tour taking in the historic sites of ►Sukhothai, ►Si Satchanalai and ►Kamphaeng Phct.

Modern city on an ancient site

King Rama Thibodi of Ayutthaya (generally known by the name of U Thong) conquered Phitsanulok in 1362. It had already become an important town in the **Sukhothai kingdom** by this time. King Liu Thai was able to regain the city from U Thong by diplomatic means and for seven years it was his residence. As of 1438 the town was finally absorbed by Ayutthaya along with the rest of the Sukhothai kingdom, and the crown princes of Ayutthaya ruled there as viceroys.

History

▶ VISITING PHITSANULOK

GETTING THERE

By car:
From Bangkok on Routes 1/32/117 or Route 11 (380km/236mi). From Sukhothai on Route 12 (58km/36mi).

By bus:
Several times a day from Bangkok Northern Bus Terminal

By rail:
Station on the Bangkok – Chiang Mai line

By air:
Daily from Bangkok and Chiang Mai

INFORMATION

Tourism Authority of Thailand
209/7-8 Boromtrailokanat Road
Tel. 0 55 / 23 10 63, tatphlok@tat.or.th

WHERE TO STAY

► Mid-range
① *Topland Hotel & Convention Center*
68/33 Akathodsarod Road
Tel. 0 55 / 24 78 00, fax 24 78 15
www.toplandhotel.com
260 rooms, restaurant, coffee shop, beer garden, swimming pool. Though it looks like a typically dull concrete building from outside, inside it has very comfortable rooms and attentive service.

Phitsanulok *Plan*

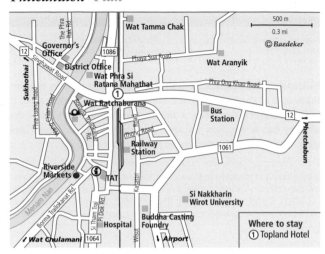

In 1563 the town fell to the Burmese. When the same invaders razed Ayutthaya itself in 1767, Phitsanulok briefly became the capital of a small independent state, it was absorbed back into King Taksin's new kingdom of Siam in 1770. A terrible fire in 1955 destroyed practically all of Phitsanulok. Although some temples have reopened, they have sadly been rebuilt in a rather faceless modern style.

What to See in Phitsanulok

★★
Wat Phra Si Ratana Mahathat

Tour ▶

The most important building in Phitsanulok is on the edge of the old town next to the Nan bridge. Wat Phra Si Ratana Mahathat is instantly recognizable by its 36m/120ft-high, Khmer-style prang with a gilded upper section built in 1482. The wat itself came into being at the end of the 15th century in the reign of King Boroma Trailokanat (1448–1488) and was a symbol of his dominance over the newly conquered region. It is likely, however, that its appearance has been radically altered from its original form by multiple restorations. The steep roof of the viharn with its colourfully glazed tiles (Bangkok period) has three steps. The coffered gable is decorated with gilded carvings. Slender pillars flank the portico and give the entire building a conspicuous lightness of appearance. The Buddha statues on both sides are outstanding example of the Sukhothai and Chiang Saen styles. The carved ebony doors with mother-of-pearl inlays date from 1756. Although the three aisles inside the viharn are lit only by narrow slits in the low side walls, the interior is one of the most beautiful sacred spaces in Thailand. The columns topped with lotus buds and the braced beams are decorated in dark blue, red and gold. The murals are more recent than the other work. The images to the right

Statue of Phra Buddha Jinarat – a masterpiece of the Sukhothai style

depict the enlightenment of Buddha while those to the left show him giving up his earthly wealth and turning to religion. The centre of attention is undoubtedly the statue Phra Buddha Jinarat (»the victorious king«), a masterpiece of the later Sukhothai style that was cast in bronze around 1350. It shows a seated Buddha making the gesture of calling to the earth in a finely chased aureole in front of a dark blue backdrop decorated with stylized golden flowers and a pair of figures that hover overhead. Several copies have been made of this statue; one commissioned by King Chulalongkorn is housed in Wat Bencha-ma Bo-bitr in Bangkok. Some of the other Buddha statues that surround the central figure are also of great beauty. It is also worth noting the lovingly carved teak pulpits, the larger of which is used by groups of monks for readings of Buddhist scripture in Pali, while the smaller one is used when they are read in Thai. A terrace from which the central prang rises adjoins the viharn. A stairway leads up to the relic chamber. The gallery that encircles the prang has some lovely Buddha statues in the Sukhothai, U Thong, Chiang Mai and Chiang Saen styles. The wood carvings are also very beautiful, as are some Chinese and Thai ceramics. The gallery is also connected to the bot. When exiting the temple com-

◀ Phra Buddha
Jinarat

? DID YOU KNOW ...?

■ When Phitsanulok was made a capital city and the viceroy made his entrance, legend has it that the Phra Buddha Jinarat statue wept tears of blood. This is one of the main reasons why the statue is so highly revered.

pound via the main exit, look out for a giant statue of Buddha in a standing position as well as two more modern Buddhas at the back.

✳
Wat Ratchaburana

Opposite Wat Mahathat, on the same bank of the Nan, the ruins of the old temple of Wat Ratchaburana have been used in the building of a new wat. All that remains of the old temple is a single impressive chedi. A pretty bell tower and the sanctuary itself complete the ensemble. The sanctuary has a carved wooden portico inlaid with coloured stones and some interesting frescoes with scenes from the Ramayana inside.

Buddha Image Factory

In the Buddha Image Factory on Wisutkasat Road it is possible to see the manufacturing process for statues of Buddha. The figures produced here are hand-made over the course of many weeks using many famous images of the Enlightened One as models. The most popular prototype is certainly the Phra Buddha Jinarat from Wat

⏲
Phra Si Ratana Mahathat (opening times: Mon– Sat 8am–5pm: please make appointments in advance).

Around Phitsanulok

✳
Wat Chulamani

5km/3mi south of Phitsanulok are the ruins of Wat Chulamani. The shrine with its conspicuously Khmer influence stands on an intricate three-tiered brick pedestal. Steps lead to the surviving main entrance. Other parts that remain are the side entrances with their lovely stucco decoration and a fine statue of Buddha. The small hall that has been added has obscured most of the original building. The wat was probably built during the Lopburi period and was restored early in the Ayutthaya period under King Boroma Trailokanat (1448–1488). About 15km/9mi east of Phitsanulok on Route 12, the ruins of a chedi can be seen on a hill. The view from there is spectacular. A little past the village of Wang Thong forestry officials have established a small park alongside some rapids on the Menam Kok. There are various waterfalls along the way or a short distance from the road. The most notable among them are the **Nam Tok Kaeng So Pa** falls (follow signposts about 52km/32mi from Phitsanulok).

Thung Saleng Luang National Park

Thung Saleng Luang National Park covers an area of 1280 sq km/500 sq mi some 65km/40mi to the east of Phitsanulok. Route 12 runs through a hilly landscape of mixed woodland to a mountainous massif, largely stripped of trees, that separates the Menam Nan plain from that of the Menam Pasak. The national park provides an environment for elephants, buffalo, wild boar, door and even a few tigers and panthers. It rises to a height of some 1500m/4920ft above sea level. Accommodation is available in the guest house at the entrance to the park and in some extremely comfortable bungalows. Northward on Route 12 there is a **development centre** for the inhabitants of some Meo villages that are scattered throughout the vicinity.

✴ Phrae

Region: Northern Thailand
Altitude: 163m/535 feet

Province: Phrae
Population: 25,000

The rich and bustling provincial capital of Phrae, one of Thailand's oldest settlements, is situated in the fertile valley of the Menam Yom. Since the Yom reservoir was built, agriculture has been the main economic focus of the region. It is mainly used for growing tobacco (which is dried in large brick ovens), sugar cane, maize and peanuts.

The many temples in the town are stylistically similar to those in Lamphun, since both Lamphun and Phrae were once part of the Hariphunchai kingdom. However, the Burmese and Laos have also left their mark on the town. Practically the entire length of the walls that once encircled Phrae has been either preserved or restored. Most of the major attractions lay within their bounds.

► Temples

The temples of Wat Chom Sawan, on the northern edge of the town and dating from the early 20th century, as well as **Wat Sa Bo Keo** (Nam Khue Road) have both been erected in the Burmese style, as the highly decorated altars and large, elegantly shaped chedis reveal. A Lao-style bot with tapered columns and a dainty library are the conspicuous features of **Wat Phra Bat Ming Muang Vora Vihara** (Charoen Muang Road).

Wat Chom Sawan

Wat Si Chum on Kham Saen Road encompasses a large area that includes three separate shrines, a lovely 16th-century chedi and a pretty library. The left-hand shrine houses a Buddha statue in the Lao style while the middle one also has a notable Buddha in the Sukhothai style.

✴ Wat Si Chum

▶ VISITING PHRAE

GETTING THERE

By car:
From Phitsanulok on Route 11 (180km/112mi), from Lampang on Routes 11/101 (85km/53mi) or from Nan on Route 101 (125km/78mi)

By rail:
Nearest station Den Chai (23km/14mi)

By air:
Daily from Bangkok and Chiang Mai

WHERE TO STAY

▶ Budget
Maeyom Palace Hotel
181/6 Yantarakitkosol Road
Tel. 0 54 / 52 10 28, fax 52 29 04
Not far from Wat Chom Sawan, this mid-range hotel offers reasonably priced rooms and a clean pool.

Wat Luang A slender Burmese-style chedi, a sitting Buddha and the carvings on the beams of the viharn are the sights at Wat Luang, alongside the city walls in the west of the town.

★ ★
Wat Phra Non Wat Phra Non at the end of Wichaira Cha Road is particularly worth visiting. It is named after a standing Buddha statue from the 18th century. The statue is kept in a building next to the viharn, which is itself worth seeing for its elegant proportions and beautifully ornamented gables.

Around Phrae

Wat Phra That Cho Mae The more modern Wat Phra That Cho Mae on a hill about 8km/5mi south of the town (Route1022 towards the airport) is also impressively decorated. It is dominated by a 34m/112 foot tall chedi clad with gilded copper plates and is famed for a sitting Buddha that mainly attracts young female pilgrims hoping to be blessed with large families.

Wat Phra Luang The beautiful Wat Phra Luang is situated in Sung Noen (a right turn off the main road in Sung Noen), 10km/6mi north of Phrae. The 12th-century chedi recalls the pyramid-shaped chedis of Lamphun, although it has fewer layers . The niches on all four sides house figures of Buddha. Covered stairways lead to each of the entrances to the library building, which have some fine sculptures. The octagonal bell tower is a further interesting feature. The viharn with its lovely carvings is of a later date.

★
Yom reservoir The beauty of the mountainous landscape can be fully appreciated on the journey to the Yom reservoir near Song (28km/17mi north of Phrae, Route 101 to Kong Kwang, then on the 103).

★ ★ Phuket

G / H 2

Region: Southern Thailand	**Province:** Phuket
Altitude: 2m/6ft	**Population:** 146,000 (whole island) 52,000 (town)

Phuket, the largest island of Thailand, is fringed with palms and rubber trees and famous for its long, white, sandy beaches and azure sea. The provincial capital that shares the name still exudes an old-fashioned charm with houses that exhibit both Chinese influence and occasionally that of Portuguese colonial times.

Climate Phuket has a remarkable climate. The rainy season starts earlier than on the other side of the gulf, for example. During the monsoons, the rain falls not constantly but once or twice a day in what are often very heavy showers. Some say that the sub-tropical character of the island is at its most enjoyable at precisely this time of year. Rain falls least often in the months from December to March (about five days of rain per month). The day-time temperatures are about 28–32°C all year round.

History

The Mon (Khmer) were probably the first people to live on Phuket. They came across the Andaman Sea from Pagan in what is now Myanmar and named the island »Iunsalan«. They established three settlements, Thalang, Kathu and Phuket. The Mon were later joined by Indonesian nomads going by the name of Chao Ley or Chao Nam (»land people« or »water people«). Their descendants are still found on Phuket today (where they are often called »sea gypsies«). King Ekatotsarot (1605–1610) was the first to allow Europeans to trade with the local populace. This quickly prompted the French, Portuguese and Dutch to open trading stations. The British discovered large deposits of tin on Phuket. The island was besieged by the Burmese in 1785. There followed two more such sieges, and when

Centre of the action: Bang La Road in Patang

the third siege in 1800 ended in the fall of the town, the Burmese razed it to the ground. Two sisters called Chan and Muk led a resistance movement that managed to repel an attack on their home town of Thalang. They confounded the invaders into thinking that Thalang was full of soldiers by having all the women dress in military uniforms. Between the airport and the town there is a bronze memorial to the two heroines called the Two Sisters' or Heroines' Monument (Route 402). In the early 19th century, waves of Chinese immigrants flooded to Phuket, attracted by its mineral wealth. They have intermingled with the native population, but Chinese heritage is still quite apparent in the town. About 50,000 of Phuket's inhabitants are »authentically« Chinese. After King Rama V had assumed Phuket into his realm, the island took its official place in the kingdom of Siam in 1933 and the town of Phuket was named the capital of the new province. The name Phuket derives from the language of Malaysia (»bhukit«) and roughly translates as »hilly island«. The province is now home to some 146,000 people. The capital and the surrounding island owed their prosperity to the systematic mining of the tin deposits. Nowadays, however, most of the tin mines have closed due to the dramatic fall in the price of the metal during the 1980s. They are often the only blot on what is otherwise an unspoiled landscape. Apart from tin, deposits of tungsten have also been found on the island. Its agricultural products include rubber and copra (sliced and dried pulp of coconut, used as the raw material for coconut oil).

Tourism Since planning permission was granted for building at Patong Beach in 1980, Phuket has been transformed from a remote island with deserted beaches into a tourist playground, with all the problems this entails. The main towns present the usual picture of high-rise hotels, restaurants catering to foreign tastes and pleasure palaces. The airport is the hub of services to southern Thailand, and its 2.9 million passengers a year make it the second-biggest international airport in the country. Prices have risen well beyond the means of local inhabitants, while investors from Bangkok and abroad have profited enormously from the boom. It has, nevertheless, been recognized that the tourist swarm needs to be limited and channelled. It remains to be seen, however, whether the ecologically responsible thinkers at the TAT, in the provincial government and in local businesses will succeed in gaining the upper hand.

Phuket Map

Where to eat
1. Khanasutra
2. Raja Thai Cuisine
3. Tokyo House

Where to stay
1. Banyan Tree
2. Le Royal Meridien Phuket Yacht Club
3. Club Andaman Beach Resort
4. Kamala Beach Hotel & Resort
5. The Old Phuket
6. Ban Rawai Bungalows
7. Dewaana Patong Resort

Sarasin Bridge
Mai Khao Beach
402
268 ▲
Nai Tang Nat. Park
Nai Yang Beach
Ko Pa Yu
▲450
Po Bay
Ko Reat
Ko Nakha Yai
Talang   ▲366
Khao Phra Thaeo
Ko Nakha Noi
Bang Thao Bay
Cape Son
Cape Yabu
4025
Surin Beach
2 Sisters Monument
Sapam Bay
Ko Rang Noi
Kamala Beach
Ko Rang Yai
Ko Maphrao Yai
Kathu
402
Cape Nga
Patong Beach
4029
4020
Phuket
Ko Siray
▲529
4022
4021
Makham Bay
Karon Beach
4023
Ko Poo
Kata Beach
4028
Ko Taphao Noi
Ko Taphao Yai
4024
Chalong Bay
Kata Noi Beach
Cape Phanwa
▲263
Ko Lon
Nai Harn Beach
Cape Ka
Rawai Beach
Ko Mai Thon
Cape Phromthep
Ko Bond
Ko Kaeo
5 km
3,1 mi
© Baedeker

► VISITING PHUKET

GETTING THERE

By car:

From Bangkok on Route 4 to Ban Koke Loi, then via Route 402 and over the Sarasin bridge to the island (860km/534mi). From Surat Thani via Routes 401/4 (290km/180mi). From Nakhon Si Thammarat on Routes 401/403/4 (340km/211mi).

By bus:

Air-conditioned buses from Bangkok Southern Bus Terminal (journey time 13 hours approx.)

By air:

Phuket has an international airport. Several scheduled and chartered flights land every day. From Bangkok the flight takes just about an hour.

INFORMATION

Tourism Authority of Thailand

73-75 Phuket Road, 83000 Phuket
Tel. 0 76 / 21 22 13, 21 10 36, 21 71 38
Fax 21 35 82, tatphket@tat.or.th

WHERE TO EAT

Rather than eat in hotel restaurants, try out one of the hundreds of alternatives along Patong Beach or at other beaches around the hotels. Phuket town also has some interesting restaurants of its own.

► Moderate

① *Khanasutra*

18–20 Takua Pa Road, Phuket town
Wonderful Indian restaurant with beautifully designed interior in the town of Phuket.

② *Raya Thai Cuisine*

48 Dibuk Mai Road, Phuket town
Tel. 0 76 / 21 81 55
Raya Thai is situated in a well-to-do

Chinese-Portuguese villa and serves good Thai meals.

③ *Tokyo House*

Phang-Nga Road, Phuket town
Tel. 0 76 / 25 67 35
Genuine sushi restaurant for homesick Japanese.

WHERE TO STAY & EAT

► Luxury

① *Banyan Tree Phuket*

33 Moo 4, Srisonthorn Road
Cherngtalay
Tel. 0 66 / 32 43 74, fax 32 43 75
www.banyantree.com
123 villas, 5 restaurants, 2 bars, spa and a touch of class. The guests here are probably in the finest hotel on Phuket and can no doubt afford it. Every villa has its own private swimming pool that cannot be seen from outside. Absolute discretion is assured here, even when no members of the royal family are currently staying.

② *Le Royal Meridien Phuket Yacht Club*

23/3 Moo 1, Vises Road, Rawai
Tel. 0 76 / 38 02 00, fax 38 02 80
www.phuketyachtclub.lemeridien.com
110 rooms, restaurants, bars, pool, spa, beach, water sports. Very pleasant hotel built into a hillside with comfortable rooms and large patios. Fabulous view of the ocean.

► Mid-range

③ *Club Andaman Beach Resort*

2 Hat Patong Beach Road
Tel. 0 76 / 34 05 30, fax 34 05 28
www.clubandaman.com
270 rooms, 3 restaurants, 2 bars, swimming pool, children's pool and much more
The hotel is centrally located on

Patong Beach but nevertheless has quiet rooms and is situated amid marvellous tropical gardens.

④ *Kamala Beach Hotel & Resort*
96/42-3 Moo 3, Kamala Beach, Kathu
Tel. 0 76 / 27 95 80-5, 27 95 78
Fax 27 95 79, 27 95 86
www.kamalabeach.com
200 rooms, restaurant, 2 bars, swimming pool, fitness centre.
A modern hotel with very comfortable rooms alongside Kamala Beach on the west of the island of Phuket. The beach is well suited to families.

⑤ *The Old Phuket*
192/36 Karon Road, Karon Beach
Tel. 0 76 / 39 63 53 56
Fax 39 63 57
www.theoldphuket.com
83 rooms, 2 restaurants, 2 bars, pools, fitness centre, sauna, spa.
The hotel building in the Sino-Portuguese style of the 19th century is a ten-minute walk from Karon Beach. The rooms are furnished with excellent taste and are highly comfortable at a very attractive price.

► Budget
⑥ *Ban Rawai Bungalows*
21/7-11 Vised Road, Ban Rawai
Tel. 0 76 / 38 15 71, fax 38 15 71
banrawai@email.de
11 bungalows, restaurant, bar, close to the beach.
Comfortable bungalows in nicely tended gardens.

⑦ *Devaana Patong Resort*
43/2 Raj U Thid 200 Pee Road
Patong Beach
Tel. 0 76 / 34 14 14-5, fax 34 17 06
www.devaanaphuket.com
53 rooms, 2 restaurants, coffee shop, 2 bars, spa, fitness centre.
Economically priced hotel not far from Phuket's tourist haunts. Nice, comfortable rooms.

SHOPPING

Wherever there are tourists, Thailand's businesspeople are not far behind. Patong Road is a magnet for shoppers and has a splendid selection of wares on offer. Many shops, from bespoke tailors to jewellers, are also in or close to the hotels.

Phuket also has some very high-quality accommodation such as the Evason Phuket Resort.

What to See in Phuket Town

The town
The town of Phuket sits on a picturesque bay on the south-east coast of the island. It was built in the mid-19th century to supersede the old town of Thalang that had been destroyed by the Burmese in 1800. The influence of Chinese immigrants can be seen in the two-storey houses with their tiled roofs and wood carvings. The arcades, which make it possible to walk and shop undisturbed by the weather, are also typical of the town. All around the town centre are houses with superb gardens that were built by rich Chinese and Malaysians who had made their fortunes in tin and rubber.

The Simon Cabaret in Patong is famous throughout the land.

The oldest and finest **Chinese temple** on Phuket is Put Yaw on Ranong Road. It attests to the influence of the Chinese population. The main temple is dedicated to Kuan Yin, the goddess of mercy.

Governor's residence
The old governor's residence close to the Put Yaw temple is now the headquarters of the provincial government. The building was erected in colonial style in the 1920s. The stucco ornamentation and the capitals atop the columns of the entrance gate are remarkable. The building was used as a location for the American Vietnam war film *The Killing Fields*, where it portrayed the palace of the Cambodian governor. The building opposite the residence, now the provincial court, was built in Portuguese style in 1916.

Markets
The lively market on Rasada Street (daily 5–11am) provides for the everyday needs of the people and is the place where the locals meet. There are more daily markets on Ranong Road and Ong Sim Phai Road.

Festivals on Phuket
The inhabitants of Phuket really know how to celebrate a festival. The **Songkhram festival** for the Thai new year is particularly noisy (and wet). Chinese inhabitants also celebrate their **New Year** (January/February) as well as the ten-day-long **vegetarian festival** (end of September/start of October) that offers the fascinating evening spectacle of hypnotized people walking barefoot over burning coals and yet suffering no injury (▶ Practicalities; Festivals, Holidays and Events).

Phuket Plan

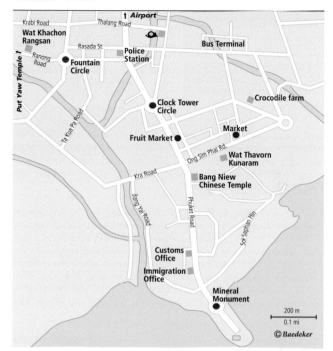

Airport

Krabi Road
Thalang Road
Wat Khachon Rangsan
Rasada St.
Ranong Road
Put Yaw Temple
Fountain Circle
Police Station
Bus Terminal
Ta Kua Pa Road
Clock Tower Circle
Crocodile farm
Market
Fruit Market
Ong Sim Phai Rd.
Wat Thavorn Kunaram
Kra Road
Bang Niew Chinese Temple
Bang Yai Road
Phuket Road
Soi Saphan Hin
Customs Office
Immigration Office
Mineral Monument

200 m
0.1 mi
© *Baedeker*

Around Phuket

The island of Phuket is world famous primarily for the quality of its beaches. Its snow-white sands lapped by blue, crystal-clear seas are not only a magnet for sunbathers but also for water-sports enthusiasts. The water quality still matches their expectations and it is hoped that a major programme for waste water disposal put in train by the provincial government will help to maintain the status quo. The prettiest beaches lie some way outside the town of Phuket. Transport connections are excellent, however. The best-known and thus the most popular beach is Patong Beach, which stretches along the opposite side of the island from the capital. The beaches on the southwest coast are much quieter and have largely been spared the tourist invasion. Most of the luxury hotels on Phuket are not around Patong Beach but further to the south. For instance the Le Meridien Phuket and Karon Villa hotels are at Karon Beach, which is only separated from the neighbouring Kata Beach by a rock promontory. **Nai Harn Beach** is even more exclusive. Here a skilled architect with an excellent feel for the unique landscape designed the Phuket Yacht Club

★ ★
Beaches

i **Red flags**

■ Particularly during the monsoon season (May to October), the beaches of Phuket can develop severe undertows. Red flags on the beach indicate that conditions are dangerous for swimming. Take the caution of the natives as a good example.

(now part of the Le Meridien hotel chain), which is skilfully built into the cliff face.

Heading eastwards to the most southerly point of the island, the road leads to **Rawai Beach**, formerly known only to insiders. At one time this was almost exclusively the realm of the sea gypsies, but now the tourists have discovered it and a suitable infrastructure has built up around them. This part of the island was very badly hit by the tsunami. For those really seeking to get away from it all, the beaches in the north-west are the places to go. The accommodation, however, is hardly on a par with that of the grand luxury hotels.

Phuket Aquarium

Opening hours:
8.30am–4pm daily
Guided tours of the research station by appointment:
tel. 39 11 26

On the road leading south from Phuket, there is a crossroads. At the end of Sakdidet Road, (Route 4023), 6km/4mi from the intersection, is Makham Bay (Ao Makham), where the Phuket Aquarium is situated. The aquarium reopened in 2005 after extensive renovation and expansion. It includes a marine biology institute where the lives and conditions facing marine fauna are being studied. Fish and other aquatic creatures are displayed in enormous tanks, but the major attraction is a glass tunnel that leads right through one of the giant aquaria.

Wat Chalong

Wat Chalong was built in pure Thai style. Situated 8km/5mi southwest of Phuket (Route 4021), it includes a gilded statue that commemorates Abbot Luang Pho Chaem, a miraculous healer who was based here in 1880. Wat Chalong attracts many Buddhist pilgrims every day. It was also once the home of another highly distinguished monk by the name of Luang Pho Chaung.

Coconut palms

9km/6mi further south, just before Rawai, is a remarkable botanical rarity, a coconut palm with a trunk split into four. The tree is more than 80 years old. The trunk first split when the tree had lived for twenty years and another twenty years later both trunks split into two again.

Ban Rawai

Vichit Road continues as far as the village of Rawai, which is populated by »sea gypsies«. They belong to the Moken people, whose origins can be found on the Andaman and Nicobar Islands. There are some Moken nomads who live entirely at sea, while others pursue a semi-nomadic lifestyle. They believe in spirits and have retained their own customs. All attempts by the Thai government to integrate them into mainstream society have so far failed. The men of the village mostly work as fishermen or captain their own boats. Ban Rawai was another village badly hit by the tsunami: the loss of 62 fishing boats

Setting sail for a journey by junk from Phuket

deprived many families of their livelihood. The village itself has a small fishing harbour and a beach fringed by coconut palms and pin oaks. Boats can be hired for trips to the outlying islands. Heading south from **Rawai Beach** (Hat Rawai) then back to the north along the west coast, the road passes the beaches of **Nai Harn**, **Kata Noi**, **Kata**, **Karon** and **Karon Noi** before reaching the main beach resort of **Patong Beach**.

A side road just before Kata Noi Beach leads south-west to the most southerly tip of the island and a viewpoint called Three Beaches View. As the name suggests, it offers a view of three of Phuket's loveliest beaches.

★★
Three Beaches View

The longest beach on Phuket was once one of the most beautiful. Patong Beach today is lined with multi-storey hotels and hundreds of shops, restaurants and bars. It can certainly no longer be described as quiet.

Patong Beach

✳
Nam Tok Kathu

Route 4029 leads north-west away from Patong Beach towards Kathu (5km/3mi). 3km/2mi further to the north is the waterfall Nam Tok Kathu, one of the loveliest sights on the island. Among the **beaches** scattered along the often craggy west coast (north of Patong) are Kamala, Surin (the largest mosque on Phuket is just 2km/1.5mi northeast of the beach and welcomes visitors outside prayer times) and Bang Thao Beach.

Hat Nai Yang National Park

The north-west strip of coast on the island is part of the Hat Nai Yang National Park (about 30km/19mi from Phuket town on the airport road, then follow the signposts). During their breeding season sea turtles come up to these beaches at night to lay their eggs.

Khao Phra Thaeo Game Reserve

The forestry and game reserve at Khao Phra Thaeo, encompassing a range of hills in the north-east of the island that rise to a height of 445m/1460 feet, is home to buffalo, boars, elephants and monkeys, as well many tropical birds. There are some lovely nature trails through the reserve (information from the TAT in Phuket).

✳ ✳
Boat trips

A trip by boat to the fabulous islands around Phuket is a must. The following islands are all worth a visit: Ko Maphrao, Ko Nakha Yai and Ko Nakha Noi (all off the east coast; the last-named includes an oyster farm), Ko Bond, Ko Kaeo, Ko Raja Noi and Ko Raja Yai (off the southern tip) and the tiny Poo Island (off the west coast near Kata-Beach). Day trips (by boat from Po Bay) also go out to ▶Phang Nga with the famous »James Bond rock«. For a trip to ▶Ko Phi Phi, it is worth planning for a two-day stay.

✳ ✳ Phu Kradung National Park

C 3

| **Region:** North-east Thailand | **Province:** Loei |
| **Altitude:** 1200–1300m/3940–4265ft | **Area::** 350 sq km/135 sq mi |

The national park of Phu Kradung was opened as early as 1925 and lies on a high plateau belonging to the Phetchabun mountain range. Its steep cliffs, fascinating flora and fauna that are untypical for the region and the pure, dry and usually very refreshing air are the distinctive features of the park.

Walks and rambling trails

A network of attractive trails criss-crosses the national park and leads to various waterfalls and viewpoints. Amid the verdant tropical greenery that is vaguely reminiscent of a European landscape, animals such as gibbons, red deer and fallow deer, wild boar and many kinds of butterflies and birds (including woodpeckers, peacocks and

The Phu Kradung National Park even has a few tigers. →

▶ VISITING PHU KRADUNG NATIONAL PARK

GETTING THERE

By car:
From Bangkok on Route 1/21/203 (520 km) as far as Loei. From Khon Khaen on Route 12 to Chum Phae, then on the 201 (209km/130mi) to Loei.
From Udon Thani on the 210/201 (143km/89mi) to Loei. From Loei Route 201 leads to the village of Ban Phu Kradung (75 km47mi) then it is another 7km/4mi to the park entrance.

By bus:
Services from Loei, Chum Phae and Udon Thani

By rail:
Nearest station Udon Thani

WHERE TO STAY

To the north-east of the park offices there is some simple accommodation in log cabins as well as some space for camping.

rare hornbills) make their home. Sometimes it is possible to see bears, panthers and even tigers.

The **ascent to the plateau**, usually starting from the village of Ban Si Than, is very steep in places and leads through jungle and bamboo forest punctuated by rocky outcrops. Steps have been cut and handrails erected to ensure safety. It takes four to five hours to reach the open pine groves of the plateau. From the rugged cliffs there is a magnificent view of the countryside. The azalea and rhododendron gardens on the plateau are especially lovely when they flower in March and April. Lots of waterfalls and ponds invite the fearless to take a cool dip.

i ### Dress up warm

■ The national park is in one of the coldest parts of Thailand. Temperatures on the elevated plateau can drop below freezing in the winter. It is best to avoid the park at weekends or holidays since it is a popular destination for trippers from Bangkok.

Around the National Park

Loei The small town of Loei lies 50km/30mi from the border with Laos, at the northern end of the Dong Phaya Yen mountain range that separates the Menam Chao Phraya and the Mekong. The town has developed into a modest economic focus for the region. The forests, some fertile agricultural land and extraction of copper, manganese and other ores have all contributed to its wealth. A lively and ever-changing night market takes place daily on Charoen Rat Road.
In February, Loei hosts Dok Fai Ban, the annual cotton festival, for one of the area's major products. It includes processions and the sale of cotton products.

45km/28mi outside Loei (in the direction of Udon Thani) is the elephant cave Tham Erawan. The cave was apparently a refuge for people in prehistoric times. Some holes and crevasses allow light to filter into the high vaulted caverns. The climb to the cave past a huge statue of Erawan is rather strenuous. 53km/33mi north of Loei the lovely village of Chiang Khan is beautifully situated on the banks of the Mekong, which forms the border with Laos here. It is possible to hire boats to navigate the rapids 4km/2.5mi to the south.

Tham Erawan

Prachinburi

D 3

Region: Eastern Thailand
Altitude: 9m/30ft

Province: Prachinburi
Population: 25,000

90km/56mi north-east of Bangkok is the town of Prachinburi, formerly a waystation on a trade route that led from India, though Burma and on to Cambodia and China. The town is particularly charming during the rainy season, when it is accessible only by boat along narrow canals. The Menam Bang Pakong river flows through the plain that is bordered to the north by a chain of mountains.

Prachinburi was first established by the Mon and retained its importance during the period of Khmer dominance. There are no particular attractions in the town itself but in the surrounding country, where the Menam Bang Pakong flows through a plain bordered by mountains to the north, there are some charming places to see.

Charming little town

Around Prachinburi

One of the most extensive archaeological sites in Thailand lies about 23km/14mi south-east of Prachinburi at Si Mahaphot. Countless finds have been made here, the remains of Hindu temples from the 6th and 7th centuries (Dvaravati period). Many of the discoveries are on display near the dam. The prime building material was **laterite**, which occurs in large quantities in the area. Buildings were then ornamented with stucco. Some of the best finds have been a standing Buddha, probably dating from the 8th century, and various statues of Vishnu that are probably from the 7th and 8th centuries. Only the excavations at Nakhon Pathom and Lopburi have produced comparable results to those of Si Mahaphot.

✶
Si Mahaphot

It is worth seeing the nearby dam, built in 1200 under King Jayavarman to provide a reliable water supply for the fertile countryside. Remains of laterite foundations that may have been part of a sluice can still be seen.

Dam

Wat Ton Po

✳

A few miles out of Prachinburi on Route 3070, the old temple of Wat Ton Po that is the goal of many a pilgrim. Its centre point is a fig tree with a large seated Buddha statue, surrounded by an octagonal colonnade and two terraces.

Muang Phra Rot

Before reaching the excavations of Muang Phra Rot the road passes a large pond with laterite edging stones that have been sculpted into animal forms in the Dvaravati style. The town that is the subject of the excavation was built by the Mon and was defended by two earthen banks with a moat between them. The fortifications can still be seen quite clearly. Where the centre once was, there is now a station for the treatment of leprosy. Close by it is possible to see remains of many Hindu shrines. The top of one roof in the shape of an octagonal dome is reminiscent of the Mamallapuramin temple in south-east India.

Wang Takrai Nature Park

✳

Take Route 33 north out of Prachinburi as far as Nakhon Nayok, then a right turn after another 6km/4mi. After a further 11km/7mi the turn-off leads to Wang Takrai Nature Park. This is one of the most beautiful reserves in Thailand. It covers an area of 80 hectares/ 200 acres and was set up by Prince Chumbot in 1955. A memorial to him is situated on the bank of the river. When the prince died in 1959, his wife carried on her husband's work and opened it to the public. She created a botanical garden with both native and imported flora and magnificent trees in a park dotted with lawns. There are bungalows that provide overnight accommodation.

Chao Pu Khun Dan

The road to the park passes the cliff temple of Chao Po Khun Dan, named after a close associate of King Naresuen (1590–1605). Beneath the rock wall there are several statues of Buddha. The gold leaf has been sponsored by inhabitants of the region in thanks to the spirit Chao Po Khun Dan who guards the mountains.

▶ **VISITING PRACHINBURI**

GETTING THERE

By car:
From Bangkok on Routes 1/305 to Nakhon Nayok, then Routes 33/319 (135km/84mi altogether).

By bus:
From Bangkok Northern Bus Terminal.

By rail:
Station on the line from Bangkok to Aranyaprathet (Cambodia).

WHERE TO STAY

▶ **Budget**
Wang Takrai
22/1 Mu 1, Nangrong Road
Nakhon Nayok
Tel. 0 37 / 31 22 75
14 rooms, restaurant.
Simple but nicely kept guest house. Good base for tours of the Wang Takrai nature reserve.

A road that strikes off to the left just before the park entrance leads 5km/3mi to the waterfall of Nam Tok Nang Rong, which plunges into the valley over three rocky cascades. A stone stairway leads up to the rocks, where the natural spectacle can be viewed. It is particularly impressive during the rainy season. There are many trails through the thick forest. Another waterfall can be accessed from Nakhon Nayok via Routes 3049/3050. The water cascades from rocks 70m/230ft high onto stone blocks in the valley below. There are several small restaurants in the vicinity of both the waterfalls mentioned here.

Nam Tok Nang Rong Waterfall

✶ Prachuap Khirikhan

F 2

Region: Western Thailand
Altitude: 3m/10ft
Province: Prachuap Khirikhan
Population: 27,000

The provincial capital of Prachuap Khirikhan, a jewel that remains largely undiscovered by tourists, is situated right on the Gulf of Thailand. The sweeping arc of coast with its fine sands is bordered to the north by a mountainous promontory and to the south by high rocky cliffs. The verdant mountains of the Tenasserim range, the backbone of the Malay peninsula, form an impressive backdrop.

There is not much to see in the town itself, although the fishing harbour is interesting early in the morning and the typical Thai market in the town centre is worth a visit.

Attractive small town

Close to Kap Prachuap three limestone islands rise from the sea. Their untouched beaches can be reached by boat from the harbour, as can the cave temple of Tham Khao Kham Kradai, which is situated inside a rocky outcrop to the north of the bay. It is greatly revered by the local people.

Islands

▶ VISITING PRACHUAP KHIRIKHAN

GETTING THERE

By car:
From Bangkok via Route 4 (280km/174mi)

By rail:
Station on the Bangkok Hualampong – Malaysia line (318km/198mi; journey time 5 hours approx.)

By bus:
From Bangkok Southern Bus Terminal (journey time 6 hours approx.)

WHERE TO STAY

The few guest houses in Prachuap Khirikhan are not particularly comfortable. Some rather better equipped hotels can be found in ▶Hua Hin.

Rocky islands in the beautiful bay at Kap Prachuap

Khao Chong Krachok The mountain of Khao Chong Krachok that looms over the town is split by a natural arch of rock through which the sky on the other side of the mountain can be seen (hence the name »mirror mountain«). The mountain is populated by hordes of wild monkeys, which have been known to attack people. From the summit there is a fantastic view of the town and the coastal region. There is also a small monastery with a Buddhist shrine at the top of a stairway with 398 steps.

Around Prachuap Khirikhan

Nam Tok Huai Yang In the jungle close to the Burmese border, 35km/22mi south of the town, the Huai Yang waterfall cascades 120m/394ft into the valley below. It is a spectacular sight, especially during the rainy season. Avoid visiting at weekends when it gets too busy.

The border region near Myanmar Not far away is the old caravan trail through the Maw Daung pass to Mergui in Myanmar (Burma), part of a route that leads to Moulmein. The mountain of **Maw Daung** is 1350m/4430ft high and lies beyond the border in Burma, making it inaccessible today. Particularly at night, a lot of smuggling goes on between Thailand and Myanmar. Further to the south, pineapple fields and palm groves give the plain its characteristic appearance, with the typically jagged peaks of the limestone mountains towering in the west.

Bang Saphan The small town of Bang Saphan, 77km/48mi south of Prachuap Khirikhan (Route 3169), has a 6km/4mi-long, gently curving beach (south of the town on Route 3374). It starts at a mountainous outcrop covered with thick vegetation called Khao Mae Ramphung. Close by is the charmingly sleepy island of **Ko Thalu**, which is best reached in a rented fishing boat.

Ranong

G 2

Region: Southern Thailand   **Province:** Ranong
Altitude: 3m/10ft   **Population:** 24,000

Ranong is the first Thai town on the Indian Ocean when approached from the north. Its houses are built in Chinese style with Portuguese influences. The nearby mountain jungles, a fascinating range of islands and its proximity to Myanmar all contribute to the town's unique charm.

Across the strait it is possible to see Victoria Point, the southernmost tip of the Burmese mainland. There is above average rainfall in Ranong between July and September.

View towards Myanmar

As in so many places in Thailand, it is worth visiting the fishing harbour of Ranong, particularly early in the morning when the boats are returning to port with their catch. It is also interesting to wander through the town along the main street. The two-storey houses have arcades on the ground floor. The old harbour at the mouth of the Ranong river has been replaced by a modern port that can accommodate ships with a greater draught.

The image of the town

Around Ranong

The boat trip to the island of Ko Pha Yam is full of interest. It passes by natural banks of shellfish, where Japanese experts have now helped to set up oyster farms (with visiting allowed). The route also leads past mangrove swamps where crocodiles live and countless mountainous islands decked with greenery.

Ko Pha Yam

 VISITING RANONG

GETTING THERE

By car:
From Bangkok on Route 4 (570km/354mi). From Surat Thani via Route 401 to Takua Pa, then on Route 4

By bus:
Several times a day from Surat Thani

By rail:
Nearest station at Chumphon (120km/75mi)

By air:
Nearest airport in Surat Thani

WHERE TO STAY
► **Mid-range**
Jansom Hot Spot Ranang Hotel
2/10 Phetkasem Road Tambon Bang Rin, Ranong 85000
Tel. 0 77 / 82 25 16, fax 82 1 8 21
220 rooms, restaurant, bar
Comfortable hotel amid marvellous scenery and to close to some hot springs where bathing is allowed.

Hot springs There are three hot springs about 3km/2mi from the Thanom Thara hotel. The most active of them spurts 500 litres/110 gallons of water at a temperature of 70°C every second. A small wat has been dedicated to the spirit of the spring. A rope bridge leads to a small garden with a mineral water basin where bathing is allowed.

Tin mines The road leading to the hot springs continues towards the village of **Hat Som Paen**, where a tin mine still produces the metal using traditional methods. The village temple Wat Hat Som Paen presents an idyllic picture with its sacred carp swimming in the surrounding ponds. Many of the former tin-producing strip mines that lie alongside the road to the south at Kapoe, Khuraburi or Takua Pa have now been closed down.

Nam Tok Bunyaban Drive 18km/11mi north of Ranong on Route 4 to see the waterfall of Nam Tok Bunyaban, and 31km/19mi further along the deep ocean channel of Menam Kraburi (also called Menam Pak Chan) to the fascinating cave of Tham Phra Kayang where there are many statues of Buddha.

Kraburi Another 13km/8mi from the cave, the town of Kraburi nestles among mountains. From there, Route 4 leads down through the narrowest part of the Malay peninsular, the Isthmus of Kra, towards Chumphon. At this point the distance between the Andaman Sea and the Gulf of Thailand is just 60km/37mi.

Mobile delicatessen

★ ★ Ratchaburi

E 2

Region: Western Thailand
Altitude: 5m/16ft

Province: Ratchaburi
Population: 82,000

Ratchaburi was once at the mouth of the Mae Klong on the Gulf of Thailand. In the course of time, however, the river has silted up so much that the coast is now 30km/19mi from the town. Ratchaburi is surrounded by extensive rice fields that extend to the sharp limestone peaks in the west.

From the time of the Dvaravati kingdom, in the Lopburi era, and in-to the periods of the Sukhothai and Ayutthaya empires, Ratchaburi was an important trading centre. Indeed, it remains so even in the present day. The area has been settled since the Bronze Age. Wat Ma-hathat in the town dates back to the Dvaravati era and at Ku Bua, some 12km/7mi away, one of Thailand's most important archaeological exca-vations has revealed another town dating back to the late Dvaravati peri-od. Ratchaburi was then under the dominion of the Khmer until Ram-khamhaeng, King of Sukhothai, ab-sorbed it into his own kingdom. A stone inscription that he himself carved in 1292 contains a report of this event. Ratchaburi along with the provinces of Suphanburi and Phetch-aburi was then inherited by the founder of the Ayutthaya empire, King Rama Thibodi I (U Thong). In 1768 King Taksin, the predecessor of the Chakri dynasty, drove out the Burmese occupiers and added the town to his new kingdom of Siam.

History

 **▶ RATCHABURI**

GETTING THERE

By car:
From Bangkok via Route 4 (100km/62mi); or alternatively on Route 35 to Pak Tho then back onto Route 4 (105km/65mi)

By bus:
Several services daily from Bangkok (Southern Bus Terminal)

By rail:
Station on the line from Bangkok to southern Thailand

What to See in Ratchaburi

Among the many temples in Ratchaburi from both ancient and modern times, Wat Si Ratana Mahathat is one of the most notable. It acquired most of its present appearance during the Lopburi period. Some older parts date from the 9th and 10th centuries, whilst some stucco ornamentation and murals were added in the Ayutthaya era. The large prang has some very fine stucco work and is flanked by two smaller prangs. The murals inside the central prang date from 1500 and are among the oldest known examples. They depict Bud-

★
Wat Si Ratana Mahathat

dha against a yellowish background in friezes arranged one on top of the other. The flowing lines and a certain natural quality of the movements stand out. The bot has several very good Buddha statues in the Dvaravati style.

✹ ✹ Floating market of Damnoen Saduak

Directions and tips

The best way to visit the floating market at Damnoen Saduak, 5km/ 3mi west of Ratchaburi, is to go by car or by bus from Bangkok Southern Bus Terminal. The jetty at Damnoen Saduak is the starting place for taxi boats and river buses. Travel agents in Bangkok offer tours but to enjoy the full experience of the market means getting there early, so that it is necessary to leave Bangkok around 5 o'clock in the morning. Organized bus tours do not depart until after 9 o'clock, which leaves hardly any opportunity to experience what really made the floating market famous.

Market for goods, channel of communication

Whereas little remains of Bangkok's own floating market, which once caused it to be dubbed »the Venice of the East«, Ratchaburi province has managed to retain its own example of the genre, with considerable assistance from the Thai tourist authorities. The market at Damnoen Saduak gives some idea of what life in Bangkok must once have been like. In order to cater for the flood of tourists, the market was moved in 1984 from its original location of Klong Ton Khem, where it had been since 1856, to the canal of Damnoen Saduak. Floating markets not only fulfilled the function of trading in essential goods, they also had an important social function as a meeting place for communication, as traders came from near and far. The canal system is confusing, with about 200 klongs linked by narrow channels. Brisk business takes place along the canals (sometimes goods are even bartered rather than bought and sold). Women row skilfully past growling motor boats, their rickety little skiffs brimming with all kinds of wares. The full spectrum of produce from Thailand's agricultural is on display: fruit and vegetables, meat and fish. The many souvenir sellers are less picturesque; their produce comprises the usual gewgaws sold all over the country, except that here they are that bit more expensive.

Around Ratchaburi

Boat trip to Samut Songkhram

To the south-east of the floating market a dense network of canals extends through the fertile vegetable-growing land. About 40km/ 25mi south-east of Ratchaburi at the mouth of the Mae Klong, which flows down from the Tenasserim mountains between Thailand and Myanmar, lies the town of Samut Songkhram. The swampy country west of the town is the site of huge salt pans, where brine is evaporated to make salt. A boat trip up the Mae Klong and through the canals is a journey through a charming landscape, part cultivated and

A symphony of colours: the beautifully displayed wares at the floating market

part primeval undergrowth. Some of the houses that line the banks at intervals are built in the traditional Thai style. The interesting temples in the vicinity, all accessible by boat, include the wats at **Ban Y San** (on a hill to the east of the village) and **Ampawa**, where Rama I, the founder of the Chakri dynasty was born.

In the limestone mountain of Khao Ngu north-west of Ratchaburi there are a number of cave shrines with sculptures from the early Dvaravati period, such as a bas-relief with a Buddha statue some 2.50m/8ft high.

Khao Ngu

In 1961 excavations at Ku Bua, 12km/7mi south-west of Ratchaburi, revealed the foundations of a town that possessed about 40 different temples. Its rectangular site covered an area of 49 sq km/19 sq mi. Water was provided by means of a canal that ran right through the middle of the town, which must have been a cultural centre during the Dvaravati era (8th-12th century AD). The foundations of the **viharn of Wat Klong** are clearly visible. The terracotta ornaments that adorn the brick buildings are such excellent depictions of figures that they are almost like ceramic friezes, including a royal figure with his slaves and soldiers. They are some of the finest relics of the Dvaravati culture. Some stone tablets and wheels of life from the site are now on display in the Bangkok National Museum.

✷ Excavations of Ku Bua

★ ★ Samut Prakan

E 3

Region: Eastern Thailand	**Province:** Samut Prakan (Paknam)
Altitude: 3m/10ft	**Population:** 63,000

The provincial capital of Samut Prakan, about 20km/12mi south of Bangkok on the east bank of the Menam Chao Phraya, not far from where it enters the Gulf of Thailand, is popular among the travel agents in Bangkok as a destination for day trips. It has an old town centre and a small harbour but no historic attractions.

★
Shell museum, marine museum

At the northern edge of the town off Route 3 (the Sukhumvit highway) is an establishment called the Shell Museum of Thailand, where a wide variety of shells from all over the world are exhibited. The marine museum, also on the Sukhumvit Highway, features some accurately detailed models of ships and royal barges, and other exhibits such as sailors' uniforms andweapons (opening times of both museums 9am–4pm daily; admission fee).

★
Crocodile farm

The crocodile farm at the southern edge of the town (777 Taiban Road) is the second-largest of its kind in the world and is home to approximately 35,000 crocodiles. The owner of this extensive enclosure, which resembles an American-style pleasure park, started in 1950 with a few dozen animals. It is claimed that the motive for the enterprise is to assist in the preservation of these endangered creatures. However, there is obviously money-making potential, as the farm includes a plant for preparing crocodile leather as well as a shop where crocodile products are on sale (opening times: 8am–6pm daily; guided tours: 11am, 1pm, 3pm, Sundays and holidays six times a day; admission fee). The guided tours are interesting and well worth joining in. One outstanding attraction is a crocodile 5.9m/19ft in length that weighs more than 1.1 tons and is the largest such animal in captivity anywhere in the world. Apart from crocodiles, the farm is also home to tigers, chimpanzees, snakes and ele-

? DID YOU KNOW …?

■ The »Washinton Agreement of Endangered Species«, which also includes reptiles, allows the export of crocodile skins if they come from domesticated ones. Before buying shoes, bags or belts, check to see if they have an internationally accepted certificate. But importing crocodile skin products is forbidden in the EU!

phants (that can also be ridden). Day trips or half-day tours of the crocodile farm are on offer from many travel agents, often combined with trips to ►Nakhon Pathom and the floating market of Damnoen Saduak (►Ratchaburi).

Ancient City - Muang Boran

The estate popularly known as Ancient City is one of the biggest open-air museums in the world. It has been financed by rich citizens from Bangkok at a cost of more then US$ 200 million. The 80-hectare/200-acre site is laid out in the shape of Thailand itself. It took ten years to build and its main attractions consist of 65 copies of some of the country's most beautiful and culturally important buildings, scaled down to one-third of their original size alongside some full-size exhibits. Some of the models depict buildings that now exist only as ruins, such as **Si Sanphet Prasat**, the royal audience hall of ancient ►Ayutthaya. Most of the individual exhibits are placed in positions on the site that correspond to their relative positions in the country. The roads that lead between them are wide enough for a car.

Opening hours:
8am–5pm daily
Admission fee

The anthropological museum in the north of the extensive compound contains exhibits from more than 1000 years of history and from almost every part of Thailand. The exhibition is housed in a set of buildings in the central Thai style. The museum also provides an insight into everyday life in the form of musical instruments, pottery and implements for fishing or rice cultivation.

Anthropological museum

A collection of stone and bronze sculptures, ceramics, wood and mother-of-pearl artworks from different civilizations in Thai culture is housed on the upper storey of Ho Kham (gilded hall). The highlight of the exhibition is a hand-carved representation of 70 episodes from the life of Buddha. The Ho Kham building itself is an authentic reconstruction of the former governor's residence in ►Lampang, itself an outstanding example of Thai art. The entire building was made of wood, with not a single nail.

Ho Kham

Among the reproductions in Ancient City there are also some full-size buildings, including houses that once stood alongside the canals of Bangkok but were moved to make way for road building in the 1970s. Some major temple and palace buildings that now exist only as ruins, such as the throne room of Si Sanphet Prasat from ► Ayutthaya, or which have

 SAMUT PRAKAN

GETTING THERE

By car:
From Bangkok via Route 3 (33km/21mi)

By bus:
Several services daily from Bangkok (Southern Bus Terminal). Organized tours are on offer by practically all travel agencies in Bangkok.

Ancient City Open Air Museum *Samut Prakan*

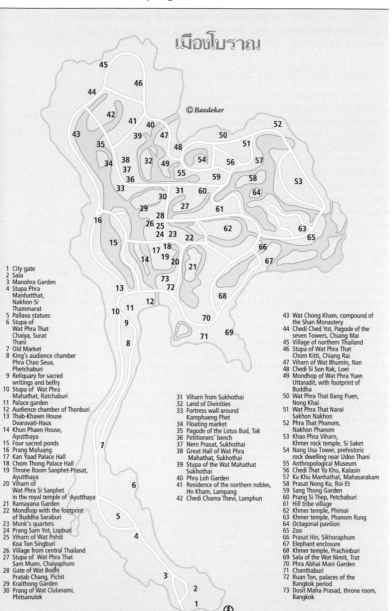

เมืองโบราณ

© Baedeker

1 City gate
2 Sala
3 Manohra Garden
4 Stupa Phra
   Manhatthat,
   Nakhon Si
   Thammarat
5 Pallava statues
6 Stupa of
   Wat Phra That
   Chaiya, Surat
   Thani
7 Old Market
8 King's audience chamber
   Phra Chao Seua,
   Phetchaburi
9 Reliquary for sacred
   writings and belfry
10 Stupa of Wat Phra
   Mahathat, Ratchaburi
11 Palace garden
12 Audience chamber of Thonburi
13 Thab-Khawn House
   Dvaravati-Haus
14 Khun Phaen House,
   Ayutthaya
15 Four sacred ponds
16 Prang Mafuang
17 Kan Yaad Palace Hall
18 Chom Thong Palace Hall
19 Throne Room Sanphet-Prasat,
   Ayutthaya
20 Viharn of
   Wat Phra Si Sanphet
   in the royal temple of Ayutthaya
21 Ramayana Garden
22 Mondhop with the footprint
   of Buddha Saraburi
23 Monk's quarters
24 Prang Sam Yot, Lopburi
25 Viharn of Wat Pohdi
   Koa Ton Singburi
26 Village from central Thailand
27 Stupa of Wat Phra That
   Sam Muen, Chaiyaphum
28 Gate of Wat Bodhi
   Pratab Chang, Pichit
29 Kraithong Garden
30 Prang of Wat Clulanami,
   Phitsanulok

31 Viharn from Sukhothai
32 Land of Divinities
33 Fortress wall around
   Kamphaeng Phet
34 Floating market
35 Pagode of the Lotus Bud, Tak
36 Petitioners' bench
37 Nern Prasat, Sukhothai
38 Great Hall of Wat Phra
   Mahathat, Sukhothai
39 Stupa of the Wat Mahathat
   Sukhothai
40 Phra Loh Garden
41 Residence of the northern nobles,
   Ho Kham, Lampang
42 Chedi Chama Thevi, Lamphun

43 Wat Chong Kham, compound of
   the Shan Monastery
44 Chedi Ched Yot, Pagode of the
   seven Towers, Chiang Mai
45 Village of northern Thailand
46 Stupa of Wat Phra That
   Chom Kitti, Chiang Rai
47 Viharn of Wat Bhumin, Nan
48 Chedi Si Son Rak, Loei
49 Mondhop of Wat Phra Yuen
   Uttaradit, with footprint of
   Buddha
50 Wat Phra That Bang Puen,
   Nong Khai
51 Wat Phra That Narai
   Sakhon Nakhon
52 Phra That Phanom,
   Nakhon Phanom
53 Khao Phra Viharn,
   Khmer rock temple, Si Saket
54 Nang Usa Tower, prehistoric
   rock dwelling near Udon Thani
55 Anthropological Museum
56 Chedi That Ya Khu, Kalasin
57 Ku Khu Manhathat, Mahasarakam
58 Prasat Nong Ku, Roi Et
59 Sang Thong Garden
60 Prang Si Thep, Petchaburi
61 Hill tribe village
62 Khmer temple, Phimai
63 Khmer temple, Phanom Rung
64 Octagonal pavilion
65 Zoo
66 Prasat Hin, Sikhoraphum
67 Elephant enclosure
68 Khmer temple, Prachinburi
69 Sala of the Wat Nimit, Trat
70 Phra Abhai Mani Garden
71 Chanthaburi
72 Ruan Ton, palaces of the
   Bangkok period
73 Dusit Maha Prasad, throne room,
   Bangkok

been totally altered over the years, such as the Dusit Maha Prasat from the Grand Palace in ► Bangkok, have also been replicated at one third of their original size but otherwise in perfect detail. The model of Si Sanphet Prasat stands out for its high halls with their splendid wooden ceilings, gilded walls with reflecting mosaics and stucco ornamentation. In Dusit Maha Prasat one particularly fine detail is the accurate reproduction of the murals, which depict national ceremonies, religious festivals, military parades and court life at the time of King Rama I (1782–1809). The carvings and ornamentation of the doors and windows are excellent.

Reconstruction of the Si Sanphet Prasat temple

At the north-east corner of the site, a hill 54m/177ft high that represents the »no-man's-land« between Thailand and Cambodia affords a lovely view of the area. The hill also has a copy of ► **Khao Phra Viharn**, a temple that in its original form was a destination for pilgrims and kings one thousand years ago. The original is approached via a climb, which is easier in the mornings when it is cooler, starting from a small river and leading to four terraces with stone ruins that once were topped with gabled roofs in the Angkor Wat style. The model Khao Phra Viharn has an authentic reconstruction of those roofs.

Gardens

Seven gardens are scattered across the site. Their waterfalls, rocks and tropical flowers represent an idyllic Thai landscape. The Garden of Gods, for example, includes a bronze image of the Indian moon god Chandra spurring his ten horses that seem to be flying over a waterfall. The Manohra Garden depicts a fair maiden with the legs of a bird amongst her sisters. A shrine to Brahma close to the entrance is also called the »royal stand«, since Queen Elizabeth II of England sat here when she attended the opening ceremony in 1972. The elephant corral and a small zoo in pretty parkland are also worth a visit, especially if children are in the party. The zoo contains open enclosures for elephants, deer, gibbons and many species of exotic birds. The floating market in Ancient City features wooden buildings built in traditional Thai style, many of which are reconstructions of actual buildings.

✱ Samut Sakhon

E 3

Region: Western Thailand	**Province:** Samut Sakhon
Altitude: 5m/16ft	**Population:** 68,000

Samut Sakhon, once an important port, is situated on the Gulf of Thailand at the mouth of the Tha Chin river. Now in the shadow of Bangkok, the harbour is mainly used for fisheries. A little to the north of Samut Sakhon, a tributary by the name of Klong Maha-chai flows into the Tha Chin. It originates in Thonburi, and there-fore it actually connects the Menam Chao Phraya and the Menam Tha Chin.

✱
Harbour

The harbour is not to be missed. It is a lively place from early morn-ing to late in the evening. The mornings are the most interesting time, when the fishing boats land what is generally a healthy catch. The quay is right in the centre of town and the tall clock tower near-by makes a good landmark and point of orientation. Samut Sakhon is also renowned for its excellent fish restaurants.

Wat Yai Chom Prasat

Wat Yai Chom Prasat is a few miles to the north of the town on the banks of the Tha Chin. The entrance to the Ayutthaya-style viharn has some beautifully carved doors. The wat can also be accessed by water (see above).

Wat Chom Long

Having rented a boat it is well worth taking a trip south to Wat Chom Long, right on the gulf at the mouth of the Tha Chin. The route goes past various villages on stilts that are home to fishermen and their families. The extensive grounds of the wat are laid out as at-tractive gardens, and although most of the buildings are recent there is a notable and well-preserved viharn from the Ayutthaya period.

 VISITING SAMUT SAKHON

GETTING THERE

By car:
From Bangkok on Routes 4 or 35 (35km/22mi)

By rail:
Station on the narrow-gauge Mae Klong railway from Bangkok Thon-buri to Samut Songkhram

By boat:
Via charter boat from the Menam Chao Phraya via Klong Mahachai from Bangkok (a two-hour journey but a delightful one)

WHERE TO STAY

Samut Sakhon is certainly worth seeing on a day trip from Bangkok, but has nothing that can be recommended in the way of accommodation.

✱ ✱ Saraburi

D 3

Region: Central Thailand
Altitude: 30m/100ft

Province: Saraburi
Population: 68,000

The provincial capital of Saraburi is a transport hub on the edge of the central plain. Here the vast expanse of rice fields edges towards lovely hills that are occasionally punctuated by startling, jagged limestone outcrops. Buddhists pay particular reverence to two holy places in the immediate vicinity, Wat Phra Buddhabat and Wat Phra Buddhachai, while the Chinese make pilgrimages to Hin Kong. The town itself has no specific attractions.

Around Saraburi

5km/3mi south of Saraburi close to Route 1 (take a right turn onto the 3042) is Wat Phra Buddhachai (»temple of Buddha's shadow«). The natural appearance of a huge limestone rock that soars vertically out of the landscape has given it the title »shadow of Buddha«. A steep stairway hewn out of the rock leads up to the wat that is now dedicated to this shadow. The view of the mountainscape from this point is glorious. At the end of Route 3042 paths branch off to the left and right to the waterfalls Nam Tok Sam Lan and Nam Tok Bo Hin Dad.

✱
Wat Buddhachai

The town of **Hin Kong** is about 8km/5mi south of Phra Buddhachai on Route 1. Some 4km/2.5mi north of it a cluster of Chinese temples stands on the slope of a mountain. Many Chinese pilgrims are drawn to this spot. A Chinese cemetery is close by.

✱
Chinese temples

▶ VISITING SARABURI

GETTING THERE

By car:
From Bangkok via Route 1 (110km/68mi)

By bus:
Several buses a day from Bangkok Northern Bus Terminal

By rail:
Station on the line from Bangkok to Ubon Ratchathani

WHERE TO STAY

▶ **Budget**
Sara Buri Hotel
478 Sut Ban That Road
Saraburi 18000
Tel. 0 36 / 21 16 46
Fax 21 15 00
85 rooms, restaurant.
Centrally located hotel with pleasant, air-conditioned rooms.

Wat Chanthaburi At Sao Hai, 8km/5mi west of Saraburi, the 19th-century Wat Chanthaburi is worth a look. The viharn still has its original murals.

Phu Khai Nature Park The small park called Phu Khai about 16km/10mi north of Saraburi has developed from its original function as a botanical garden. Many tropical trees, shrubs and fabulous blooms are on view there. At the edge of the park is a plantation of teak trees that have been sponsored by the ministry for forestry.

Wat Tham Si Wilai On the way to the temple of Phra Buddhabat (along Route 1 in the direction of Lopburi) the road passes the cave temple of Wat Tham Si Wilai. The extensive cave system has beautiful stalagmites and stalactites.

✷ ✷ Wat Phra Buddhabat

Buddha's footprint The magnificent Wat Phra Buddhabat (from »Buddhapada«, a Sanskrit word signifying the symbolic presence of Buddha) is 24km/15mi north-west of Saraburi. It is a jewel in the crown of Thai architecture and one of the holiest places in the country. The temple gains its name from a footprint of Buddha that is worshipped here.

History The chronicles of the temple are intertwined with history and legend. In around 1615 King Songtham of Ayutthaya (1610–1628) sent some Thai monks to Ceylon to pay homage to a footprint of Buddha there. Ceylonese monks from the island maintained, however, that one of the five »true« footprints of Buddha on earth was to be found somewhere on Siamese soil. It was not long before a hunter unearthed the footprint. A wounded stag led him to a foot-shaped recess in the earth that was filled with water. The hunter had suffered for many years from a severe skin disease but as he drank of the water here, the disease was healed. When the king was told of this miracle, he ordered that a temple be built on the site. In 1765 Burmese invaders destroyed the shrine on their way to launch the fateful attack on Ayutthaya. The current buildings were erected at the command of King Rama I around 1800 and are scattered across several hills.

> **! *Baedeker* TIP**
>
> **Pilgrimage**
>
> Twice a year Wat Phra Buddhabat is the destination for hundreds of pilgrims. One festival is held along with an annual market in January, while the other is a movable feast that takes place some time between March and October.

The buildings The mondhop containing the legendary footprint is richly decorated in blue and gold. Three flights of stairs flanked by a balustrade formed by the body of a five-headed naga lead up to a terrace with its own white balustrade. Twenty slender columns support the tiered, pyramid-shaped roof, adorned with glazed tiles and topped with a dainty canopy over its ringed spire. Countless bronze bells are suspended over the terrace, all of which have been sponsored by pilgrims. The doors have beautiful mother-of-pearl inlays and the floor inside, including the footprint itself heaped with offerings, has a carpet woven with silver threads. The artistic coffered ceiling is also of note. The temple complex on this mountainside also includes a viharn that is used as a small museum (for offerings and relics of the temple), a small bot, a Chinese temple, a Hindu temple and several chedis. From the ridge, the view over the temple roofs and chedis is

A footprint of Buddha is worshipped at Wat Phra Buddhabat

breathtaking. At the foot of the temple there is a bustling trade in wooden sticks bearing religious symbols (for ringing the bells), in amulets and religious objects, as well as food and drink.

✷ **Sattahip**

E 3

Region: South-east Thailand
Altitude: 7m/23ft

Province: Chonburi
Population: 52,000

Sattahip was formerly a base for the US fleet and air force. Nowadays it is the home of the Thai navy. It is situated to the south-east of Pattaya amidst jungle-covered mountains, beautiful beaches and rocky capes. In comparison to Pattaya, it is a quiet spot. There are more fine beaches near the fishing village of Ban Pala.

The town and its harbour
A wide avenue skirts the beach. The fishing harbour and its fish market are at their liveliest during the afternoon. The old naval base that was established around 1920 (follow signposts from the coast road) was replaced by modern facilities some years ago. The water is deep enough here to accommodate even the largest battleships or the enormous freighters that dock at the civil harbour. Thailand has never become a major maritime nation since the Thais have tended to concentrate more on inland and coastal shipping.

✱ Chong Samae San fishing harbour
South-east of Sattahip at the tip of a peninsula is the picturesque fishing village of Chong Samae San, or just Chong for short. The town has several good fish restaurants. The bay is protected by rocky promontories and is a starting point for trips to some of the fairytale islands and snow-white sandy beaches that lie offshore. Among their number are Ko Ai Raet, Ko Samae San, Ko Chang Klua, Ko Nang, Ko Chan, Ko Chuang and Ko Rong Khon.

? DID YOU KNOW …?

■ During the Vietnam war American squadrons of B52 bombers were stationed at the air force base of U Tapao. The base was not disbanded until the 1980s after the Thais politely but firmly requested the Americans to withdraw their forces. Since then the airfield has been put to both civil and military use. Plans to expand the airport into an international hub to cater for large numbers of tourists and boost the economy of the region have been quietly shelved.

About 18km/11mi north of Sattahip some holiday villages and hotels have been built around the idyllic fishing port and resort of **Bang Sare** with its fine restaurants and beaches. From here, it is also worth paying a visit to the craggy island of Ko Khram, which has a lovely beach for swimming on its northern coast. Further north towards Chanthaburi there are more beaches at **Sim Wong Village** and **Sonprasong Beach**.

▶ VISITING SATTAHIP

GETTING THERE

By car:
From Pattaya via Route 3 (30km/
19mi; from Bangkok 180km/112mi)

By bus:
From Bangkok Eastern Bus Terminal

WHERE TO STAY

▶ Mid-range/Luxury
Ambassador City Jomtien Hotel
21/10 Sukhumvit, km 155
Na Jomtien, Sattahip
Tel. 0 38 / 25 55 01, fax 25 57 33
4500 rooms, multiple restaurants,
bars, shopping arcades, spa, beach,
swimming pools and much more.
The biggest hotel in Thailand offers

accommodation in various categories,
but is suitable only for travellers who
like hotels of this kind. Effectively a
whole town in its own right, the
Ambassador provides every facility
needed for an enjoyable holiday.

▶ Budget
Sea Sand Club
Km 163, Sukhumvit Road
Bangsaray, Sattahip
Tel. 0 38 / 43 51 63
Fax 43 51 66
46 rooms, restaurant, bar, beach.
Nice little hotel with the atmosphere
of a family guest house right next to
the beach – and not far from Pattaya.

✶ ✶ Si Satchanalai

C 2

Region: Northern Thailand   **Province:** Sukhothai
Altitude: 68m/223ft   **Population:** 12,000

**The old town, a little off the beaten track for tourists and much
less well known than Sukhothai itself, is one of the most fascinating ruined sites in Thailand. All the exquisite glory of the early
Thai kingdom was expressed in buildings of outstanding artistic
quality.**

This, the »twin city« of the first-ever Thai capital at ▶Sukhothai, lies
at the very northern edge of the central plain on the right bank of
the Menam Yom as it wends its way through the surrounding rocky
but verdant terrain. In the late 19th century, the new town of Si
Satchanalai was founded about 11km/7mi from the ruins, along with
modern Sawankhalok.

**Twin city on the
river**

Si Satchanalai was built in 1250 at the same time as Sukhothai and
was the second royal town in the Sukhothai kingdom (the seat of a
viceroy, who was usually the crown prince). Two Thai princes from

History

the surrounding region had succeeded in ousting the Khmer rulers of Sukhothai in a bloody war. One of them was declared King Si Indratitja of Sukhothai, Si Satchanalai and the surrounding regions. He was succeeded by his own son, then by King Ramkhamhaeng, one of the most potent figures in Thai history. In the 17th century Si Satchanalai was conquered by the kings of Ayutthaya. It was given the new name of Sawankhalok and declined in importance. During the following century, once more under siege by the Burmese, the city was abandoned.

✱✱ Old Si Satchanalai

Si Satchanalai was laid out in a near rectangle. The earliest, 16th-century wall was 5m/16ft high. Some parts of it and its moat are still in existence. The enclosed area is dominated by two hills that were once crowned by wats. From the top there is a fine view of the ruins.

City and temples A massive stairway that has been partially preserved leads up the eastern hill to **Wat Khao Phnom Pleung** (»temple of the holy fire«) on the summit. On the other hill there is still a lovely bell-shaped shaped chedi that belonged to **Wat Khao Suwan Kiri**. The chedi also has the remains of some stucco ornamentation and a huge Buddha statue. A third hill called **Khao Yai** lies to the west near the city walls, but all that remains of its temple **Wat Chet Yot** are ruins with traces of some fine sculpture on the door gables.

✱✱
Wat Chang Lom One of the most remarkable temples of old Si Satchanalai is Wat Chang Lom in the centre of the town, of which a vast laterite chedi is still quite well preserved. Construction of it began during the reign of King Ramkhamhaeng in 1285 and was completed in 1291. The bell-shaped chedi intertwined with lotus leaves stands on top of two tall square pedestals. The taller one has 20 niches that used to hold

 VISITING SI SATCHANALAI

GETTING THERE

Car:
From Sukhothai Road 101 (55km/33mi)

Bus:
Regular connections from Sukhothai and Phitsanulok

Train:
Closest railway station is at Sawankhalok (29km/18mi)

Plane:
Closest airport is at Phitsanulok (114km/67mi)

ACCOMODATIONS

Theree are no recommendable accomodations in Si Satchanalai, but there is a large number in nearby ►Sukhothai.

Buddha statues 1.4m/4.5ft high. Some of these, showing Buddha in the posture of subjugating the Mara, have survived. Emerging from the bases and separated by candelabras are life-sized sculptures of 39 elephants, which really seem to be supporting the building. Archaeological investigations and restoration work have revealed some columns topped with capitals behind these sculptures. The conclusion has been that the walls of the lower base once followed a different line and were altered either during the Sukhothai period or in the Ayutthaya era.

Wat Chedi Chet Theo is a magnificent sight with its 32 chedis of various shapes and styles arranged in seven rows. The chedis contain the ashes of members of the royal family (or of the viceroys' families). Look closely at the Sukhothai-style central stupa in the form of a lotus bud (as at Wat Mahathat in Sukhothai) as well as various stupas in the Srivijaya style, which first came into fashion during the Sukhothai epoch when King Ramkhamhaeng conquered areas of southern Thailand in the 13th century. Many of the stupas are built in a mixture of these styles, a majority of them in the time of King Loei Thai (reigned 1347–1370) and are distinguished by their elegant proportions. Some still have some lovely stucco bas-reliefs, e.g. the stupa in the middle of the northern row, which has a meditating Buddha beneath a naga, the heads of which clearly show the influence of the Srivijaya style. In one chedi at the north-western corner and another behind the lotus-bud stupa are traces of murals. **Wat Utthayan Yai** still has a chedi and some remains of the main shrine.

The centre of the ruined town is dominated by the chedi of Wat Chang Lom

Wat Nang Phaya (»queen's temple«) has a lovely bell-shaped chedi on a square base. On one outer wall of the ruined viharn beautiful ornamental plants made of stucco still surround the narrow slotted windows like fine carving.

✷
Wat Nang Phaya

Between the shrines and the Menam Yom is the area once occupied by the royal palace. There are still some chedis here. To the south of

Old royal palace

Old Si Satchanali *Plan*

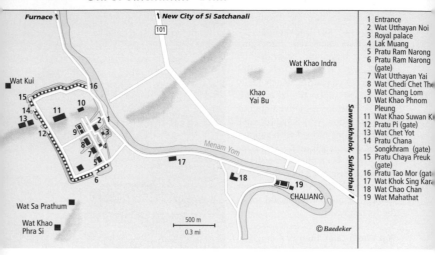

Label	Name
	Furnace ↑
	New City of Si Satchanali
	101
	Wat Khao Indra
	Wat Kui
15 16	
14 11 10	Khao Yai Bu
13	
12 9 2 1	Menam Yom
8 3	
7 4	17
5	18
6	19
	CHALIANG
	Wat Sa Prathum
	Wat Khao Phra Si

Sawankhalok, Sukhothai ↓

500 m
0.3 mi

© Baedeker

1 Entrance
2 Wat Utthayan Noi
3 Royal palace
4 Lak Muang
5 Pratu Ram Narong
6 Pratu Ram Narong (gate)
7 Wat Utthayan Yai
8 Wat Chedi Chet The
9 Wat Chang Lom
10 Wat Khao Phnom Pleung
11 Wat Khao Suwan K
12 Pratu Pi (gate)
13 Wat Chet Yot
14 Pratu Chana Songkhram (gate)
15 Pratu Chaya Preuk (gate)
16 Pratu Tao Mor (gat
17 Wat Khok Sing Kara
18 Wat Chao Chan
19 Wat Mahathat

these is the Lak Muang shrine, built over the town's foundation stone and topped by a spire shaped as a lotus bud. It is surrounded by four chedis in Sukhothai style.

Chaliang A pretty path that runs about 2.5km/1.5mi along the river leads to Chaliang, the site of the important **Wat Phra Si Ratana Mahathat** temple. On the way it passes the 14th-century **Wat Khok Sing Karam/ where several columns and chedis survive. The remains of the co-lumn-encircled bot are an unusual feature. It was not built around an image of Buddha, as normal, but covered a small chedi with a Buddha statue in its niche.**

Wat Chao Chan A few hundred yards further the laterite prang and some of the stuc-co ornamentation of Wat Chao Chan have been reconstructed. One of the ruined shrines still holds remains of a standing Buddha, while parts of a reclining Buddha can be seen in one of the others.

Pottery kiln
Route 101 towards New Si Satchanalai, then left and by boat 4km/2.5mi on the Menam Yom ►

In the northern part of Si Satchanalai are remains of a kiln, where the famous **Sawankhalok pottery** was fired according to a Chinese method. As early as the 13th century the kilns of **Ban Ko Noi** (prob-ably the oldest in Thailand) and their Chaliang ware were well known. The clay found in this vicinity is particularly well suited to hard-firing, and when King Ramkhamhaeng brought back the knowledge of such ceramics from a visit to China, he decided to in-troduce the technology to Thailand. He invited some Chinese potters to settle around Sukhothai and Si Satchanalai. The Chaliang ware was primarily used for everyday purposes but, under the guidance of the Chinese, a new »Sawankhalok ware« came into being that was distinguished by beauty of form and a silky glaze. The products were the equal of China's own **celadon ceramics** in terms of quality and became a major export from the Sukhothai kingdom to Indonesia, Japan, the Philippines and Borneo. Apart from jugs, teapots, bowls and crockery, figures were also made for use as toys or as offerings to guardian spirits. Thais have maintained these pottery skills down the centuries, even though there has been no development in terms of form or style since the 15th century. The centre of modern ceramic manufacture is around Chiang Mai; but the artistic perfection of the ceramics from Si Satchanalai, Sukhothai and Sawankhalok has never been equalled.

Chaliang

Chaliang, about 2.5km/1.5mi upstream of Sukhothai in a loop of the Menam Yom, was formerly a Khmer outpost. The Khmer shrine of Phra That, forerunner of the later Wat Phra Si Ratana Mahathat, was built at the narrowest part of the loop so that it could be accessed by land from one side only. An inscription sponsored by Ramkhamhaeng in 1292 states that the king had excavated relics from the old Khmer prang in 1285 (probably meaning the one at Wat Chang Lom) and commissioned a new chedi to house them at Wat Chang Lom, the building of which had taken 6 years. Legend has it that he had previously dedicated a month and six days to worship of the relics. The lovely chedi, which survives with its beautifully designed tiered base, dates from the early 15th century (early Ayutthaya style). It may be, however, that the base of this chedi was actually part of King Ramkhamhaeng's original building. The figure of a sitting Buddha on the north side of the prang has been heavily restored. On the west side of it, there are still some remains of a shrine containing a bronze footprint of Buddha. In a small niche nearby a fine stone sculpture depicts Buddha under the hood of the naga. The nine-headed snake has some artistic texturing and a bas-relief of a relaxed striding Buddha is one of the finest images of the **Sukhothai era**. The stucco relief dates all the way back to the time of King Ramkhamhaeng and is located in a small shrine east of the prang, where another standing Buddha can be seen.

**★★
Wat Phra Si
Ratana Mahathat**

Even the perimeter wall is interesting. It is made up of broad cylinders more than 1m/3ft in diameter and was built between 1285 and 1288 under King Ramkhamhaeng. The pillars have heavy, roof-shaped laterite capstones. Three taller pillars form the entrance gates; above the centre pillar there is fine stucco decoration featuring figures and ornamentation. Unusual and impressively sculpted faces adorn the four corners. They may have been influenced by the tower of faces at the Bayon temple in Angkor Thom (now in Cambodia), which was a major stylistic exemplar.

Perimeter wall

Chedi The compound also features a large 14th-century chedi of Ceylonese influence that was erected by Mon monks. The mondhop called Phra Ruang at the eastern edge of the compound is dedicated to the son of a snake goddess.

Buddha statue at Wat Phra Si Mahathat in Chaliang

Si Thep

D 3

Region: Central Thailand   **Province:** Phetchabun
Altitude: 128m/420ft   **Population:** 9000

A visit to this town, situated in the valley of the Menam Pasak amid jungle-covered mountains, can only be recommended to those with a serious interest in the history of Thailand and plenty of imagination. The organized intervention of archaeologists is still proceeding hesitantly, although some excavations are underway. The best finds from Si Thep can be seen in the National Museum of ► Bangkok.

History

It is a matter of debate as to whether Si Thep was of any importance before the Khmer made it their own. Researchers have certainly established that the region around Si Thep boasted one of the earliest settlements in Thailand. This theory has been advanced by excavations that discovered Brahman statues and pictures. The discovery of various stone tablets with Khmer inscriptions has certainly proven, however, that during the period of the Khmer empire Si Thep played an important role.

City boundaries

It takes some effort to trace the outline of the oval Mon walls and the later rectangular walls of the Khmer. Some remains of the walls are still visible, along with various prangs and traces of five temple complexes. Stone images unearthed by the excavations including some of the oldest and finest Hindu art can be viewed in the National Museum in ►Bangkok. An outstanding Buddha statue with a Pali inscription on the base can also be seen there.

Thamorat Cave

Traces of Buddhist art (images carved into the walls that have not been dated) have been found in a cave in the Thamorat hill west of Si Thep.

 VISITING SI THEP

GETTING THERE

By car:
From Phetchabun southwards via Route 21 (132km/82mi), from Saraburi on Route 21 in the opposite direction (123km/76mi)

By bus:
From Saraburi and Phetchabun

WHERE TO STAY

In Si Thep there are no places to stay that can be recommended. If modest comfort is enough, rooms are available in some of the basic guest houses in the town.

✳ Songkhla

H 3

Region: Southern Thailand
Altitude: 4m/13ft

Province: Songkhla
Population: 85,000

Songkhla is a provincial capital in the far south of Thailand and one of the prettiest seaside resorts in the country, although it remains practically untouched by tourism. Its original economic importance has declined in favour of the neighbouring town of Hat Yai, not least because of the airport that has been built near the latter.

Scenery Songkhla is almost completely surrounded by water on a promontory between the Gulf of Thailand and Lake Songkhla, at 80km/50mi long and up to 20km/12mi wide the largest inland lake in South-East Asia. White sandy beaches lined with casuarina trees and tall palms extend for mile after mile along both the lake shore and the sea. The scenery between the sea and the mountains is outstandingly beautiful, but the lake no longer provides a living for the once countless fishing families because it has been completely emptied of fish.

! *Baedeker* TIP

Chinese Lunar Festival

Every September Songkhla celebrates the Chinese Lunar Festival. Thais of Chinese heritage pray to the moon and the queen of the heavens, asking for good luck in the future. The celebrations involve colourful dances featuring dragons and lions as well as sporting contests and other folk events.

Harbour The once important harbour, protected in a bay (and formerly known by its Malay name of Singora) is now used only by coastal traffic due to silting. Larger ships anchor between the islands of Ko Meo and Ko Nu (»cat island« and »mouse island«).

What to See in Songkhla

The town The town centre has shifted several times over the centuries. Some remains of fortifications belonging to the old town of Songkhla, as it existed until the 17th century, can still be seen near the modern village of Khao Hua Daeng. They were erected by a sultan, who rebelled against the dominion of Ayutthaya. In the course of the reconquest, the town was destroyed, later to be rebuilt on the grounds of Laem Song. The present town to the south of the bay dates from the middle of the last century. Some remains of forts and the old walls can be seen near the police station. Many inhabitants of Songkhla and its environs are Malaysian or Chinese and a typical Chinese business quarter can be found on Phatthalung Road. In the arena on Rajchu-

▶ VISITING SONGKHLA

GETTING THERE

By car:
From Nakhon Si Thammarat on Routes 401/41/4/43 to Hat Yai, Route 407 (220km/137mi) or the coast road, Route 408 (160km/100mi)

By bus:
Several buses a day from Bangkok Southern Bus Terminal

By air:
Nearest airport in Hat Yai with two flights a day from Bangkok

INFORMATION

Tourism Authority of Thailand
1/1 Soi 2 Niphatuthit 3 Road
90110 Songkhla
Tel. 0 74 / 24 37 47, 23 85 18
Fax 24 59 86
tatsgkhi@tat.or.th

WHERE TO STAY IN HAT YAI
▶ Mid-range
Novotel Central Sukontha
3 Sanehanusorn Road
Tel. 0 74 / 35 22 22
Fax 35 22 23
www.centralhotelsresorts.com
237 rooms, 3 restaurants, coffee shop, bar, spa. New hotel belonging to the Novotel chain right in the centre of town with very comfortable rooms. Large shopping arcade in the neighbourhood.

WHERE TO STAY IN SONGKHLA
▶ Budget
Princess Resort
163 Kaew Beach
Singha Nakhon Songkhla 90280
Tel. 0 74 / 33 10 59
Fax 33 10 58
143 rooms, restaurant, bar, swimming pool. Well recommended hotel with comfortable rooms a little outside the town centre.

tid Road bullfights (animal versus animal) take place on weekend afternoons.

The **governor's palace** that dates from 1878 (home of the Na Songkhla family) is a wonderful edifice, built in Chinese style and featuring some splendid carvings. Nowadays it is used as a museum. There is another museum at **Wat Matchimawat**. Both contain valuable bronze sculptures from the Srivijaya period that exhibit distinct similarities to the early art of central and eastern Java. Ceramics from the Srivijaya and Ayutthaya periods are also on view as well as everyday implements and many curiosities (mostly found at Sathing Phra). In the 16th-century Wat Matchimawat there is an ancient Buddha statue that is almost 2000 years old and once had a lotus crown made of pure gold. For security reasons, the crown is now kept in a safe and is only set upon the statue on major feast days.

Museums

⏲
Opening hours:
Wed–Sun
9am–4pm
Admission fee

Fishing harbour of Songkhla

Wat Klang ★ Although it is ancient, the 19th century Wat Klang is still well worth a look. The brick Reussi sala, and the bot guarded by Chinese lions are decorated inside with frescoes of hermits practising yoga, done in the less attractive Bangkok style. Reliefs by a Chinese artist adorn the base of the bot.

Viewpoint ★ Two hills dominate the town. On the smaller of the two (Khao Noi) there is a small park, while the larger one (Khao Tang Kuan) is crowned by a temple that offers a marvellous view over Songkhla and its surroundings.

Beaches ★ **Samila Beach** on the bay is highly popular with Thais, especially at weekends, whereas the beach on the gulf coast is often devoid of people. At one end of Samila Beach is the fishing village of **Ban Kao Seng,** which is populated by Moslem fishermen. During the day, their brightly painted boats are left on the beach.

Around Songhkla

Wat Suwan Khiri ★ At the southern end of the narrow strip of land opposite Songkhla lies the temple of Wat Suwan Khiri. It was funded by the Na Songkhla family in the early 19th century. The small chedi and the Chinese bell tower are very lovely, as are the viharn and its decorative frescoes. The Na Songkhla family, whose original ancestor was Chinese, have provided Songkhla with its governors for generations. The family is supporting the efforts of the Thai royal family to enhance the integration of southern parts of Thailand.

A boat trip along the mountainous promontory north of Songkhla passes many picturesque fishing villages built on stilts. Further north the lake is split into two by towering limestone cliffs called **Thale Sap** and **Thale Luang**. In the lagoons of the briny swamps there are many Sunda gavials (Siamese crocodiles); the cliffs are the nesting places of sea swallows, the nests themselves considered a delicacy in Chinese cuisine. One destination for such a boat ride could be the island of **Ko To** with its two temples.

✶
Bay

On the spit north of Songkhla there are religious sites dating from the Srivijaya empire that now exist as fascinating ruins. The most important is probably Sathing Phra, right on the seashore 30km/ 19mi from Songkhla (easy to get to by car or bus or by ferry across the strait). The stupa with niches on three sides is in the finest Srivijaya style. The neighbouring shrine contains a statue of Buddha and some interesting frescoes. The stucco ornamentation on the gables probably dates from the Ayutthaya period. Archaeological digs have unearthed bronze sculptures from the 8th to the 12th centuries, some of which are displayed at the National Museum in ►Bangkok while others are in the museum of Songkhla. Some have some very clear Javanese influence while others are in the Khmer style. Trips that can be recommended include visits to a **coconut plantation** where monkeys have been trained to pick the nuts or to **Wat Khao Tum**, which is built on a cliff.

✶
Sathing Phra

◄ Day trips

✶ ✶ Sukhothai

Region: Northern Thailand
Altitude: 66m/217ft

Province: Sukhothai
Population: 36,000

The former capital of Sukhothai, the historically and artistically important nexus of the Sukhothai period, lies to the north of the central plain. The expansive terrain fringed by distant hills is the catchment basin of the Menam Yom. The ruined town is 12km/7mi from the modern centre of Sukhothai and can easily be reached by bus, rental car or taxi.

For 140 years, Sukhothai was the capital of an important kingdom. According to legend the city was established in around AD 500. One of its rulers was King Chao Aluna Khmara (a.k.a. Phra Ruang), who was alleged to be the offspring of a human being and a naga princess. Phra Ruang is therefore the name given to the dynasty of eight kings that ruled the great kingdom. The first of the Phra Ruang monarchs was Si Indratitja (1235–1279), who was able to wrest the land from Khmer dominion. His kingdom comprised little more than the two towns of Sukhothai and ►Si Satchanala.

History

Reign of King Ramkhamhaeng While Si Indratitja is important as the founder of the first uniquely Thai culture, the legacy of his grandson Ramkhamhaeng (1256–1317) is even greater. His kingdom ranged from Vientiane in the north-east, westward as far as Pegu in what is now Myanmar and south to Nakhon Si Thammarat, covering almost two thirds of the present area of Thailand. The king is hailed as the inventor of the Thai alphabet and was instrumental in the development of porcelain and faience using Chinese techniques.

i Sukhothai period

■ The era of the Sukhothai empire and the artistic style with which it is associated covers the period from the mid-13th to the mid-15th century.

His eventful reign (which also saw the first establishment of diplomatic ties between a Thai ruler and China) was celebrated in later times.

Fall and rise of Sukhothai Under Ramkhamhaeng's immediate successor Loei Thai (1299–1347) most of the newly gained territories were lost again, nor was it possible for his son Liu Thai (1347–1368) or Mahadharmaraya I to restore the former extent of the kingdom. Ayutthaya's

▶ VISITING SUKHOTHAI

GETTING THERE

By car:
From Bangkok on Routes 1/32/117 towards Phitsanulok, then Route 12 (430km/267mi)

By bus:
From Bangkok Northern Bus Terminal (440km/273mi), Sawankhalok, Phitsanulok

By rail:
Nearest station Sawankhalok (38km/24mi)

By air:
Nearest airport Phitsanulok (58km/36mi)

WHERE TO EAT

The night-time establishments on Charodvithithong Road in New Sukothai provide some reasonably priced and enjoyable places to eat. Some of them have menus in two languages, while some offer such delicacies as fried beetles or larvae. An El Dorado for the intrepid.

WHERE TO STAY

▶ Budget

① *Ratchathani Hotel*
299 Charodvithithong Road
Tel. 0 55 / 61 10 31
Fax 61 28 78
81 rooms, restaurant, bar, swimming pool
Nicely kept hotel with well equipped rooms and a good restaurant.

② *The Sukhothai Resort*
99 Mu 7, Tambon Sarmruen
Tel. 0 55 / 68 16 98
Fax 68 16 97
80 rooms, restaurant, coffee shop, swimming pool. Relatively new hotel in a splendid location between Sukhothai and Si Satchanalai.

Sukhothai *Plan*

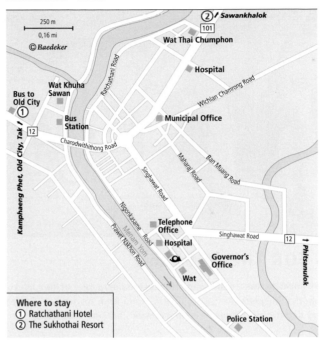

250 m
0,16 mi
© Baedeker

② ✦ Sawankhalok
101
Wat Thai Chumphon
Hospital
Wichian Chamrong Road
Wat Khuha Sawan
Bus to Old City ①
Bus Station
Ratchathani Road
Municipal Office
Charodwithithong Road
Kamphaeng Phet, Old City, Tak ✦
12
Mahavat Road
Ban Muang Road
Singhawat Road
Ngonkasime Road
Prawet Nakhon Road
Menam Yom
Telephone Office
Hospital
Singhawat Road   12
Governor's Office
✦ Phitsanulok
Wat

Where to stay
① Ratchathani Hotel
② The Sukhothai Resort

Police Station

King Boromaraja I conquered Sukhothai in the year 1378, and in 1438 it was formally incorporated into the Ayutthaya empire. When the Burmese razed Ayutthaya in 1767 Sukhothai's inhabitants also fled their homes. Only eleven years later, however, Rama I, the first of the Chakri dynasty ruling from Bangkok, established a new Sukhothai on the left bank of the Menam Yom. As this town was largely destroyed by fire in 1968, most of the buildings in the town centre are very recent.

What to See in Sukhothai

In 1988, after some 25 years of work supported by UNESCO funds, King Bhumibol opened the ruins of old Sukhothai to the public. 193 temples had been excavated and partially reconstructed. Since opportunists had increasingly been offering antiquities plundered from Sukhothai to art collectors around the world, UNESCO had taken the step in 1978 of declaring the ruins a world heritage site. Nowadays they are subject to strict security. Every building on the site is furnished with a plaque in English that describes its date of construction and other interesting facts.

UNESCO World Heritage Site

KING FOR THE PEOPLE

King Ramkhamhaeng was a noble and effectively modern ruler of his subjects in the Sukhothai kingdom. An inscription in stone from his time, a kind of government declaration, is preserved in Bangkok's national museum.

»The land of Sukhothai thrives and flourishes. There are fish in the waters, there is rice in the fields. The ruler levies no tax upon those subjects who use the roads to drive their cattle to market or ride their horses to trade. The trader in elephants may do his business, the trader in horses alike. Merchants in gold and silver may buy and sell gold and silver. When a humble man or a rich man dies, all his possessions, his elephants, his wives, his children, his granaries and rice, are inherited by his son. When his citizens are in dispute, the king will adjudge the case to determine the circumstances and the reason for the disagreement and will then rule with wisdom and justice. He will tolerate no thief or dealer in stolen goods. When he sees the riches of another, he does not rage. When someone rides up to him upon an elephant to beg the king to protect his land, the king shall grant his generous aid. If a man with no elephants, no horses, no gold and no silver should come to the king, he will be granted means by which to establish a household. If prisoners are taken in war, they are neither put to death nor beaten. Above the gate shall hang a bell and when any member of the nation has a grievance that wracks his body and causes his heart to weep, he should ring this bell. King Ramkhamkaeng, the ruler of this kingdom shall hear his call and listen to his case so that he may make a wise judgement. Let him therefore be praised by the people of Sukhothai… King Ramkhamkaeng and… all have faith in the religion of Buddha.«

Within the Walls of the Ruined City

The old centre of Sukhothai was bounded by three earthen banks separated by two moats. Three of the four gates (»pratu«; Kamphaeng Hak in the east, Na Mok in the south, Oa in the west, and San Luang in the east) were defended by forts, of which it is still possible to see some remains. Apart from 21 wats, four ponds have also been brought to light: Thapang Thong, Thapang Ngoen, Thapang Trakuan and Thapang So. There were not only temples within the town itself, but also others spread over a wide area around it.

Old city centre

> ! *Baedeker* TIP
>
> ### See Sukhothai by bike
> The ruins of Sukhothai are very extensive, and on foot it is only possible to scratch the surface of what is there. The alternative is to hire a bicycle at the main entrance in order to move quickly and conveniently between the individual temples and other religious sites.

The Ramkhamhaeng museum was opened in 1964 and includes numerous finds such as statues, stucco work and ceramics found in Sukhothai, Si Satchanalai and Kamphaeng Phet, the three main towns in the kingdom. There is a good overview of the development of the Sukhothai style from its beginnings, when Khmer culture was still the primary influence, until its Ayutthaya-influenced later period. Particular highlights include a striding Buddha said to be the finest of its kind, a sitting Buddha from Wat Chang Lom in ►Si Satchanalai (both on the ground floor) and a bronze sitting Buddha (upstairs). There are more statues and some pottery kilns in the gardens of the museum. The entry price includes a detailed brochure written in English.

★ ★
Ramkhamhaeng museum

Opening hours:
9am–4pm daily except for holidays
Admission fee

The most magnificent wat within the present ruins was Wat Mahathat next to the former royal palace. However, its wooden buildings have not survived. This wat alone once covered an area of some 40,000 sq m/10 acres and included 185 chedis, 6 viharns of various sizes, a bot and 11 salas. The whole compound was enclosed by a perimeter with several gates. The most impressive part of the compound is at its centre, where the main chedi, a viharn and a bot are all located. The tall and finely structured chedi in pure Sukhothai style is topped by a spire in the form of a lotus bud. The central section is similar to Khmer prangs, and the tall rectangular base is adorned with figures representing a procession of 40 worshippers, each of whom is one metre in height. The niches in the four chapels at each corner have some lovely stucco work, rosettes, scenes from the life of Buddha, gods and demons in battle and all contain Buddha statues, as do the ledges around the base. Four Khmer prangs in the middle are aligned to the points of the compass. A tall stairway leads up the eastern side into the central chedi. Some pillars still remain of a small 14th-century viharn in Ayutthaya style with a sitting

★ ★
Wat Mahathat

Wat Sra Si is in the centre of a beautiful lotus pond.

Buddha statue, as well as a huge bot (40 x 15 m/130 x 50 feet). The columns making up the five aisles of the bot present a particularly stunning sight. This bot once contained the gilded figure of Phra Buddha Shakyamuni, which King Rama I had removed to Wat Su-that in ▶ Bangkok at the end of the 18th century. In the mondhops on either side are 8m/26ft-tall standing Buddhas set into protective niches. The ruined chedis around the centre probably contained the ashes of members of the royal family.

Wat Si Sawai was encircled by two walls and a moat and was built in **Wat Si Sawai**
Khmer style in the 12th–13th centuries, thus predating the founding
of the city of Sukhothai itself. After
being initially dedicated to a Hindu
cult, it was converted to a Buddhist
shrine with the addition of a bot
and a viharn. The three brick
prangs, each with seven tiers and
clad in stone and stucco, are quite
distinctive. There are still Buddha
statues in the gables of the upper
storey. All three prangs encompass
a cella. The one in the tall centre
prang is linked to the bot by a gal-
lery, while the other two can only be accessed from outside. Fragments of reliefs that originally adorned the walls of the prang can be
seen in the Ramkhamhaeng museum. The rectangular temple complex also includes a chedi and two other shrines.

> ## ! *Baedeker* TIP
>
> ### Loy Krathong in Sukhothai
> Every November Loy Krathong (Festival of Light),
> possibly the loveliest festival in Thailand, is held
> in honour of this holy place. It transforms the
> lake into a wonderful sea of light made up of
> thousands of floating candles.

West of Wat Mahathat is an island in the middle of the lotus-covered　★
pond Traphang Ngoen (»silver pond«). Upon the island are the　**Wat Traphang**
beautiful chedi of Wat Traphang Ngoen and the pillars of a large vi-　**Ngoen**
harn. The niches of the chedi contain Buddha statues; its spire has
the form of a lotus bud.

Wat Chana Songkhram has a bell-shaped chedi in Ceylonese style　**Wat Chana**
and a raised platform with the bases of two vanished shrines. The　**Songkhram**
small ruined building to the south of the wat was erected over the
symbolic foundation stone of the town, the Lak Muang.

Wat Sra Si is also on a small island and must once have been spectac-　★★
ular. It includes chedis that display a Ceylonese influence. All that re-　**Wat Stra Si**
mains of the large viharn are six rows of columns and a fine sitting
Buddha making the gesture of Bhumisparsa-mudra. The bot of Wat
Sra Si is in the middle of a pond covered with flowering lotus. The
buildings of the wat on the shore are recent and still inhabited by
monks. The old laterite chedi in Ceylonese form is badly ruined. A
stone Buddha footprint that was brought here from Wat Phra Bat
Yai was apparently discovered by King Liu Thai in 1359.

Some sections still remain of the beautiful stucco ornamentation on　**Wat Mai, Wat**
the richly decorated base of the viharn at Wat Mai, although there is　**Trakuan**
nothing left of the prang but its base. A bronze image of the Buddha
under a Naga was found here and is now preserved in the Ramkhamhaeng National Museum in Sukhothai. Numerous Buddha statues in
early Sukhothai style were found in the ruins Wat Trakuan, of which
only one fine chedi and the base of a viharn remain to be seen. They
display a rather unique mixture of Ceylonese and Chiang Saen styles.

Old Sukhothai *Plan*

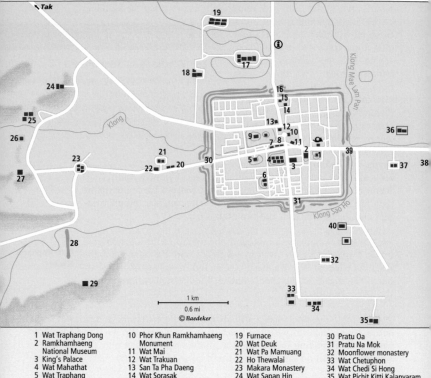

Tak

19

17

18

24

25

26

16
15
14

13
12
9
7 8 10
11
2

21
20
30
22

23

27

5
4
3

6

39

36

37
38

31

40

28

29

1 km

0.6 mi

© Baedeker

32

33
34

35

1 Wat Traphang Dong	10 Phor Khun Ramkhamhaeng	19 Furnace	30 Pratu Oa
2 Ramkhamhaeng	Monument	20 Wat Deuk	31 Pratu Na Mok
National Museum	11 Wat Mai	21 Wat Pa Mamuang	32 Moonflower monastery
3 King's Palace	12 Wat Trakuan	22 Ho Thewalai	33 Wat Chetuphon
4 Wat Mahathat	13 San Ta Pha Daeng	23 Makara Monastery	34 Wat Chedi Si Hong
5 Wat Traphang	14 Wat Sorasak	24 Wat Sapan Hin	35 Wat Pichit Kitti Kalanyaram
Ngoen	15 Wat Son Kheo	25 Wat Phra Bat Noi	36 Wat Chang Lom
6 Wat Si Sawai	16 Pratu San Luang	26 Wat Chedi Ngam	37 Wat Traphang Thong Lang
7 Lak Muang	17 Wat Phra Pai	27 Wat Tam Hip	38 Wat Chedi Sung
8 Wat Chana Songkhram	Luang	28 Phra-Ruang-Damm	39 Pratu Kamphaeng Hak
9 Wat Sra Si	18 Wat Si Chum	29 Wat Phra Bat Yai	40 Ashokarama

San Ta Pha Daeng ✳ San Ta Pha Daeng, built in the 12th–13th centuries, is one of the most important Khmer ruins on Thai soil. The shrine rests on a base 3m/10ft high and has four porticos. Five beautiful stone fragments showing Hindu gods and goddesses in the style of Angkor Wat were found here.

Wat Sorasak ✳ Wat Sorasak was built in 1412 during the later period of the Sukhothai empire. A stone inscription at the describes the history of and reason for its construction. The ruined chedi in Ceylonese style is supported by 24 stone elephants. The niches contain Buddhas sitting in »western« style with legs hanging down. Through the Pratu San Luang gate leading out of the central area are two more shrines and a pottery kiln.

North of the City Wall

The extensive moated grounds of Wat Phra Pai Luang enclose one of the oldest and most important shrines in the whole area. It was probably built in around 1200. Only the most northerly of the three stucco-ornamented laterite prangs is still standing. The gable on the shuttered door shows Buddha surrounded by worshippers. The tiers of this chedi as well as the base of the ruined east chedi are adorned with lovely stucco figures. Only the outer walls, the foundations and remnants of four rows of pillars remain. Excavations of the mondhop revealed statues of Buddha in the four basic postures. This wat is believed to have been the major shrine of the old town during the period of Khmer control, before the Thais moved the centre further south to the area of the present-day ruins.

✷ Wat Phra Pai Luang

The mondhop of Wat Si Chum, a solid, windowless block (22 x 28 x 15m/72 x 92 x 50ft) stands on a base 4.30m/14ft high. The walls are 3m/10ft thick. The roof can be reached via an entrance in the southern wall. The roof of the corridor was once adorned with beautifully carved stone tablets (one can be seen in the Ramkhamhaeng Museum in Sukhothai and another is in the National Museum in Bangkok), showing in sweeping lines some scenes from the life of Buddha. The images, which are of outstanding quality and display the in-

✷✷ Wat Si Chum

In Wat Si Chum

fluence of Ceylonese and Indian painters, resemble the temple walls of Polonnaruwa on Sri Lanka. Inside the mondhop there is a colossal statue (14.70m/48ft high) of a sitting Buddha that was formerly gilded. It is probably the Phra Achana mentioned in an inscription of King Ramkhamhaeng from 1292. In front of the mondhop is a bot covering an area of 21 x 12m/70 x 40ft, the 13 pillars of which are made of the mineral limonite covered in stucco and are still standing. To the north of the mondhop are the ruins of a small viharn and a brick building with a statue of a sitting Buddha.

Ceramic kiln A pottery kiln, one of 13 that apparently stood here (there is a model in the Ramkhamhaeng museum), is another notable survival. The manufacture of ceramic goods and tiles started here in around 1300, when King Ramkhamhaeng brought several hundred potters from China, and lasted until the mid-15th century, when production was disrupted by war.

West of the Wall

Ruined temples Not many of the ruins to the west of the old centre are worth seeing nowadays, but some have been restored. **Wat Pa Mamuang** was a key religious centre during the Sukhothai period. Inscriptions in Pali, Khmer and Thai (now exhibited at the National Museum in Bangkok) describe its history. The base of the mondhop, the bases of several chedis and ruins of the bot are still visible. At **Wat Tuk** only parts of the mondhop, the viharn and some chedis remain. **Ho Thewalai** stands on a high platform accessed by a stairway; eight columns of this Hindu shrine still remain. The base of the chedi at **Wat Chang Rob** is supported by 24 elephants (► photo on p.478). In front of it there are a few pieces of debris and laterite columns from the former viharn.

✱
Wat Sapan Hin Wat Sapan Hin lies on a rise at the edge of the Yom plain, from which there is a good view to the mountains of Si Satchanalai. A stone-paved path leads to the monastery and gives it the name »temple of the stone bridge«. Every October King Ramkhamhaeng celebrated the Thot Kathin Festival at the end of the Thai fasting period. Tall, stucco-clad laterite columns once supported the viharn. An impressive 12.5m/40ft standing statue of Buddha in Sukhothai style now stands in the open, leaning against a brick wall with its right hand making the gesture of protection. Nearby is a statue of a sitting Buddha also in the Sukhothai style.

✱
Wat Phra Bat Noi Another interesting remnant is the temple of Wat Phra Bat Noi (»wat of the Buddha footprint«) with its extraordinary chedi in mixture of Thai and Khmer styles. The middle section on its square base

King Ramkhamhaeng still watches over Sukhothai. →

has a niche on every side, each containing a small Buddha. The lower part of the spire has vertical ribs that are decorated mainly with Hindu motifs, as are the niches with the statues. The footprint from the viharn is in the Ramkhamhaeng museum.

Wat Chedi Ngam The bell-shaped chedi of Wat Chedi Ngam rises from a richly decorated foundation. The base of the bell is decorated with a lotus frieze and each of the sides of the middle section has a niche for a Buddha statue. In front of the chedi and about three feet lower are the laterite pillars of the viharn with four small stone chapels.

South of the Wall

✳
Wat Chetuphon On the way to Wat Chetuphon are the ruins of **Wat Kampang Lang** with the foundations of the chedi and viharn and the remains of **Wat Ton Chan** with a chedi in Ceylonese style. Wat Chetuphon has one particularly fine example of the sculptor's art in classic Sukhothai style, a striding stucco Buddha, the only one of a set of four that has been quite well preserved. The other three showed Buddha in sitting, standing and reclining postures. They once adorned the outer walls of the mondhop, a solid brick building in the centre of the temple compound. The chedi is built in the form of another mondhop and contains the Buddha statue Phra Si Arijya Metria (»Buddha of the future«). Preserved parts of the window frames of the viharn look a little like wood carvings. The slate walls, sculpted in imitation of carved wood, are a unique feature of Wat Chetuphon.

Wat Chedi Si Hong Wat Chedi Si Hong is notable primarily for its 14th-century sculpted decorations on a laterite base. Upright, angel-like figures carry vases in their hands while making a gesture of prayer. Their clothes demonstrate Ceylonese influence as well as aspects of Khmer art. Between the figures are some lion statues. The laterite columns of the viharn are still standing, and the bases of two chedis remain in the vestibule.

Wat Pichit Kitti Kalanyaram The tall, bell-shaped chedi of Wat Pichit Kitti Kalanyaram is visible far and wide. Built in 1403, its square base has sides 15m/50ft long and is embellished with some beautifully sculpted moonstones, which are common in Sri Lanka but quite rare in Thailand.

East of the Walls

✳✳
Wat Traphang Thong Lang Wat Traphang Thong Lang along the road to New Sukhothai has some beautiful stucco reliefs on the façade. The bas-relief on the southern side is possibly one of the best of its type in the Sukhothai style. It shows the Enlightened One striding down steps while descending from Tavatimsa heaven, Buddha protected by parasols, accompanied by the Hindu gods Indra and Brahma as well as worship-

pers. It is thought that this may be the first-ever image of a striding Buddha, a representation that was invented during the Sukhothai era. Another bas-relief on the northern side shows with slightly less skill how Buddha tamed the elephant Nalagiri, which had been set loose by his cousin Devadatta to attack him. The relief on the western wall shows Buddha under a mango tree performing the miracle of Sravasti. Paintings of this kind can be seen in Polonnaruwa (Sri Lanka) and Pagan (Burma).

A little further east lies Wat Chedi Sung with a towering and impressively tiered chedi, a beautiful balance of immensity and elegance. The stucco-clad 14th-century chedi is one of the finest religious buildings exhibiting Sukhothai architecture. The tall sub-structure on a square base displays features of the Srivijaya style, whereas the slender bell-shaped upper part on its octagonal base exhibits definite Ceylonese influence.

✷ Wat Chedi Sung

✷ ✷ Surat Thani

G 2

Region: Southern Thailand
Altitude: 8m/26ft

Province: Surat Thani
Population: 57,000

Surat Thani lies on the fertile plain at the mouth of the Ta Pi on the Gulf of Thailand. The region has been settled since the Neolithic period and was the terminus of an important trade route from Ta Kuapa, a short-cut to the South China Sea, during the first millennium AD. After good roads were built, the town developed into a major trading post between Thailand and Malaysia.

In the town there is little to see, but the scenery between Surat Thani and Ta Kuapa on the Andaman Sea on the other side of the peninsula is among the most attractive in Thailand. The dolomite cliffs rise as much as 1000m/3300ft from the thick tropical rainforest. The beauty of the offshore islands is breathtaking.

Entrancing scenery

One temple worth seeing is Wat Dei Tamaram on Na Muang Road, even though it dates from modern times. It has a splendid tall viharn with beautifully decorated gables. A much older building is right next door, its entrances guarded by fierce-looking demons. The life of the temple complex is also interesting.

✷ Wat Dei Tamaram

The harbour of Ban Dong (the old name of the town) is a lively area, and the markets are marvellously colourful.

Harbour of Ban Dong

About 60 islands are scattered off the coast near Surat Thani. Many have pretty beaches with holiday developments, comfortable hotels

✷ ✷ Islands

● VISITING SURATTHANI

GETTING THERE

By car:
From Bangkok via Route 4, from Chumphon on Route 41 (645km/400mi). From Nakhon Si Thammarat on Route 401 (135km/84mi)

By rail:
From Bangkok Hualampong (651km/405mi, journey time 11 hours; night train recommended, reservations necessary)

By air:
Daily from Bangkok; also a destination for charter flights

INFORMATION

Tourism Authority of Thailand
5 Thalad Mai Road; 84000 Surat Thani
Tel. 0 77 / 28 88 18-9, fax 28 28 28
tatsurat@tat.or.th

WHERE TO STAY

► Mid-range
Saowaluk Thani
99/99 Kanchanadit Road
Tel. 0 77 / 21 37 00
Fax 21 37 35
280 rooms, restaurant, bar, swimming pool, discotheque. Comfortable hotel a little way from the town centre with reasonable room prices.

► Budget
100 Islands Resort
19/6 Moo 3, Bypass Road
Tel. 0 77 / 20 11 50
Fax 20 11 59
www.roikoh.com
120 rooms, restaurant, bar, swimming pool, spa, sauna, fitness centre. Pleasantly furnished rooms in friendly colours. The pool is splendid.

and idyllic fishing villages. Almost all have a varied landscape of rocky cliffs, dense vegetation and tranquil bays with white sands. The largest islands are ► Ko Samui,► Ko Phangan and Ko Phaulai. 40 small islands to the north-west of Ko Samui have been included in the **Ang Thong Marine National Park**. The shimmering green of the salt-water lake Thale Noi on Ko Mae is an unforgettable sight.

✳ **Surin**

D 4

Region: North-east Thailand	**Province:** Surin
Altitude: 145m/476ft	**Population:** 40,000

Surin, on a wide plain on the southern edge of the Khorat plateau in eastern Thailand, is the centre of silk manufacture and weaving in Thailand. It partially occupies the site of an ancient Khmer settlement. Every year in the third week of September the town hosts an elephant rodeo that attracts many visitors.

> ! **Baedeker** TIP

Elephant rodeo at Surin

The reason that the elephant rodeo has been held in the otherwise sleepy town of Surin since 1960 is easily explained. The mahouts (elephant drivers) from here are said to be the most skilful in the land. With the help of more than 200 elephants they put on performances that include battle tableaux. The festival lasts for several days and closes with a colourful procession.

Whereas the provincial capital Surin is bursting at the seams when the elephant drive takes place, it is otherwise a quiet and delightful place with good facilities for tourists, from where several important Khmer temples can be visited.

Delightful holiday spot

What to See around Surin

The north-east of Thailand, particularly the strip between the railway line to Ubon Ratchathani and the Cambodian border, is speckled with important Khmer ruins. 30km/19mi south of the town at Prasat is the temple of Prasat Pluang, an 11th-century Khmer shrine. A quadrilateral tower on a tall base with beautifully sculpted door lintels survives.

Prasat Pluang

▶ VISITING SURIN

GETTING THERE

By car:
From Bangkok on Routes 1/2/24, Route 214 from Prasat (460km/286mi)

By bus:
Several buses a day from Ubon Ratchathani

By rail:
Station on the Bangkok Ubon Ratchathani line (420km/261mi, 6–8 hours) During the elephant rodeo, special trains run from Bangkok (bookings with travel agents).

WHERE TO STAY

▶ **Budget**

Tarin
60 Sirirat Road
Surin 32000
Tel. 0 44 / 51 42 81
Fax 51 15 80
240 rooms, restaurant, bar, pool. Modern hotel in the centre of town with comfortable rooms. During the rodeo it is expensive and always booked out.

HERALDIC BEASTS ON SAFARI

About 2000 wild elephants and 3000 tame ones currently live in Thailand. A hundred years ago there were as many as 100,000. The mighty creatures have always played a major role in the life of Thailand. They once graced the flag and the coins of the country, and a stylized elephant still appears on the Thai coat of arms.

Elephants were always seen as sacred animals. Ganesha, the Hindu deity with the head of an elephant, is worshipped in Thailand as much as elsewhere as the god of science and art. Even Buddha is supposed to have lived as a white elephant in a previous incarnation. One of the key episodes in Buddha's human life was his meeting with a wild elephant set on him by his cousin. Purely by the power of his love, he tamed the elephant and halted its attack.

White Elephants

White elephants, even though they do not really exist as a zoological entity, are still highly revered in Thailand. **32 characteristics** distinguish such an elephant from its contemporaries. It should possess 20 rather than 16 toenails and have red eyes. Such elephants are not completely white, however, being distinguished rather by the white patches on their heads or ears that may be large or small. The number of such elephants possessed by a king during his reign is said to be indicative of how the happy those years shall be for the ruler and his people.

In this respect, the years of King Bhumibol must be a particularly glorious period, since as many as 16 white elephants have been found during the king's reign, of which eleven are still alive. They are captured in a solemn ceremony, declared to be sacred and sent initially to the Dusit zoo. From there they are transferred

Long ago wars were fought on the backs of elephants and reparations were paid in the form of elephant herds. Later the animals were essential for logging in the impenetrable northern rain forests

to magnificent stables in the grounds of the king's Chitralada residence, where they are lovingly tended.

Working Elephants

Working elephants live a rather more prosaic existence. **Their assistance is still essential in the rainforests of the north.** During their working lives, between the ages of 25 and 60, elephants work eight hours a day. Between April and May they are allowed a kind of holiday. They are taken into »elephant training schools« at the age of three to prepare them for their future lives. One such state-run school is situated near Lampang, but elephant corrals exist near many of the tourist centres, where it is often possible to watch the training and the work of the pachyderms. A mahout, or elephant trainer, undergoes years of training himself in order to learn the 85 pressure points by which he can guide his charge using his feet or an iron hook.

Elephants are usually placid, but during the winter months they can be become unpredictable. This is due to a secretion that comes from a gland on their heads during the mating season and runs into their eyes. It is also true that elephants have a proverbially good memory (including recall of unpleasant incidents) that has surprised many a mahout, and cost some their lives.

Elephant Festival

The best elephant trainers and riders are said to come from the area of Surin in north-east Thailand. This may have been the reason why the Thai tourist authorities instituted a great elephant rodeo in the region. The spectacle starts on the third weekend of November, lasts several days and has become a large and colourful festival. About 200 elephants are brought from all over the country to be judged for their skill, strength and obedience to the mahout in front of the spectators. Members of many of Thailand's various tribes also perform dances in full traditional costume. The days of the festival not only offer plenty of opportunities for a splendid photograph but also give an insight into the lives of people in the Thai countryside.

Prasat Yai Ngao From here, Route 24 leads 51km/32mi east to **Sangkha** and Prasat Yai Ngao, which consists of two brick prangs decorated with splendid sculptures (including a five-headed naga).

Prasat Phnum Pon A few miles south of Sangkha, **Ban Don** was built amid the ruins of a very early Khmer temple, the 7th-century Prasat Phnum Pon. The lintels and pillars have remarkable sculptures, garlands, hanging flowers and medallions decorated with leaves.

Tak

C 2

Region: Northern Thailand   **Province:** Tak
Altitude:: 111m/364ft   **Population:** 22,000

High mountains flank the already broad valley of the Menam Ping (one of the major tributaries of the Menam Chao Phraya) around the idyllic provincial capital of Tak, where impressive scenery makes a short detour from Sukhothai on the way to Chiang Mai well worthwhile. The town's proximity to Myanmar (Burma) means that the culture of the neighbouring country is much in evidence.

»Gateway to the north« The picturesque old town still has many wooden houses built in traditional Thai style. A monument, Sala Somdet Phra Chao Taksin Maharat, commemorates the most famous son of the town, King Taksin (1768–1782), the founder of the kingdom of Siam.

Wat Sibunrung Tak only has one interesting temple: the viharn of Wat Sibunrung has a marvellously carved gable, a nice chedi and a magnificent statue of Buddha in the Sukhothai style.

 VISITING TAK

GETTING THERE
By car:
From Sukhothai via Route 12 (80km/50mi), from Kamphaeng Phet on Routes 1/104 (60km/37mi).

By bus:
From Bangkok Northern Bus Terminal (420km/261mi) or from Surin and Kamphaeng Phet

By air:
Four times a week from Bangkok

INFORMATION
Tourism Authority of Thailand
193 Taksin Road, 63000 Tak
Tel. 0 55 / 51 43 41-3, fax 51 43 44
tattak@tat.or.th

WHERE TO STAY
▶ Mid-range
Mae Sot Hill Hotel
100 Asia Road, Mae Sot
Tel. 0 55 / 52 26 01-8, fax 53 26 00
www.centralhotelsresorts.com
Very comfortable mid-range hotel

Around Tak

Route 105 leads westward through mountainous jungle past Lan Sang National Park with its attractive waterfalls and villages inhabited by Meo, Lisu and Lahu hill tribes to Mae Sot on the border with Myanmar (98km/61mi).

★
Lan Sang National Park

Mae Sot is a pretty, lively little town in the valley of the Menam Moei, which forms the border with Myanmar at this point. The temples in the town are in the Burmese style; the most interesting of them is 5km/3mi outside the town on the Burmese frontier. Its viharn has Buddha statues, one of which is particularly notable for the gems that hang from its earlobes.

Mae Sot

66km/41mi north-west of Tak is the Yanhee reservoir, created by the King Bhumibol dam, that rises to some 154m/505ft. The dam on the Menam Ping is intended to eliminate that flooding that frequently plagued the region and permit controlled irrigation of the fertile land. The energy from the hydro-electric station is transmitted all the way to Bangkok. The reservoir, a paradise for water sports enthusiasts, and its hotel are a popular place to visit for the locals.

King Bhumibol dam

Ban Tak 20km/12mi north of Tak shows how life goes on in the villages. This one is a particularly charming spot on the banks of the Menam Ping. Its stilt-houses look splendid at sunset.

Ban Tak

★ ★ Trat

E 4

Region: South-east Thailand   **Province:** Trat
Altitude: 6m/20ft   **Population:** 14,000

Trat is a bustling market town on alluvial land next to the Gulf of Thailand and close to the Cambodian border. Its main attractions are the islands off the coast such as ▶Ko Chang and the gemstone mines in the neighbourhood.

Thai territory narrows beyond Trat to an 88km/55mi-long strip of land with some fabulous scenery.

Scenery

The town does have economic importance in its own right. Like the neighbouring town of ▶Chanthaburi it is a major centre for. There are dozens of mines around the two towns. Most use strip-mining techniques to extract rubies, sapphires and other precious stones. It is possible to visit some of them without joining a guided tour, but many such organized tours are on offer from travel agents in Pattaya, from which most trips to Trat begin. Another economic staple of the

Baedeker TIP

Thai harvest festival

The region around Trat is one of the most important areas in Thailand for the cultivation of fruit. The main harvest times are mid-May and mid-July. The end of the harvest period is of course a reason to celebrate a festival. Rambutans, durians and mangosteens are the main stars of the annual fruit festival with its procession, gardening contests, beauty contests and all sorts of other entertainments.

region is the large-scale cultivation of fruit and vegetables. Many sorts of fruit grow well here and are distributed to all parts of the country for sale at the markets.

In the1970s the province became famous throughout the world for its massive camps, where Vietnamese and Cambodian **refugees** had fled to escape the regime of Pol Pot. Hundreds of thousands escaped across the open sea, often in small boats. When the participants in the Cambodian civil war made peace in 1991, many of the refugees returned to their homeland.

What to See in Trat

Temples There is not much to see in Trat, as its temples date almost exclusively from recent times. The exceptions are **Wat Chai Mongkol** with various overgrown chedis from the Ayutthaya period and the **Bupharam temple**, where according to legend some of Buddha's ashes are kept. Trat is the ideal base for crossings to ►Ko Chang, Thailand's second-biggest island.

● VISITING TRAT

GETTING THERE

By car:
Trat is 75km/47mi from Chanthaburi on Route 3

By bus:
Regular buses from Bangkok, Pattaya and Chanthaburi

INFORMATION

Tourism Authority of Thailand
100 Moo 1
Trat-Laem Ngob Road
23120 Trat
Tel. 0 39 / 59 72 59 60
Fax 59 72 55
tattrat@tat.or.th

WHERE TO STAY

Trat has several small guest houses offering modest comfort and some small hotels (information from the TAT bureau).

✶ ✶ Ubon Ratchathani (Ubol • Rubol)

D 5

Region: North-east Thailand   **Province:** Ubon Ratchathani
Altitude: 125m/410ft   **Population:** 80,000

The »royal town of lotus blossoms« lies on the banks of the Menam Mun in north-east Thailand. The region used to be dubbed »the poor-house of Thailand« before the first fruits of the national development programmes of the 1980s began to emerge. The town itself has few attractions, but is a base for visiting the important temple of Wat ► Khao Phra Viharn on the border between Thailand and Cambodia.

The splendid temples in the town are modern without exception and have little importance in terms of art history, but it is still worth seeing **Wat Si Ubonat Thalam**, where there is a fine viharn amid the extensive grounds, and **Wat Supattanaramworwihan**, which was founded by King Rama IV and has elements of three different styles, Khmer, Thai and European.

Temples

A further interesting temple is Wat Phra That Nongbua near Chayankun Road, with a pair of stupas modelled on the Bodhgaya temple in India. The central stupa is the tallest building in the town. It is worth looking at the stone reliefs on the base that were added in 1977 to celebrate 2500 years of Buddhism.

**✶ ✶
Wat Phra That
Nongbua**

▶ VISITING UBON RATCHATHANI

GETTING THERE

By car:
From Bangkok on Routes 1/2124 (630km/391mi)

By bus:
From Bangkok North-Eastern Bus Terminal (672km/418mi, journey time 10 hours)

By rail:
From Bangkok Hualampong (575km/357mi, 10–12 hours)

By air:
Once a day from Bangkok

INFORMATION

Tourism Authority of Thailand
264/1 Khaunthani Road
34000 Ubon Ratchathani
Tel. 0 45 / 24 37 70, 25 07 14
Fax 24 37 71
tatubon@tat.or.th

WHERE TO STAY

► Budget

Regent Palace Hotel
265-271 Chayangkun Road
Tel. 0 45 / 24 50 46, fax 25 54 89
120 rooms, restaurant, bar, discotheque. A short distance away from the town centre, nice rooms at reasonable prices.

Around Ubon Ratchathani

Wat Phokhakaeo

✴ There are some interesting attractions in the region to the east of Ubon Ratchathani (Route 217). The lovely Wat Phokhaokaeo with its buildings of red-baked bricks lies 43km/27mi along the road. Look at the beautifully carved doors and window shutters of the viharn on its square base – as well as at the marvellous view of the countryside.

Sao Chaliang

✴ ✴ Beyond the entrance to Kang Tana National Park, just before **Pa Tham** is the natural obelisk of Sao Chaliang. First take Route 217 to Phibun then Route 2222 to Khong Chiam before heading north on Routes 2134 and 212. Wind and weather have fashioned an imposing group of rocks, which the locals believe to be the home of both good and bad spirits.

Cave paintings of Pa Tham

✴ ✴ One of the biggest surprises for researchers into the history of Thailand was the discovery as recently as 1987 of the cave paintings at Pa Tham. Previously it was believed that the settlers of this region had made little contribution to the cultural history of the land. The paintings high above the banks of the Mekong are the most extensive of their kind in Thailand. Over a length of some 150m/500ft there are about 300 extraordinarily well-preserved paintings. They are 3000 to 4000 years old and use brown and red pigments to depict the ordinary life of fishermen and hunters. The great attention to detail in the depiction of implements, animals and people is remarkable. The cave paintings are accessed via a plateau from which a path 1km/1100yd long leads along the cliff.

! *Baedeker* TIP

Candle festival in Ubon

Every year at the start of the Buddhist period of fasting (mid- to late July) Ubon celebrates its candle festival, a series of religious festivals commemorating the first sermon of Buddha after his enlightenment. Beautifully decorated candles of up to two metres in height are carried through the streets. The best candles win prizes and are then donated to temples throughout the region.

Follow the path a bit further (half an hour's walk) to see some more paintings. At various points there are fine views over the Mekong, the longest river in South-East Asia.

Amnat Charoen

The busy little town of Amnat Charoen is 75km/47mi north of Ubon Ratchathani on the way to Mukdahan and about 50km/30mi from the border with Laos. It has no particular historical or artistic importance but is the site of an important religious shrine at **Wat Buddha Mongkol**. The temple is situated to the south-west of the town near a place that bears the same name as its major attraction, Ban Buddha Mongkol. The wat's 16m/52ft Buddha statue is a modern creation. It stands on a pedestal 5m/16ft high in front of some shady trees and is clad with thousands of tiny glass mosaic pieces.

Buddha im Wat Buddha Mongkol

Every February the shrine hosts a major religious festival that draws pilgrims from near and far. The temple also has a bronze Buddha that was found in a pond on the property when the temple was renovated in 1962.

Thanks to its stunning scenic location, it is worth taking a short trip from Amnat Charon to the reservoir of Lam Dom Noi. It was completed in 1971 and is also known as Sirindhorn reservoir after the second daughter of King Bhumibol and his wife. The reservoir is close to the Lao border and is reached via Route 217 (about 85km/53mi from Ubon Ratchathani).

✱
Lam Dom Noi reservoir

✳ Udon Thani

C 4

Region: North-east Thailand   **Province:** Udon Thani
Altitude: 186m/610ft   **Population:** 85,000

Udon Thani is the last major town before the border with the neighbouring country of Laos and lies on the plain of the Menam Luang, a tributary of the Mekong. Since the withdrawal of the American soldiers who were based here during the Vietnam war, many of its night clubs and bars have closed. A shopping trip to the market is entertaining. Not far to the east of the town is the important archaeological site of ▶ Ban Chiang.

Around Udon Thani

Udon Saeng Tawan

The **orchid garden** Udon Saeng Tawan is situated about 2km/1.5mi from the town in Soi Kamol Wattana. It is an opportunity to admire a myriad orchids and smell their intoxicating fragrance, particularly in the mornings (before 1pm). Aromatic oils are also distilled at the garden as ingredients for perfumes.

✳
Wat Phra Buddhabat Ban Kok

A strange and thoroughly untypical landscape 65km/40mi north-west of Udon Thani is the home of Wat Phra Buddhabat Ban Kok. Sandstone blocks burst and hollowed out by erosion are its characteristic features. Monks at the wat are often happy to act as guides to the remarkable scenery. The temple has a picturesque site on the barren summit of a thickly wooded ridge. It possesses one large chedi

 VISITING UDON THANI

GETTING THERE

By car:
From Nakhon Ratchasima via Route 2 (200km/124mi)

By bus:
From Bangkok North-eastern Bus Terminal (560km/348mi)

By air:
Several times a day from Bangkok

INFORMATION

Tourism Authority of Thailand
16/5 Mukmontri Road
41000 Udon Thani
Tel. 0 42 / 32 54 06-7
Fax 32 54 08, tatudon@tat.or.th

WHERE TO STAY

▶ **Budget**
Charoen
549 Phosri Road
Tel. 0 42 / 24 81 55, 24 61 21
241 rooms, restaurant, bar.
Good medium-range hotel with rooms of an adequate standard and pleasant service.

and several smaller ones. Its modern-day wat is modelled on Wat Phra That Phanom in ►Nakhon Phanom. Wat Phra Buddhabat Ban Kok is mainly notable for its symbolic footprint of Buddha. Archaeological discoveries have indicated that the area was settled at a very early period (5000–6000 BC), as its rocks and caves provided good shelter for a nomadic people. In the 9th century, some offshoots of the Khmer people must have settled here. Names based on old legends have been given to the rock features, beneath some of which recent Buddha statues have been placed. On the walls are bas-reliefs of sitting and standing Buddhas from the Dvaravati era.

✳ U Thong

D 2

Region: Central Thailand   **Province:** Suphanburi
Altitude: 186m/610ft   **Population:** 16,500

U Thong is on the edge of the central plain. In the north-west the towering Burmese highlands form an impressive backdrop. The heyday of the town was the time of the Dvaravati kingdom, when it may have been the country's first capital city, as well as the Khmer period when it was a major cultural centre. It also developed an artistic style of its own, particularly in terms of sculpture.

The history of old U Thong goes back to Neolithic times (from which some tools have been discovered). According to one Chinese source, U Thong was the capital of the Funan kingdom (1st– 6th centuries), the oldest empire on the continent of South-East Asia. When the Dvaravati kingdom split up, U Thong mutated from being a vassal state of that empire to becoming an independent domain in its own right. U Thong was also the first capital of this kingdom, but in the 11th century it fell into the hands of the Khmer. After another period of independence, its king U Thong moved his residence to Ayutthaya in 1350 and took the name King Rama Thibodi I (reigning from 1350 to1369).   **History**

▶ VISITING U THONG

GETTING THERE

By car:
From Bangkok via Routes 4 or 338 to Nakhon Pathom, then via Routes 321/ 324 (100km/62mi)

By bus:
From Bangkok and Suphanburi

By rail:
Nearest station Suphanburi (30km/ 19mi)

WHERE TO STAY

In U Thong itself there are no good places to stay. It is better to go on to ► Nakhon Pathom.

✱
Museum
🕐
Opening hours:
Wed–Sun
9am–4pm
Admission fee

The distinguishing feature of the U Thong style (▶Art and Culture) was work in sculpture (although the U Thong period has left no legacy of architecture at all). The museum was opened in 1976 and presents an overview of the three stylistic periods of U Thong sculpture. Some stone tools are also on display (from Neolithic times) as well as baked clay reliefs influenced by Indian Dvaravati art (4th–5th centuries), some bronzes, terracotta figures and sculptures from the Dvaravati periods (6th–11th centuries) and examples of Srivijaya art. There is also a plan showing the layout of the town. Some foundations can still be seen scattered across the surrounding countryside. The fortified town was an oval area measuring some 1600 x 830m/ 1750 x 900yd.

Refreshment is good for monks too.

✶ Uttaradit

C 3

Region: Northern Thailand
Altitude: 81m/266ft

Province: Uttaradit
Population: 32,000

Uttaradit is situated in the broad basin of the Menam and has been rebuilt following a major fire that almost completely destroyed the old town in 1967. Since the building of the gigantic Pa Som reservoir 45km/28mi north-east of the town, Uttaradit has experienced a boom triggered by the growth in agriculture.

A monument in front of the provincial administration building commemorates Governor Phraya Pichai Dat Nak, who repelled an attack by the Burmese army in 1772. The Chinese-style Wat Tha Thanon has a sitting Buddha statue.

Monument

Around Uttaradit

The interesting Wat Phra Boromathat 5km/3mi outside the town (on Route 102) exhibits some Lao influences and features excellent carvings on the gables of the viharn porch, which protrudes far beyond the viharn walls. It also has murals from the Ayutthaya period and a group of fine chedis from the Sukhothai period.

✶
Wat Boromathat

Not far away is **Wat Phra Tan Sila Aat**, which has a stone footprint of Buddha as well as four bronze ones. Next door is a pretty Chinese temple with magnificent teak beams.

Nearby is another interesting temple: **Wat Phra Yeun Phra Bat Yukon** with its graceful mondhop, line of slender columns and bronze Buddha images in the Sukhothai style. A little way to the south of Uttaradit on the left bank of the Menam Nan is the lovely **Wat Phra Fang**, also from the Sukhothai period.

▶ UTTARADIT

GETTING THERE

By car:
From Phitsanulok on Routes 12/11/1045 (130km/81mi); from Sukhothai via Route 101 to Si Satchanalai, then Route 102 (105km/65mi)

By rail:
Station on the line from Bangkok to Chiang Mai (485km/300mi from Bangkok Hualampong, journey time 8 hours approx.)

Route 1045 heads eastwards to the beautiful Sirikit reservoir, named after the wife of the present king and featuring a dam 160m/525ft high and 800m/875yd long. It is the largest dam in Thailand and was completed in 1973. The surface of the reservoir (also called **Pa Som**

Sirikit reservoir

reservoir) covers some 22,000 ha/85 sq mi. An intricate system of canals allows not only irrigation of the surrounding land, creating some high-yield agriculture, but also provides energy for the populace. On the shores of the reservoir there are a few fishing settlements with stilt-built houses. It is possible to drive to the top of the dam and around the lake. A toll must be paid at a gate set up about halfway between the village of Tha Pla and the dam itself.

✶ Yala

H 3

Region: Southern Thailand   **Province:** Yala
Altitude: 15m/50ft   **Population:** 74,000 (province)

Yala is the busy capital of a densely populated and flourishing province in the very south of Thailand close to the border with Malaysia. The townspeople are mainly of Chinese descent, but most inhabitants of the province are of Malaysian extraction and Moslem; the local language is Malay.

Wat Kuhaphimuk lies at the edge of the town. It has been a cave temple for some 1200 years. An attractive park nearby contains a fine and well-proportioned viharn built in recent times. In the limestone cliffs above the park (10 minutes walk) there is a cave with a reclining Buddha 24m/80ft long, which is highly revered. The temples for the Chinese population are well worth seeing.

✶
Wat Kuhaphimuk

> ! **Baedeker TIP**
>
> ### Cooing doves
>
> Every year in March Yala hosts the Zebra Ground Dove Festival. More than 2000 banded doves that are bred locally sit on their caged perches and compete with their cooing. Winners are determined in several categories. Doves that coo with particular skill can be worth up to 20,000 on the open market.

Around Yala

In the mountains around Yala there are many caves, some of which have been made into **cave temples**. Among the most interesting of these are Tham Koo Ha Pimsak (with a 25m/82ft Buddha statue) and Tham Silpa, which still possesses remains of 13th-century murals that are believed to be the oldest such paintings in Thailand (take Route 409 from Yala towards Hat Yai and follow the signposts).

Route 410 leads southwards through mountainous landscape covered by dense tropical rainforest, peppered with the limestone outcrops that are so typical of southern Thailand. After 133km/83mi of twist-

✶ ✶
Scenery

← *Decorated banyan tree alongside the pathway*

● VISITING YALA

GETTING THERE

By car:
From Songkhla via Route 408 to Nathawi, then Routes 42/409 (128km/80mi); an alternative is to switch to the coast road at Chana. From Pattani via Route 410 (43km/27mi)

By bus:
From Bangkok Southern Bus Terminal to Hat Yai (1000km/620mi, 14 hours) and by local bus from there

By rail:
Station on the line from Bangkok to Malaysia (from Bangkok Hualampong

1055km/655mi, journey time 20 hours; sleeping compartments available)

WHERE TO STAY
▶ Mid-range
Royal Princess
Phichit Bamruang Road
Tel. 0 73 / 51 10 27
Fax 51 50 40
rsvnctr@dusit.com
117 rooms, restaurant, bar, swimming pool. The best hotel in Yala with very comfortable, air-conditioned rooms and a good restaurant.

ing roads (maybe with a brief stopover at the Bang Lang reservoir or the hot springs 20km/12mi beyond the village of Ban Ayerweng) the border town of Betong, deep in the mountains, is reached. The population here has mainly Chinese roots. Beyond the Malaysian border, the road forks: one way to Singapore, the other to Butterworth on the Indian Ocean.

✳ Yasothon

D 5

Region: North-east Thailand	**Province:** Yasothon
Altitude: 68m/223ft	**Population:** 22,000

Yasothon is one of the most recent provincial capitals of Thailand, and there would not be much reason to go there if it were not for the fabulous spectacle that takes place in May to the delight of natives and tourists alike. Towards the end of the dry season the popular festival of Bun Bang Fai is celebrated for a whole week throughout the province.

Benefits of the bamboo rocket festival The festival seeks to alert the rain god **Phraya Thaen** to the period of dryness. For weeks before the event, the people of Yasothon put together their rockets, to be powered by a mixture of saltpetre and charcoal. They make the shells mainly from tubes of bamboo and light a fuse of saffron yellow fabric to shoot them as much as 600m/

⏵ VISITING YASOTHON

GETTING THERE

By car:
From Bangkok on Routes 1/2 to Ban Wat (near Phimai), then Routes 207/202 (530km/329mi). From Ubon Ratchathani via Route 23 (98km/61mi)

By bus:
Buses run from both the centres named above

By air:
Nearest airport Khon Kaen (180km/112mi)

WHERE TO STAY

▶ Budget
Yot Nakhon
143 Uthai-Ramit Road
Yasothon 35000
Tel. 0 45 / 71 16 62
Fax 71 14 81
66 rooms, restaurant.
A hotel in the centre of Yasothon with nice rooms and a highly recommended restaurant.

2000ft into the sky. The rockets are taken to the launch site on the edge of town in a colourful procession. The faces of the men are covered in thick mud, in order to disguise from Phraya Thaen the fact that humans are behind this attempt to appease him. The governor himself gives the signal to start the proceedings and those rockets that do not explode on the ground are greeted with great cheering from the crowds as they ascend into the heavens. What is more, just once in a while it really does rain the next day.

Wat Thung Sawan in the east of the town is notable for its remarkable Khmer-style construction. In **Wat Mahathat** the main shrine and the graceful library (Ho Trai) provide the architectural interest.

A small offering of fresh flowers

That Luk Khun Mae, which lies about 7km/4mi south of town on Route 23, exhibits a mixture of both Lao and Khmer stylistic influences.

That Luk Khun Mae

The village of Ban Si Than is known for its hand-woven silk and cotton fabrics. It is 20km/12mi outside the town on Route 202.

Ban Si Than

INDEX

LIST OF MAPS AND ILLUSTRATIONS

PHOTO CREDITS

AKG p. 74, 105
Baedeker-Archiv p. 108
Beck p. 7 above, 44, 149, 183, 261, 272, 297, 302, 316, 323, 356, 399, 471
Bilderberg p. 170/171
F1 p. 4, 57, 110/111, 188/189, 201 above centre, 294
Father Ray Organisation p. 101
Fausel p. 11, 61, 123, 127, 214, 243, 249, 266, 306, 312, 382
Frei p. 113, 250, 440
Friedrichsmeyer/Spielenburg p. 202, 237
Gstaltmayr p. 14, 15 Mitte, 36, 73, 89, 156, 159, 171, 177 below, 180, 185 below, 185 above right, 187 left, 191, 205, 231, 235, 263, 285, 287, 289, 304, 314, 331, 345, 348, 357, 361, 364, 373, 387, 393, 403, 415 below right and left, 444, 447, 451, 458, 466, 474, 478, 485, 493, front cover inside
Häusler p. 13, 177, 189, 221, 232, 343, 354, 419
HB Verlag / Sasse p. 3, 6, 8, 9 above and below, 10 above and below, 18, 22, 34, 42, 50, 55, 67, 69, 95, 119, 124, 131, 140, 143, 150, 155, 160, 173 below, 186, 187 right, 193, 194, 201 below left, 215, 225, 226, 239, 253, 257, 264, 277, 293, 310, 326, 358, 367, 379, 384, 394/395, 408, 423, 428, 455, 468, 473
Höbel p. 245, 282, 301, 443
IFA Bilderteam p. 38, 172, 200, 201 above right, 259, 328, 391

Ihlow p. 397
Kubsch p. 173 centre
Lahr p. 223, 338, 462, 477
Laif p. 2, 7 unten, 15 above and below, 16 above, 40, 47, 173 above, 209, 271, 332, 350, 415 above right, 415 above, 416, 490, 493, back cover outside
Mandarin Oriental Hotel Group p. 211, 248
Mauritius p. 25, 32, 181 above, 336, 438
Mielke p. 5, 17, 97, 142, 152, 401, 426, 431
pa p. 100, 102
pa/Stockfoodp. 132 centre, 133 centre and right, 181
Patterson p. 12/13, 53, 61
Peter p. 185 above left, 275
Petrich p. 181 below, 204
Randebrock p. 111, 132 left, 390
Stadler p. 216, 409
Stockfood p. 132 right, 133 left
Thailändisches Fremdenverkehrsamt / Gstaltmayr p. 120, 129, 131, 185 centre, 230, 268, 319, 324, 488
Weigt p. 16 centre, 16 below, 92, 177 above, 199, 220, 296, 298
Zefa p. 433

Cover photo: IFA Bilderteam/Alastor Photo

PUBLISHER'S INFORMATION

Illustrations etc: 219 illustrations, 48 maps and diagrams, one large map
Text: Heiner Gstaltmayr, with contributions by Prof. Dr. Wolfgang Hassenpflug, Silwen Randebrock, Anita Rolf, Hanny Tichy, Reinhard Zakrzewski
Editing: Baedeker editorial team (Rainer Eisenschmid, John Sykes)
Translation: John Sykes
Cartography: Franz Kaiser Sindelfingen; MAIRDUMONT/Falk Verlag, Ostfildern (map)
3D illustrations: jangled nerves, Stuttgart
Design: independent Medien-Design, Munich; Kathrin Schemel

Editor-in-chief: Rainer Eisenschmid, Baedeker Ostfildern

1st edition 2008

Copyright: Karl Baedeker Verlag, Ostfildern
Publication rights: MAIRDUMONT GmbH & Co; Ostfildern

Printed in China

DEAR READER,

We would like to thank you for choosing this Baedeker travel guide. It will be a reliable companion on your travels and will not disappoint you.
This book describes the major sights, of course, but it also recommends the most interesting events, as well as hotels in the luxury and budget categories, and includes tips about where to eat, shopping and much more, helping to make your trip an enjoyable experience. Our author Heiner Gstaltmayr and the editorial team ensure the quality of this information by making regular journeys to Thailand and putting all their know-how into this book.

Nevertheless, experience shows us that it is impossible to rule out errors and changes made after the book goes to press, for which Baedeker accepts no liability. Please send us your criticisms, corrections and suggestions for improvement: we appreciate your contribution. Contact us by post or e-mail, or phone us:

► **Verlag Karl Baedeker GmbH**
  Editorial department
  Postfach 3162
  73751 Ostfildern
  Germany
  Tel. 49-711-4502-262, fax -343
  www.baedeker.com
  E-Mail: baedeker@mairdumont.com

Baedeker Travel Guides in English at a glance:

► Andalusia

► Dubai · Emirates

► Egypt

► Ireland

► London

► Mexico

► New York

► Portugal

► Rome

► Thailand

► Tuscany

► Venice